Film Hieroglyphs

Film Hieroglyphs
Ruptures in Classical Cinema

Tom Conley

With a New Introduction

University of Minnesota Press
Minneapolis • London

Portions of chapter 2 originally appeared as "Writing *Scarlet Street*,"
MLN 98 (December 1983); reprinted by permission of The Johns
Hopkins University Press. Portions of chapters 3 and 4 originally
appeared as "Apocalypse Yesterday," *Enclitic* 10–11 (1982); "Objective
Burma!" *Enclitic* 13 (1983); and "Manpower," *Enclitic* 14 (1984); all
reprinted with permission.

Published by the University of Minnesota Press
111 Third Avenue South, Suite 290
Minneapolis, MN 55401-2520
http://www.upress.umn.edu

Library of Congress Cataloging-in-Publication Data

Conley, Tom.
    Film hieroglyphs : ruptures in classical cinema / Tom Conley, with a new
Introduction.
        p. cm.
    Includes bibliographical references and index.
    Originally published: Minneapolis : University of Minnesota Press, 1991.
    ISBN-13: 978-0-8166-4970-9 (pb : alk. paper)
    ISBN-10: 0-8166-4970-7 (pb : alk. paper)
    I. Motion picture plays—History and criticism. I. Title.
    PN1995.C63 2006
    791.4309—dc22
                                        2006015938

Printed in the United States of America on acid-free paper

The University of Minnesota is an equal-opportunity educator and employer.

12 11 10 09 08 07 06   10 9 8 7 6 5 4 3 2 1

Contents

Acknowledgments

Too long in the making, this study owes much to critical readings by Terry Cochran, T. Jefferson Kline, and Paul Smith. They have worked with the manuscript from its inception and have offered patient and effective counsel at all of its stages. Many have encouraged its completion and offered timely support at various stages of its making. I thank the Graduate School and Fred Lukermann, former Dean of the College of Liberal Arts of the University of Minnesota, for their support and encouragement. I am grateful to Kerry McIndoo and Julie Silverman, for their preparation of the manuscript, and to Mary Byers, for her patient and encouraging emendations.

On the horizon of the book is the deeply mourned Michel de Certeau, whose studies of history are, I believe, crucial for the dynamics of film and memory. His death, a severe loss to his readers and friends, has marked the pages that follow.

I owe much to George Bauer and his work on Duchamp, Sartre, and film; to Réda Bensmaïa, practitioner of film and adept of bilingual writing; to Hannah Charney, whose vision mixes the tracks of image and writing; to Roger Dadoun, critic of Fritz Lang, for his friendship and collaborations in Paris and Minneapolis; to Brian Henderson and Richard Macksey, who maintain that analysis, imagination, and history are strands of the same fabric; to Marie-Claire Ropars-Wuilleumier, a friend, whose concept and practice of the film-text inform every chapter; and to Hayden White, whose supportive remarks about history and ideology, drawn from cinema, have been precious.

The central and final chapters on Raoul Walsh were begun, long before they were written, with Walter Conley (1899?–1974), who for years taught me more about film, I believe, than could any textbook. Much of the study, dedicated to his memory, lives in dialogue with him.

I am indebted to David and Francine Conley, their childhood nourished with celluloid, for their unrelenting pleasure at seeing countless projections over and again. Verena Conley, the most patient and supportive of all, has withstood the many antics and mimicry that go with film writing. To her this book is dedicated.

Hieroglyphs Then and Now

Personne n'est exempt de dire des fadaises. Le malheur est de les dire curieusement. *Nœ iste magno conatu magnas nugas dixerit.*

No one is exempt from uttering banalities. The ill fortune is in uttering them in an overwrought fashion. *Surely this man is going to great length to tell me great inanities.*

—Michel de Montaigne, *Essais*

In spite of its overwrought fashion, and at the cost of its author having uttered many banalities, the grounding hypothesis of this book was forthright and simple. Each of the chapters was built on the assumption that classical cinema, roughly what came before and immediately after the Second World War, could be studied as forms and shapes of writing. Writing was understood in the strong critical— and then forcibly Gallic—sense as *écriture. Écriture* had been understood as a continuous process of tracing, marking, and tracking. It was a substantive complement to *écrire,* a verb then understood, and championed by Roland Barthes, to be one that had to be taken in an intransitive sense.[1] For Barthes and others, writing did not just transcribe speech or refer to things and phenomena in the world at large but, more compellingly, drew attention to and enabled a glimpse of unforeseen relations that flickered in the movement of its aural and graphic form. Writing could be marshaled to call into question the presence—if a presence there ever was—of what its writers and, in the most literal sense, its printed characters were said to designate.

Cinema, the book argued, was a mode of *écriture* that made manifest the effects of this complex definition of "writing" in classical cinema, an area in which it would otherwise seem invisible. Classical cinema was defined as one whose scenarios were assumed to tell good stories in films that followed the order of seamless or invisible editing. They followed Aristotelian poetics and, as a result, demanded that the narratives being told have a beginning, middle, and end. But the matter of the writing conveying the stories was shown to interfere with the designs that would have served the step-by-step procedure of standard narrative design. Wherever writing intervened in classical cinema, the book took pains to show there emerged a host of other and different meanings—some contradictory, some unconscious, others of strong ideological charge—that could hardly be subject to the control of the scenario or screenplay. Writing was seen to complement and deviate from the contexts in which it was said to be found. It was remarked, further, that graphic forms in the field of the image not only confirm what happens in the narrative but also, and more decisively, allow the viewer to "read" the film against the grain or gist of its meaning. Because writing is *not* of the matter of film, its form intervenes and brings forward things that cannot be assimilated or entirely controlled by the film or its editing. Writing, it was felt, can thus acquire unforeseen critical force and even suggest, especially in the areas between the images in which it is found and even in its own characters, the presence of other dimensions of the film that often need to remain unnamed or even, on occasion, are unnamable.

The gap between what a film would wish to say or mean and the impact of writing in the field of the image was discerned as an effect of *rupture:* wherever graphic traits interceded in the film (in the credits or the icons, in signboards within landscapes, in subtitles, in toponyms on maps shown in the field of the image), it was sustained that the illusion of reality seen within the frame became subject to graphic treatment that might forcibly call cinematic illusion into question. Whatever was visible became equally legible. Writing that begged to be both "seen" and "read" in the same act of cognition summoned the mimetic dimension of the film. In the rift or rupture between its visible and legible form, a critical relation could be established, and from there the film could be put to uses other than those shown in its narrative effects, in ways other than its treatment of themes or other than the emotions its rhetoric would awaken or inspire. In this way *Film Hieroglyphs* argued, if not for a creative treatment of cinema, at least for ways of reading and seeing cinema in a fashion other than those that the medium had dictated in its narrative and mimetic order. It argued for vigilant reading and constructive dialogue with cinema.

An irony in the history of *Film Hieroglyphs* still resounds in the title. Because it intended to make *écriture* equivalent to cinema, the manuscript was initially sent to the editorial staff of the University of Minnesota Press under the title "Film Writing." The marketing department of the Press quickly changed the title for fear of confusion with a manual whose purpose was to teach readers how to write a successful scenario or how to develop a screenplay from a first to a final treatment. The book, the editors rightly reasoned, was anything but practical. At that point the concept of the hieroglyph came forward. Following the dense and still vigorous pages of Marie-Claire Ropars-Wuilleumier's *Le Texte divisé: Essai sur l'écriture filmique* (The divided text: an essay on filmic writing) (1982), the book had all along exploited the concept of the hieroglyph to draw attention to the visible, legible, and emblematic aspects of writing. *Hieroglyph* was inspired from her meticulously superimposed readings of four canonical texts bearing on the concept of *écriture filmique,* in other words, of film writing.[2]

The first, drawing on the early work of Jacques Derrida, proposed that *écriture* was by its own nature *not* a series of signs transmitting voice and thus relaying presence as it would be felt in a religious, philosophical, or even an everyday continuum in which truth or verisimilitude would be privileged. Rather, writing was understood to be a process of tracing, of spacing, and of an autonomy that it bore in respect to its writer or reader. For Ropars-Wuilleumier the texture of *De la grammatologie* was (and is) strongly cinematographic because its concept and practice of writing are constituted "by sight and outside of voice, in space, and against time."[3] The graphic character of *écriture,* like an image that refuses to disappear before the eyes or to be lost in the visual register of memory, suspends whatever meaning that would tend to cause the forms that convey it to disappear.

In the second, Ropars-Wuilleumier complicates the issue when she places writing in the context of Emile Benveniste's binary equation of expression *(énonciation)* and statement *(énoncé),* in which, in an utterance or a locution, the presence of the speaking subject—a character who makes a statement in a sound film—is eradicated. The expression and expressivity of a statement, like a signifier, cannot entirely be associated or affiliated with the state, being, or seeming place of its origin. To see becomes an act of speech, what one reader of Beneviste (by way of Maurice Merleau-Ponty) envisions as a rupture between things seen and things stated or heard: "This act makes of things seen the expression of the invisible texture that ties them together. It is the perception of an invisible solidarity in and through the 'terms' of objects seen." Seeing is "speech," but a speech "that is silent and that relates to language."[4] An act of seeing or of speaking entails a splitting of the self and a consequent displacement from a stable position that would otherwise give the speaker or viewer a guarantee of veracity.

In the third, Freud's studies of figurative languages and their relation to the unconscious are mapped onto the work of the philosopher and the linguist. The unconscious, argued the founding father of psychoanalysis, is best discerned through "figurative" language, indeed, what he calls the graphic traits of dreams. Noting the manner in which Freud "reads" dreams in the *Traumdeutung,* Ropars-Wuilleumier observes closely the appeal he makes to Chinese writing or "hieroglyphics" to specify what he is getting at. Hieroglyphs are "figurative enigmas" that now and again are "dreams" and "rebuses." In the passages that Derrida translates from the *Traumdeutung,* "montage" (a cinematically charged term) characterizes the syntactic articulation of the dream-figures, what Freud had originally called *Zusammensetzungen* (32–33).

At the locus of montage Ropars-Wuilleumier brings forward the teachings of Eisenstein for her fourth reading. She notes that the director of *October* aimed at a film-writing or *ciné-écriture* when he envisioned montage as what would allow cinema to be inscribed in "the general perspective of systems of expression and meaning." It would pertain to writing or figuration, especially hieroglyphs (35); for Eisenstein the latter are taken to be nonalphabetic forms, found within language, that are not subordinate to speech. Montage, the principle of cinema in its purest condition, is described as a "hieroglyphics."[5] In glossing one of Eisenstein's articles on montage (first published in French as "Hors cadre" [Off-frame]), Ropars-Wuilleumier recalls what Benveniste had implied to be the "artistic" qualities of language that go hand in hand with its signifying attributes.[6] The observations of the linguist are marshaled to prevent montage from becoming a synthetic or ideated form. In accord with Eisenstein's essay on cinematography and the ideogram, in which the cinematic hieroglyph can be seen to have both figural and conceptual dimensions, she argues that any dialectical synthesis of the components of the ideogram is impossible because the former (the figural element) subverts or denies any resolution on the part of the latter (the concept): "In the hieroglyphic context of 'Hors cadre' it is not a question of conferring upon cinema a signifying capacity analogous to that of the sign; cinema will be a writing—and herein not the least of the paradoxes of this article—insofar as it can produce conceptual meanings comparable in abstraction to that of the sign; but this linguistic productivity can be fully realized only if the operation goes forward in full autonomy in respect to the content of the initial raw material—the image" (38).

The image contains and is made of figural matter, and thus Eisenstein collapses, long before debates on the virtue of cinema as a "language," anything that would make a shot the equivalent of a word, or a sequence the equivalent of a sentence. Eisenstein discovers in *ruptures,* or in negations, of the representative dimension of shots the power of montage as a hieroglyphics, a term that becomes tantamount to a cinematic language of its own order. The initial division of shots—and not the shots themselves—yields "signification" that is not only irreducible to representation but furthermore, at the utmost, remains "independent of it" (39). The formulation in Eisenstein's work in 1929 anticipates a remark, made in 1938, in which he asserts that today the juxtaposition of two fragments of film resembles their product more than their sum.

Ropars-Wuilleumier concludes that Eisenstein's articulation of montage stands close to Derrida's theory of writing because rupture plays a principal role in the signifying process. When the image is seen and read as a hieroglyph, the Eisensteinian principle of the abrupt collision of volumes, masses, luminosities, and spaces contained in the frame (47) leads to a rethinking of the shot because the concatenations within and between individual shots cannot be contained or limited to a single theme, a dominant signifier, a major constructive principle, or even any semblance of unified space. Single or unitary meanings cannot be found because of multiplicities of form made manifest in the frame—things are seen, things are read, things are at once seen and read, things are noted that resist seeing and reading—in the midst of the passage of images. Thus when Eisenstein calls the shot a "multivocal hieroglyph," he clears the way for a cinema that can be identified as *écriture*.

On this basis *Film Hieroglyphs* found its title. It set forth to study the ideogram as Derrida had developed it in the gist of his own essays, and so too the rebus and the concept of *Bilderschriften* dear to Freud. And following Benveniste's emphasis on "artistic language" that cannot be assimilated into alphabetic forms, the book placed under the concept of the "filmic icon" image-signs that were traits, bearing reference to cinematic writing, that complicated narrative designs or could, because of their disruptive qualities, cause the film to reflect—and reflect on—its own process. Instead of taking a directly theoretical itinerary as had the author of *Le texte divisé,* the book appealed to the delineations and confusion of images and writing in the tradition of surrealist painting and cinema. The work of Marcel Duchamp (though hardly mentioned in the opening pages) served as a foil and a model for study of cinema in which the fruits of experiment and chance would not seem obvious. The chapters were written before the cinematic taxonomies of Gilles Deleuze became assimilated into lexicons of film theory. In order to respect the realm of "classical" cinema, allusion to Godard's art of combinations of letters, texts, intertitles, and broken words between and about images, both in his films of the 1960s and in his *Histoire(s) du cinema,* was left aside.

But some of the guiding principles of Deleuze 's theory and Godard's cinema were not. What goes by the name of classical cinema effectively belongs to the regime of the "movement-image" because film of that moment tends to motivate perception, action, and affection in the "sensori-motor" realm of the viewer. Thus the two chapters on Raoul Walsh, for whom the three fundamental ingredients of good cinema are, in the director's own words, "action, action, and action," would typify the taut and gripping effects that his features and so many others of his time promote in their spectators.[7] So too would the narrative designs of early and high film noir, whose pertinent traits are nascent in *La bête humaine,* flickering in the chiaroscuro of *High Sierra,* crystallized in *The Killers,* and modulated for apocalyptic effects in *White Heat.* In *Film Hieroglyphs* the films that Deleuze would affiliate with the weakening of the movement-image are still assumed to be classical by dint of their "sensori-motor" appeal: each of the six tales of *Paisan* is an integral and gripping narrative about contact and rupture, but the overall effect of the six fragments attests to Eisenstein's dictum that the juxtaposition of any two fragments—be they shots or episodes—is greater than their sum. When Deleuze alludes to the fourth tale of Rossellini's mosaic epic to suggest the ruins of Florence (a cityscape composed of heaps of bricks, debris piled and scattered helter-skelter, bombed-out buildings, and heaps of rubbish), he uses *Paisan* to attest to a nascent cinematic space and time that are both within and outside history. It is the setting of a paradoxically originary and touristic world through which two personages scurry en route to a devastating destiny.[8] Inasmuch as Rossellini heralds a new cinema he remains faithful to classical composition; yet, as the book argues, the film betrays the marks of a hieroglyphic style.

The hieroglyph shows that in the most traditional films that would appear to belong to the regime of the movement-image the time-image is present. Visible letters and signs confer on the shot in which they are seen an ambiguous depth of field, indeed, an unsettling continuum of unresolved duration. In Renoir's *La bête humaine,* shards of letters, as they will be made manifest in Godard's cinema that acknowledges its debt to Renoir, would be images of destiny that symbolically seal the fate of the hero Jacques Lantier (Jean Gabin). They are of the same grist from the outset of *High Sierra,* when convicted criminal Roy Earle (Humphrey Bogart) is "pardoned." In these and other sequences a copresence of visible and legible forms draws attention both to perception and to what is perceived. The shots are seen and read synchronously. As a result, what would be a phenomenology of cinematic perception in the narrative register becomes something vastly different when located in the field of the image.

The hieroglyph bears more than a casual resemblance to Deleuze's concept of the *fold,* an abstract pleat creased between things *said* and things *seen.* The hieroglyph does not allow what is observed on the screen to refer solely to the world being recorded, nor does it permit voice to bear witness to an original or authentic speaking subject. To the contrary, when speech is seen on the screen as something detached from its origin, a "being-language" comes forward. So also, when the luminosity of a shot acquires more interest than its composition, a "being-light" is shed on "forms, proportions, [and] perspectives" that have nothing to do with an intending or intentional gaze or aural sensitivity on the part of the viewer. By way of Deleuze's reading of Michel Foucault, the hieroglyph converts cinematic intentions into shapes and qualities in duration independent of speakers and seers who might otherwise be a guarantee of their presence. The hieroglyph thus transforms a phenomenology of cinema into an epistemology, that is, into a problematic condition in which things heard and spoken or seen become elements of knowledge, but of a knowledge occulted because the hieroglyph remains a site where we cannot see that of which we speak, nor can we speak of what we are seeing.[9] The most classical films, or those based on invisible editing, open themselves to different interpretive trajectories wherever the graphic aspect of language unsettles meaning and redirects cognition along unforeseen paths.

Throughout Deleuze's work on cinema, ruptures and conflations of sight and legibility recur. At the beginning of his discussion of the frame and the shot, and of framing and editing in *L'image-mouvement,* he posits that the image on the screen can be either rarefied when it becomes black or white, or saturated when deep-focus photography allows things to multiply or to compress the space in the enclosing rectangle of the frame. Whether rarefied or saturated, the frame "teaches us that the image is not merely given to be seen. It is as legible as it is visible" (24). Along an almost identical line in *L'image-temps,* he argues that when duration replaces movement as a commanding element of modern cinema, it is "with a new conception and new forms of montage" that the eye "accedes to a function of clairvoyance." There occurs a mystical or suspended moment when, he reiterates, "the elements of the image, which are not only visual but also sonorous, enter into internal relations that require the entire image to be 'read' no less than seen, [to be] as legible as it is visible."[10] When each of the two remarks, the first at the beginning of *L'image-mouvement* and the second at a similar point in *L'image-temps,* are superimposed over each other, it can be said that the movement-image of classical cinema becomes a time-image of postwar cinema, especially wherever the hieroglyph is present or where it intervenes in the narrative order. Here and elsewhere in his two volumes of theory, the hiero-glyph seems to be what ties the two types of image to each other and, as a con-sequence, to make their distinctive traits—however much Deleuze argues for their difference—difficult to ascertain.[11] Had *Film Hieroglyphs* paid heed to these and other combinations of writing and of letters and sounds in the field of the image in a theoretical vein, it might have arrived at similar conclusions.

Were the book to be rewritten, it would have to reconsider not only Deleuze but also theorist Jacques Rancière. Rancière intuits that most cinema is based on a contrariety emerging from the difference between an *active* agency of a cre-ative director (a scenarist, actor, set designer, or director of photography, and the like) who imposes a style or a vision on the medium and a *passive* counterpart—the camera itself—that owns an "expressive power" that brings to light what is "written directly onto things, independently of any will to mean or to make a [complete or integral] work." It belongs, he adds, reaching into Romantic aes-thetic theory, to the "silent writing of things."[12] The grounding contrariety of cin-ema is composed of a passive visual faculty, *opsis,* implied to be what both reads and sees things in the same gaze, that which works against "the Aristotelian priv-ilege of *muthos*" of the stories or narrative it sets out to tell (17). Rancière likens cinema to a fable that, in an honored meaning belonging to early modern print culture, is an illustrated poem or an emblematic (or hieroglyphic) combination of images and texts. Its constitutive elements are at odds or in a differential rela-tion with each other.[13] The hieroglyph and its spatialization of meaning would be vital to this definition of cinema that Rancière finds in some of the most preco-cious writings of film theory, including those of Louis Delluc and, by inference, Elie Faure. In a revised version the book would examine how classical cinema is related to concepts and practices of the *fable.* It would discern how, in turn, the interface of texts and of writing makes the contrarieties that Rancière dis-cerns a vital interpretive element of the medium.

The reader will see that the eighty illustrations that punctuate the text seem to be either quaintly fuzzy or of resolutely poor quality. They appear as if taken from a dusty album of photograms belonging to an archaic mode of reproduction. None of the illustrations bears a legend or a title in a list of figures. During the editing of the manuscript it was felt that the text adjacent to each image— what was above and what was below—provided enough explication. On some occasions the writing in the image completed sentences in the text above that led into them.[14] Today the illustrations appear so deficient in respect to what was made of them that they could hardly be qualified as photograms.

For this reader their graininess recalls the spirit of the time in which the book was written, a moment that preceded the advent of the videocassette and the DVD. The pictures were shot from 16-millimeter copies of films of diverse provenance. Some were duplicates that had for some reason reached a public domain; others belonged to the Hennepin County public lending library; still others had come from distributors whose names (such as Kit Parker, Swank Pictures, and Blackhawk Films) have almost become history. Each and every one of the 16-millimeter prints had been run almost endlessly through the gates of three archaic projectors (a Kodak Pageant, found in a closet of the Department of French and Italian at the University of Minnesota; later, when the College of Liberal Arts made one available, a Kodak Athena; and, when all other projectors failed, a portable Bell and Howell that could barely pull the film from one reel to the other). Each of the photograms was shot through a Duplikin lens, set on a bayonet mount of a 35-millimeter camera, that reduced the scope of the original frame on the filmstrip. Daylight photography (mostly in the winter of Minnesota) required multiple takes of the same image at different shutter speeds and f-stops. The most adequate illustrations were chosen from a sizable number of photograms examined on contact sheets. The process of image duplication was archaic by today's standards, but then so also were, by their very nature, the "scenes of writing" that were taken up in different films and in various cinematic traditions. The book now reminds us of what seems to be an antediluvian age when film theory and pedagogy thrived on a minimum of technological support. It is hoped that the time and the history of the book—and also the excitement of close analysis and the stakes of "reading" a film—can be seen through the ways the images were reproduced and tipped into their textual surroundings.

A final and parting irony can be found in the third illustration of the first chapter, which engages a comparative study of *Boudu sauvé des eaux* and *La chienne*. The prologue of *Boudu* is a scene on a makeshift stage where a rotund and aging satyr (whom viewers will discover to be Edouard Lestingois), playing a flute, seduces a young nymph (who will be Anne-Marie Chloë, Lestingois's maid and mistress). This is followed by an establishing shot of Lestingois's bookstore that brings the film into the ostensibly real time and space of Paris, circa 1932, on the Quai Voltaire, facing the Seine, adjacent to the Pont des Arts, from which Boudu will jump only to be saved when Lestingois spots him while scanning the cityscape through a telescope. In *Film Hieroglyphs* the shot was selected to play on the idea of the signature of Renoir's film as a reproducible autograph, a form that figured prominently in the philosophy of deconstruction.[15] Renoir's "signature," it was hypothesized, could be found in the reproducible "autograph" written into the field of the image, the paradox being that the guarantee of uniqueness and authenticity found in the word "autograph" in the field of view is undone by the mechanical writing and the reproductive function of the film in which the word becomes visible. Thus on the windowsill of the second floor, a signboard reading "autographes" is shown attached to a protective iron balustrade to the left of the name of the bookstore and its owner: "V. Lemasle, autographes (à l'entresol)" (V. Lemasle, autograph manuscripts [on the mezzanine]). On a panel near the ground (and under the shop windows) is written "Ancienne Maison Lemasle" (formerly LeMasle Establishment). It was then argued that the name of the store in the image brings a realistic effect of on-location filming and an immediate and recognizably urban geography. "The name may have been a given, unmotivated place-name that happened to be where the film was shot" (6), but the innuendo of a "former male" could refer to the sylvan world of the old satyr and young nymph shown in the prologue (and soon to be alluded to in the present time of the film when Lestingois quotes strains of romantic poetry that parody Victor Hugo's "Le satyre").

The observation did not fulfill what the book set out to do. Herein lies a banality of the kind Montaigne discerns in most of what we utter, read, and write: the visible writing placed squarely in the center of the frame went unnoticed. Behind the panels of windows are seen three sets of Baroque maps that, thanks to hindsight, can be identified as folios stripped from seventeenth-century French and Dutch atlases in the line of Guillaume Blaeu and Jodocus Hondius. The maps tell the viewer that the film is *not* in the spaces they represent; nor do they indicate in any way where the narrative will go. They merely bear a matte quality that begs them to be read and seen as both visible and legible objects in a field where other pieces of writing are seen. Where the bookstore is seen in extreme depth of field, the maps have the paradoxical effect of flattening the image and of turning into a hieroglyph. The surroundings of the maps locate the film and its viewer, but the maps themselves call into question the notion of the "location" and the "autograph" of the film. They also beg us to ask how, as elements of pictured writing found in a movie, they might be discerned. In light of the theory noted here, we can ask how these maps ought to be "seen" and how they might be "read." Each of the folio sheets (of Europe, the Netherlands, Africa, and other countries) is composed of legible and visible signs and, like the film itself, each unsettles the discursive and optical qualities of the image in which it is placed.

At the time of the writing of *Film Hieroglyphs,* these maps were invisible to its author. Now, in what might be seen as a companion and a sequel, in *Cartographic Cinema* the same pages of the Baroque atlases serve as a visible point of departure for a broader treatment of space, cartography, and film. The first section of a chapter on Renoir in that new book begins from a close-up of these maps, and from there it reaches broader conclusions about the relation of cartography to cinema. What was sought in the name of the hieroglyph then has now become a map. An instance of blindness visibly obvious in one book becomes what the author would hope to be a guiding insight for what might be a sequel.

July 2006

Notes

1. When he or she writes "the subject is constituted as immediately contemporaneous with writing, being effected and affected by it: it is the exemplary case of the Proustian narrator who exists, despite the reference to a pseudo-memory, only while writing." "Ecrire, verbe intransitif?" in *Essais critiques IV: Le bruissement de la langue* (Paris: Seuil, 1984), 30. The essay originally appeared in English, "To Write: An Intransitive Verb?" in Eugenio Donato and Richard Macksey, eds., *The Languages of Criticism and the Structuralist Controversy* (Baltimore, MD.: Johns Hopkins University Press, 1970), 131–45.

2. In his careful reading of Ropars-Wuilleumier's essay, David Rodowick notes that as "a model for cinematic signification, the hieroglyph is of interest because of its mixing of phonic, graphic, and figural matters of expression, as well as its fundamental polyvalency. In the hieroglyph, a phonetic element can symbolize an object, transcribe an element combinable with other phonemes, or, through the juxtaposition of connected figures, formulate an entirely new concept" (in *Reading the Figural, or Philosophy after the New Media* [Durham, N.C.: Duke University Press, 2001], 89–90). These and subsequent pages sum up the importance of her work in the field of film theory in general, and they situate the theory in a context that goes as far as the line of divide between analog and digital cinema.

3. Marie-Claire Ropars-Wuilleumier, *Le texte divisé: Essai sur l'écriture filmique* (Paris: Presses Universitaires de France, 1981), 24. Here and elsewhere, translations from the French are mine.

4. Michel de Certeau, "La folie de la vision," *Esprit* (June 1982), 97–98.

5. At the beginning of his epochal essay "The Cinematographic Principle and the Ideogram," Eisenstein calls cinema "so many corporations, such and such turnovers of capital, so and so many stars, such and such dramas," and cinematography "first and foremost, montage." Montage finds its principle in the "copulation (perhaps we had better say, the combination) of two hieroglyphs" that yields a product in the form of an ideogram. Ropars-Wuilleumier builds her theory on these pages (29–30) of the seminal essay in Jay Leyda, ed. and trans., *The Film Form* (1949; reprint, New York: Meridian Books, 1957), 28–44.

6. "Hors cadre" first appeared in French translation by Jean Schnitzer, in *Cahiers du cinema*, no. 215 (September 1969), 21–28. The title became that of Ropars-Wuilleumier's journal, *Hors cadre*, published through the Press of the University of Paris–VIII (Vincennes-à-Saint-Denis), which for a decade studied how cinematic principles inform and even traverse different disciplines and practices.

7. Action has been tantamount to his signature as auteur. See my "A for Auteur and F for Fake: A Case for Raoul Walsh," in Jeremy Braddock and Stephen Hock, *Directed by Allen Smithee*, with a preface by Andrew Sarris (Minneapolis: University of Minnesota Press, 2001), 249–68, especially 257.

8. In the situation of the immediate postwar years Rossellini discovers "a dispersive and fragmentary *[lacunaire]* reality . . . , especially in *Paisan*, a series of fragmented meetings, cut into pieces, that call into question . . . the action-image." The city is seen "in demolition or reconstruction," and "spaces of any kind whatsoever proliferate, an urban cancer, a dedifferentiated fabric,

rundown areas *[terrains vagues],* that are opposed to the circumscribed spaces of earlier realism" (*L'image-mouvement* [Paris: Minuit, 1983], 285–86).

9. In his work on Foucault and in his two volumes on cinema, Deleuze invokes Blanchot's "Parler, ce n'est pas voir," a dialogue-essay that cuts a line of divide between what can be seen, what can be heard, and what can be known (*L'entretien infini* [Paris: Gallimard, 1969], 35–45). Deleuze's gloss of Foucault, which depends on Blanchot, in which he converts phenomenology into epistemology, is summed up in *Foucault* (Paris: Minuit, 1985), 116–17. I have tried to explicate these difficult and beautiful pages in "Folds and Folding," in Charles Stivale, ed., *Gilles Deleuze: Key Concepts* (Chesham, England: Acumen Books, 2005), 172–73.

10. *L'image-temps* (Paris: Minuit, 1985), 34.

11. In the last chapter of *L'image-temps,* Deleuze asserts that "silent cinema needs to interlace *[entrelacer]* to the maximum the image seen and the image read" (283–84). "Interlace" cannot fail to refer to Maurice Merleau-Ponty's use of the entrelacs of language seen and language heard in *Le visible et l'invisible.* In a careful reading of Deleuze's writings on film, Jacques Rancière shows that the difference between the movement-image and the time-image is at best hypothetical and in practice indiscernible (in *La fable cinématographique* [Paris: Seuil, 2001], 162–63).

12. *La fable cinématographique,* 15.

13. I have tried to work through the concept of the cinematic fable in two essays. The first, on the latent combinations of words and images in *Winchester 73* (Anthony Mann, 1950), is "A Fable of Film: Rancière's Anthony Mann," *SubStance* 33, no. 1 (2004), 91–107. The second, on figure, ground, and writing in *The Man from Laramie* (Anthony Mann, 1955), a western that figures in *La fable cinématographique,* is "Landscape and Perception: On Anthony Mann," in Martin Lefebvre, ed., *Landscape and Film* (New York: Routledge, 2006), 291–314.

14. See the shift from description to image in the treatment of *Boudu sauvé des eaux* (5–6), the montage of text and image on the end of *Paisan* (122–24), the relation of the text on *La bête humaine* to an illustration of a title card in the front credits (132–33), a billboard seen in passing in the opening shots of *The Killers* (156), and the name of the gasoline station that figures in the printed writing above the figure of the protagonist of the same film who is looking at his imminent demise (161).

15. Jacques Derrida, "Signature événement contexte," in *Marges de la philosophie* (Paris: Minuit, 1972), 365–93.

Film Hieroglyphs

Introduction

The "seventh art" has been a heterogeneous medium from its origins, at once narrative and pictural, "diegetic" and mimetic. Since Lumière and Méliès, film has been a benchmark of reality and the most efficient narrative medium since the nineteenth-century novel. At the same time, its own form appears to call into question the narrative powers that have charmed billions of spectators. Wherever a film lures a viewer into its fiction, it also makes obvious how its modes of fabrication are working. In a study of narrative inspired by his reading of Proust, Gérard Genette has argued that a story (an *histoire*) is a sum of events understood in a totality, as an abstraction in whatever medium that conveys them. A tale (a *récit*), he adds, amounts to the oral or written discourse that tells it, while narrative can be called the act producing the discourse.[1] A gap, similar to the slash that separates a signifier from a signified in the world of semiotics, or the unconscious from the conscious in psychoanalysis, is given between the story and its tale. As viewers of cinema we know this well when we allow ourselves the leisure of forgetting the dialogue or movement of the voice and images, or when we turn our attention to memories—by daydreaming in the dark—in distracted play with details that move and disappear on the screen. Other films come forth and block the reading of the movie before our eyes; or thoughts about the day—about desire, trauma, pleasure—come forth in myriad ways to interfere creatively and loosen our attention from the laws of an imaginary contract we have signed to honor the projection seen on the screen. In this way impressions are produced that belong neither quite to themselves nor to the narrations from which they might be inspired. They are tantamount to secret "readings" of film whose value resides in their evanescence. Once these impressions are cast into language after their dialogue between unconscious and narrative registers, they begin to summon issues that ground fabulation, film, and the symbolic exchange of language.

My aim in this book is to consider what seems to be working in that median area, between spectators' fantasies and the facts of the film, and how the viewing of film can be an act of reading and, more cursively, of writing. The study of film, of no matter what kind or period, entails rewriting and reworking the medium for the sake of creative interpretation. I will use as my point of departure the hypothesis that the fuzzy area between film and its massive reception, or the ostensive truth of its form, constitutes its heterogeneity, its mixes of codes and figuring floating between its "stories" and its "discourses."

One of these improbable areas concerns the presence of alphabetical and iconic writing within the field of the moving image. Writing is never the film itself, but both the image and script are together, within each other, in various degrees of tension that cannot be resolved. Often it appears that writing falls into the film "by chance," fugaciously, unbeknownst either to the storyteller or to the spectator. It prompts wonder, divagation, distraction, or even confirmation of what the film is arousing. At other times the mix seems to be determined to serve the purpose of narrative. But it is also crafted to lock the spectator into a double bind, and to strategize communication by virtually producing a collective unconscious designed to behave according to pregiven patterns of interpellation. Certain patterns of writing and image tell us that an industry is selling commodities or producing ideology wherever it can fabricate and control the fantasies of a global population.[2] But if it can be remembered that the unconscious is in fact what knows no control, and whose order works in ways always other than what it is told, then the slide area of creative conflict between dialogue and narrative can be used as a critical and analytical agency. The chapters that follow propose to open onto that zone and offer ways of working within and in ways marginal to strategies of control, whether on the part of the industry, the critical field of its reception, or even the rules of common sense or cognition narrative encourages its viewers to use.

Our work can begin with a figure that Alexandre Astruc used to launch an aesthetic politics that the New Wave would mobilize, that of the *caméra-stylo,* or the camera-pen.[3] With a camera a cineast could, paradoxically, trace an image. In the late 1940s, Astruc's figure of writing offered a highly literate view of film and inspired a generation of filmmakers who conflated cinema and literature. His reflections showed that movies could be read in order to be seen, and that, in the wake of Proust and Sartre, all literature could be seen as a montage or, it can be added, an extended hieroglyph of moving letters. With this figure, both cineast and viewer can mobilize at once the narrative force of writing, its highly allegorical appeal, and its divided essence — its aural and visual "tracks" — to engage a rethinking of itself. Writing, Astruc suggested, is no less a binding of a figure and a discourse than a post-Freudian self is a unit fashioned from mutually alien parts. The image connotes timeless abstraction in its pictural form, while the literal shape of writing, when inserted into the field of the image, denies any stable presence of meaning. The shape of its lines enhances the image, but its meanings distort it. The film may indeed "write" a story of images, but its traces of script change the narrative that is engaged. Implict in the concept of the *caméra-stylo* is a film hieroglyph, a writing that unites and divides word and image; that invokes memory to recall analogous forms of legibility and meaning, which serve and contradict what is before our eyes; that fashions rebuses or unforeseen combinations of pictures and writing that are controlled neither by the film nor by the viewer. Alterity of writing in respect to what it ostensibly transcribes, Astruc suggested, might spur an existential commitment to representing and interpreting the world—to changing patterns of events through the distortions and tensions it produces. And, he implied with the metaphor, film can never be identical to writing but must be imbued with it. Writing may inform film but can never dissolve into an image. Only a sense of the utter difference that exists between the two, or what more recently has been termed a *différend*, could be used to initiate an active and critical relation between filmmaking and film viewing.[4] Astruc's figure of speech had clearly Sartrian undertones that were useful for his time, but today needs specificity to rencw it for more effective ends. It may be useful thus to graft the notion of a hieroglyph onto that of the *caméra-stylo*. In order to lay an analytical foundation for a practice of interpretation, I will sketch the points where writing and film become hieroglyphic. A general sense of filmic writing and reading will be developed for the sake of foregrounding the following chapters that engage the tenets of the introduction.

Title, Credits, and Film

A spectator's range of cognition is framed by the relation the introductory credits hold with the film that follows. Cognitive limits and a ground for interpretation are set in place between the title and the film. Aesthetic, ideological, and political dimensions of the narrative spectacle emerge from movements generated between the graphic traits of the titles, the information they provide, their generic conventions, and, especially, their recurrence within and throughout the film. From cognition of the first word that heralds a film, a mechanism of delay and deferral is set in place. The title, posed as an enigma above and before the images, finds its solutions in the spectator's work, which must, almost contractually, aim at forgetting them, at rediscovering the fantasies of their impact, or then finding their manifold meanings throughout the narrative and its images. Sometimes the experience of viewing confirms what is suggested in the title's apparent meaning; often it is betrayed. Otherwise, by way of allegory, its sense is verified when a film and its title happen to interpret each other. Frequently the visual design of the credits inflects the composition of the feature as a whole.

In this respect the relation of credits to the film resembles an unconscious dimension of literature, in which its force of meaning derives from movements that are common to emblematic traditions in literature. An initial figure is posed as a somewhat arcane, stenographic shape above a picture or inscription—which can be a body of text as well as a drawing—mediated by a subscription, or explicative materials below.[5] From the study of the superscription, the image, and the gloss beneath, a triangular course of visual and textual interpretation is established. It moves between different discourses, one of two languages (superscription and subscription being of different tongues), modes of representation (an image and two texts), and of discourses of two different aspects (one dense and arcane, the other explicative and prosaic).[6] In filmic terms, a reader's or spectator's sense of process and discovery—or of interpretation—is begun in the delays that come with the difference in time and modes of cognition, as in emblematics, spent in the displacement between an initial viewing of the credits and the reading of the film. A title can be a superscription, the credits a subscription, and the film a central "inscription." No less pertinent, the illusion of participation or spectatorial enrichment happens when the viewer abstracts or "figures out" what appears to be the whole of the film, that is, a synthesis of writing—insofar as it produces and concretizes the moving pictures—and the pictures themselves. Viewers produce the illusion that they are "learning" or "working through" a relation that needs to be—because it has already been done by the director, the cutters, and the editors—"elucidated." The intelligence of the spectator is almost entirely built into the mechanism that the relation of writing and credits establishes with the narrative of images.

The system can be at once arcane and simple. At times the credits, if they are superimposed on the images that begin the narrative, can produce self-contained rebuses that sum up, duplicate, or mirror the figurative process of the entire film. At other times, when scripted over a blank or abstract background, letters or words tend to inaugurate a rapport of nonidentity with the film, and the narrative can become something other than what is announced. In either instance, the instability yielded by the placement of credits over and within a moving picture has the effect of unfixing the linearity of the general narrative design. Writing induces a linear reading of an image, but its own nondiscursive traits can jostle or complicate its meaning enough to make of its signs a tabular, pictural, even tactile ensemble of letters. It invokes an alienating effect within its own form, such that what is read as an apparent title in orthogonal fashion, because of the presence of the image at the initial—hence most provocative and enticing, or most underdetermined—moment of the viewing, can be subjected to graphic analysis. In this way the letter of the title no longer holds truth in a spectator's faith in an illusory grammar or natural extension of things. As a function of the pictural surface, the letters of a title can be broken apart, splayed, and recombined. The viewer is free to see writing as a compositional design that has everything—as well as nothing—to do with what is meant. At these moments viewers can play constructive havoc with the limits of a film's ostensive meaning. By appeal to interpretive tactics common to poetic analysis,[7] they can force the film, because of its only illusory sheen of truth associated with the writing of its title, to become validly other than what it says it is. Such alterity within a field of meaning brings forth glimpses of an unconscious dimension of film. Spectators begin to study the mix of its elements and detect what programmatic ideologies, whether of a film industry, a director's "point of view," or a filmic analysis usually derived from institutional pedagogy, cannot strategically control.[8]

The rapport of credits to a film is further complicated by the profusion of advertisements and marketing that already interpret the rapport of image and writing before a viewing takes place. Most often, the configurations in trailers, newspapers, or magazines that herald a film will duplicate what is obvious in the difference within writing and the image track in the film. Here, however, the work of subliminality, or what might be called a poster-unconscious,[9] or a configuration of forms and shapes that baits the viewer, elicits the same will to interpret or to "come and see"—or to inaugurate a scene of visibility, to *commencer*—what is effected in the credits.[10] Spectators move to and from pregiven writing and pictures and those in the film. Scenes represented in newspapers are discovered in the ways they match or differ from the imaginary constructs they elicit. Hence, both before and after the viewing, if the overall strategy of promotion works, a matrix of ambivalence will determine what a film means. Yet in the play of the relation of credits and writing to the image, the allegorical structure (an aspect usually based on what is thought to be a consumer's desire) can be loosened or flattened.

Such loosening can be seen through a pictural metaphor taken from the canon of classical painting, in whose conventions signatures are set in the lower right-hand corner of the frame. At the moment the writing is apprehended along the margins, a mode of intellection apparently changes; we read what we have been seeing. In retracing the signature, all of a sudden, we decipher the work in a different register. Yet with a signature the work immediately acquires symbolic stature, is subject to archival or historical control, develops abstract worth, and is commodifiable. A signature puts a painting into circulation. Or, if the title of the painting is placed where the proper name is generally assigned its place, the words tend to direct or to "freeze" the pictural mass into an order that is iconically determined by the directions of the title's meaning. When Marcel Duchamp paints the uppercase title in Geneva-like type, in a red miming the color of Courbet's signature at the lower left-hand corner of his *Nu descendant un escalier,* the four words ask the viewer to find an anthropomorphic mass where there is none. But at the same time, the image inflects the writing so that the diagonal, almost futuristic motion of the scene finds itself motivated in the reversal—back and forth, up and down—of ''nu descendant un escalier,'' by which the vectors of a palindrome emerge from the words to suggest how the effect of vertical and diagonal motion is both erotic and imaginary. The *nu,* of new decency, is of no code or sex other than its own symmetry in writing and in suspension in the mind's eye of the painted image. The *nu* also *un*ifies and *un*does the scene on the stairway. Duchamp's title as signature both anticipates the picture and translates its effect into its own graphic or ''n(e)utralizing'' play. That the words are situated at an optical origin, the corner, of the tableau is hardly surprising, for the writing theorizes the optical and intellectual motion of lines, a body, and letters. In the credits of a film, what holds for the writing in respect to the visual composition plays a no less powerful a role.

Writing in the Film

The silent tradition had carefully developed an effective way of placing writing within the field of the image. On strictly pragmatic levels insertion of toponyms—on mailboxes, shop windows in the background, books or photos placed on desks adjacent to the players—could assure the viewer of narrative continuity when the sign of a person, a name, or a place needed to be designated in the plot. Markers inserted in the visual field allowed the film industry to avoid recourse to intertitles that broke the continuity of the images. Silent cinema quickly drew a line between a desire to retain a pure flow of shots without undue interference of titles and the need to use writing for the sake of continuity. Titles were kept to a minimum, but, when present, they engaged the complexities and ironies at work on the image track.[11] They were part of the complex rhythm that the cutters and director sought in the ensemble of shots and overall montage. Placed within the image and in a fashion ensuring a realistic effect, by which the words would be informative but also a ''natural'' part of the composition, writing could obviate the use of intertitles or destine them for more varied symbolic purposes. The titler could work with subtle counterpoint, for example, when the audience had acquired the habit of lipreading.[12]

In mediating writing and the image, both silent and sound cinemas projected the spectator onto various fields of ambivalence and contradiction. Beyond the expediency of effective combinations of writing on and off frame, the mix produced a dissonance or difference that European directors were especially able to exploit. For in a tradition that had developed from experiments in cubism, the collage, the readymade, or in surreal painting, bits of writing were inserted into pictural fields for the effect of flattening all illusory depth taken for granted in the compositional traditions inherited from the Albertian Renaissance. Pieces of script inserted in a painting neutralized its depth of illusion but also offered points allowing a gridding of other spatial relations. Interplays and contrasts resulted, but with the overall virtue of inaugurating movements to and from image and figure. The image, seen in terms of tones and fields of color, whose intersecting edges drew lines of force throughout the interior of the frame, was disturbed by writing, which precipitated an incomplete act of intellection—reading—in the more sensuous play of visual forms. Yet the image fractured the intellectual dimension where letters, ticket stubs, shards of newsprint, or stenciled numbers did not sustain continuous reading. Figures could be seen in a tabular or painterly relation with words. From the combination of image and text a sort of gaze was fashioned, through which the spectator could discern forms evident less with applied study than by chance or distracted attention. The eye roved. It mixed visual shapes with those of discourse. Scattered figures had the effect of pulling a depth of field, the stuff of the classical tradition of painting, up to a single plane all the while writing became invested with its own tabular and pictural depth enticing and disallowing penetration.

In a very real way, a graphic urgency of unconscious forms resulted from the heterogeneous mix and splice of the two media. Through the agency of translation, where a figure was transformed into color and form, and vice versa, painters and collage makers could fashion paradoxes of identity and difference. In their rebuses, one shape both canceled and identified the other of which it was a part. Image and figure affirmed and betrayed each other, revealing their hidden rhetoric not through steps of rational procedure but by means of a visible obviousness. Braque, Schwitters, and Gris no doubt led the visual arts into intense play of form that showed exactly the risks of placing illusion or two-dimensional creations onto planar surfaces. From the period of what Apollinaire called "analytical" cubism to Picasso's return to representational painting toward the end of the First World War, the visual revolution in painting had immediate impact on artists working with cinema. Cineasts could, in the path of Apollinaire's *Calligrammes,* also say, "We too are painters." Experiment with writing in a lexicon of compositional tension took place in mixed media. Where it was studied in its virtualities, a vanguard cinema—such as that of Richter or Duchamp—resulted. When it relegated its unconscious play to apparent thematic control, narrative and "classical" film resulted. Yet one tradition could not help but play on and off the other. With artistic experiment, writing became a function mediating and conflating surfaces, depth, and forms; with narrative work, writing was folded into illusion for the sake of a strategic production of the unconscious that subtended narrative. The two traditions appear to meet especially forcefully in the 1930s and 1940s, when directors who had been spawned in the world of European cubism emigrated to California and renewed experiment within the film industry.[13] The tensions at work between the two traditions, it will be seen later, pervade Hollywood cinema to the extent of developing much of its aesthetics from the plastic heritage of European painting and film.

With writing conceived as a compositional element in the visuals of film, the narrative that it helps to convey is both aided and subverted. Hence, illusion and narrative passivity are broken: the spectator sees how any concatenation of meaning is fissured from within the division of speech and writing or broken with the shift by which one "track" is altered by the other. Writing appears to generate the elemental fissure; it leads to and draws away from image and voice. It can be observed that the developing industry cashed in on the difference in order to produce sustained contradiction long after painters and vanguard filmmakers had articulated tensions in mixing the two media. Yet since, as in the trope of irony, contradiction cannot be controlled by a single source of language, the artful spectator could then—and now—deflate even the most grandiose narrative enterprise. It is here that film writing, like interpretation, discovers over and over again its creative origins.

Sometimes viewers see the act of reading or writing performed in a film. On these occasions both silent and sound films literally spell out the difference of image and writing. In *Tierra sin pan* (*Land without Bread*, 1932) Buñuel has one of the children from a remote town in the hills of southwestern Spain write, on a blackboard illumined by reflectors keylighting a sequence taken in a classroom, a cursive rendition of what the sound track had said it was inculcating in the children: "Respectad los bienes ajenos." The boy chalks the Golden Rule in a hesitant but firm hand, revealing in script the ultimate lesson of the film, which the voice of the colonial narrator cannot grasp. The basic law of ethnography comes into being within the world seemingly alien or even hostile to any "inscription" of a Western camera. All of a sudden, Buñuel's film begins to write and to emblematize its mission to respect the alterity of the Hurdano world that it is simultaneously desecrating. Or when Anna Karina scripts a description of herself on gridded paper on the plastic tabletop of a café in *Vivre sa vie* (*My Life to Live*, 1962), her hand traces the instant that the film inaugurates, reflects upon, and translates. Its lived, organic time coincides with its own shift into the absolute here and now of the character's life. The vanguard filmmakers seem to theorize what, in the Hollywood tradition, the dying Humphrey Bogart writes with a lead bullet onto a shard of paper on the mountainside of *High Sierra* (1941): that an absolute present of the film coincides with the tracing of the message.

André Bazin has shown how the act of writing in Bresson's *Journal d'un curé de campagne* (*Diary of a Country Priest*, 1955) determines an obvious and self-canceling present of eternity in the lap dissolves combining the image of the hand writing the journal, the voice-off reading the same words, and the events within the image just as they take place. The impact of these moments is no different when we catch Al Pacino, in the role of a reborn Scarface, speaking into a receiver by a telephone canopy in Brian De Palma's 1982 remake of Howard Hawks's film of 1932. As Pacino, playing Tony Montana, carefully slurs his diction, next to his mouth is written, almost as a phylactery in the field of view, the

word PHONE. His act of speech, because his mouth is aimed at the writing heralding the public telephone, forces the viewer's eye to rewrite the word in allegorical harmony with his character. "Phone" becomes *Phon(è)* or speech, which
yields *phony,* or even a bestial *faune,* an epithet fitting both Pacino's role and the
film in general. In historical and pragmatic terms, what had been ancillary to the
image in narrative now generates and mirrors its own meaning all the while it
tells where the spectator can locate its raison d'être in the identities of verbal and
visual composition. These crucial moments in film indicate how spectators can
discover where the medium acts out, as it registers writing taking place, its own
principles and technical conditions.

The Written Reference: The Allegorical Dimension

Writing, it has been observed, is used to make narrative unravel in silent cinema.
At the same time it possesses the virtue of being able to allegorize, that is, to
problematize the relation of its part to the whole of the film. In this sense a piece
of script can serve as a visual *mise-en-abyme* or interior duplication that sums up
the seemingly greater problems of character and intrigue within a given shot. In
New Wave cinema, the ubiquitous presence of book titles next to characters underscores and offsets the filmic language as if to construct a filmic hieroglyph. In
A bout de souffle (*Breathless,* 1959), Godard places the title of Maurice Sachs's
Abracadabra in extreme close-up while, voice-off, Jean-Claude Belmondo, portraying Michel Poiccard, speaks frontally to Jean Seberg (Patricia Franchini) and
the spectator about his father's background as a musician. The effect is double, as
the speech-off collides with the cabalistic writing of the near palindrome of the
book's arcane title evoking the very witchcraft of Godard's compositions. Mystery and death are displayed all the while the film translates the figure of one
musical instrument into another. Belmondo's father, whom the English subtitle
invokes in the writing, "Sure, he was great with a clarinet," affronts the figure
of a Sachs, or the homonym of a saxophone. Clarinet and sax form a rebus-pun
summarizing the way the film is constructed.[14] The moment divides the two principal tracks, revealing exactly how the gap is generally "sutured" for the sake of
continuity; Godard's style uses a written reference to sum up a compositional
process that supersedes the narrative, inspired from many anterior versions of the
Orpheus myth, recounting the love of two childish characters attempting to free
themselves of their cultural patrimony.

The rebus is a miniature allegory scripted into the film. Allusion to Sachs's
novel displaces the story but also summarizes its musical and graphic components. The close-up interrupts but also makes the writing and image cohere. In
other films graphic inscriptions may not be so immediately significant; they may
require extensive decipherment if they are being used to translate and duplicate
the film in figurative syntax. In the opening shots of Bertolucci's *The Conform-*

ist, behind the scrolling credits, a contemplative Jean-Louis Trintignant moves in a space adjacent to a window on the right—supposedly, because of the flashing neon marquee to the right and outside, a hotel room in the convention of theater and classical cinema. Along a vertical axis the sign flashes, in art deco majuscules, "La vie est à nous." On the one hand, the writing sets up a skewed visual order where the letters plunge downward and contrast the extended horizontal path of the credits. But on the other, both the reference and the neon-flash effect make the writing disappear and appear. Reference is made both "on" and "off" in relation to the original title, *Il conformista,* which is simultaneously a novel by Moravia and a production by Bertolucci. A close-up of the marquee cuts *estan* out of *La vie est à nous,* further complicating the mix of languages already seen. But the marquee is also an allusion to Jean Renoir's film of 1936, *La vie est à nous,* which was dedicated to the Popular Front. Renoir, Bertolucci, Moravia: who is betraying whom, in what language, for what nation, and why? Allusion to the filmic and political left of the prewar years is on the visible right, while Trintignant, the Fascist who is betraying the left, will be placed in the middle of the frame, immobilized by the cinematic and historical forces that frame him. A geography of tension is established by the tabular aspect and the allusion to film within the film.[15] The spectator is visibly caught between opposing forces that the textual and historical allusion—both the Popular Front and the Spanish Civil War—draws into the film through the horizontal and vertical configurations of the frame duplicated within the image and, later, the narrative.

Allusive snatches of writing often arrest the narrative by summing it up long before it comes to visible completion. The ambiguities of a film's design are set in miniature or are enclosed in the whole. Because of its imaginary totality, writing can introduce a unity contrary to the overall flow of images. Here powers of allegory break up the continuity it apparently underlines. The foreign totality of written interpretation within and constitutive of the film invests the narrative with renewed force. In properly literary terms, the film establishes "a double approach, a double attention to the surfaces of works and their psychic effects and significance."[16] Image and writing produce conflicts manifest among the image track, the field of reference in the writing (as if it were an element integral to the compositional design, its own possibility of future division into allegorical subunits, and an imaginary field of visibility). In this latter direction the title of a book or a film within a film can—with effective distortion—lead beyond and through the limits it appears to designate. The spectator can supplement the film with a wealth of information that the title cannot or does not control.

When, in *Boudu sauvé des eaux,* Lestingois sighs with ingenuous disgust upon discovering that Boudu has spit on a handsome edition of Balzac's *Physiologie du mariage,* his reaction, couched in allusion to the nineteenth-century novelist's parodic sketches of the double standards of middle-class conjugal life, refers not only to the bookseller's household that perpetuates the same duplicity.

Nor does it simply align Renoir with the cult of force and dissemination (which defies legal control) associated with Rodin's sculpted myth of an ever-virile Balzac. The book associates writing with a world lacking physical drive, an environment where water, an element that has no pictural border to contain it, is necessarily absent. The book's title refers to a hidden emblem, seen at least five times in the film, of a sprinkling can adjacent to the upper end of the spiral stairway in the apartment's narrow passage. Shot with a lens of long focal length, the can is flattened against the floral decor of the wallpaper background. The liquid in the container can only water flowers on wallpaper, thanks to a visual conundrum announced by reference to Balzac in spittle. Years later, however, Renoir, playing a music critic in *La règle du jeu,* sighs dejectedly to the woman he loves unrequitedly, "All I can do in life is spit . . . ,'' as if he were recalling a lifelong paradox of cinematic virtue begun in *Boudu.* The webbing of allusions caught in the title does not fashion a moral allegory so much as it grounds Renoir's study of interior and exterior space. The allusion to liquid, in moving from *La physiologie du mariage* to the emblem of the sprinkler, entails lenses of different focal lengths and ranges of inversion. His allegory, as the later films confirm, veers away from a comedy of class and leans toward cinema.

Often the presence of writing reveals a seemingly unconscious allegorical dimension that both controls the narrative order of a film and, like Renoir's allusions, exceeds the strategies for which it is used when it envelops the camera into its field of analogy. In the Hollywood of the 1930s and 1940s, where continuity dictated that the film rarely be overtly reflective of the industry's own mode of production, visible allegories of film within film would appear to be few and far between. But they are often insinuated polymorphously in the tradition. Mitchell Leisen's *Arise, My Love* (1940), a sort of Sturges-style screwball comedy turned engagé, has Ray Milland and Claudette Colbert fall in love and convert to the anti-isolationist cause of the late prewar years. Together they impel the American public to respond to the crimes committed in Europe under fascism. Finished prior to Roosevelt's declaration of war on December 8, 1941, the film weaves a romantic narrative around all the sites of Europe where violence has been wrought. Milland, a freewheeling soldier of fortune who aimlessly used his talents as an aviator for the Republican cause in the Spanish Civil War, has been convicted as a criminal under the Franco regime and awaits his death in Burgos at the hands of a firing squad. The year is 1939. Portraying an eccentric journalist in Europe writing nostalgic stories about Americans lost from current view, Claudette Colbert flirts her way into the prison, in the guise of Milland's despondently hysterical (or just plain wacky) spouse, to obtain a pardon from the Spanish commandant ("Oh, these Americans,'' waxes George Zucco, playing the role of the pardoning officer, about the couple's apparently zany attraction for each other). They are permitted to leave, but then steal a squad car, drive recklessly over the countryside to an airfield, plunge through a barrier, and get away with an idle plane parked by a hangar. They take off, ascending into the empyrean ahead of the gunfire of soldiers who follow at their heels. Their ventures lead them all over Europe and end with the refrain that rings with renewed love for America. "Arise, my love," they tell the viewers in harmony, to warn everyone of the European cataclysm that threatens the world. The personal drama of two screwballs becomes collectively urgent.

Their patriotic cause gets complicated by the graphics of filmic allegory. When the couple brakes the speeding car, runs to the hatch on the starboard side of the aircraft's fuselage, starts the engines, and finally takes off, the title of the film returns through Milland's voice. Framed in medium shot in profile, revving the engines, as Colbert bounces about at his right side, Milland exclaims, "Here it is, as in the Song of Solomon, two, ten: 'Arise, my love, my fair one, and come away.'" He accelerates (motor noise is heard *off*, in crescendo), pulling the guiding stick toward his belly to raise the aircraft's stabilizer. After the take-off, thrashing her typewriter, Colbert exclaims to the flier—at this early moment in the film, "Don't you think we've had enough climaxes for today?!" *My Love* now points to Milland's phallus, represented—as a phallus should be—detached from his body and as an abstraction, in the shape of the airplane's "stick" between his legs. The social cause of the film is entirely a function of its libidinal comedy, which continuously portrays its subjects under the blade at once of Hitler and symbolic castration.

The implicit equivalence also arches the movie toward self-reflection, or broader consideration of the film's own degree of allegorical potency. In the shots immediately preceding the reinscription of the title, the couple scrambles into the plane. They are shot scurrying from the car (behind or adjacent to the camera) to the doorhatch. Colbert runs back for her typewriter, lugs it under her arm, drops it as she raises her skirt while clambering into the plane, and picks it up.[17] She defers the action to promote the spectacle, but also allures the viewer into reading an inscription, next to her hips, printed on the fuselage for a calmly realistic effect: the letters KJNO, a sort of license number stenciled on the aluminum panels, give the craft the air of a Russian Stormovik left over after the defeat of the Republicans. The mark would be evidence of the Soviet alliance with the Communists against the Fascists. But, K-J-N-O also spells K-I-N-O, or the Russian noun for cinema couched in vaguely Spanish apparel. The airplane is obliquely named as a sort of "motor of history" in the guise of the film industry, in other words, another lure or phallus suscitating desire (in the near homonym, it might be added, of "Arise, my love," "Arouse, my love," or "A ruse, my love") and determining the parade of events in the film as, partially, an object of its own self-promotion. The anti-isolationist cause of the film is thus tied to the war as a mechanism of desire and gains manifold force when read in terms of the graphics that betray it.[18] The mode of desire the industry uses for its economy is insinuated in the allegory being advanced.

Seen thus, relations of graphics to erotic rewriting of a film within a film prevail in Hollywood and invariably figure what is at work in its industry. Its rhetoric of desire often overrides both genres and stars. The allegorical dimension of the literal surface of John Huston's revered *African Queen* (1951) very much betrays Katharine Hepburn's recent best-selling memoir about its filming. That everyone suffered pain while working on the dark continent is evident in the soundtrack recording of the incessant buzz of insects, or the image track, which shows leeches all over Bogart's torso when he pulls his boat through the marshes. The plot, much like *Arise, My Love,* and *It Happened One Night,* has to do with two different protagonists "getting there." They must reach a destination, the sea, but if they are to get there, they must also get together. The underside of the narrative is of course reflected in the title, with the African Queen being Hepburn all the while the drama brings together two aging figures from opposite ends of the social and geographical ladder. They work when they go about their affairs: when, after one of many allegorical mishaps, Bogart has to repair the bent driveshaft connecting his boat's motor to its propeller, a series of lap dissolves speeds up the time of labor expended to straighten his shaft. The hero plunges under water to fish out and hammer into place the long iron rod under the stern. Above, Hepburn bends over the gunwales to encourage her captain. Below, Bogart buoys up in the bubbles. Within a few fleeting instants of the several dissolves an allegory of filmic writing is traced: Bogart's body and Hepburn's body are edited to be seen evanescently in deviant sexual poses. Writing out the number 69, they engage fugaciously in oral copulation and confirm, in their configuration, what Hepburn and Bogart constantly ask each other on the sound track: "Do you think we can do it, Charlie?"[19] *It* becomes a shifter, a floating figure with numerous referents in the allegory (the trip, the political gesture of sinking the enemy boat), as well as the ineffable dimension of eros written into the lap dissolve and the filming of the two bodies engaged in fellatio. The film transliterates a scenic drama and mythic structure of voyage or quest into an erotic comedy whose basic enigma asks if two aging subjects, with their symbolically rotting pudenda, can find love in old age. In this respect the film twists back to self-allegory, in which it plays with Bogart's own physical decrepitude — when he was dying of stomach cancer[20] — and a graphic "typing" of Hepburn in the stock of airy roles habitually assigned to her in the industry. The junctures of the film — here the lap dissolves — concretize its relation to a consciously unconscious program far more than does the narrative or the myth of its production on location in the Third World. Patterns of this type of allegorical writing have changed little in the industry since *The African Queen.*

An erotic writing is scripted between the bodies as they are posed, matched, and dissolved in the framing and editing. They become figures in a rhetoric of camouflage. The film confuses the political and erotic registers in its moments of transition and slippage. These effects, which both screen and reveal these dimensions, seem obvious wherever image and writing are combined. But in *The African Queen* a different grammar emerges from the overlay of images. The film cannot denote its overriding conflation of decomposing sex organs and death within its characters; it must shunt the confusion into the gaps between sequences and in the innuendo of speech that floats free of images that would otherwise locate its meaning. Hence, the indeterminate ''it'' of ''Can we do it?'' finds a referent only in the camouflage of montage.[21]

The Signature

A debated term in literary and cinematic theory, the signature calls into question the qualities of the proper name. Who authors a film? Are the persons who are said to sign their names adequately ''represented'' or motivated by it? Do the literal form and combination of figures in the signature codify a historical subject once and for all, or is the name itself an indication of a conventional, serialized commodity? The questions raise issues as old as the dialogue of Hermogenes and his interlocutors of the *Cratylus,* but they also are centered on current dialogues taken up in literary and cinematic theory. In the former realm, the signature has been seen less and less as an apothegm giving bona fide cause or essence to the person who writes it than an act, a theatrical event, that stages a play of identity, origin, conscience, selfhood, or alterity.[22] It has been the area, since the impact of Michel Foucault, where the notion of the author, the individual writer, or the subject has been almost entirely erased. In the latter, where the concept of the auteur as a director has depended on the signature as a loosely defined unit summarizing a particular ensemble of tendencies, of themes — or even of visual traits that run through and across films of different stripe — issues of origin are no less problematic. From a standpoint that used the signature to analyze the great body of films produced in Hollywood or France in the 1930s and 1940s, critics (mostly of French extraction, after Astruc, and aligned with the early vision of *Cahiers du cinéma*) often and successfully challenged the imperium of entertainment. Like it or not, Hollywood was a haven of real artists. Canny interpretations of the medium were made in the name of the signature, introducing lateral or transversal categories into the history of film. Certain auteurs, in the line of Jean Renoir, were seen producing elsewhere in many films one total, unfinished, conceptual Film — like Mallarmé's fabled but necessarily fragmented and unfinished *Livre* — of a given proper name. Genres, styles, and technical limitations were crossed: Lang, Hawks, Ford, Wyler, and Welles had specific styles in their choice and interpretation of stories; their decors and locations; their preferred actors and actresses; their camera work and their editing.

Yet, as literary analysis has shown, the personal signature has been personal only insofar as it appertains to a generally recognizable collectivity. The signature has to be both conventional and special, both a product of an industry and evidence of a given touch or tact of its own. At once a type, a historical trait, and an interpretation of themes, the signature is (or was) both evident but seen "erased" in a greater play of collective forms. Certain films and filmmakers, however, have been seen doing more than "signing" their films allusively in the tensions of the individual artist and the common traditions of film. They literalize their style in and through an arcane body of obsessions that bind thematic and visual problems no less cohesively than a rebus conflates the difference between voice and image. Some filmmakers weave a hidden, always scriptural language of forms in and across their works. In the European tradition, where the association of film and art has been postulated far more willingly than in Hollywood, the rapport of the auteur, the signature, and the film appears less strained.[23] In the classical studio years of America, where the director was a piston in an industrial cylinder, that relation is evinced in blur along the edges and margins of a conventional visual rhetoric. Since the signature is more subtle and problematic in its articulation in the visual medium, it is paradoxically all the more obvious and hence, in its obviousness, all the more unconscious, or of a "difficult" visual fabric.

On the same score, the resistance that the directorial signature encounters in Hollywood becomes part and parcel of the visual expression—and repression—that the entertainment industry created. The "law" of the signature turns into that of classical film, in which it is seen only in its evanescence as writing returning from and disappearing into oblivion, like the "repressed" of Freudian name, but only recurring otherwise and elsewhere throughout an entire oeuvre. Its modes of return are many and often require pictural reading that studies the ways a sign is placed in the frame in relation to other elements of the compositional body.

A constant trait prevails and can be located through appeal to the concept of the *objet de perspective,* or perspectival object. Coined by Guy Rosolato to study the visual and verbal fields at work in clinical practice, the term applies to the way subjects (or patients undergoing psychoanalysis) visualize or indicate through the bias of speech nodal points in their descriptive relation to the world they see and live. He calls it a "signifier for a representation of the unknown," by which, in a clearly Freudian operation, a child spots a figure that covers an imaginary lack (usually of maternal origin);[24] it is seen, repressed, or translated into other areas of physical exchange, such as that of the body with its transitional objects (and in certain respects, these could be the experience or the memory of films) that brings forth pleasure but also fears of confusion and death if it is lost from view. A narcissistic object serving as a wall built in defense against the Other, against desire as a function of the phallus and bliss (128), it acquires spatial and plastic qualities wherever the subject expresses fear of the unknown: the *objet de perspective* may be akin to a vanishing point in classical painting, where the lure of a resolution of pictural and narrative tensions appears to offer an escape from physical constraints but actually does not; or it may be an appeal to an imaginary space of resolution that is the "happy ending" of a film—such as the rays of dawn that crown the unsettling conclusion to *Mildred Pierce*—that promises none. It figures a concentrated point of attention that captures what a subject chooses to see, simply because in it resides what cannot, because of its paradoxical evidence and accessibility, be seen. Rosolato's concept, built in part over Merleau-Ponty's study of the relations that hold between the eye and the mind, shows that "we see only what we are looking at";[25] that is, we see only what our drives determine to be significant according to the ways our bodies animate our relations with the world. What subjects discern locates where they are, but the same objects also elude their visual grasp of things.

Perspectival objects can also be analogous to signatures in film. They constitute a recognizable order of meaning, but their quasi-metaphorical status at once protects and projects their mystery. A spectator quickly discerns series of visual or lexical units that characterize an "auteur"—for instance, deep-focus photography, John Wayne, Monument Valley, Maureen O'Hara, Victor McLaglen, low-angle shots in interiors that pull ceilings down into an already small space, Latin crosses tipped into the montage, in other words, traits common to John Ford's autograph—in order to have the film respond to the information announced in the credits, or have it make coherent aesthetic sense. Each of these shares much with a cipher, or a determining mark that identifies coordinates of tension in the film and leads the eye to seek resolution at the vanishing point of its narrative or image. The *objet de perspective* complicates, however, when conventions of cinema use classical perspective to locate bodies or objects in filmic space. Studio traditions depend on vanishing points for the purpose of having spectators see a visual exit or *deus ex machina* where the characters in the film do not. The triangular relation scaffolded among the viewer, the figures on screen, and the spatial depth effectively shows where narrative and visual solutions, each displaced in the same space of a given shot, produce the literal ambiguities of a classical film.

In an empty tavern, Johnny Ringo (Gregory Peck), in Henry King's austere masterpiece, *The Gunfighter* (1950), begs his estranged wife for enough time to see his eight-year-old son before he continues his solitary journey through life. The camera locates the couple in profile, facing each other in front of and below a pendulum clock on the wall immediately behind and between them. The dial provides information about time passing according to the Aristotelian "unity" to which the film subscribes. Its triangular relation with the two figures contributes much to the film's realistic effect by narrating the tale toward classic closure, but all the while it also allegorizes the gunfighter's existential plight by forcing the viewer to compare the way time has "run out" for the aging hero now undone by his former ways. But as an *objet de perspective,* the clock forces the eye to apprehend it in the frame as a literal point that promises the contrary of vanishment into absolution. The clock flattens the depth of field it establishes, and its position in respect to the characters divides the screen into halves and separates the image track from the sound track. It becomes a "signature" to the film and is almost a filmic icon, that is, an object that turns into a rebus with a shard of writing literalizing the film's script. In this scene, the clock makes Peck's name, Ringo, turn into its own graphic center, its bull's-eye of death at its own narrative end, in Ring-O, or an endless closure of circles within each other. If a broader analogy can be followed, it signals how the closure of figures in space becomes a convention in Henry King's work, from *Jesse James* (1939) to *The Sun Also Rises* (1957).

In the tradition of the novel and classical cinema, these visual points become synonymous with the appearance of letters that disengage themselves from the semantic field of the text or the image. Adrift in syntax, they carry meaning along one axis of intellection, that is, an axis associated with the effort the spectator engages in to make the images carry narrative meaning, but virtually nothing on another, in the drift of space. The letter sallies forth from an image field because it belongs neither to narrative nor to image, just as an uncanny mark (a name, a cipher, a number) can become visible in a body of writing when it does not fit in the syntax. In both instances the letter marks and delimits a characteristic space according to the style of an author and a convention. But neither quite yields meaning that a spectator would like to derive from the field of images. Letters become laden with psychic energies whose particular dynamics are caught in an overall matrix of force and tension set between cognition and the traits of the auteur.

An illustration of the problem can be taken from the European tradition: in Vittorio De Sica's model of neorealism, *Ladri di biciclette* (1948), poor Ricci finally obtains employment when his wife pawns the family's sheets to redeem his bicycle. An old man has just come to pawn his binoculars. Then Ricci arrives with his sheets (and, as it were, an allegory complementing the optical apparatus as a sort of crumpled screen). After a stunning vertical pan that records the thousands of cubicles in which similar bundles of sheets—and, by direct implication, similar movies—are pigeonholed, a sense of the utter gratuity of the story is gained. But the irony is confirmed later only by an *objet de perspective* that becomes visible at the moment a Roman urchin, hiding behind a car, responds to an older gang leader who stands on the sidewalk next to Ricci as he attends to his labors. The hoodlum is seen stalking his way across a row of parked vehicles. He runs forward, grabs Ricci's bicycle, jumps on the saddle, and pedals downward into a throng of traffic and people. Just prior to this initial theft, Ricci had been pasting to the wall the lower left edge of a poster displaying the body and name of Rita Hayworth. A promotion for *Gilda* doubles and mirrors the perspective: Ricci has struggled to obtain a job mounting posters from, it is implied, the degrading Hollywood entertainment industry at a time when Italy would be better off handling its social problems. The spatial relation of the corner of the poster and the corner of the whole frame makes De Sica's enterprise identical to what his film puts in question. It is ideologically alike but also, along the edge between the poster and the frame, irrecuperably different. The unresolved irony of the rapport of the name of Rita Hayworth, the edge of the poster, her curves, Ricci's mucilage daubed over her calves, and his wet brush become funny and, in their allure, no less maddening. The psychic ambiguity by which the name-in-the-film, Rita Hayworth, is translated into increased constraint, is found in the shot detailing the sequence of the theft. The establishing shot of the thief creeping up the sidewalk between the wall and the cars takes as its visual cue of depth an uncanny, almost fuzzy letter in the background in the center of the frame, an uppercase P that apparently, but only apparently in the graphic Esperanto, signifies a space in the depth of field reserved for "P" . . . arking. It is we who supply the letter with meaning when we see its placement in a vanishing perspective thresholding the area in which the theft takes place. The ostensive meaning, however, is canceled later in the film, at the moment when, seen from another, diametrically opposite view, we discern the same letter P once again, now above a crowd of cars and bicycles that fills the median ground between the point of view of the shot (the enraged and desperate Ricci, who has been reduced to sitting with his son on the curb) and the modern Coliseum in the background, filled with a mass of raving spectators who could be memories of the barbaric Rome of Juvenal's time or a soccer match of the postwar years. The perspective object, the P, recurs like the repressed, and it "keys" Ricci's complementary theft in exactly the same visual rhetoric that seemingly had catalyzed that of the youth much earlier in the film. The irony of Ricci-Rita Hayworth gives way to a more mutual, but also more maddening, mirror of the P-cipher. It defies meaning, but it also schematizes the enigma of reversal in the film all the while it manifests a larger signature — that of De Sica, whose work plays on serial, even alphabetic, relations of humans who are alienated within an arbitrarily numerical environment, as that of the perspective shown in *Umberto D* (1952) and, later, *The Roof* (1957).

In Hollywood, the signature and perspectival object have protean expression but are no less prone to bait the viewer. Certain directors sustained their identities through the tensions fanning among their styles, the studios that employed them, and their own oeuvre developing within the industry. Raoul Walsh, whom we will study in detail in chapters 3, 4, and 7, made 120 films from 1914 to 1964, in various studios, and in an astonishing range of genres spanning the western, the war film, the comedy, and the musical. Upon first glance his status as an auteur can be attributed to relentless movement and action. Psychological complexity plays a minor role in films that move so quickly. Yet, as Andrew Sarris has keenly observed, Walsh's depiction of the male "with pathos and vulnerability" subtends the trademarks of action and violence.[26] Furthermore, his tendency to isolate males bonded in self-contained units, generally in military quarters, men's jobs, or in prisons (*What Price Glory? They Drive by Night, Manpower, White*

Heat), as Pamela Cook and Claire Johnston have implied, reverses into a proto-typical feminism, in which males are females who also live in menacing conditions, a depiction that runs against the grain of Hollywood ideology.[27] The signature subverts the ideology of the industry from within its own cadres.

Here Walsh's autograph would still be thematic, neither graphic nor pertaining to the realm of the unconscious. On another level, the director writes his own name directly into his films, enabling each work to be linked to another, and to grow into a manifold and coherent, but paradoxical, body marked by recurring visual figures that lure the viewer into envisioning a total opus. It has been noted that the reinscription of credits into the film can have uncommonly decisive effects. In *Saskatchewan* (1954), a fairly innocuous travelogue-like western that shares much of its plotline with Walsh's *Distant Drums* (1951, a variant on *Objective, Burma!* [1945], which shared much with *The Naked and the Dead* [1958], which harked back to *Sadie Thompson* [1920] . . .), the intrigue hinges on the successful crossing of Alan Ladd and Shelley Winters from the land of the film's title, Saskatchewan, to an American sanctuary in the Dakota territories, marked on a map shown early in the film as "Fort Walsh." The adventure has the protagonists travel from the Canadian wilderness to a reassuring place-name of America. Or is the ruse more cunning? Do they go from the side of the title, the first words scripted in the credits, to the name-of-the-director, the last graphic sign before the image track begins the narrative? Is it an imaginary travel à la André Gide, where no one goes anywhere except in a name, in a sort of "voyage d'Urien"? Can it be a highly self-referential adventure that displays the illusory world of cinema in its writing that flattens the depth of the lush landscape?

The question might be approached through *Colorado Territory*, a film that a median viewer of 1947 would recognize immediately as a remake of Walsh's *High Sierra* (1941), a prototypical film noir now shot on a low budget, but in Western guise. The themes of one film seem transposed onto the other. But, at one point, when the reincarnation of Roy Earle (Humphrey Bogart), named Wes McQueen (Joel McCrea), waxes in brief nostalgia about how good, hard-boiled, hard-working, dedicated, professional criminals are not "the way they used to be," and how punks and saps are asked to do the jobs of real "men" now dead and gone, he appears to reiterate the words of "Doc" (Henry Hull) in *High Sierra,* who lamented that there were no more Dillingers, and that Earle needed not a good American girl but a "fast-steppin' filly" to befriend him. *Colorado Territory* would simply be quoting verbatim the plot and plight of the earlier film; Walsh would be seen as an auteur in the diacritical space between the first film and its reformulation in another genre and context. But across the history of the Second World War, it now refers allegorically to the death of veterans of the First World War. By extension, the nostalgia inflects *Colorado Territory* in alluding to actors and directors who are being supplanted by "punks and saps," that is, self-involved youths who have neither resolved their oedipal crises nor learned the craft of action movies from the silent era. In the film the aging "veterans" could only be the hard-boiled directors who refuse, in 1947, to yield to "sensitive" films that espouse existential estrangement.[28] The self-referential presence of cinema in the bandits' discussion would appear tenuous in the narrative, except when, on his deathbed, McCrea's interlocutor, responding to the thief's question about why outlaws are not what they used to be, wonders inquisitively, "O, a cockeyed world . . ." Walsh here inserts a footnote to his oeuvre. Reference is made to *The Cockeyed World* (1929), the bawdy sequel to *What Price Glory?* (1928). Connections between the ribald banter of Edmund Lowe and Victor McLaglen in that film would apparently have nothing to do with *Colorado Territory* except to weave a subliminal tissue of titles that bind a sundry number of films into an oeuvre.

But the graphics and the tendency of allegory to supersede narrative make the allusion something of a perspectival object. The reference is to *The Cockeyed World,* of "men" bonded and isolated from women, and of "veterans" who live and fight together through campaigns and across continents—here the players being Sergeant Flagg (McLaglen) and Harry Quirt (Lowe), who live and love their fraternal attractions, animosities, common desires, and homoerotic fantasies from icy Vladivostock to the torrid Caribbean. Their tenuous eros would cause the quotation to relive the "partial object," in a general sense, of men coping with their desires. But the perspective is all the more ocular—hence graphic—when the viewer realizes that Walsh had lost an eye while filming *In Old Arizona* (1927) on location, just before the filming of *The Cockeyed World,* and that the latter film is fraught with allusion to death fantasy, and its near equivalent, the experience of enucleation. From a traumatic event in a director's life a general obsession is built to cohere with the entire convention of film. It acquires a graphic acuity of the precarious eros it thematizes. In its attention to ocular conditions within its narrative, the object embodies, negotiates, and also, when seen from a broad perspective, turns into the art of an auteur. A personal obsession in the form of an interfilmic reference is scripted into a film in order, it appears, to betray constructively the world of Walsh as well as to display some of the basic oedipal dynamics on which the industry had capitalized.[29] The relations are clear but visible only when freed from fabulation. For this reason, one final concept requires discussion before detailed analysis can begin.

The Filmic Icon

The moments in which combinations of image and writing seem to concretize the dynamics of a film also invite transversal, analogical study. At times they meld narrative and visual elements into rebuses. They establish where the film represents its unconscious in conspicuously superficial ways. Where the classical film is patterned according to allegories designed to "grip" the spectator—such would be the limited effect of the inscription of names and places, as in *To Live and Die in L.A.* or in *Fatal Attraction,* in which figures are marked to be marketed[30]—there also exist films that do not set a controlling, strategic limit on their play of figures. The latter types tend to let their narratives connect rebuses for the sake of extended combination. They use narrative creatively, tactically, and without a unifying intention or calculated effect. This is what viewers can make of Walsh's opus in transversally graphic terms. At given points a body of films will be determined by a filmic icon, or an image-text that knots visual and scriptural configurations into inseparable entities.

At the point of these conflations an inscription of writing embodies and summarizes an image, or an image translates a scriptural form into written allusion to itself. It yields an infinity of reflections that move to and from picture, writing, and cinema. Marcel Duchamp may have theorized the problem in *Anemic Cinema,* where his rotor wheels spin to essay the relations of reading, seeing, montage, and retinal suspension. Puns are strung into cock and bull sentences in spirals moving from the circumference to the center of the frame (whose overall design alludes to the front of Ubu's garb in Alfred Jarry's *Ubu roi* of 1896). When the wheel turns before the camera, the words adhere into movement, and movement into a montage of infinitesimal stoppages that translate letters into film. The montage of letters theorizes retinal suspension at the basis of the cinema while simultaneously mobilizing a poetics of movement. Hence "anemic" cinema—hardly a medium in need of Geritol—is nothing more than a spiral anagram. The film theorizes rotative movement through the tension of a double decipherment that comes with the mirroring of *cinema/anemic*. A sense of space is obtained by spiral, circular, and lateral movement afforded by filmic motion the letters are keying. Such is the filmic icon that plays on the relation of words to images that invoke broader issues of cinematic movement.

Do similar icons mark narrative films? Given the concepts of the signature and the perspectival object, the answer may be yes. At moments a paradoxically spatial writing falls into the storyline and suddenly knots up its structure of relations and its visual properties. A composition of text and figure in the design of a shot will produce an icon combining heterogeneous elements of script, scenario, and cinema. One becomes identical to the others, in an ideogram or verbal picture in an auteur's own predispositions or obsessions; in the conventions of the industry; in the "style" or "aura" of a period of filmmaking. The narrative is wrapped in Freudian "hieroglyphs" of cinematic and verbal shapes that condense the entire duration of a single film or even an oeuvre. Certain films orient their narrative to iconic points where the convention of unfolding stops, where the film arrests and virtually translates its constituent elements—figures, words, and images—into itself. If these moments occur within an opus, they might be called, pursuant to stylistics, "auteuremes," a term that might be translated from its formalistic air into minimal authorial units, or figure-icons, that summarize and complicate broader paradoxes or ambiguities running through a body of films of one signature. They are ciphers that put into view recurring configurations. When the self-translation of a rebus is totalizing, the innate ambivalence of the auteureme tends to mark the film as an absolute symmetry of verbal and pictural elements, or as a cinematic hieroglyph.[31] The latter betrays and also subverts any continuity of edited images. It will be shown that Lang, Walsh, Rossellini, and Renoir produce these rebuslike icons that effectively disrupt the artifice of the camera within the conventions of classical cinema or invisible editing that tend to exclude its presence.

A filmic icon in narrative can serve as a point of transition from theory to practice, and it can lead us from the introduction to the body of this study. The first shot of Michel Simon in *Boudu sauvé des eaux* is taken in medium close-up, of the tramp, reclining against a tree whose trunk is wider than his body. Inattentive to his affection, the dog exits off-screen left. Boudu's head swings left and right in search of the lost mutt. He barks gruffly, "Chien! Chien!" The dog has just been seen—but not named—up to the point of his double utterance. Now it is named, but only after it has left: once departed, the dog becomes a *chien*. And later, once gone, Boudu becomes *Boudu*. Akin to Duchamp's experiments with language and image that play on delayed meaning in simultaneously verbal and visual registers, Renoir (as he did in his silent cinema) works with visual indexing in retinal and aural suspension. But in the viewer's ken, that is, the viewer who knows that Boudu is the second part of a diptych including *La chienne* (1931), the bum's raucous words, "Chien! Chien!" add up to a filmic icon summarizing the visual dissolution of the masculine canine while recalling the title and ending shots of the feminine counterpart, *La chienne,* in which Legrand (also Michel Simon), a bank clerk and Sunday painter, becomes the tramp who is now . . . Boudu. A transubstantiation occurs before the narration is put in gear: the second film begins where the first, like the dog, has uncannily disappeared, or been left adrift in visual and audible memory. The same viewer would ascertain that Renoir conflates sexual codes by having *chien/chienne* serve as a single unit binding the two films, no doubt because, at the crucial moment in *La chienne,* when Lulu is lying on her bed, Legrand (Simon—who, because he is tall, is indeed "le grand") utters to her in a deadpan tone, as if he were virtually writing the name of the film into its narrative center, "Lucienne, tu n'es plus une personne, tu es une chienne" (Lucienne, you're not a person anymore, you're a bitch). In Lucienne, the epithet *chienne* becomes the vanishing point, the *objet de perspective,* of Legrand's viewing desire in the same shot. The transformation from Lucienne to chienne spots a pivotal shift in the narrative—unraveling its enigma to the duped lover—as a change in the visual shape of a word in the image. Lucienne does not portray the abstract essence or type of a bitch but is merely scripted—visually, anagrammatically, anamorphically—in Lulu's Christian name, Lucienne. Lulu is read twice (lu-lu), becoming the elision of the nickname and formal name, just as Boudu barks "Chien! Chien!" twice, to collapse the narrative about the name and to make it visible.[32]

The moment of the tramp's words in *Boudu* summarizes a critical instant and its implications in *La chienne*. It also heralds another crucial element in Renoir's gallery of filmic icons. A decisive transitional shot that divides the long sequence of life in the Lestingois household from the ethereal liberation by the riverside (the place-name that Boudu chants in the same first sequence, in the melody of the words, "Au bord de la rivière . . . "), registers a gathering of listless individuals sitting in an outdoor café. They are seen, immobile, just before the opening bars of "The Blue Danube" are heard. In the background two violinists begin the music that will seem to waft the camera down along the river. The characters are set, like figures in a tableau vivant restaging the elements and ambience of Auguste Renoir's great painting, *The Afternoon Boating Party* (1881, Phillips Collection, Washington). In the lower left-hand corner of the tableau, a figure no doubt allusively present in *Boudu*, a young woman plays face-to-face with a black poodle. The originary love of humans for dogs, that eminently neolithic moment in Auguste Renoir, scaffolds a filmic icon for Jean Renoir: Boudu's first appearance offers a pictural element taken from his father's work in a rebus. Boudu is a male avatar of the young woman in the painting but also a reincarnation from *La chienne*. An intertextual combination of pictures, doubled names, and motion moves the apparent story of Boudu away from the apparent transcription of René Fauchois's boulevard comedy into a graphic and painterly meditation on film, art, autobiography, and the tensions of familial and sexual paradox. Renoir *père* often painted women with dogs.[33] The film knows this; from this moment it opens a universe of pictural and erotic relations that the son transacts through both his father's heritage and his own cinema.

The iconography is located in impressionism and the classical tradition, but it also forges scenes of textual origins that mix painting and cinema. These are decisive for alternative readings of narrative and can, I will argue in this book, be useful for articulating analytical practice. Hollywood offers problems that are not quite of Renoir's stamp. Classical cinema produced conventions that changed—to continue as conventions—only after the impact of Renoir on the New Wave.[34] When Hollywood fashions its filmic icons, it appears to forge them for calculatedly limited effects. But, given the tradition of the highly literate cinema of the European model within the American industry, it is often—even perversely—subject to losing the control it establishes.[35] A spectator's tactical analysis of the unconscious as an effect of surfaces and rebuses can question the world of psychology that seems to saturate Hollywood narrative. It requires the memory of experimental or vanguard cinema that had built its icons without investment in spatial or narrative illusion. Study of the ways that, even in its classical phases, film icons can betray and invert the Hollywood model will be taken up in the chapters that follow.

Credits in their mix of figure and image are seen within the pictural frame; allegorical configurations as they are crafted; the vagaries of a film's signatures and perspectival objects; and no less, filmic icons: these working concepts will inform the method of investigation here. All are clearly interrelated and often synonymous, and all insist on the importance of graphics as a pervasive element of cinema. They are crucial to the medium because, as foreign elements integral to the image, they define it by their own alterity within cinema. Like literature, the heterogeneity of film thresholds an activity—a pleasure—of analysis allowing spectators to rewrite and rework discourses of film into configurations that need not be determined by what is immediately before the eyes. Reworking of this order can lead, it is hoped, to creatively political acts of viewing. In this way, the literal aspect of film writing can engage methods of viewing that need not depend entirely upon narrative analysis. They may follow a transversal course but ultimately favor a relation that every spectator holds with the discourses of film, with memory, with the body, with adventure, but with an alert sense of critical practice.

I will begin by taking up Renoir and the filmic icon. His studies of painting, writing, and motion in the narrative of poetic realism will underscore the methods I use to review American films that owe much to the same problems he encounters in the years 1930–39. It will be seen how Fritz Lang, who remakes *La chienne* in Hollywood under the name of *Scarlet Street* (1946), the second panel of a diptych with *The Woman in the Window* (1945), rewrites Renoir. In deference to Renoir's concept and heritage of the director who spends his life making "one film," Raoul Walsh, an unlikely auteur, will be studied in terms of his autograph and the filmic icons in the style of Hollywood. In contrast to Walsh's commitment to history and its representation through the American industry, a contrastive view of Rossellini's war trilogy will be offered. The literal view of the medium as Renoir and Rossellini had defined it will be compared, finally, to the heritage of film noir. By conclusion it will be seen how the classical tradition yields the elements of a powerful, active process of viewing that knows neither time nor history.

1

The Filmic Icon
Boudu sauvé des eaux

In the introduction it was seen how shards of writing in a film draw attention to tensions of difference that determine the medium. The spectator is required to decipher the moving image in various ways at once; the contradictions that seem to hold among them open the medium to interpretations that can work multifariously. Sometimes these cannot be controlled by either the film or the viewer. Placed in a field of movement, pieces of writing, letters, or fragments of script arrest the eye and force it to see the film heterogeneously. Flattening the fictive depth needed for a narrative, written elements betray its field of illusion. At the same time, they often play informational or other semiotic roles in accord with the scheme of narrated images. Writing imposes binds such that in the act of viewing, the spectator is forced to work in various directions at once.

In the twenty-fifth shot of *Boudu sauvé des eaux* (*Boudu Saved from Drowning,* 1932), the bum calls out, "Chien! Chien!" His words are voiced, on one level, to bring back the dog that just left him and, on another, to recall the film *La chienne,* in which Michel Simon portrays an artist as a old tramp.[1] From the divided relation of the metaphor of the "dog" in the current story to its literal, graphic identity with the title of Renoir's feature completed just a year earlier, the words of Boudu's speech, "Chien! Chien!" can be seen to be uttered not only to suggest that the protagonist has just lost his visible identity (the bearded bum looks like a mutt), wants to retrieve it, or, failing the dog's return, that he must take solace in suicide. The reiterated name becomes a filmic icon cuing problems of visibility and language in *La chienne, Boudu,* and the rest of Renoir's work.

Michel Simon beckons across the barrier of one film to gain an identity recently lost in another.

The beginning of Boudu is born from *La chienne*. Its ending also glides from the margin of one film to another. When the weeping Anne-Marie Chlöe (Sévérine Lerczinska) and Emma (Marcelle Hainia) huddle about Lestingois (Charles Granval), who is framed next to clumps of fig leaves, and ask where Boudu has gone, he surmises, not knowing the answer, that perhaps the bum has followed "the thread of the waters," *le fil de l'eau,* which implies a narration.[2] That he has, but the utterance is a memory-icon, in the masculine — as *chien* is to *chienne* — of Renoir's very first film, *La fille de l'eau* (The girl of the waters, 1924). No matter how intertwined the genders or the allusions, the connections work within and beyond the narrative, the confines of the immediate frame, and a larger body of films. They infuse their referents with the uncanny reminders that pertain both to images and fragments of spoken and graphic language.

As a concept the filmic icon has the mobility of being something the spectator shares half way between the film, in the unconscious registers of language and image, and of concretizing what appears to be a series of recurring obsessions in a filmmaker's work. *Boudu* embodies them in its writing. Names and allusions drawn from a panoply of authors and artists abound; the film uses puns to distort words in speech and in their placement in the frame; it essays writing as a transversal mode that works through both language and picture. Above all, the representation of scriptural elements makes the process of cinema increasingly visible. The construct of an illusion is shown within the illusion itself.

It would be easy to assert that *Boudu* represents an antidote to the deadening effects of writing — its fabled gravity, its force of repression, its inability to translate the far richer tones of speech, and its stasis. From this point of view, the bookseller Lestingois, the stocky, repressed, repressive, and tired bourgeois hero, would be the contrary to the tall, irrepressible, comic, energetic, and nonchalant Boudu. Both would be part of a classic pairing that sets the limits of a tension — of especially oedipal origin — doubling one visual center into axes tagged as "good" and "bad" or positive and negative. The opposition would thus map a convenient geography for the viewer, and put forth problems that, for the sake of viewing more and more films, will never be resolved.[3] Or likewise, the reciprocal of Lestingois's wife, the haughty, snobbish, bourgeois Emma, and the mistress, the myopic and self-involved "Anne-Marie Chlöe," would offer no ground for reconciliation of different cultural and sexual codes. The filmic icon neutralizes these polarities in the interface of narrative structure and concrete writing.

The problem can be studied in the relation of Boudu to the telescope through which Lestingois first catches sight of him. In the forty-second shot, the bum walks along the quay Conti by the Seine. He is flattened and pushed into a medley of moving cars and pedestrians in front of endless lines of bookstalls selling

literature and lithographs. He ambles forward, as if lost in the urban press of cars and people, before turning right abruptly and up the steps of the bridge from which he will soon jump to his death. Up to that shot in the film, the camera had used extreme depth of field to show where Boudu was located — and lost — in the space of the city park. Lenses of short focal length tended to make of Boudu a cipher establishing a spatial relation of a scene according to its depth of field. An object giving perspective to a picture, a piece of *staffage* in a contemporary landscape, his character also recalls the tramps in the filmic tradition of bums who, since Chaplin, embody imaginary counterparts to the social classes in which they circulate.

When Lestingois sees him, Boudu is seen wandering along the quay through a lens of long focal length. It conflates figures and ground, hence reversing the visual texture used in the prologue and opening sequence that crosscut his outdoor life with the interior of Lestingois's cramped household. The long take records the city life and follows Boudu squashed against it. Outside as well as inside, cars and people seem jammed together. Trucks roll by and display on the panels of their cabs characters that move laterally across the frame; when a bus rolls across the frame, the place-names of its itinerary are marked on a strip below its windows. The movement of vehicles is foiled by the arrested view of *bouquinistes'* displays of books and lithographs behind the moving traffic. Squashed into the cityscape, Boudu moves with the flow of forms in front of him. Several

Their sadness disappears.

shots later, however, the mode of the representation of Boudu walking down the street is folded into the narrative. In a shot taken from the western wall of a room of the apartment, a wall whose window looks over the city below, Anne-Marie toys with a telescope that Lestingois, when he enters, appropriates. It is "his instrument" and more properly belongs to his array of effects. As he surveys the quay through the monocular lens, an iris-shot in close-up reproduces the perspective that had flattened Boudu against the background. Lestingois remarks on two ladies' legs and ankles (which Anne-Marie tosses off, not needing to see what the shot is showing) and then discovers the tramp on the bridge.

All of a sudden the unnamed origin of the first telephoto shot of Boudu has a marked origin in the telescopic effect of what Lestingois is seeing. The first shot of Boudu in the city retrieves its point of view through the optical style, explained after the fact of the establishing shot, in Lestingois's view through the telescope that doubles the camera lens. Technical properties of the entire sequence come forward. Boudu was constrained as much by an extended camera lens—with its clear erotic connotations—as by melancholy following the loss of his cherished dog. The sequence serves both to disengage the means showing how the image is made and to align expression of ocularity with Boudu's moving body. He literally focalizes the telescope; he is not a metaphor of the instrument but an extension or embodiment of it. Henceforth his function in the film keys the ways that visibilities are composed and indicates how the visual fields are organized.

As a telescope, Boudu becomes a filmic icon and a manifestation of filmic writing. The optical instrument is presented as an object bearing a technical and masculine privilege. Lestingois rips it from Anne-Marie, who has just fondled and caressed it in a way that already parodies the identity of the telescope and the phallus: in the first shots of the film's prologue, in the bogus theater of sirens and dryads, Lestingois's failed ''flute'' (shot 3)—that he despondently tosses to the ground—complements the mediated relation of the married bookseller with his live-in mistress-maid. The first shots (3-4) detail the cultivated frustration such that Anne-Marie's stroking of the cylinder would be tantamount to fondling a partial object that replaces what her desires cannot hold; likewise, its detachment from Lestingois's body makes it a sign of power that no one controls. The phallus is Boudu's icon, for he is literally in and of the telescope. His role as optical instrument and figure of its mechanism serves to indicate the degree to which the other objects in the frame are both invested with and devoid of libidinal charge.

Now if Boudu is the figure of the ''phallus'' in the identity of the production of his image and his identity as a force—a sort of ''human beast''—showing how figures in the film produce their desire, he is also a shifter, or a cipher, that locates how and where the others are positioned. All eyes tend to move toward Boudu, but since he is in passage in the film, his erotic force is sensed through his movement across a static background. He advances in every cardinal direction, to the center and margins, and even beyond the frame. Time and again the camera cuts him off at the neckline on the upper edge or shows his body in partial view because he exceeds the given space of the apartment doors, rooms, or windows enclosing him. In this respect he is not a body to be likened to an ''irrepressible'' force of character that no one can contain, but rather as a trickster whose movement calls attention to the texture of the image. In the same guise he is eros itself, jolting everything that falls within his view. His passage produces visibility. In literary or allegorical terms, he is an agon who calls into question the codes and rules of a given social space. Avatar of a Panurge who impugns the humanism of his sanctimonious friend Pantagruel, or of the famous Winnebago tricksters known for having an uncontrollable phallus so long that they must carry it in a backpack,[4] he confers value upon the bookseller's world by negation and disruption. But in Renoir's terms, the archaic trickster is also the icon of visibility that reflects on the film from within its narration.

Boudu collapses figure and ground or image and writing in terms that also conflate sexual difference. Once the identity of Boudu and the telescope is made across the narrative gap of the first shot portraying him in the telephoto lens, and Lestingois's discovery of what he wants to see, the narrative can only become a field of tension whose properties are at once discursive and iconic. The film goes

in all directions at once. The scene thresholding Anne-Marie and Lestingois looking left and out of a window appeals to a tradition of painting common to French eighteenth-century scenes of daily life and owing much to Vermeer, a tradition that puts bourgeois figures holding secular objects in rooms illuminated by an erotic shimmer coming across the frame. But the sequence also refers to recent memory of the first shot of Lestingois's store (shot 9) that heralds the sign overhead, ANCIENNE MAISON LEMASLE. The name may have been a given, unmotivated place-name that happened to be where the film was shot, but with the relation of eros, writing, and visibility centered in Boudu's character, Lemasle can be invested with the sense of the ''male,'' or of the ''former'' male's domain, perhaps that of the world of sylvan creatures repressed into printed memory and recent liteature. Such a reading concurs with the relation of frustration making up the Balzacian scenarios spelled out by allusion to the *Physiologie du mariage,* a book mentioned twice in the film. It is indicated visually by Lestingois catching sight of Boudu's spit left on a first edition. The tramp motivates the name through his intermediary position between abstract and literal visions of things.

One of the most crucial iconic attributes of Boudu's role involves, on the one hand, establishing visual and verbal identities in erotic and graphic registers and, on the other, replacing logical oppositions with visual and aural equivalences. Boudu is an amphibologist. His work begins in scenes of visual closure that parallel acts of gratuity between the bourgeois and the bum. The imperfection of the sequence as a failed "montage" is obvious. The editing seems rough, but none-theless a first "gift" of life is given to Boudu (shot 31) by a little girl who tenders five francs to the apparently despondent bum slouched on the end of the park bench. The rationale for the gift follows the gesture, in the girl's deadpan words, "Pour acheter du pain" (to buy bread). Two shots later, Boudu renders the money to a rich blade who is about to tip him for opening the door of his expensive convertible. The system of gratuity—a paradox in terms—is inverted when the poor person bestows wealth upon the rich. The moment of exchange in the city park is immediately mirrored in the loose montage that cuts to Lestingois seizing an occasion to give two books to a student just after his penny-pinching wife exits from the desk where she has been taking inventory. Lestingois's gift to the "Youth" (Jean Dasté, soon to be Captain Jean in Vigo's *L'Atalante,* 1934) in the name of bourgeois social progress, mirrors the 100 sous Boudu passes onto the rich youth who needs nothing. But Lestingois's gesture also evinces his own pen-chant for poaching. The jolt of pleasure he obtains by stealing from himself rep-licates what he gets when fornicating with the maid in his own home. His book-shop elicits desire merely because it offers a visual and social frame for transgression.

If Lévi-Strauss is correct in noting that "incest is fine, as long as it's kept in the family,"[5] in respect to a total social taboo, Lestingois also explicates one of the rules of Renoir's cinema, for throughout the oeuvre a social order or class is endogamous and self-isolating. Like the aristocracy at La Colinière in *La règle du jeu* (*The Rules of the Game,* 1939), it must continue to function that way until an order from without perturbs it enough to force it to realize how it works, throw it into disorder, and somehow bring it back to order with a different sensibility. The structure is religious in nature, and so pervasive that it binds films as vastly different as *Boudu, Toni* (1934) and *Le crime de M. Lange* (1935).[6]

In this way Lestingois's concomitant theft and act of generosity support the erotic practice of his social class, but its coincidence with Boudu's revolutionary gesture marks it as an element of unbound montage and as a prototypical visual scenario that will recur as a filmic icon throughout later films, first *La bête hu-maine* (1938), in which Renoir, as Cabuche, plays a poacher, and then *La règle du jeu,* where Marceau, also a poacher, inspires La Chesnaye, an "impure" aris-tocrat on the upper rung of the social ladder, to take rabbits from within his own domain. Something of a focal inversion works in conjunction with social and lit-erary upheaval. Boudu's "gift" unleashes a contagion of gratuitous acts that con-stitute the field of visual desire and the operation of social order. Boudu's gift leads to that of Lestingois, who then gives back to Boudu the life that he might have lost, which in turn allows Boudu's undirected libido to revive Emma and collapse the bourgeois practice of mixing philandering with philanthropy. The contagion of gifts made through the montage retains its focal properties throughout the film, and with the consequence of conflating graphic, visual, and social elements into inseparable units.

The most obvious of these entails lenticular inversion with the gift and with contemporary reflection on the practice of reciprocity. *Boudu,* finished in 1932, bears inflections of Marcel Mauss's "Essay on the Gift" (first published in *L'Année sociologique* in 1923–24), which hypothesizes that a gift is a "total social fact." Its dialectical process impels obligation. Giving promotes speculation on receiving, which in turn promotes a continuity of exchange essential for the definition of a social space. In that same essay, Mauss nonetheless does not steer clear of data showing how, in certain times of prestation, materials are consumed in ways that make reciprocity problematic.[7] And Mauss was clearly working within the context of debates that André Gide's *Les caves du Vatican* had launched in 1913, on the *acte gratuit,* or gratuitous act, that works—"deliberately" as it were—free of any social or linguistic control. Gide's novel of 1913 did not fail to grow out of the obsessions with poaching, incest, and homoeroticism expressed in his earlier novels. René Fauchois's play no doubt capitalized on the aftereffects of these debates, but it is Renoir, changing the play quite drastically, who takes up the gratuity and obligation as identities in social and visual terms.[8] An optical revolution, he implies, can have consequences no less telling than social upheaval. If the former is not of the substance of the latter, then a cognitive revolution must somehow accompany a total cultural change.

A change in vision, like the revolutionary dream of changing the language of everyday life, constitutes both the end and the impossibility of a social reform. As trickster or hermeneute, Boudu is the perspectival object who engages one revolution in order to effect another. Social and visual revolutions conflate in the last shot of the film, where an uncanny skewing of perspective comes with the passage of a collective of tramps marching right and upward, beneath the spire of Notre-Dame de Paris and the sky over Paris in the background. In the visual and graphic field of his own film Renoir foments an utter change, seen concomitantly in the film, in the way the world is apprehended.

The rapport that the *acte gratuit* holds with social theory was no doubt fairly obvious to viewers in 1932; spectators probably could not fail to see the film engaged in post-Sorelian dialogues about *élan vital,* the Freudian unconscious, and the aftermath of surrealism. The memory of Proust's fresco of the social imaginary (the last volume of *A la recherche du temps perdu* being published in 1927) was fresh, and the equation of force with social masses in the work of Faure and Céline was in the air. But the aesthetic revolution that Boudu prompts has something both very "old" and "new" in the fabric of the film's writing and visual articulation. It deliberately arches back to Flaubert by dint of its proper names. A pent-up wife named Emma, out of place in the dusty bookstore in which she wears flowing silk dresses, cannot fail to allude to the character at the center of *Madame Bovary.* And Lestingois, when he tenders a copy of Voltaire to the

"Youth" of the film, can only be a light parody of Homais, the bumpkin reformer whose ideas about "social progress" were an obvious anachronism in 1857.[9] When Lestingois receives a medal of honor for saving Boudu, further allusion is made to Homais's award of the Legion of Honor in the sardonic irony of the novel's last sentence. Clearly Renoir encourages his spectators to "see" Flaubert in and through Boudu. The intertextual and filmic mix allows the film to work through the novelist's political devotion to "art for art's sake" in visual terms that acquire revolutionary aspect.

The first evidence of Boudu rewriting *Madame Bovary* and its impact involves tensions that characters establish with windows and objects. Bric-a-brac abounds, signaling visual relations, when seen unconsciously, that are coded merely to impart an "effect."[10] Their scatter in the interior of the apartment tells viewers that they are the "objective reality" of a bookstore by the Seine in 1932, and that, when they are glimpsed in movement during any of the pans, they draw attention to the cinematic properties of the moving camera. At the same time they are simultaneously eroticized and neutralized, through the codes the filmic icons have established. In this sense they become equivalent to letters or to writing seen in an image field; when apprehended, all of a sudden we are prompted to ask why indeed we have arrested upon them, and for what cause. Conflation of the act of viewing with the relay of reflexion shares the effect of a doubly erotic movement that Boudu embodies.

In the fourteenth shot, a cloth on the balustrade is foregrounded, in an effect of *repoussoir,* as if to threshold Anne-Marie looking down the spiral staircase at Lestingois below and musing on the coming night of bliss in his arms. Casually unfolded on the surface, the textile also signals that it is the base on which fruits or objects are placed in the tradition of still-life painting. The scene of a painting is given, but only later, when longer takes of the stairwell and corridor are given, a watering can comes into view above the cloth. It marks the end of the hallway and defines one of the cardinal points of the apartment. But, as the watering can is not a typical element in still lifes, it jostles the ensemble. Because a sprinkler generally has a practical function in most households, the object tends to be invisible. (If a distortion of Marxian terms can be ventured, use value is generally in inverse proportion to sight value, just as a commodity becomes visible only when it loses its exchange value.) A casual viewing might allegorize it in terms of the field of force that the film articulates between things wet and dry, or those repressed and free. It would partake of water, flowers, and nature unbridled, released, a sign of archaic force, as opposed to dust, books, flowery language, and the spiritual constipation of the French bourgeoisie. The can could have an ironic role in its gratuity in the apartment where Anne-Marie dusts artificial plants and sings songs about springtime in the woods, or where flowers are found in books or on the wallpaper behind the watering can, but never in vases. The object fits

into the iconic network, however, as a rebus-joke signaling filmic issues that supersede the allegory.

Boudu is a perspectival object in the spatial plan of the film. Because Boudu animates people and things about him, the can forms a link in a visual chain associating the kitchen faucet spewing water, glasses of wine and water overturned, and eventually the capsizing of the nuptial skiff in the river. The issues of writing and film, figure and ground, and of gift and need are engaged in the signifying network that runs in multiple directions and is glimpsed at once in signs, objects, and sequences. The image of the can evokes its name, *arrosoir,* which also fits in a skein of figures devolving from *arroser,* to sprinkle, which in familiar speech means to piss. Yet the can displays an erect spout, implying that it will sprinkle sperm and not urine. A phallus detached from the bodies of the characters who climb, descend, and then turn around it, next to the spiral staircase, the watering can becomes an arouser, a fetish object that eroticizes its milieu because it is detached, gratuitous, and impractical in the area in which it is placed. It forms a verbal and visual collage that ramifies into the literary field of the film.

Two particular scenes seem to be inserted for the sake of extending the same joke: early in the film, a message is left in the store about a gentleman seeking an early edition of *Les fleurs du mal* (also, like *Madame Bovary*). The sprinkler figures in the association of the flowers on the wall before which it stands erect, and then the book of "evil" flowers—or metaphors—that its literal, visual aspect collapses. Metaphor is generally taken to be an abstraction, but here the filmic composition literalizes its movement. Thus, later in the narrative, when the client finally comes to get his copy of Baudelaire, the camera uses two shots in deep focus to record Boudu's point of view, from the threshold of the doorway to the shop, which looks onto the street, and the gentleman approaching the shot across the noise and traffic of the city. The din on the sound track evokes urban change in the passage from the nineteenth to the twentieth century, in a motorized metamorphosis of what Baudelaire had called the "bric-a-brac of modern life."[11] At this moment Baudelaire's reproduction of "modern" (as opposed, in the *Querelle des anciennes et des modernes* in which he played a role, to the "classical" or pompous vision) of Paris, an important element of *Les fleurs du mal* is drawn into the realistic, documentary aspect of *Boudu*. Baudelaire's presence is renewed through the objects that figure in the mix of writing and images. In the first shot, Boudu looks knavishly up and left so that the cigar he puffs is on the same eyeline as the name "Lestingois" painted in the glass of the door behind him. He virtually "inspires" his savior by drawing the name into his lungs and, like the effect of the spout on the watering can hovering in indeterminate space, Boudu disperses his benefactor's letters into the atmosphere. Boudu's atomization of Lestingois occurs just as he sends the client away, when he tells the collector of *Les fleurs du mal* that metaphors—that is, abstractions, or things invisible—are not here. They can be sought in a flowershop and not a bookstore. The play of the name of the book with the act of smoking further complicates the sequence, since the sight of writing being "smoked" alludes to the Symbolists, who assiduously studied *Les fleurs du mal* in order to fashion "poem-symbols" that etherealize language.[12] Following their meal, when Boudu and Lestingois retire to the living room to smoke cigars, the deep-focus photography carefully locates one figure in the background and the other in the foreground. As Lestingois smokes his cigar, the tip moves about but holds over Boudu's mouth. For an instant they literally smoke each other in superimposition on the same visual plane. The film and the memory of many literary texts form a collage of visible language. The cinematography confirms what is begun with the relation of the watering can to the stairwell and wall, and now orients the narrative toward far more polymorphic configurations of bodies, objects, and letters in space.

The sprinkler is seen momentarily in its uncanny setting both in deep focus, from afar, and also in soft focus and close up from the wall. It corresponds to the deep-focus and telephoto shots describing Lestingois's sight of Boudu's suicide and promotes a confusion of literary and visual fields. At the same time it shows how and where the "visual pleasure" of the film depends on disbelief or a mute gaze prompted not by the story but by the camera's literal view of its objects. In fact, it tends to neutralize what a spectator's desire might seek in the visual field. The can is at the head of the stairs, poised so as not to water the flowers of the wallpaper against which it is placed, and it is also above the curvilinear balustrade adjacent to the bust of Voltaire. Its chain of literary analogies is extended by

metonymical association with these two other items. The spiral stairs can be likened to Boudu's phallus because, as an *escalier-à-vis,* they are what lay over (as Boudu, in *escale* in the apartment) and screw (with *vis* recalling both the effect of turning and the French epithet for the male member, as well as alluding to sight). Its name and visual shape are associated with water, such as the great screw of Archimedes that transports vital fluids upward, hence becoming a political sign of force that crosses barriers or levels of classes, and an icon of unbroken movement that the frame cannot contain.[13] Like the *arrosoir,* the spiral staircase flattens its erotic dimension in its function as a filmic agent. It stands as if detached from the profusion of square and oblong forms in which it is placed. It can be seen, therefore, as a visible antithesis to the frontal take or the ever-divided frame that had used doorways, windows, and the metallic columns to multiply its effects of closure. Since the film uses panoramic shots to offset the closure, the shape of the spiral staircase virtually mirrors the circular movement of the camera. In fact, the sixth shot of the film pans exactly from a view of the staircase—as if its sight were inspiring the camera movement—to the windows on the left, immediately binding the camera play to the object. A concomitant play of camera and object animates the decor.

The erotic moment of the panoramic recurs in the film, in the famous shot that reframes a scene in a café looking over a river, a scene that vaguely resembles Auguste Renoir's *Boating Party.* The shot moves downward, when musicians begin "The Blue Danube," to an indeterminate area, between sky, earth, and water, that is bereft of anything real, before catching a view of Boudu dressed in a tuxedo and sporting a bowler hat, looking right with the air of a rascal.[14] A pan of 360 degrees follows, enclosing the origin of the field of view within and making the camera more than merely implicitly present.[15] After capsizing and floating downstream, isolated, in silence, Boudu climbs ashore, exchanges his clothes for those on a scarecrow, obtains another gift of bread, and ambles down a hillside. In the wind and agitated vegetation he lies down in the grass before a dappled goat enters the frame—as if it were an avatar of his dog—and eats a piece of the bread. When Boudu tosses his hat into the river, an allegorical reading would have him jettison his bourgeois ways, symbolized by the formal attire, to become "free" after living through the nightmare of life in the bookstore and the lettered world. But the pan that follows the hat moves by a construction of vertical rods placed in the water, tilts up to reframe the space, and extends its depth of field (with slight rack-focus pull), inscribing the river and the other shore beyond some rowers in the deep middle ground. It continues its career right, records some effects of modern industrial life—a crane and a building site—and moves toward an iron-girdered bridge in the background. It would be easy to see the bridge as a return-of-the-repressed, or the place where Boudu had first attempted suicide. As in *Toni* (1934), where the bridge is the gratuitous beginning and ending of the narrative, the return to the original space of birth and death would buckle the film into an eternal return of circularity. But the pan ends on the edge of the river where, in the foreground, a tuft of reeds marks the distance between the world of civilization far away in the background and the bushes and river and the foreground.

The reeds correspond to the pan by establishing the end of the career and by offering a literal equivalent to the name of the shot. Pan is both the shot and the god of nature; the reeds are the reincarnation of Boudu in the form of an image-sign of his new floral life. The reeds are such a charged image in the French literature and art that inform the film that their immediate view transforms the errant hero into a mystical trace of writing and movement. Pan, the hidden god of the film, is materialized in the passage of the shot that marks a tension between between the bridge and the reeds. And the reeds, if they do not refer directly to Pascal's aphorism fixed in the minds of every French citizen, that "man is only a reed, but a thinking reed," or to many pictures that appeal to the mix of pagan and Christian belief, such as Jacques Callot's,[16] they invariably arch back to writing: for the origin of *roseau* is *calamus,* which means both a stalk and a stylus, or writing instrument. Boudu is thus seen under the sign of a turning image that writes, the panoramic shot embodying Pan that ends with concrete evidence of the god as filmic movement. They are seen in an almost Ovidian metamorphosis that turns cultural forms into a mystical shape of "natural writing." The panning camera operates a transformation that begins with the sign of the turning stairwell and ends on the secret writing of natural shapes and objects. The shot manifests, if Alexandre Astruc's figure of the *caméra-stylo* can be recalled, a style of depthless inscription that figures its objects as part of a secret code of cinematic, alphabetic, and natural forms in continuous metamorphosis.

At this moment the film uses emblematic process to bind and separate the various elements of its infinitely extending composition.[17] The final pan of Boudu ends its inscriptive moment in the image-sign of Pan, in the writing instrument of nature, that complements the initial pan in the bookstore that seems to be inspired by the spiral staircase and its hidden name. Like Boudu, each object seems to have a simultaneously veiled and literal relation with the camera. If the erotic and visual registers are extended to details of editing manifest in the relation that objects hold with the characters, the point becomes clearer. The watering can and the spiral staircase elicit sensuous drive by virtue of their shape and their partial, detached status in respect to the decor and the humans who circulate almost oblivious to them. They appear to supersede the humans: in the first shot of Emma entering the shop from the funeral (shot 18), her hand that momentarily holds onto the erect doorhandle suggests that she grasps the memory of the member of which she has been deprived in the bourgeois ménage. That shot is prepared by Anne-Marie's entry into the kitchen (shot 16), where she goes up to the checkered wall on which a row of pots are hanging. She picks one at random, turns it about, and spins it by the handle in her palm. Like Emma's hand briefly

clasping the erect door latch, Anne-Marie's fetching and twisting of the pot does not carry any immediate narrative continuity following Lestingois's command to prepare the soup (shot 12). Rather, she fondles the handle as a detached member while daydreaming about sharing Lestingois's body in the evening. The women are holding these "knobs" or extensions with the same unconscious gusto that Lestingois will exhibit when he strokes his telescope. The decor turns every "object" into a sign of "partial," "transitional," or "perspectival" forces[18] that concretize cinema and desire as drive, or primary process, marked between signs and visual forms.

Writing figures as a switching element that turns the eye from one area to another and back again. Sometimes it shifts abstractions back into what they are, from a partial object to a "door handle," that is, from the memory of an anticipated pleasure to simply an object as a spatial index. At other times, writing dismantles the illusion of narrative or montage. Its function might best be seen in the sequence depicting Emma's seduction and Lestingois's being awarded the medal of honor. Twenty-nine shots make up the sequence.[19] Boudu returns from the barbershop, its sign framed in a countertilt offsetting the icon of the barbershop and the writing on the glass, *service antiseptique*. His gait rhymes with the music-off of a hurdy-gurdy player attended by an indolent bystander slumped over his bicycle.[20] The shot locates the organ of desire, and its presence, *off*, in two shots of Emma, draped in her flowing dress that lends a charge to her figure.

She is shot as a water-nymph, a tableau vivant of Jean Goujon's relief sculptures of dryads pouring water from urns on their shoulders. The music becomes the same flow infusing the space of the bedroom with indifferent lust. Prior to meeting Boudu, Emma had been associated with the "boudoir" when she had been powdering her face ('J'ai mes nerfs, oui, j'ai mes nerfs," [Yes, yes. I've got my touchy points]). Boudu enters the "boudoir" as if to conflate his name with the place, thus to reinvent it by identifying it with his body.[21] Opposites of social class and of verbal identity collapse. The seduction in this way is an effect of filmic language, of hieroglyphs.

Crucial also is the foregrounding. When Emma lies on the bed, in a foreshortened, Mantegnesque pose (shot 1) next to the sculpture of embracing plaster *putti* on the mantelpiece, she raises her left arm and shields her eyes with her forearm. The hurdy-gurdy music seems to be all that she can see. Is she reproducing Flaubert's romantic cliché that has Emma Bovary close her eyes in order to see? Or, in line with Baudelaire, since she is in the guise of a dryad, does she allude to an ironic observation that would have her make love to herself in word and image?[22] Might her gesture refer to a surreal icon of "adventure," in which Man Ray drew figures of Eluard's poetry? If so, Emma's gesture would refer to a textual icon that matches visual and verbal collaboration.[23] The shot refers to the very scene that foregrounds Lulu's murder almost congruently in *La chienne,* but it also melds into a single image a more pervasive identity of desire and murder.

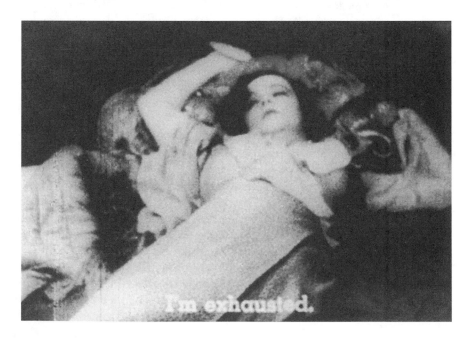

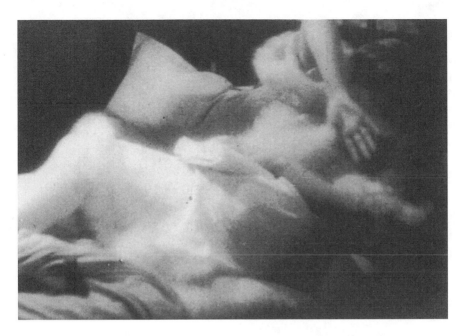

In *La chienne* Lulu closed her eyes with her forearm in order not to see her jealous lover plunge a letter opener into her belly, before he looks at the book she had
been reading. In *Boudu* Emma seems to anticipate the same, but she now exudes
the same sign as an erotic venture. It rhymes sensuously with the organ music *off*.
But its literal effect forces the viewer to see the graphic of desire in the name of
the "organ grinder," the *orgue de barbarie,* a barbaric organ, that soon will be
manifest in the figure of Boudu, cleanly shaven, having lost only the look of his
barbarity in the barbershop. Although the shot marks a diacritical relation with
La chienne, it suggests how all of Renoir's scenes depicting the act of love vac-
illate between tenderness and murder. It gives far more credibility to Lantier's
(Jean Gabin's) murderous love with Flore (Blanchette Brunoy) in *La bête humaine,* and it also shows why Henriette (Sylvia Bataille) at once thrusts away and
draws to her lover, Henri (Georges Darnoux), in *Partie de campagne* (1936). Life
and death are dedifferentiated just as are word and image. In the latter sense the
sequence in *Boudu* shows how writing is figured in the visuals, and how the film
flattens its depth by being infused with the evanescence of names within what is
shown.

Emma's seduction indeed returns to the letter. Thanks to a shifting role of writing, the foregrounding to the seduction establishes the alternate montage that
brings the civic and sexual orders together. The camera dollies in to the print of
the bugle boy over the bed, his right hand holding the instrument he blows with
his mouth (recalling the eroticized orality in the cigar-smoking sequences) and

his left hand on his genital region. The camera trucks forward, evincing a slight focus pull that marks the limit of Renoir's apparatus. The sudden blast of music-*off* cues the trombone-*on* but disallows synchrony of sound and image. They are seen as being absolutely gratuitous. Emma and Boudu's climax is produced by a bogus illusion. Literal and abstract registers conflate once more. When Vigour prances into the bookstore, proclaiming to a stolid Lestingois, "Victoire, victoire, vous l'êtes" (Victory, victory, you're it), the pun on cuckoldry and civic achievement afforded by the indeterminate reference of the direct object would seem to belong to the gentle farce of Fauchois's boulevard theater, and not to cinema. "Victoire, victoire" are two image-signs that script the path of convergence that the montage had been articulating, on the one hand, from the trajectory of the public domain (Boudu sauntering down the street; the shot of the hurdy-gurdy player, the long take of Vigour leading the dancing children in the street outdoors, and the triumphal entry into the same space where Boudu's body had been deposited after his attempted suicide) and, on the other, that of the inner, erotic space (Boudu bounding up the spiral staircase after Lestingois tells him with a paternal air that "Madame," his "mother," will scold him [shot 14], the flirtation with Emma in close-up, and the shot—21—trucking toward the print over the bed). The two orders trace the abstract line of a V: Vigour heralds Victoire in such a way that the film's script writes the configuration of the montage that resembles the letter V, which, as cause, also figures the erotic effect of

Emma's sex. The editing seems to be both done and undone by the doubled graphics of speech that are ostensibly independent of the editing.

Is the sequence a precocious analogue in film to the literary montage of images and letters that Flaubert had crafted in the *comices agricoles* sequence of *Madame Bovary*? In the novel, the conversation of seduction is crosscut with the speech of the local mayor, appropriately named Lieuvain (a montage of a "vain place," a *lieu vain,* and *levain,* or the yeast needed for the baking of bread), that praises the French soil, its fertilizers, and its farmers. Both discourses are woven with clichés. Rodolphe Boulanger (that is, Rudoph Baker) offers tempting words to Emma while the public official embroiders a metaphor that moves from the earth and agrarian labor to the production of wheat that ends with the work of the baker. The converging lines of the two speeches mirror each other's circumstantial words. The literary montage depends on a common graphic sign that buckles the contrapuntal structure, in the word *boulanger,* which puns on the name of the seducer, his effect, and the ultimate social figure uttered in the speech of civic dedication. The explosive moment depends on the retinal persistence of an arresting mark in the literary and filmic texts alike, since, like *boulanger,* the V of Victoire and Vigour (and Emma) emblematizes the contrapuntal movement that it keys: it provides a miniature cipher that reflects the sum of the sequence.

The film thus exudes a complex relation with writing and appears to produce, between its time and its appropriation by the New Wave, what few other films have done with graphic and visual media. *Boudu* does not simply "use" or "evoke" writing or other texts in order to broaden the film's field of allusion or to satirize gently the nineteenth-century heritage of the novel and lyric. Film and writing combine and remain paradoxically autonomous and identical. They form effects by which one tradition utterly changes the other. This is what the concept of the filmic icon specifies: for both writing and image, indeterminacy and destabilization of meaning are engaged. Cognition remains divided between one set of "tracks" (sound or image) and others (writing in the film and interfilmic and textual markings). Something other, both in and out of the narrative, something almost unconscious, is produced in the attention the film draws to its own problems of creation through translation and transformation of image and writing. For this reason *Boudu* and all films that "write" themselves thus cannot be said to own any symbolic or thematic registers independent of their own conflations and disruptions of discourse.[24] If the film does have a theme and a politics, they are committed to showing the viewer how to see, how to read, and how to write the sensory world in revolutionary ways. A hieroglyph is born of lenticular experiment. It is also shared with other filmmakers throughout the early and middle classical periods of sound cinema. The following chapters will examine how this film writing devolves and with what consequences.

2

The Law of the Letter
Scarlet Street

In Fritz Lang's *Scarlet Street* (1945), Kitty March (Joan Bennett) orders a rum collins in a basement bar. Her companion, Chris Cross (Edward G. Robinson), has just requested a cup of coffee. He hesitates, and then decides that he might as well have a drink with the lovely lady. "Make mine the same," he asserts to the barkeep. They sit down at a table and, seconds later, puckering his lips around the straw and sipping his cocktail, Chris interrupts to tell Kitty of his impressions of the current art scene. Turning her head away from Chris—as if she were about to spit a lemon seed away from the table—and commanding the frame in the right-hand foreground, she quips, "You're never appreciated in your own country." To which Chris responds, stuttering, "That's . . . that's one way . . . of looking at it." His words, like the two rum collinses posed on the table, already signal two ways of looking at the same thing. At this instant the film reflects on its own painterly and scriptural mechanism. "That's . . . that's . . . " fails to indicate its referent by dint of repetition. Chris's remark crosses over what is entailed in any act of showing or representing a figure in a work of art or a film. Fritz Lang, a European in America, was so esteemed by the Nazis in 1933 that he was offered an eminent position in Goebbels's arm of the government. To be "never appreciated in your own country" is, historically, only one way of looking at Lang's career. To see how self-exclusion, obtained by doubling, operates within one film is another way and will be our concern in this chapter. Obliquely, the two characters tell of the production of *Scarlet Street*. Chris and Kitty ultimately indicate how to read the film as a long rebus.

In chapter 1, I argued that filmic icons are constructed through webbings of visual and graphic relations. In *Boudu sauvé des eaux*, networks of mutually inflecting combinations of writing and speech are made that produce, arrest, and theorize the composition of narrative in film. A nodal point of visual and scriptural orders, each rebus, like a visual calligram, is a unit of picture and writing. Each opens upon a broad, almost unconscious maze of signs disrupting most orders of comprehension.[1] A transfilmic creation results when fragments recur and run back and forth through the director's creations.

In his American cinema, Fritz Lang appears to touch on a filmic unconscious that has affinities with Renoir's oeuvre, but in a highly different context and with even more literal effects. No doubt Lang took much from the French director; he may have used the same formal issues that had been developed in the early 1930s in order, a decade later, to turn them into expressions of extreme confinement. Lang completed his version of *La chienne* (1931) in *Scarlet Street* (1945) and modernized Renoir's treatment of Zola's *La bête humaine* (1938) in *Human Desire* (1954). From these outward signs a rapport is clear but may be more complex than a cursory view of sources might indicate. It appears as if Lang develops a series of filmic icons that are invested with a highly Freudian and even more intensely scriptural cast.

Scarlet Street never received good press in the United States, nor in circles of film criticism has it acquired the aura that Renoir's films have obtained since the 1960s.[2] The reconstruction of *La règle du jeu* (1960), the seminal influence of André Bazin in *Cahiers du cinéma*, and the interfilmic creations of the New Wave directors resurrected Renoir's work of the *entre-deux-guerres*. The American phase of Fritz Lang's career remains far more problematic. The opus does not quite cohere like Renoir's. Some critics view the early German period as Lang's only substantial legacy in film history. Noël Burch has argued that Lang's experience in Hollywood (1936–56) betrays the innovations that produced *M* and the *Mabuse* trilogy.[3] But Lang's American period is resurrected in 1963, in *Le mépris (Contempt)*, when Paul Javal (Michel Piccoli), a scriptwriter working with Lang (who plays himself as a director working under a tyrannical, Goebbels-like American producer, Jerry Prokosch, played by Jack Palance), meets the aging god and lauds *Rancho Notorious*. There Godard opens a dialogue, for Lang tells Javal that he really prefers *M* to the western of 1951. The interfilmic debate that Godard tips into the film may have prompted scholars as diverse as Raymond Bellour, Jean Douchet, and Reynold Humphries to reconsider the American contributions.[4] After the demise of author-centered monographs of the 1960s, Lang's American years resurfaced in studies of the conventions of film noir and feminism.[5]

Scarlet Street is so closed and self-contained that the narrative involves what it means to be lost in a maze of maddeningly doubled forms. The plot seems to threshold a more intensive study of visual and verbal repetitions. Nothing takes place only once or from one way of looking at things. Every statement and sequence, as if mapping Freud's remarks on the double in "The Uncanny," is reiterated a second time.[6] Repetitions of this kind raise theological questions about the status of transgression as the basis for all representation. Because of the depth of this tradition, the film reflects on the act of mimesis through its maniacal replication of images and graphic discourses. The film's writing subtends the narrative but also is staged as a mode by which viewers or readers can detect its other, unspoken political dimensions. The textual figures seen in the frame serve as an element that reads the film.

Christopher Cross, a cashier and Sunday painter who works for the Hogarth Company, a New York firm that ostensibly deals with graphic productions, is awarded a watch for twenty-five years of service at the company's annual spring stag party. With a co-worker, Charlie, he begins to venture home, parts company, and gets lost in the labyrinth of Greenwich Village. On the way, he witnesses in the distance a man and a woman who seem to be engaged in an act of violence. Chris runs forward, hits the assailant with the tip of his umbrella, and fells him. He discovers the woman, wrapped in a transparent slicker that glistens with raindrops, under the street lamps. By the time Chris hails a policeman, the man he knocked down has fled. Chris walks the woman home, but first they share a drink to get acquainted.[7] Chris falls in love. He arrives home early in the morning and stays up all night to paint a picture of the carnation she gave him upon their departure, and then receives Charlie, whom he invited to come by on Sunday.

Thrilled by his rejuvenation, the cashier takes a critical view of his life as a henpecked spouse of a shrew named Adele (Rosalind Ivan), whose first husband, a police officer, had mysteriously disappeared years ago. Chris writes to arrange a date with Kitty. Unaware she lives with a pimp named Johnny (Dan Duryea), Chris gives Kitty money and eventually steals from the Hogarth Company to support her. He paints—but fails to sign—his work in a new studio his embezzled money has allowed her to rent. Johnny tries to pawn the unsigned paintings after he learns from an artist (Vladimir Sokoloff) in Washington Square that they may be valuable. Damon Janeway (Jess Barker), a critic, happens upon the works. His associate, a dealer who owns the Dellarowe Gallery, buys them. Kitty signs the paintings and poses as their creator. Her fame grows. Enchanted by their success, Chris continues to paint under Kitty's signature until Adele's first husband, Homer Higgins (Charles Kemper), returns from the depths—the East River, into which he had plunged, he later admits—with the intention of blackmailing Chris so that Chris would have to remain married to Adele. Chris double-crosses Homer by having him "discovered" with Adele in their apartment. "Freed," Chris goes to live in the studio with Kitty, but as he enters he catches sight of Johnny kissing Kitty. Confounded, humiliated, and enraged, Chris murders Kitty with an icepick. Johnny is convicted for the murder and sent to Sing Sing to be executed. Chris's boss, J.J.(Russell Hicks), then learns of the theft of funds from the company and is impelled to fire his cashier. Overwhelmed with guilt and remorse, Chris tries to commit suicide but fails, and he becomes a tramp. The film ends at Christmas time, with a shot of the hero trundling down an avenue in central Manhattan, as the tune of "O Come Let Us Adore Him" leads to the end credits.

The plot superficially duplicates *La chienne*. Names, places, and contexts are changed. The tall Legrand becomes the squat Chris Cross, and the blond street vamp, Lulu, is now the brunette Kitty (Joan Bennett, wife of the film's producer, Walter Wanger). The pimp, played by Dan Duryea, who had a reputation as a "type," matches the sleaze of Renoir's Dédé (Georges Flamand).[8] Renoir has a fake signature, "Clara Wood," put to Legrand's paintings, a name Dédé draws from a winning filly at the Longchamp racetrack. Legrand kills Lulu with a letter opener, whereas Chris murders Kitty with an icepick that Johnny had taken from Marchetti's store.

Despite the similarity of narrative, the endings diverge. An errant bum, Chris is confined in the solitude of his guilt after the debacle of his life. Legrand announces the coming of Boudu when he skirmishes with another tramp for the privilege of opening a car door.[9] Legrand's adversary is Alexis Godard (Gaillard), the analogue to Homer Higgins, the first husband of Adele (whose name is the only one kept in the second version). They share a cigarette. Yet at the same moment in the plot, Chris is enveloped in a swirl of smoke turning about an axis, an X, visibly marked in the furrow between his two eyes. Renoir's beggars are oblivious to the daring shot that has Legrand's self-portrait recede to a vanishing point as the car that carries it drives away. (The painting marks a point that matches the converging lines of the backdrop in the opening of *Boudu*.) The bums cross the street before the puppet-theater intertitle of the epilogue sets up the film's ending. Lang has Chris walk off into the distance. Rather than using a puppet-show cornice for the film, Lang has the end credits, subtitled "A Universal Release," written below "The End," to mark his character's confinement of guilt and remorse.

In contrast to *La chienne* or *Boudu*, a highly local study combines a Freudian concern with the double and the letter with mimesis in general. Just as Renoir made a diptych of his two "Parisian" films starring Michel Simon, Lang makes two "New York" films with Edward G. Robinson, Joan Bennett, and Dan Duryea—*The Woman in the Window* (1944) and its complement, *Scarlet Street*, in the following year. Renoir's films exude a humanism recalling the vast sweep of his oeuvre. "It takes all kinds to make a world," says Godard to Legrand as they look at the paintings in the window before them. To which Legrand replies, "Let's go. Life is beautiful," but in a tone that makes the viewer share the ironic vision of the camera. If Lang holds a critical view in respect to his story, it is through the filter of Freud, for whom there can be no distance between a spectator and a story because both are caught in the same symbolic process. Lang has

Chris Cross live through a tragic psychogenesis, by which he does not grow into the world through trial and error but rather remains a "case"— or a "case history"—living in an arrested stage of development. He is unable to discover a perspective for his life because he cannot work through oedipal relations over the passage of time.[10] Chris Cross is a little old boy who has married a bad mother, happens upon a bad woman, and internalizes all his spite.

The Freudian view pivots elliptically around two scenes that form a pair of "primal" moments. The first, of course, is his first view of Kitty and Johnny together. In Freud's reading of the child "seeing" the parents in coitus, the scene is a necessary trauma in the development of the subject. Lang has it take place through the girders of the elevated subway (the "El"),[11] in extreme distance, and through a series of frames within frames. For Chris it becomes the discovery of his own genital relation indicated at the tip of the umbrella he pokes at Johnny. The second, when he looks through the glass partition of the studio and beholds Kitty and Johnny embracing, leads to the murder of Kitty. Chris no longer pushes with his bumbershoot; he now plunges the icepick five times into the body of the woman he loves unrequitedly. These two moments form the two centers that describe the filmic ellipse in which both character and viewer are caught.

But psychoanalytical methods are hardly inaugurated in *Scarlet Street*. In the general industry their implicit conclusions were used to imprint viewers and to yield effects determining the imaginary and social fabric of the lives of millions. The notion of the primal scene has been used—even massified—to make viewers regress to infantile states so that their affective energies could be manipulated for immense profit. There is no doubt that Lang saw the work used against itself in the industry, and that, once "free" enough to direct his own film, he could theorize the ideological use of psychoanalysis in his own cinema. One of the modes of articulating a critique within the terms of the industry, it seems, was through the interfilmic relations he established with his own work. Like Renoir, he could produce transfilmic icons embodying cinematic process and forming nodal points, or obsessively recurring configurations dismantling the field of illusion in narrative. Another involved the binding of psychoanalysis to a mix of images and writing. In this way a highly political view could be bound to the psychoanalytical process of his film. Their agencies seem to be at work in the modes of writing seen in *Scarlet Street*.

Psychoanalytical process depends on writing understood in a broad sense. Writing is not opposed to voice, nor does it merely transcribe maternal or paternal speech into alphabetical scripture. Rather, writing is in and of speech; the two are inextricably combined, plural, and of each other. The analyst studies the patient's writing as a voice conveying recurring marks that cannot be grasped in semantic registers that represent events. The more significant and difficult areas of meaning are held within the plurality of verbal writing. "Written" speech appears to share a direct rapport with the concept of the pictogram that analysts use in their treatment of patients. In the course of an analysand's remembrance through speech, the act of recall reaches back as closely as possible to "primary" moments of trauma that cannot yet be designated as phantasms. Verbal translation is made of shards of memory-images. Patients must recover pictograms, nodes of a pictural and verbal order, unlike the structure of grammar, that are composed associatively, like a hieroglyph or a rebus combining graphic signs and images of things. The process is "regressive" insofar as it conduces to a private discourse knowing no common symbolic code; but, no less, because letters, voice, and pictures are mixed, they are accessible to those—especially the Freudian analyst—who is "supposed to know" how to decipher them and prod the analysand to continue to make them manifest.[12] They are often associated with alphabetic forms that concretize verbal pictures, or with splinters of symbolic language analysands use to protect themselves from the limiting world of social forms. The loss of the private use of these shapes commingles with the gain of their rearticulation into poetic language.[13] Such a process that gains access to subjectivity has often been associated with the dialogic properties of authentic art. In this view both the study and the creation of art engage total psychogenetic activities that open the subject, like a Freudian patient, onto simultaneously destructive and constructive, liberating and repressing activities that collapse and separate at once images and letters, pictures and writing, and, of course, signifiers and signifieds.

In the study of film the process would seem to be of a doubly delicate essence, for the strategist—the Industry—knows its power and with it can re-create psychogenesis on a grand scale. Dominant cinema can initiate symbolic activity in a controlled way, thus luring a subject into illusions of living through creative transformation while being rocked, as in a manger, in the passive assimilation of feature-length films. The "cure" would amount to implanting a desire to spend more money on more films and to "buy" the products and ideologies that the films purvey. For Lang or certain directors working within Hollywood, the creative *tactic* involves creating a bogus likeness of the *strategy* of prevailing films, replete with inscriptions that question ideology-producing illusions.[14] The key would be to make failed or overwrought allegories that show where the representations are illusions, in other words, to stage psychodramas whose travails are askew or out of perspective. Irregularities—what Eisenstein calls "the basis of all art"—would prompt a different, new, and totalizing mode of viewing tantamount to creation.

These same tactics prevail in the relation of writing and image in *Scarlet Street*. The film draws on the heritage of the collage and montage to articulate an unconscious writing that doubles strategies used to program a subject's desires.[15] Graphics in the image arch toward and draw away from the "primal scenes" of division and separation. They are initially manifest in the mix of written, aural, and visual codes but cannot fail to inflect the politics of the film. For the same reasons *Scarlet Street* appears to be studded with scenes moving to and away from Chris Cross's two primal moments. Through the presence of writing, of ciphers, or of a pictogrammar embedded in the images, an unending process of regression to undifferentiated images and scriptures is afforded. Continuous breakage and rupture become obvious. This grounding contradiction makes the operation of viewing equivalent to a "working through" of the film's discourses that goes with a highly critical view of the industry and its formatting of visual pleasure. It can be followed from any point of departure and then ramified through various shots or sequences. Those mixing letters and images are crucial for articulation of what Lang's film writing seems to entail.

The camera frames and cuts Chris Cross's departure from the stag party in a series of carefully designed low-angle shots. We look down when he and Charlie descend the stairs of the brownstone as the camera tilts down by a sign indicating a "Hack Stand." The two old men exchange nostalgic words about times and lives past. The two men—literal hacks—are nearing the end of their failed careers and can do no more than "kill time," or have avocations, their conversation implies, similar to going to the movies. They share an umbrella. It points to a neon sign over a shop window in the background scripting JEWELRY in uppercase letters. As a function of these characters, Chris Cross is marked by words within the same words, in a Saussurean play of anagram[16] that renders him precious, delicate, and of rare talent. J.J. has just praised him as a jewel of a character, a "fourteen-carat, seventeen-jewel cashier." Now he is marked by the word to which his umbrella points. When subjected to movement, the allegorical stability of the jewel as a precious commodity is lost when the letters disengage and recombine under the wavering tip of the bumbershoot. Short, squat, squeamish, fearful of J.J., Chris is the obverse of the jewel, seen in light of a jeweler, and hence can only be a Jew.

But with the echo of J.J.'s voice, the J of JEWELRY is the point where the two characters of opposite social rank begin to meet. Yet JEWELRY allows other inflections to bear upon the protagonist, to mark and endow him with traits running in directions other than the narrative. JEW (EL) RY: thus the word that is a mannequin enclosing another term, the El, to be heard during the first primal scene, is first anticipated in the center of JewELry. If it is subtracted from the word, the remainder is Jewry, which brings forth the phantasm of genocide at the moment of the liberation of the concentration camps in 1945, a time synchronous with the production of the film. Jewry will be what is redeemed (in the pawnshop) through the passage of Christopher Cross. EL subtends the sign of the Hell of the unimaginable dimensions of the camps.[17]

The same letters of the film recur so often that their self-reflective dimension encourages confirmation of their essence across the image tracks and sound tracks. A graphic rhetoric slowly emerges and forms an unconscious register of

the movie. The missing H of Hell enclosed in Jewelry is supplied by J.J.'s monogram stolen from lithography, in

$$J.J.$$

as seen in the boss's office or on the door of a company car. J and H are two
centers of the same monogram, but they are also linked to their words in the film:
(H)ell; (H)itler; H(iel); (H)ogarth. J.J.'s name identifies the scenes of domestic

life and "Marriage à la Mode" that Lang takes from William Hogarth (1697–1764), or the Hogarth Press, which published the *Standard Edition* of Freud's works. J.J. is in the same business, the circulation of prints and broadsheets, as his English namesake.

Likewise, equivalence of a character and a letter inaugurates a visual and aural stutter that punctuates the doubling that recurs time and again throughout the film. Chris Cross transfers (in a Freudian sense of transference) the I that designates himself onto the identical letter, J, that is repeated in the doublet of his other. Synonymy of I and J makes Chris a function of his boss, and vice versa.[18] After receiving the commemorative watch during the stag party, Chris looks up and stutters, "Well, I . . . I don't know how to thank you, J.J." The doubling is inscribed again, when he adds, "J.J., I . . . I am really grateful for all you've done." Each character is determined by the paradox of an identical difference. The slight curve at the base of the J allows for a zero-degree differentiation of social rank, and all the more because I and J are adjacent in the alphabet as well as in the narrative, which implies that Chris indeed merits a better station in life, and that J.J. is where he is only by force of circumstance and unchanging social conditions.

The ornate flourish of success and individual selfhood, the American dream of autonomy, the signature has its effective monetary worth in the arc of J.J.'s monogram. The straight and curved lines of the letters are set in coincidence. One functions as the complement of the other in perfect circularity, and both are enclosed in a circle drawn around them.[19] J. J. Hogarth's monogram belongs to a heraldic tradition that uses devices to self-authorize or give to its bearer an allure of privilege that is produced only in the aesthetics of its self-enclosing symmetry. It conveys immense ideological force, for as a logo it endows its user with an effect of self-legitimizing or self-incorporated power. The medallion describes the same closure as the shape of the pocket watch that Chris was awarded for his years of unstinting service. Both reflect the social reversals of identity that the sightlines and visuals articulate elsewhere.

In the contrapuntal shots taken from either end of the festive table at the party, J.J. is the first to name the character facing him. The silhouette in the foreground is suddenly put into circulation. He is tagged as "Chris Cross." Viewers are tempted to laugh at its overdrawn motivation that confuses proper and common names, and visibility with abstraction. Chris Cross or criss cross? Chris (X) cross? J.J. and Chris who (chi) cross? A temporality is written in the name, a temporality of action that takes place, or a passage, moving from one condition to its transfiguration, from Chris to Cross, from i to o, from a linear, orthogonal mode to a closed, completed, circular form.[20] The name crosses, marks, x'es a signature that bears the name of a subject in process. The pun gives way to a greater problem of indicating, naming, and signing that marks Chris as a piece of jewelry, a Jew, and a victim of Hell. Like other figures in the film, he is destined or written by highly conventional associations surrounding the graphic units that determine his essence.

These signs are traps that the film sets to elicit apprehension of differences that constitute naming, indicating, and seeing. All of the names have a visual allure, an overwrought "look" that points to themselves and to the overall visual network of the film. They show how the names fix the characters in space and time, and how those baited into motivating a name (that is, to accord it a "natural" part of that to which it refers) are caught within the force of containment at work in any act of nomination.[21] At the end of the stag party, when J.J. offers a cigar ("They cost a dollar apiece") to Charlie and Chris, Chris is the third to receive the match. Superstitious about the destiny of the third person sharing the same light (allusion being made both to fate and to the experience of soldiers in the trenches of recent wars), the middle and index fingers of Chris's right hand form a cross in close-up. In relation to his name the act and its sign duplicate the effect of his proper name. A self-indexing occurs. From this point the character is written and ciphered doubly, and even determined before the first primal scene that follows in the narrative.

At the end of the film, after Chris has lived through trauma, his bungled attempt at suicide is set in the most banal volume of Hollywood cinema, a hotel for transients. A flashing neon sign outside and above the window provides a cliché that connotes the pulse of the fearful heart as it designates a city slum. But the on-and-off of the light beyond the window evokes the return and loss of visibility in the context of symbolic genesis that the film has developed at length.[22] The vertical cast of the flashing letters—the lower bar of what we ascertain (mistakenly) to be a T is an I (or simply a line that has no semiotic status) above an E and an I.

I

E

L

Is Chris Cross in the lower depths of (H)EL(L)? Or is the I, the vertical bar of the T of "Hotel," a hidden sign that refers to (H)iel (Heil, Hitler) that recalls the Nazis and the extermination of the Jews? Does the EL become a visible pulse of the scream of the Third Avenue El heard in the first primal scene? Or more simply, do the graphemes function as a transition between the former shot, where Johnny is heard shrieking in Sing Sing, when they "pull the switch" and ELectrocute him?[23] Or does the sign trace over what it has caused to disappear, the HO(T) of the hotel, appropriately, the heat of the voltage running through Chris's body as he imagines Johnny's electrocution, which has just been announced in the preceding shots? Would the absent HO refer to other networks of writing that run through the film?

Simple as the letters are, their indeterminate status as marks tends to knot the lines of reference in the thematic weave of the story. The characters of the film are numerical and figural functions of the letter-marks that flatten the perspective of illusion. On this ground alphabetic characters appear to mediate the signless mark seen everywhere (an alphabetic figure that a beholder seeks to invest with meaning) and the totalizing function of language that unconsciously supplies its users with conventions of meaning—the capital of its pragmatic use and the power it has to produce illusion. For this reason, contrary to the A-genre films, *Scarlet Street* acquires political force either where it does not convince or in moments when its meaning is painfully evident. This is spelled out in Adele's name. For Chris she embodies a domestic Hell; but the name literally tells us to read the allegory of the film in its imperative dimension, that is, to add L, thus to make an LL of EL, an "Add Hell" or a conjugal Hell of her figure. The verb folded into her first name conjures up the same doubling of initials in the monogram of J.J. and the letters CC and SS of the title and principal characters of the feature: Adele, Add L, A DD LL.

It would be easy to find the H reflecting the same function of doubling forms. Since the emblematic dimension of names and letters lays stress on the pictural silence of the film—its mute, hieroglyphic surface—and since we never hear the word Hogarth pronounced on the sound track, the insistence of its mark becomes overbearing. It is caught in the exclamatives, the stammerings and particles of apostrophe. "Ho, Ho, the boss is stepping out," remarks one of the members of the company during the dinner party, underlining how J.J. leaves the circle of old boys. He exits to a car in which a smiling blonde is waiting. J.J. goes from a puerile scene to a genital world. The Freudian narrative of psychogenesis that the sequence entertains is flattened by the image of the car. The lady who looks out is denoted as another Woman in the Window, in reference to the other panel of the diptych adjoined to *Scarlet Street*. H H of the "Ho, Ho, the boss is stepping out" (spoken *off*) doubles Hogarth who is stepping out on while he remains *in* frame. Language becomes visible when the image duplicates the vocal description. The rebus forces the viewer to see other vocal shards as literal manifestations of language. Following the same logic, anyone who is "stepping out" of frame encounters a return to an originary fear of the letter (of the boss, of the officer in the first primal scene—an avatar of the agents of the SS—and so forth).

Redundant combinations of image, figure, and voice yield what appear to be unintended ciphers. In this way the film virtually reads its own genre and array of forms. Objects are doubled no less than the characters of the players' names. They recur and "return" relentlessly as if providing a key to unlock the film's hidden language. There are two sequences that use company safes in the decor of the world of business.[24] One prints "J.J. Hogarth" on its two doors, and the

other, set in the pawnshop under the El, has on its doors "V. NICHOLAS." In the first, Chris is seen in his cubicle just before, in a contrived moment of suspense, J.J. descends from his office "upstairs" to take a draft of cash before

going out. A black janitor has told Chris that he will soon let Chris out of there.[25] Mortified by a confusion of remorse, passive aggression, fear, and desire when readying to pilfer some bills for Kitty, Chris is interpellated by the voice of the benevolent boss, *off:* ''I'm glad I caught you just in time, Chris,'' utters a voice we ascertain to be that of J.J., just before he enters the frame and faces the window of the cashier's office.[26]

The shot and reverse shot establish continuity through the mirroring of the name CASHIER on the glass. The configuration of bodies and letters literalizes the economy of the film. Below CASHIER an S is cast eerily onto Chris's forehead, as if to tell us that Chris is turning about, croSSed, in a serpentine drama of reversal and doubling; that we have in the name of Chris Cross a sad, melancholy case, a near-psychotic like M, taken and cited from Lang's earlier German film of that letter. Furthermore, in a transliterated German, Chris is a psychotic box, a vault or case on display, a *Kass hier,*[27] or he is a reptile, a snake, an infrahuman Jew that curls around the dark regions of the Third Avenue ''El,'' like a rat inhabiting his own grim paintings of the New York cityscape. In the hieroglyphic dimension obtained across the reverse shots, the letters of CASHIER are read in the opposite direction. In the first shot taken from Chris's point of view, we discern, mirrored,

ЯƎIHꙄAↃ

next to J.J. First, the only perfectly reversible letters in the doubling are I and H, as if they make identities of "I" and "He" across the glass separating the boss and the employee. But S turns around and embodies the two curves of the C, backward and forward, next to the equally reversible A. Only when the shot is mirrored from the same axis, on the diametrically reversed angle of the same sightline, does the adverse, in a numismatic sense that goes with the scene, reveal the reverse. Reference is made to the "Scarlet Letter" of *Scarlet Street*, as Hawthorne's A of Adultery branded on the forehead of the adulterer. His crime, therefore, is double: he is a thief and an adulterer, determined by the plot of a capital letter. Yet the adultery, in part due to Adele's irascible character, is written into ADuLtEry, the word that spells out the effect of the cause in the name-of-the-spouse in a slippage between Hawthorne and Renoir. The icon A also embodies the drama of the angularity, the anguish of accession to visibility, of passage from an imaginary state to that of a subject inscribed in social process. He is visibly "adulterated" or drawn into the symbolic domain by the law of the letter cast upon him.[28] When the ciphers are traced on Chris's forehead, a simultaneously vertical and horizontal reading of letters is prompted. Transgression of linear scansion disengages a crucial—and unconscious, traditionally repressed—dimension of the film. Cashier is placed over Chris. On him is branded the S that resembles the snake he portrayed curling about the El. The entire configuration of letters yields

CASHIER

S

in an emblem by which a horizontal and vertical reading in acrostic baptize Chris as an ass. As Chris turns to move toward the safe, he taps his head with his finger, visibly indicating that the rebus must be read in the various directions and with attention to the hieroglyphic, secret code of filming. The pathos of the melodrama does not permit viewers to see him "like" an ass, since the tradition of heraldic letters and blazonry (studied in Freud's *Psychopathology of Everyday Life* and *Jokes and their Relation to the Unconscious*, two texts that the film seems to study) appeals to the tradition of enigmas constructed through mirror writing.[29] Seen on the glass, in reverse, the C initiates a reading leading back and forth from CA to AC. Thus it goes from CA-AC, and thus to CA-CA, to and from cacke and caca, signs of waste, money, and shit. The arcane configuration reveals exactly what cannot be adequately represented or designated as such in the medium of cinema.

The rapport that is held between Chris and excrement, thematized in the anality of the protagonist's condition, has an uncanny literal equivalent in the film's childish mirror writing. He is the force that has been the only figure of an un-named, irrecuperable, totally generous figure in a world of general social stop-page and immobility. His sign implies a nameless, liquid state in contrast to the arrested environment in which he circulates, and for whose movement he is re-sponsible. When he first seeks money to sustain Kitty, Chris tries to get a loan. He enters an office whose name is seen only in reverse, on the other side of a frosted glass that carries the blazon of the "Globe Loan" Company next to a picture of the planet Earth. This is not the first time we have seen this "globe." It cues a memory of the Universal Studio logo that wound the ring of "A Uni-versal Production" around a sparkling globe in an illuminated galaxy. The em-blem of the Universal production is now written into the narrative: Chris cannot procure the five hundred dollars he needs for Kitty because he lacks a "co-signer," that is, a double of his signature, the double being the film that has, ironically, excluded him from freedom by containing him within its borders. The reversed writing of the sign on the door of the loan office is written in a way that triples the circles of the O of Hogarth. This is equivalent to the desire to draw a circle around—to trademark—what one imagines, to fetishize by copying, or to name in the name of repetition that is either love or an act of painting. The em-blem reconfirms the expression of narcissistic innocence that Chris had used to describe the fantasy-work of painting. "I draw a circle around what I like, and that is why I love to paint," he avows during their first date, a lunch, in boyish euphoria to Kitty, with a figure that doubles the economic pattern of the film but that also locates the enigma that designates Chris as the most "precious" shape held within it.

The Globe Loan Company is a double of the main office and the safe that incarcerate the cashier. An infinitely constraining world, a modern prison à la Piranesi, it articulates space within spaces by the penchant to duplicate narrative instances through both letters and objects. The safe in J.J.'s office is matched by the safe in Nick's pawnshop. Johnny takes two paintings to the broker for ap-praisal. The only inkling of the shop's location is revealed in the first painting, which had portrayed the shop window below the El. "Nick," the gruff broker sitting stolidly on his desk in profile in a medium shot, tells Johnny that the art is worthless. The S-like snake curling around the iron girder "is strictly from the Bronx" and has no business slinking around the space by his own window. "Take that junk," he barks at Johnny, "back where you got it, in Washington Square." Nick refers to the traditional array of kitsch in the annual spring show in New York, that is, art painted well after the leading trends on 57th Street, the site of the Dellarowe Gallery. He tells Johnny to bring him some jewelry next time, just the way he had the last, and to get the paintings out of there. Literally, in Nick's words (which double Adele's), the art stinks. The broker's name is painted in letters on the safe just behind his pudgy face. Allusion to the gift-figure in the film is found in (Saint) "Nick," or Chris (of Christmas), who, by refusing to name his art in writing, makes a truly precious object, an allusion to Santa Claus, the opposite of "jewelry."

Johnny speaks to "Nick" but V. NICHOLAS is printed on the vault. Johnny's "Oh, hi, Nick" on the sound track cuts the visible word in half, leaving the division of V. NICH and OLAS. According to the logic of the filmic icon, it is not unwarranted to disengage the O—the perspective object in the Globe Loan office—in order to see in the broker's name another emblem of the hole in the frame. Like everyone else, the broker is broke. In the circularity of the scene, the effect of the jewelry, the "fourteen-karat, seventeen-jewel cashier," causes Nick to ask Johnny to bring some jewels the "next time" (just as does the globe of the Universal logo) he "comes around." With the AS(S) produced by the word CASHIER and the shadow of the S over Chris's head in the preceding sequence, an analogous shape is inferred, in A S O L, the circle in which the money of the film is traveling. The literalization of an ineffable sign—asshole—comes across the writing divided and doubled on objects that recur uncannily throughout the film.[30]

The way Nick sits arrested on his desk typifies the general stoppage and blockage of both the body and the economy of the film. All holes are sutured or, better, corked up. Only the illusion of love, a sort of Chris-tmas gift, provides an imaginary opening and sense of passage. Once again, the splintered graphics of the film show why. In the sequence depicting his first encounter with Kitty, Chris stands gazing at the object of his desire. He is placed before a sign we would easily misread as ABSOLUTELY NO CREDIT in the dingy setting, yet we see SOLUTELY CREDIT, that is, a rebus of an unblocked (A) S O L, a solution of credence and solvency. Ab- and ass-solute, dissolved, flowing, madly in love, Chris sucks his rum through the straw. In a currency heightened by these letters and by the drip of the morning rain seen outside the window above, the unlikely hero indicates his relation with the closed circulation of the film. It appears that movement is unblocked only when names have not yet been fixed to what they signify.

When Chris did no more than "draw a circle" around what he liked to represent, Johnny points at what the camera proceeds to double or render ambivalent. He salutes in mannered, half-open, half-closed style. He extends his arm with his palm up and fingers together when he points to the virtual worth of Chris's letter sent to Kitty. He does the same when he says good-bye to Chris as he leaves with Millie in their new studio. When Janeway asks who has authored these nameless paintings, he points not to anyone in frame but to the next shot, which places both Kitty and Janeway facing the camera. Clearly the camera "signs" them with a triple attribution that includes the spectator. Kitty responds to his indexical act, gasping, "No, Johnny, no," in a doubled negation erasing the denial that in turn can be taken as a yes. The paintings "come around" to Johnny between the image of indication and the ambivalent referent. Their trajectory is emblematized

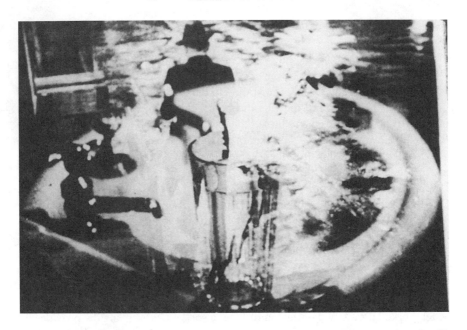

in the curvature of Johnny's palm, which points forward but also back to itself. Kitty registers the very shock that had marked Chris's face when he witnessed the primal scene under the El. Now she repeats a sign of panic and anguish that had been Chris's first entry into a sexual and symbolic domain: aghast, eyes rounded, and lips opened to form a circle, Kitty's face registers the fear of being named. Johnny's rounded palm that had initiated the exchange is the icon of the hand that holds the coin of Kitty.

Johnny's "style" amounts to his manner of naming ambiguously. He wills to have the world in his hand. Cupped, it is ready to receive the coins that it seeks. A self-enclosing gesture, a personified logo, the hand is related to the general problem of naming. It is coded as a Midas effect, in which the signified is turned into waste. Thus, when the "boys" catch sight of the woman J.J. has hired for his pleasure, a shot of two windows between a picture overhead locates the view that looks down from the banquet room onto the street below. "Look!" is shouted *off*, before a hand indicates what could be either the window, a picture, or the street beyond. An infinitesimal gap between aural and visual sign—a failed synchrony—calls into question the relation of viewing and naming. Only when the men crowd to the windows (in a medium close-up in profile) and ogle, and when one voice exclaims, "Hey, boys, get a load of that dame!" does the reference freeze. In the subsequent shot, in close-up, and from a perspective that the group could only imagine, the referent appears. The blonde looks out of the car window. As a filmic icon, she skews visual continuity. From the standpoint of arrested sexuality implied by the sight of the men gazing at the scene from an undisturbed locus, in isolation, "Get a load of that dame" is not merely a slangish turn. It equivocates on an undifferentiated mass of inert matter that is not the blonde but the anal mass that embodies the men who are looking. "Loads" of shit, as it were, the men gain their pleasure in an act of visibility that bends the erotic sign of the female back to an axis aligning money and unexpended waste. The cohort who utters the words is the paunchiest of the revelers and, like Johnny, what he indicates about the status of the other comes back to describe himself.[31]

Doubled and reversible indication also holds in Charlie's inquisitive gesture regarding Chris's Sunday painting. After Charlie enters the apartment adorned with glass and elegant floral wallpaper of mottled aspect broken by doorways and prismatic passages, Chris leads him to the studio. Only later is it confirmed that he paints in the bathroom. Adele enters in her slip and hastens away, but only before Charlie's gesture of indication reveals that the studio embodies the "same thing," or matter of the same essence, as the painting. "You mean to tell me," he exclaims wryly, "that when you look at *this,* you see *that?*" A rebus, the statement uttered *off* while the camera holds on the sink literalizes the equivalence in all acts of indication (*this* on one side equals *that* on the other, or that the *is* of *this* is the same as *at* of *that*). The gestural mode in the cutting of the shots is identical, as Charlie indicates not only the objects in frame but those seen in the next shot. In the narrative register, he implies that Chris does not see a faucet, sink, and toilet when he looks at a flower in a glass. The ambivalent referent, since plumbing is in question, is an emblem of a "pipedream," an ambiguous indication that confuses painting with excrement and stoppage.[32]

The implicitly Freudian register allows developmental, economic, and historical elements of the film to inflect one another. The time is the Depression, signaled as bodily constipation, suggesting that arrested stages of psychic and economic development are similar. In this respect, historical and aesthetic borders become infinite and inclusive of the process of meaning exceeding contingent time. Writing cues regression. When Kitty and Chris say goodnight for the first time, they are apposed to the sign marking Tiny's Bar from which they have exited below. The sight of the name interrupts the scene and brings history back into it. Tiny would also refer to Edward G. Robinson, who is coded as old, fat, ugly, and short—that is, the Jew, the other, the human shit in the eyes of the Aryan or anti-Semitic viewer. "Tiny" functions as a double marker in a fashion identical to the characters' acts of indication. As a self-enclosing figure that draws attention to Edward G. Robinson as himself and his other roles, it also works as an element, like the vaults in J.J.'s and Nick's offices, apposed to the second marquee, *Marchetti's.* Joined to and doubled with the first, *Marchetti's* replicates *Tiny's.* Both are diminutive and a sign of the racism on which the industry thrives. But in the autonomy of the film, Marchetti returns to Tiny. It is the third term of the emblem, in the graphic presence of Edward G. Robinson that passes across the illusion of the narrative: Mark Eddie, one hears as one reads, in echo of the visual stature of Chris, a "little Edward." Given the pun read across the two signboards, a viewer is tempted to see the chiasmus of Chris (X) in Marchetti. In reading the name syntactically, as a function of space and surface, the German *March* (a fable, a coin, or impression) is crossed into the name. Joined with other allusions to contemporary Germany, the political unconscious of the film moves over, of course, to the sign of *Kitty* in homonymy with Marchetti, when she is marked (and marketed) as Katherine March. *The March of Time,* both a fragment of fable, a filmic icon, a piece of history, and an allusion to a newsreel, Kitty is framed and splintered through the name that incorporates and mints the worth of all the characters. The money of her name and others acquires worth in their autoreferential dimension. Self-enclosure heralds the same circularities in the framing of the street fragmenting the signs of Tiny's and Marchetti's.

Marchetti's grocery store is seen across the pavement adorned with a fire hydrant and two garbage cans. An indispensable figure for any cityscape, the fireplug is a visual joke that fuses bodily and historical registers. An implicitly redundant relation with the excremental plumbing of the movie is shown. The same object is foregrounded in the first shot of the film. A city street shot from a low angle with tiny figures in the background that move up and down a gallery of stairs under a canopy, a middle ground presents a doorman whistling for a car to park on the shine and gloss of the moist asphalt. In the foreground, the hydrant sets the perspective of the sidewalk in a mannered effect that conflates areas far and near. Gigantic figures of pedestrians move in the foreground, while minuscule humans are seen on the other side of the street. The hydrant offsets the doorman and figures moving in the illuminated decor in the stairwell. The music of the hurdy-gurdy lends a quaint effect, but in the flattened depth the uniformed male whistles to beckon a large female torso in the foreground whose midsection crosses over his face: what will be the narrative dimension—the arrival of a blonde at the end of a stag party—is both anticipated and canceled by the body whose sex affronts the doorman and passes by. After dominating the tiny figure in the middle field, the female in the foreground exits left before a male and a female cross right with a dog on a leash. The dog in extreme foreground— possibly a double allusion to *La chienne* and to Joan Bennett—duplicates the presence of the monkey turning the organ in the background. The dog passes by the hydrant but—fortunately for decorum—chooses not to leave its sign there. Urine is displaced from the fireplug to the city street in the glistening surface of the street. The excremental side of the scene is duplicated in the figure of the monkey (associated in European iconography as the essence of mimicry and waste). As if he were essaying Freud's stages of a child's development simultaneously across three layers of the same shot, Lang makes the camera return to a

moment of originarity right where spectators seek narrative signs that will elim-
inate ambiguity.

If the hydrant thus conflates sexual and historical elements, it becomes one of
the filmic icons that makes the illusion of the film regress to a coextensive mix of
writing and image. Variants of the hydrant figure in the play of dots, abstract
forms that seem to flatten the depth of field and to recur often enough in order to
suggest a network of arcane signs (a whorl of sequins on Kitty's purse, the globe-
shaped lamp posts, the lemon wedges on the rum collins glasses, the cigar ends
that cut perfect holes in J.J.'s mouth when he sticks it between his lips, light
bulbs in rooms, and the like) whose enigma is their literal evidence. They provide
a frame for the insertion of ciphers. One of these may be Johnny's straw hat. It
flattens his character and skews perspective. With his hat, he envisages himself
going to Hollywood to act tough with women to gain a high salary of "fifty dollars a day."[33] His hat offers a slanted line that makes the shots in which he moves
essays of visual tension and self-reference.[34]

His hat is first seen in extreme depth in the first primal scene. Seen through
Chris's eyes, its sight prompts the cashier to run forward. After having gently
poked his umbrella (toward the viewer), in the next shot, Kitty is seen squatting
on the edge of the sidewalk and gutter beside Johnny and his straw hat. The hat
flattens the decor by resembling a dot that cannot be set in the narrative. By immediate analogy, the headpiece resembles a potty seat. In the midst of the rain
and wet of the city streets, Kitty only reflects liquid on her slicker. When she
stands erect, legs spread apart (in contrast to Johnny's legs in their closed parallel
position), she is a parody of the vamp, but also set adjacent to the excremental
sign of the hole figured by the straw hat placed on the sidewalk.

Through the film hats beget each other. The hat Chris wears is more discreet
and worn with the brim turned up to favor its circularity. The artist who takes
Chris-Kitty-Johnny-Janeway's paintings on commission in Washington Square
sports the cliché of the painter with his Montmartre beret. But most tellingly, in
the pan following Johnny crossing the street in Washington Square, next to the
old man's display, we remark a woman—who for a moment seems identical to
Joan Bennett—sitting immobile and mute next to her display. She wears a broad
and elegantly two-toned sombrero. A sombrero in Washington Square? It can be
dissociated neither from the Universal logo nor from the function that doubles
and flattens perspective, but now with the explicit difference that it counterpoints
two garbage cans on which another artist, an old woman, is sketching a drawing.

The equivalence of hat and receptacle cues a visual scansion of the sound
track. Time and again the dialogue touches on waste, which cues flow, stoppage,
orality, and anality. Their apartment, yells Adele, stinks of paint. Chris responds
that "the only reason I'm married is because I'm stuck," which is the same remark he passes off on Kitty during their second date: "You walk around with
everything all bottled up." And the oval portrait of Sergeant Detective Higgins,

he avows to Charlie, is "mud done by a photographer." Where Chris is knee-deep in the muck of a life of Sunday painting to "kill time," by contrast, Johnny can't get dirty. In one of his first remarks, he admits, "Why, I had a chance to clean up at a crap game, and you gave me a dirty look." After concocting the deal that will have Kitty draw money from Chris, he concludes, "It's a cinch to squeeze out your partners." He conjures up his "pipe dream" of life on Easy Street only to tell Kitty, who groans about the task before her, to "pipe down."

Here the word binding the entire film—its mix of letters and doubled indications—is the demonstrative shifter *this*. Its ambivalence underscores the first words Charlie and Chris exchange in the bathroom about abstract painting. *This* seen in the picture is not *that* on the sink. Chris replies, in words seemingly cribbed from an art history textbook, that a "real" work comes through individually creative distortion. But Charlie's insistent *this* is soon duplicated when the next sequence inaugurates the first oral exchange between Kitty and Johnny. He picks up Chris's letter, taps it with his curved hand, and says, "I'm talkin' about this . . . " He adds, "This is a setup." *This* is spread all over the film. It points doubly, on the one hand, to what it designates in the image field, and on the other, what it remarks about its own form. It harks back to the stag party when the men look at the timepiece ("Hey, look at this!") and pass it from one end of the table to the other, taking care to hold it by the chain and not to touch it. *This* becomes concretized as a piece of writing that can be seen in its lenticular presence, anamorphically, and *that* turns into what it points to: an equivalence of time, money, and, by anagram, as *shit* it thus condenses the relation of the work to visibility and representation in general.

Here the subversive elements of the film writing become clear. Words and letters dictate that speech must be seen as plastic manifestations of script. Opposition or relay of voice and image does not appear to hold in the type of writing that the film espouses. The field of illusion in which *Scarlet Street* is produced is severely impugned. In a pathfinding study explaining how the viewer of classical cinema is seduced into making sense of the arbitrariness of sound and image tracks, that is, into constituting a "discourse" where closer inspection reveals there really is none, Rick Altman discovers that continuity depends on a hidden lawmaker who is none other than the paying consumer. Viewers choose to find or fabricate narration; they select as self-identical what the film merely puts into a relation of visual proximity. Altman notes that next to the sound track, the lure of continuity of the image exists "only in order to keep its responsibility secret. Using the ideology of the visible as a front, the sound track remains free to carry on its own business."[35] The other, repressed dimension of films emerges only when we imagine the sound track as a ventriloquist. It has been shown how Lang's objects—particularly the fire plug and garbage can—already call into question their own roles as functions of illusion. On a more pervasive scale, in *Scarlet Street* a productively "bad" ventriloquism prevails. The film simply ruptures its own effects of synchrony so as to render them undecidable. If, for this reason, the sound track could be interpreted as a band of letters, a phylactery of sorts that viewers can imagine as visible language,[36] then the force of Lang's critique of the medium and its circulation can be specified in his conflations of sound and image that work in ways unlike those of major studio productions.

Upon cursory view the script seems patently lousy: The slang is dated, insipid, or obviated in its references to economy and to the body. Dialogue is either too childish or too learned. "Jeepers, Johnny, I love you" is as ingenuous as "for cat's sake," an interjection that is too obviously aimed at the feline Kitty (or the reminder of a common Jewish name, Katz). Chris speaks too elegantly to be a cashier; Johnny has a distinctly dated verve; Millie banters in lines too obviously drawn from soap opera; and Kitty groans about love with an aggressive ennui ("Can I help it if I'm in love," she retorts to her roommate).[37] It cannot be said that the script or the players are that "bad" or, as the ideology of representation would say, "unconvincing." Rather, the speech is hieroglyphic. The voice matches names and figures seen along the image track. The concatenations require the viewer to dispense with illusion of synchrony in order to extend the rebus of writing.

It has been noted how Johnny speaks excrementally when he barks to Kitty, "It's a cinch to squeeze out your partners." As visible writing, Johnny's word explains the whole system of illusion that Lang is abusing. If cinch is apposed to Chris, with the identity of [k], it recalls, of course, the sink that is the origin of the unnamed artworks acquiring so much value in the story. They are executed next to the toilet and the bathroom sink. Yet the sink in which everyone is mired, sunk in the collective bowels of depression, refers back to the code name of illusion on which Hollywood film is based, and which sychronizes image track and sound track.

In showing how European films question the illusion of a coextensive origin of image and voice (in samples drawn from Renoir and Rohmer), Altman notes, "We often hear words spoken long before we know where they come from; these disembodied words are then associated with a specific character by means of a closer shot and lip synch" (73). In American cinema, this amounts to interpellation. Continuity in the sound tradition depends on a spectator attributing false origins of voice to a place where they really are not located. The sound tradition in America no doubt played on these illusions in order to orient spectators in directions the industry could more easily control by means of producing sutureless illusion. "Lip sync," decisive for the sound tradition, appears to be what the writing of Scarlet Street takes to task. It is posed between its presence as inscription, as a force of indication, and as a shifter or relay between the sound track and the image track. Johnny indicated that "sync," "cinch," or "sink" has the role of attributing a bogus origin to things. Seeing the world economically depends on possession of a keen perspective, while effective art depends on losing it. The

film extends the analogy to the signatures forged on the paintings. The illusion of authorship can assure a large profit by the allure of a self-given authority. The sink that backgrounded the flower and glass of Chris's first painting honoring Kitty was indeed the very sync being displaced within the field of the Hollywood studio film.

The credits also work against synchrony, but in ways different from verbal-visual amphiboly that the sound track and image track use to collapse illusion. The first credits display "Scarlet Street" on a New York-like street sign of the 1940s, seen askew, in a slowly drawn scroll to the lower right below the rays of light from the lamp on which Edward G. Robinson is overlaid—to the left of Joan Bennett. The combination of bars and the tilted framing evokes clappers that test synchrony in the production of rushes. Matching of image and sound is put forth not as a given but as a problem being visualized. The skewed framing is offset by the horizontal cast of the names of Edward G. Robinson and Joan Bennett. Unlike the characters they represent in the film, their names are bound together forever, exactly where they will not be in the narrative. The actors are figured contiguous to the film—and excluded from it—by way of the lower case *in* that tickles the viewer into ascribing a false rapport of intimacy: Is Edward G. Robinson ever "in" Joan Bennett? Is he "in" *Scarlet Street,* or do the three names (Robinson, Bennett, and the title) form the triangle of the law of the film whose mediating term is the preposition *in?* If credits conventionally play on cardinal and metaphysical virtues of direction that the West has invested into script in the emblematic tradition, by which the heading or upper part of a text is its heavenly soul or idea, and the bottom is its bodily trace, then the visible configuration of the two names resolves the narrative before it unwinds.

Likewise, "Scarlet Street" is never found in the maze of Brooklyn, Greenwich Village, or midtown Manhattan. The title is never uttered or seen in the film.[38] It is implied that, like Chris's paintings, *Scarlet Street* may be an unsigned film. Only two streets are ever named, one by a plastic echo of the written title, when Johnny tells Kitty that the whoring of signatures will land them on "Easy Street." The second is on a signboard that retitles the scene at Washington Square when Johnny picks up the paintings he had consigned to the amateur painter. He crosses by the space that had been marked by the woman in the sombrero in the first episode of the sequence. Cut into the frame — almost anamorphically — is a sign on the pavement that displays DETOUR DRIVING THROUGH A PLAY STREET. Along with the abyssal space of birdhouses, toys, and activities done for what Chris called "fun," the writing makes the scene a sign both of regression and of a collapse of symbolic continuity. Everything remains transitional or cross-referential. In the iconography of early twentieth-century film and literature, the "street" denotes an area of risk (close to the death drive of Freud), frustration, and social contradiction, as well as symbolic passage. At the end of Proust's *Remembrance of Things Past,* when Marcel steps down from sidewalk into the street, an epiphanic sense of flow is unlocked from the secondary world of symbolic forms and gains access to synesthesia and universal memory. But in René Clair's *Paris qui dort* (1923), the characters who happen into the street risk their lives, as do Godard's children of *A bout de souffle* thirty-six years later. In German films of the 1920s, the street locates mass hysteria and social conflict.

The image of the street finds its referent couched not just in two allusions in the narrative, but also in the letters of the title that stage an act of instancing and betray an obsession with the symbolic weight of writing. If Hawthorne can provide an interfilmic clue with the A cast on Chris's forehead, *Scarlet Street* alludes to *The Scarlet Letter* by literal resemblance and a common thematic concern with inscription. When the titles are superimposed in the style of a collage or a dissolve, the graphic process of the film reveals:

$$\text{S C A R L E T \quad S T R E E T}$$
$$\text{L E T \quad T R \quad E}$$
$$\text{S C A R \qquad S \qquad E T}$$

The relation of "setting" a name is identical to the verbal play of the proper name Chris . . . Cross. On another level, it can be aligned with the trauma of the body being named, or with the dialectics of the letter, as in Kafka's "Penal Colony,'' printed on the body to make the victim atone for the crime its form represents. The end of the film does just that. An X is printed on Chris's face—he is a variant of a man x-ed, a scarface—and he bears the trace of his name forever. But perhaps the title *Scarlet Street* suggests the circular concatenation of the pictural economy of the film, in which the actors and actresses are not humans but lettered configurations in spatial tension. There are curious similarities in the visual slippage from Jewry and Johnny to Janeway. The "Dellarowe" Gallery is first seen in a pan left that reads the sign in reverse, almost as "Owe a Dollar." Or, "for cat's sake" goes from Katherine to Kitty, from an adult to a feline to a child.

All the graphic doubling devolving from the alliteration of Scarlet Street flows into the production of the characters. "Johnny" is named Prince (the name is never seen, implying a multiplicity of orthography, including Prints, as in "Johnny Prints") because in every scheme he artlessly doubles a nothing. He heralds *J*aneway and *J.J.*, just as *K*itty beckons *C*hris. On the margins of the film, reframed and doubled so as to produce miniature monograms, Joan Be*nnett* and *D*an *D*uryea carry their own doubles. But what of Edward G. Robinson, who is so fittingly tabbed as Chris Cross? Does not the film theorize his role in cinema ever since *Little Caesar* (1931) and *The Amazing Doctor Clitterhouse* (1938)? Like a little boy whose only distinguishing mark can be construed to be an initial between two innocuous proper names, Edward "G." Robinson is seen in the lettered redundancies as a little trait of difference apposed to the "J" of J. J.

Finally, it must be noted that the title has its own color. Scarlet is both everywhere and nowhere in the crisp contrast of black-and-white textures. The display of flowered wallpapers, sheets of glass, flower-print dresses, arabesques, and meanders shows how the film essays the unconscious as color seen through black and white.[39] The elegant patterns of the women's dresses indicate that abstract forms, hues, and lines cannot be named or lettered. They are a ground for the invisible mottling of colors, but in ways that foster the extension of Lang's rebus of characters at play with their form. When Kitty greets someone at the door of the new studio (as if rehearsing the title of Lang's *The Secret Beyond the Door,* 1947), she says, as her hand pulls the knob and her eyes fix upon the person whose identity has yet to be seen, "It's you!" For a moment it is we who are called forward by the shifter *you. We* are named before Millie enters and is seen in a paisley dress that complements the straight borders of Kitty's robe. In this instance, the indicative "you" that she utters is also seen as a colored letter on Kitty's garb, in the design of the Y of the doubled fabric that draws the shape of the ostensible character—behind the door—into visibility before it ever enters. You, that is, *why* and Y, is the circulation in O of the film's self-enclosing system of voice and image.

In this fashion *Scarlet Street* projects its figures at once within, beyond, and through its boundaries. Yet an ultimate test of its practice of the letter takes place in extraneous scratches or shapes left on the film. In the triangular play of the mark, letter, and image as they are set against one another, the frequent recurrence of change-over cues (set in the upper right corner of the frame, signaling to the projectionist that the adjacent machine must soon be set in motion to keep the synchrony intact) becomes part of the visual motifs of circles and orthogonal lines. They are just out of sync, but figure integrally with the redundant circularities of lamplights, purses, sombreros, lemon wedges, ashtrays, glasses, and smoke rings. The cues that do not belong to the narrative of the film are suddenly perspectival objects within it. They project the film back to the booth and define broader frames of a space without depth in which the spectator is totally confined.

For this cause the logo of Universal Studios is also drawn into the broader emblematic dimension of *Scarlet Street*. The first visible sign is a globe about which the words A UNIVERSAL PRODUCTION turn in a glittering galaxy. An iconographic viewing of the planet Saturn evokes the obviously melancholic dimension of the artist that Chris Cross embodies as a forever-frustrated creator. No less than the film's subject, the logo rhymes with the letters of the end credits. The last words of the film print A UNIVERSAL RELEASE over the shot of Chris left on the street and confined by his guilt. The extraneous subtitle all of a sudden is pulled into the narrative, summarizes it, and serves to theorize the entire convention of guilt on which the ending is based. At the end, there is more of confinement than release.[40] From beginning to end, the two writings literalize the symbolic process of the film. Yet their letters, too, are in an abyssal relation. The very first mark in the film is the letter A set over the globe; it begins the career of the circle of the Universal alphabet that invokes the angularity, the saturnal view of the artist, and the abyssal economy of naming and marking. It is the A of adultery and art cast over Chris's forehead, as well as the A that begins the revolutions of the filmic mechanism. The logo bears the same conflicts as does every other word, image, and object of the film, forcing its signs to circulate by and through each other and to promote a reading that knows no control other than the maddening closure of its redundancy. In order to step out of the circles of *Scarlet Street*, it may be necessary to see the reincarnation—or incarceration—of Chris Cross as an embodiment of Raoul Walsh's *Manpower*.

3

Dummies Revived
Manpower

In *Scarlet Street* elements of writing on screen open an endless movement of meaning that collapses the mimetic frame of the film. The signifier runs through and across the work and raises issues involving cinema, writing, and the gamut of representation. The system is sustained maddeningly and endlessly, in ways that run both counter and true to prevailing styles of invisibility in the studio tradition. The letter tests its limits of illusion. It is time now to see if the same mode of analysis can work for more staunchly transparent films. In this and the following chapter, we will study two apparently stock features of the Warner Brothers studio, *Manpower* (1942) and *Objective, Burma!* (1945). One goal will be to see if the Hollywood tradition betrays its mode of invisibility in a general practice of the letter and filmic icon. These two works, both directed by Raoul Walsh, are chosen also to continue speculation, begun in the first two chapters, on the relation that may hold between the system of the ''mark'' and that of the signature of the auteur, but now within the broader history of Hollywood at the peak of its productivity and impact.

This chapter will begin where the preceding one left off, along the margins of the film, where credits, which initiate the film writing, serve to distinguish the production from the narrative. Students of the Hollywood film know well that the industry had eroded the notion of *character* since its beginnings of production. Shared by viewers and the major implements of production, both the studio and the consumer worked together to articulate the system of the star. Films were built around given voices or faces, and spectators paid money to see and hear them. Tensions between known actors and actresses (including memory of the roles they had played in previous performances), and the limits imposed by the new parts and plots, lent an illusion of continuity to the industry. An audience paid not just to see a character taken from a novel (for example, Wolf Larsen of Michael Curtiz's version of *The Sea Wolf*) but to enjoy the demands it imposed upon a known actor who was cast in it (that is, Edward G. Robinson). "Character" therefore floated between spectator and screen. Viewers went to see themselves analyzing both characters and actors in the play of image and memory established between the known star, former films, and the promise of future features. Viewers could not fail to note a complementary and reciprocal relation between Edward G. Robinson as Richard Wanley, professor of Freudian psychology in *The Woman in the Window*, and Christopher Cross, the unheralded artist of *Scarlet Street*. Both partake of a melancholy character and excel by virtue of a skewed perspective they share with the world around them. Any spectator would notice immediately that Lang's casting of the star differs from the role that Robinson plays in *Double Indemnity* (1944) or, especially, in *Manpower*.

Manpower was the seventy-ninth film in Raoul Walsh's career as a director, and his sixth film since he joined Warner Studios in 1939. The title takes up a heavy and charged theme: "manpower" was bound to have appealed to American youth in the wake of the New Deal and at the onset of war in Europe and the Pacific, and it no doubt reminded the country of the manpower needed to fuel the Allied cause soon to come. For Walsh, it would have to take up a call to arms through collective memory of the comic antimilitarism of *What Price Glory?* (1927) and *The Cockeyed World* (1929). The film would have to tell everyone to be ready to engage in combat at the slightest provocation. And too, *Manpower* would have to signal the equally potential strength of *womanpower*, of a population of segregated females—identical to their consorts at war—ready to "man" the production lines at home. By 1942 the title must have been rich enough to inflect American domestic policy through its own example.[1] In its libidinal play the film generates a self-identical allegory of history and human diplomacy. An inner writing undoes the generic structure of the melodrama and opens a space of play. In this sense, the writing of the film is not as graphically obvious as what has been remarked in *Scarlet Street*; it seems to be of another sort, of a configuration that articulates bodies and things, and that relays erotic fantasy through movement and stoppage.[2]

Already the "character," Hank McHenry (Edward G. Robinson), heralded in the lead role, is anything but the prosopopocia of manpower. The spectator knows this before stepping into the theater. The trailers and posters for *Manpower* signal the inversions that are intended. Two items emblazoning the film tell how its position in the media of 1942 undoes the psychological unity of *character*. First an endnote and photographic flyer in *Life* magazine: in the usual endnote (or "parting shot") on the issue's last page, George Raft and Robinson are photographed slugging each other in what could be seen either as a fist fight or a dance in fast tempo. A primal scene reminiscent of what Chris Cross first observed in *Scarlet Street*? Robinson is shoved—or led—about by Raft, who sports a handsome profile and the dance step for which he had been famous (since 1929, as the champion Charleston dancer of the United States). Wearing a Bauhaus bathrobe that outlines Robinson's three-piece suit and the black profile of his body and angry face, Alan Hale (playing Jumbo Wells in the screen version) is the hidden figure in the scene. His fuzzy, almost electrically charged hair provides a sparkling aureole for the star's high forehead and wavy black coiffure.

The story in subscription to the photo takes great care to establish ambiguities of character in the film, which has not yet reached the American public. In its entirety:

ROBINSON & RAFT STAGE
IMPROMPTU FIGHT ON SET

In Hollywood April 26, Edward G. Robinson and George Raft were rehearsing a scene from their new picture, *Manpower*. Cast as pals, they profoundly dislike each other off location. In this sequence Raft was supposed to stop a quarrel between Robinson and Ward Bond by gently intervening. Instead he grabbed Robinson's arm, swung him violently around. Surprised, Robinson yelled, "Not so rough, George," and yanked his arm free. Raft reported that Robinson could keep his directions to himself. As they started to swing, a still photographer caught this exceptional picture. They were separated before damage was done. A week later Raft, who in the film enacts a telephone lineman, fell from a 30-ft. pole, suffered three broken ribs, contusions of the stomach. Robinson was not on the pole with him at the time.

Who is cast as whom and why? Who is on whose pole, and what kind of pole is, as it were, at stake? Where is the story, if not among the film, the ancillary projections of it through the media, and in the anticipations incited here for the public? "Cast as pals, they profoundly dislike each other off location": The sentence, an ideological jewel, refracts the production of *Manpower*—its area "off location"—into the fiction of the story. Cast ambiguously, the syntax of the legend to the photo appears to duplicate the structure of violence at the basis of the narrative. Something is said to have "gone wrong," since the fisticuffs that *Life* captures only project the strife seen everywhere in the screen version, whose plot in "life" is superimposed upon a representation of two electrical workers in a love triangle. A quarrel was being filmed (or staged), but in the photograph when Raft, who was supposed to "break it up," only baited Robinson by swinging him around; he elicited the rejoinder, "Not so rough, George." The temperate air of *Life's* corrective words would seemingly emanate from the calmer profile of Raft. The text attributes the remark to Robinson, but the image functions in an opposite way, enjoining us to see *Raft* declaring, "Not so rough, *Edward*."

Hence through the ideology of character a myth is served up to project an imaginary reality of Hollywood and a virile world of life and film having infinite extension. The erasure of an individual, a character, a star, a scene or framed representation is carried a step further in the last caption to what the magazine calls "this exceptional picture." Equivocal shifters give the illusion that in real life—that is, on the set and location—Raft fell from his pole (from a height of thirty feet) and broke three ribs. Yet this event is reproduced in the film, such that the off-stage event in real *life* will be fictionalized in the film in a greater flux of mythography. Two keynote ambiguities are manifest. First, *Life* and "life" are to each other as *Manpower* is to "manpower."[3] The imaginary dimensions of the film can be visualized as true to life in their production of both fiction and real events. The film not only reflects reality but also produces it in the story of the hard lives and times of electrical linemen. An air of *scuffle* gives a paradoxically hurried and studied look to "this exceptional picture." The photograph makes explicit the equivocation that Raft and Robinson can be both fighting and dancing, and that the photo is signed in 1942 by both Warner Productions and the Time-Life syndicate. Because the stars are staging as well as living a dispute, the viewer must deduce that their "character" is based on ambiguities shared among all the figures in the drama and in the consuming mass.[4]

The names of Raft and Robinson serve to locate polyvalent forces in the allegorical oppositions set in movement by their dance, their banter, bodies, and gesticulations. The "character" is neither where a viewer looks for it—in a single name—nor in an image associated with the voice and body. It emerges from a montage of photos, of stories, and of scenarios. The news item in *Life*, an advertisement, amounts to a trailer with disguised credits. And in the feature, the credits begin a bizarre pan-right as the frame moves from the name in uppercase letters of EDWARD G. ROBINSON to those of MARLENE DIETRICH and GEORGE RAFT. Instead of scrolling the names up or down, the camera keeps them on the same horizontal line, connoting that they are all a function of each other. Set over an abstract design suggesting an overlay of heavy metal plates studded with rivets, the square and robust letters evoke a world of girders and bolts. The characters—now in a calligraphic sense—partake of a sadistic eros galvanized by the surfaces of steel, of nuts and bolts screwed to iron piers. The three principal characters are scripted as elements of the same decor, while the studded look of their script and background has the manifest effect of making each name a linear function of the other.

"Manpower" is given as an oedipal triangulation. The foreign, exotic German figure is necessary for the dynamic rivalry of adolescent children who must fight each other for her attention, yet with the difference that Robinson, an infrahuman of sorts, a monstrosity (as in *Scarlet Street*, where he carries the conventionalized attributes of a Jew), must be expelled from the film so that its ambiguity can be extended beyond the conclusion. Robinson is the ideal misfit and outcast of a men's society because he is *too* masculine in his attempt to reproduce manly conventions. Robinson is the deformed member of the group who must be eradicated so that a symbolic murder will give a temporary sense of cohesion to the broader order through collective guilt, grief, remorse, and expiation.

On this score the hero's anti-heroic demise prepares an equivocal ending that convinces the viewer less about the religious features of the film than its own generic confusions. After Hank McHenry falls from the pylon—he just missed being caught by Jumbo Wells, who had reached out to grab his hand—the rain clears, a bus arrives, pulls in front of Johnny Marshall (Raft) and Faye Duval

(Dietrich), who have been waiting to drive off into the light on the horizon. The vehicle sputters down the road toward a painted crepuscule. For a moment the spectator is left adrift, floating, detached from both the narrative connections and the allegorical elements that had generated its tensions. The triad of characters has just been undone. Will Raft be abandoned as Dietrich leaves to pick up her former life spent in clip joints? Or will Dietrich stay and mourn her dead husband as Raft leaves in a self-imposed exile of guilt? Will both go off in sleazy apotheosis? Or will they return afresh to start over again?

They must repeatedly produce the same tensions that were inherent both to the film and its presentation in the media. In a structure not dissimilar to *La règle du jeu*, *Manpower* at once acts out and works through the murder of the anomalous figure inserted into its codes of order. The narrative can give the illusion of progress up to the murder—as in the case of the events that take place before Jurieu's demise in Renoir's film—and can be explained by the recurring events of life regained and lost in the initial scenes and in the denouement. The final sequence redoes the beginning. In frenzied rage, Robinson inches up the pylon where his partner is perched. Under a pounding cloudburst they engage in hand-to-hand combat. As he has discovered in an earlier locker-room skirmish with his crony Eddie Adams (Ward Bond), Robinson does not yet realize he is "way out of line." He swings a monkey wrench at Raft, slips, and dangles in midair. Raft tries to swing Robinson's pendant body toward Alan Hale, who offers an outstretched hand from the safety of his steel ledge. But the connection is missed. Unable to keep his grip as he lunges toward Hale, Robinson falls to the ground and soon dies surrounded by his mourners. Filmed in a dazzling series of quick takes that make a closed montage of high- and low-angle shots and close-ups of heads and parts of bodies clinging to poles or steel rafters, the sequence ends when unbelievably, unpredictably, Robinson *does* fall. Calling for a Shakespearean finale, the tragic ending brings the community together to utter praise over the dead comrade.

Tragedy supplants farce. The initial revival of Robinson at the beginning of the film was seen as bawdy comedy. After an electrifying montage that calls the linemen to the front as if they were shock troops or the counterinsurrectionary marines of *The Cockeyed World*, the men get to the scene of a natural disaster. While riding in the truck that takes them to the front, "Pop" Duval (Egon Brecher), a veteran of wars against the rains and also the father of Faye, presages death and damnation. It is *he*, not Robinson, who first must die. His prophetic words are turned against himself, but only after Robinson acts out his death. In the first mishap he appears to be electrocuted for having divided his attention between his work and his longing for the "mouse" (or "B girl") he had just left in a dance hall in Los Angeles. His leg slips against a live wire, and he is almost shocked to death. In a chiaroscuro filmic version of Rembrandt's *Descent from the Cross*, Robinson is carried down to the truck where a co-worker administers

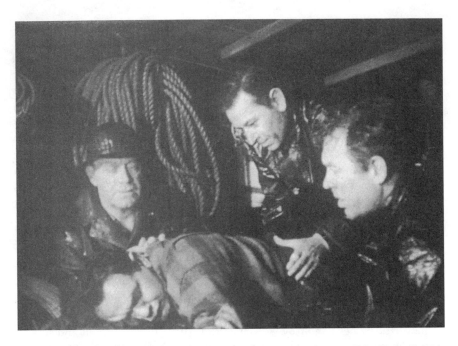

artificial respiration. After that attempt fails to bring the hero to life, Raft tries his hand and somehow succeeds, as if through faith, love, and deft touch. Robinson, who already had been cast as an incongruity in the initial dancing sequence (he leaves footprints on his partner's shoes, which prompts her to call him a ''jerk of all trades''), was virtually dead from the beginning. Given a temporary lease on life for the duration of the picture, he emerges from death only to seek it again.

Is it *Life*, life, or more of the pervasive ''death drive'' Walsh had depicted in other features at Warner Brothers since *The Roaring Twenties* in 1940? A liminal area between narrative and signature is glimpsed: crucial is how Raft resuscitates Robinson in the film's hidden writing. Limp, lifeless, and lying flat on his stomach, Robinson is attended from behind. On his knees and astraddle Robinson's body, over and behind his back, Raft leans forward and back in applying his hands and releasing them from the victim's ribs. A scene of artificial respiration is enacted upside down. A mute farce is begun that depends on the sight of males seen in anal congress: Raft enters Robinson from behind in order to give him a penal jolt that will make the body, which was just depicted tragically, in baroque tones, come to the farcical sense that the film needs for its generic mixture. The scene is coded carefully. Two men try to revive their comrade from the back. The second succeeds when, as two cutaway shots display them, a gallery of cronies stares on the spectacle as if it were a ribald skit of roughneck sex. Here ''man-power'' not only amounts to the roles of sexually isolated heterosexuals, but also

entails the erasure of codes within social divisions of labor and categories of realistic film.

In one of his typical oxymorons Voltaire once called Shakespeare a "barbaric
genius." If the concept of the auteur is respected, his epithet might be passed to
Walsh, an ardent admirer of Elizabethan drama, who continually stages abrupt
shifts between tragedy and farce here and in other features. The seeming "mixture of styles," evident in the tragic thread of *Manpower* (and which Erich Auerbach used to describe biblical narrative), is mapped in the initial shots and reiterated throughout the composition. Seen in Voltaire's enlightened view of
Shakespeare's bad taste, the film would suffer from a sort of generic contamina-
tion where, as in the ambiguities of the ending, the film's effectiveness resides in
how it appears to be unable to honor its genre. When it tries to be serious, the
pathos of the music or sound track is undone by the farce of the image track, and
vice-versa. Proximities of farce and tragedy operate polyvalently by forcing the
spectator into a position of not knowing exactly "how to buy" either one or the
other. Tension of equivocation works through amphiboly—and here the film's
writing is crucial—pervading the composition in the areas between the registers
of image and sound.

The narrative moves, ironically, from the farce of regress in Robinson's first
anal salvation to an oedipal solution, by which the female is finally, begrudgingly
it seems, accepted into the consort of males. Tragedy turns to farce, to tragedy,

and, as the ending connotes, to *you name it*. If confusion reigns in the convention of genre, the film's erotic movement—between "anal" and "oedipal" phases— also entertains a fusion of space and language, or what Eisenstein calls a "non-differentiation of perception—a well known absence of the sensation of 'perspective.' "[5] In *Manpower* the sexual dimension that fails to differentiate male and female roles is matched by an intermediate field of visual play likened to what can be apprehended only through the eyes of a child. As in *Scarlet Street*, the film forces its viewers to "regress" to an optical and erotic indistinction of planes and objects. Movement is coded in psychogenetic terms, where a dialog-ical sensibility forms part of a global apprehension of the world through indif-ference to cultural constructs. In terms that *Manpower* only implies in its puerile aspect, these forms include space, progress, narrative continuity, codes of de-marcation, or logical oppositions that determine culture and everyday life.[6]

In this fashion confusions of sexual boundaries replicate those of filmic genre. They both motivate and theorize the film's general economy on a broad scale. Farce typically involves sadism enacted either on oneself or on another, but with-out any focalizing perspective that would use moral distinctions to assuage or redeem its violence. Farce and sadism are on the same plane as tenderness. The latter can be homoerotic or turned toward a reconciliation of the sadism implicit in the ambiguity of its condition.[7] Bound together in a precarious unity that can veer toward violence (war), amity (exchange or commerce), or laughter (a ma-chinery of breakage and attachment that alternates like the system of an electric generator), farce produces manifold ambiguity when it is out of place or "out of line." Here the electrical metaphor, which precipitates so much of the comedy of the film, figures at the basis of the regressive pleasure its "other" writing is heralding.

Electricity becomes synonymous with the ambivalent drive of "manpower" and the libidinal institution of Hollywood film. The metaphor of wiring is strung through the scenario. The men are always bantering bad jokes fashioned from the stockpile of circuitry. Glass insulators are either fantasied extensions of the male body or teat-like orbs that remind the men of what they lack, and generate their lust. The men are always after connections—male and female; they will break them when they return to their locker rooms or dormitories. Everything breaks down (farce turns to sadism or dialogue becomes a fistfight) when someone blows a fuse or is "out of line."[8] Seen thus, the words make a mockery of all the seemingly "phallic" images of the film by shunting them from some shape in-volved with invisible desire (to behold and control another) to hilarity that breaks the silence in which a gaze or a force of desire is elicited.

Replete with laughter, thunder, and cacophony, *Manpower* ranks among the noisier of Walsh's films made during his tenure at Warner Brothers. The din is effectively obscene in that it rids the optical center of the film—especially the commandingly central presence of Raft and Dietrich—of a conventional heterosexual privilege. The din disperses the gaze that would see them as vanishing points of an idealized eros attained after passage through the puerile and adolescent world of work. The virtually "genital" cast of Raft and Dietrich, which opposes that of Robinson, Hale, and the other men, celebrates less an ideal of heterosexual union than a dominant order of surveillance and potential control. The more symbolically accomplished, postoedipal pair never falls "out of line," whereas Robinson, a child, like Renoir's Lantier in *La bête humaine* or Jurieu in *La règle du jeu*, attains calm only in death. Yet his position is tempered only by an ambiguous sort of control exerted by Alan Hale, another impish figure arrested in regression.

Hale's role is aligned with a fascination for water, fluid, urine, and messiness. On two occasions he slithers on his bottom on a moist surface in a practical joke played before his buddies. In the first, in a sequence in Mrs. Lynn's rooming house, he pours water on the floor and slides forward on his rump, legs spread apart, in a carnivalesque display proving that the ass is faster than the eye. A partner squats before him with a fork and knife in his hands; he will attempt to pick up the napkin with which Hale will wipe the liquid poured on the floor between their legs. In the second rendition, he performs (and is victim of) the same gag, but now more salaciously, with a woman at Robinson and Dietrich's wedding party. Dancing to the music of the Wing-Ling Chinese band, Hale spreads his legs apart and faces "Scarlet" (Joyce Compton), who giggles and squirms, bends down, spreads her legs and awaits his propulsion into her body. He falls back on his bottom, laughs, and wipes his wet bottom as the men at the table watch the two children play at sex in the piddle. And later, in another joke, Hale bets his cohorts that he can get a quarter to fall off his head into a funnel stuffed into his pants. Falling victim to the gag, he leans back for an instant while the men pour a jug of water into his pants.

In few films — *Sadie Thompson* and *Rain* perhaps excepted — does water spout so furiously. The Los Angeles Bureau of Light and Power appears to struggle in a climate more characteristic of a tropical forest than of southern California. Aligned with themes anchored in farce and literature reaching back to Villon and Rabelais, the omnipresence of Mother Nature taking her proverbial leaks is coded on the side of obscenity, a reversion to a fascination with a childish sense of fusion and flow. One shot binds its force of subjectivity — a process of oedipal passage that works in the configuration of the characters and the narrative alike — to its politics. The men are ordered to work on the Hoover Dam, a place named through the stock shot that establishes the episode. The visual toponym confirms that the troupe has been sent to work on electricity harnassed by the efforts of "man" in real historical time. The stock footage of the great convex line of the dam is seen from below, as a monolithic triumph of modern technology. Taken from above, the second shot records the great streams of water in a steady flow, in a continuous release of foam and spray. Seen in the context of the men-children's freely urinary activity, opposed to the sexual control of Raft and Dietrich, the streams make a festive froth of recent history. In fact, in the imaginary dimension of the film, the erotic "release" seen through the image of the dam entertains a paradox of work and play. Men work at and about the dam, an extended figure of the film industry, that coordinates collective ejaculation according to its own montage of orgiastic images. It virtually programs the free imagination and allows it to entertain phantasms of spendthrift play or unproductive expenditure of erotic energy. The sequence is close to what Georges Bataille had articulated (at the same moment of production of *Manpower*) to correlate the cultural manifestation of release and repression. The latter, he said, was concretized in dams controlling both hydroelectrical and libidinal currents. Dams or *barrages* replaced the lavish display of waters in mannered or prerevolutionary fountains and baths. A free spending of energy, like farce or the moments that a homeostatic culture reserves for its self-parody when it turns itself upside down, contrasts the daily control of order.[9] *Manpower* would be thus a double instance of both control and release, of a moral lesson and a piece of entertainment. Notwithstanding the cultural history of the figure of plumbing, release in *Manpower* is on the side of farce and popular economy, while the ethic of manipulated stoppage is closer to the ethic of controlling powers of repression associated with the film industry.

To imply this much from two stock shots—both of which suggest a presence of history into the fiction—might be construed to overstep the bounds of practical analysis. Yet if, as literary historians Mikhail Bakhtin and Jurgis Baltrušaitis have proposed, a history of laughter needs to be written, its main lines would arch back to orificial phantasms, in which every bodily protuberance or cavity would be comically marked by its identity with the bottom.[10] Vagina, ear, clitoris, nose, eye, navel, nipple, finger, toe, anus, penis, knee, rump, ankle, head, and arm would be cast as projections of *le bas corporel*, or lower body, which parodies and turns topsy-turvy a subject's relation with the classical ethos of control and closure. Reading *Gargantua* and the chapbooks in the medieval tradition, Bakhtin locates riotous shapes of comedy in the *carnivalesque* vision of the world as a global body of the undifferentiated swell and cavity of sensual and procreative energy. In this light the world is always expanding and lubricating itself, ingesting its own products in a congress of love, nourishment, defecation, and flatulent bliss. Parts of the human body are thrown about in name and deed, as opposed to a classical ideal that hermetically seals the orifices of the worldly body in favor of order and the clear logic of finite extension and closure. Under classical strictures the human is deprived of its protuberances and sallies: holes are bottled up.

From this standpoint the classical look of the Hoover Dam (and perhaps the Republican party in the eyes of Warner Brothers) would be the monument that the laughter of the film is fissuring; wit leads to a great orificial dilation and stream of water that pisses over the generally arid world of southern California. In line with principal theoreticians of the function of laughter in the cycles of everyday life,[11] the film would ostensibly open what is usually closed: its barrage of jokes, its banter, its play with urine and fluid would be seen as celebrating a victory of the (dis)order of a timeless Middle Age, a realm of laughter and a love of life tasted through Shakespeare, Rabelais, Cervantes, and Freud. But, the same theoretician might introduce a cyclical model—let us say a principle using the montage of the rhythms of everyday life—to show that a lustral movement that opens the closed sphincter of the world is merely temporary or regulated by the intervals an industry controls. As Victor Turner and Natalie Z. Davis have metaphorized the process, the function is likened to a societal motor that has gaskets and safety valves for blowing off excess energy with festive and windy toots. The cavalcade of bottoms and ends turned downside up amounts to control, to a corrective moment in an order coordinating the flow of libidinal energies such that force could never be "pent up" enough to precipitate a change in order.

Cast in these terms, the Hollywood film would be the valves releasing tension built up among millions of subjects who go to the movies to laugh; to identify with sexualities they cannot assume in a daily life; to regress to a communal *caca* of common "man" laughing through class conflict, opening phantasms of bodily holes closed by the Depression and the economic failures of American domestic and foreign policy. The mechanism of film would be eminently perverse in the ways it controls the force it elicits, or provides regulated doses of wit.

It can be assumed that the spectator plays on the tension of the two orders in the montage of *Manpower*, delights in a polymorphous control of individual relations between the image and narration, between what viewers discover to be an official erotic pleasure and a carnivalesque vision. Here the lines of the script cannot fail to be at once undecidably "good" and "bad." "I'll lay you three to one we've got to string up some wire tonight," George Raft snaps in his first words, which he addresses to a flossy brunette with three daisies in her hair. When he encourages Edward G. Robinson not to despair over losing a B-girl— "If the dames don't love you, I do"—Raft plays on their separate but identical status as *both* men and women, as indifferent conductors (and insulators or condensers of energy). His wisecrack has the same timing as Ward Bond's repartee, aimed at parodying Robinson and Dietrich's impossible union, "A new groom always sweeps clean." Lines of this kind are wired through the narrative—they are nodal letters, explosions of amphiboly—that persist as reminders of joking relationships that go outside of the movies and enter into the banter used to play with—to construct and to protect individuals from—the symbolic power of everyday life.

Laughter as breakage and reconstruction may seem distant from the film, but it is enveloped in the composition. The order of the first montage of the film, which initially dissolves history and narrative into spectacle, is carefully ordered.

The first twenty-three shots follow in this order (please see the Appendix for an explanation of the abbreviations used here):

shot 1
ls of the two electrical towers with factory in background against a bright sky.

shot 2
ms of the feet of one tower set in a relation of tension with the frame in deep focus.

shot 3
ls of turbine, inside, seen from above.

shot 4
Wipe and dissolve to *ls* of turbine seen in profile.

shot 5
Wipe and dissolve to *ms* of giant wheel turning in a factory.

shot 6
Wipe and dissolve to *ms* of turbine with pulley and wheels turning.

shot 7
Wipe and dissolve to *ms* of another turbine seen from above.

shot 8
Dissolve to *ls* of sky, thunder, and lightning in chiaroscuro.

shot 9
ls of insulators exploding on an electrical pole.

shot 10
ms from above of lights flickering during a medical operation. Masked figures stop their work and look up anxiously at the illumination near the camera.

shot 11
ls of a giant pylon on a cliffside over a raging river (in miniature).

shot 12
ms of the same with its grounding and leg seen in center of the frame.

shot 13
ls of the pylon.

shot 14
ms of explosion on its wires and insulators.

shot 15
ls of tower falling and crashing into the waters.

shot 16
ms of a man shouting into a telephone adjacent to a candle (''Hello? Light and Power? There's no electricity here,'' and turning aside, speaking to a figure *off*, ''Hey, honey, what's the address here?'').

shot 17
Pan across telephone switchboard with men at both sides, facing each other; shot ends in *cu* of man in profile barking into a telephone.

shot 18
ms of a white-haired figure (resembling an Irish-American cop) at a desk. He telephones while thunder roars in window in the background. Dolly in to *mcu* with voice-*off* vaguely synchronized with the telephone. Pan right following the man's exit.

shot 19
Dissolve into a men's club where cards are being played and smoke clouds the screen. Dolly in to *cu* where Irish boss barks and exits in *ms* before the camera pans and dollies right to record in *cu* (as in shot 17) a man making another telephone call on the right, to

shot 20
mcu of an Irish bartender receiving the call and then, with the camera tracking forward with him, ordering an employee to deliver the message in the adjoining dance-hall. He says: ''McHenry. Yeah. He's here. Tell that poleclimber he's wanted on the phone.'' Long dolly in through the crowd.

shot 21
Cut to *ms* of agitated motion of Edward G. Robinson dancing mechanically with a blonde and a pan left following him to a table where a brunette is seated.

shot 22
ms from above of the girls at the table.

shot 23
ms that pans up to George Raft standing behind them and in front of a poster of a woman on the wall. He remarks, ''I'll lay you three to one we've got to string up some wire tonight!''

In the beginning a montage of six diagonal wipes follows the two establishing shots of a double set of great electrical pylons. The first frames two of them as identical doubles; the second plays on the lower order of the steel girders in their relation to the frame. The allegorical process of the film favors a confused association of all objects with parts of the human body. The urge to "naturalize" a cultural phenomenon—to anthropomorphize it—is offered to reduce the tension of its alterity by bringing it into closer relation with the human form. Through this association the pylon seems to allegorize the stupendous stick figures as fake men, as delicate bodies made from erector sets posed in front of a power factory in the background. On the one hand, they could be interpreted as ideal subjects that "conduct" or "convey" the ideas or energies that are circuited to pass through them (as in the case of the perfect subject in a social compact); on the other, as humanoids, they are seen as reduced essences of humans, schematized and serialized (riveted together from mechanically stamped parts that, in order to be procreated, must be deprived of a sexual code or difference—hence telling us why two or more of the same prevail), or as farcical avatars of the great effigies of the medieval carnival, of figures that enthuse and bait because they offer an absence of human difference in their serialized identity to one other. When, in the fifteenth shot, a pylon next to the torrent of water begins to crumble and fall, teetering and tottering in a pyrotechnical crackle of explosion, viewers are asked to see why a single and solitary tower, a pylon without a partner, has to fall. Nature is enacting a catastrophic violence on its anomalies; it is expelling from its order whatever does not conform to its laws or its modes of production. The happy duality of the two pylons in the still photographs of the first shot is lost in the movement of the montage. The unity of the double in the first shot figures to be stability lost in the conflictual process. In the midst of nature a precariousness of the human order reigns. It is built on disquiet and fear, and its subjects are all close to apocalypse.

In the first two shots, the montage specifically upsets the convention of the artifice of timeless splendor and power. In the first, the still life confers a monumental look upon the towers. In the second, the view from the bottom intimates how creatural they are after all. As "almost" human shapes the pylons have bottoms, orifices, undersides, legs, arms, and privy parts; they are anchored in the earth and emanate from the same ground that Mother Nature has given to us except that, now, like Frankenstein's monster, they are "dummies" that nature charges with force. Akin to the allegory of the film in general (the tension of the sameness and difference of Raft and Robinson elicited by the identity of the two megaliths of shots 1 and 2), the pylons can be seen as structures that have grown out of proportion of the power of "men" by (implicitly) wishing to reproduce others from the organs they do not have, but that are invested in their human counterparts. By the second shot they are likened to a fabled monster of man's creation, a monster whose anomaly has the dialectical effect of offering perspective on the human condition by virtue of its *de-monstrative* qualities.[12] They are

steel dolls created by the industry — a factory of energy — that stands in the background.

Shots 3 to 7 are a cavalcade of turbines and generators setting a montage of quick dissolves that wipe diagonally across the frame. Since the film makes a farce of itself, as ostensive generators and alternators they are organs detached in one way or another, from the humanoid bodies of the first two shots. Spinning and whirring, buzzing and pulsing, their shapes become erotic through the mechanical distortion of human symmetries. A pulley is erected while the cylinders of the turbines and their rotors suggest far more than the inside of the Los Angeles Bureau of Light and Power. The shots are all taken outdoors, where sky and nature stage a psychomachia between man and his inventions. A static electricity of thunderbolts attacks the alternating current that is passing through the wires; a great explosion takes place, the direct and natural production of cataclysm at the point where artificial current runs through the wires from its generators. Already two sexualities are inferred, one natural, the other a product of human power.

The tenth shot in the series is key. A half-dozen figures in white uniforms and masks react to the light flickering from the lamp over the operating table. The terror of a loss of power takes its ultimate form in the figures of a medical team thwarted in its efforts to save a human life. But in the context of humanoids and dummies established since shots 1 and 2, the masked figures are further instances

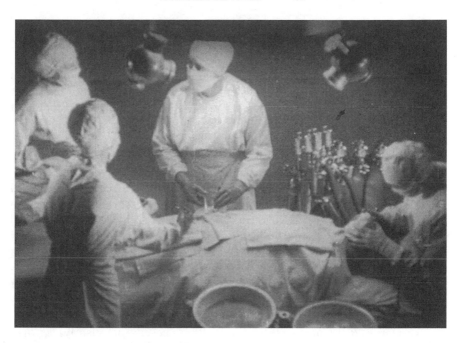

of dolls, or of subjects reacting mechanically to the play of light and dark that is imposed upon them. They play the roles of subjects that are identical to viewers of film who have been trained to react to electrical forces dosed according to the quantities and types of current wired through them. A powerful shot that implicitly theorizes a view of the role that the film can play both in its ideal material effect—it will produce millions of dolls like those in surgical gowns in the tenth shot—and its farce, the scene comically denotes how its effects are produced. Its failure to generate a total illusion is a cinematic success, for as soon as it is clear that these are dolls and not doctors, spectators ascertain where and how the fabrication masks the power the medium exercises over the imagination.

This shot would have none of its implied force if the first two shots had not allegorized the pylons as humanoid figures. Already the film entertains many more generic types than its title promises. The surgeons of shot 10 are proliferations of *The Invisible Man*, of the essence of the mute voice of Claude Rains (the rebus may have been intended with the contextual downpour of the surrounding shots), just as the previous montage of a supreme technological order aligns *Manpower* with *A nous la liberté* (1931) and *Modern Times* (1936), or each man-tower with its hidden energy crossing through it brings forth the interfilmic reference to Boris Karloff and *Frankenstein* (1931), or even, later, the dummy-figures who play crucial narrative roles in *White Heat* (1949).

The eleventh and twelfth shots appear to be set in counterpoint to the first two.

Shot 11 displays a model pylon in a studio re-creation of what its downfall "would be like" in the real world (the "real" being too, too colossal for Hollywood, for human optical powers; the film connotes that miniature representation is convincing enough), and in shot 12, when the base of the sculpture crumbles under the force of the torrents below, it is clear that the portrayal of the tower, first in its immensity, and then in the detail of its legs, reproduces the pattern of whole-and-detail that dictated the first two shots of the film. In fact, if the implication of the rhymed sequence of shots 1 and 2 and 10 and 11 is carried to its conclusion, then the repeated insistence of the *legs* projects toward an analogy associated with the name of the female lead: the product of manpower is an inhuman leg having none of the grace and curve of what Marlene Dietrich will display later of herself, as the icon (or synecdoche) for which she was known since *The Blue Angel* (1930), in the drugstore or during her singing of "He Lied and I Listened." The episode in the pharmacy makes explicit the overall metaphor of the pylon and the human body. As in Lang's editing, the druggist gazes at the image that will be shown in the next shot. In three-quarter view, he is apparently opening a bottle of Coca-Cola below the counter, as Raft—also gazing at the scene—quips to him, "Why don't you jerk yourself a soda?" Here the farce of boys masturbating over the sight of Dietrich arches back to the staging of Robinson's revival. It also draws attention to Dietrich's pose, which displays her right leg standing attractively on a metal ladder in profile. In miniature relief, the lines of the stepladder are congruent with the shape of the arms of the pylons of the second shot and the metalwork in the corner of the frame in the last shot of the film. All of a sudden, the film explains why the credits were cast over a metallic background of plates and rivets. The ambiguous "tension" of the figure is derived from the relation of the female leg to its stick-figure analogue. It produces an allegory of the Germanic body of beauty controlling a network of erector-set males.

The writing of *Manpower* is articulated with recurring figures that refer to each other by resemblance. Their enigma is the identity of film as serialized signs that have no gender, and that are able hence to confuse the boundaries of male and female in the social codes they are purported to represent. The mixed identities of male and female and man and nature are underscored in shots depicting the wedding cake in the dinner party following the marriage of Faye and Hank McHenry. The effeminate Jew is betrothed to the phallic German.[13] In *Madame Bovary*, Gustave Flaubert celebrated an ill-fated marriage with a festival that turned on a great wedding cake. The novelist used the architecture of the dessert to place into a *mise-en-abyme* the tension of the unlikely marriage and an allegory of romance battling with reality. Not dissimilarly, here two waiters serve a colossal cake with white frosting topped by two pylons. The cake is set on a table in such a way that Marlene Dietrich's face is framed between the two erections on the summit. Narrative or symbolic analysis might tempt viewers to schematize

the electrical tensions of the unresolved passion in the love triangle; yet in the greater system of the film her figure harks back to the problem of identity and difference of the towers seen in the opening montage and in the drugstore. She is a function of their form; hence the association of their steel legs with her shapely curves conditions the rhetoric of the film in general.

In this light the sequence of initial shots and their rhyme scheme weld together libidinal, fictional, and historical dimensions. The film slips from documentary and a depiction of a landscape devoid of man to an area of entire artifice. The sequence seems to be composed of three distinct segments. The first is of pure documentation, its mode and style taken from newsreel techniques or still photography of recognizable sites in Los Angeles. They give way to a miniature rendition of great landscape before when, in shots 16 to 20, the film establishes an intermediate area of ambiguity between history and the fiction that have been anticipated. In this sequence the locale, tone, and tempo of the latter are set in motion without, however, ever fixing the course of the narrative. The first off-color joke is told ("Hello? Light and Power? There's no electricity here," barks a young man into the telephone in candlelight, before turning and asking in *aparté* to an unknown figure *off* "Hey, honey, what's the address here?"), but the joke already has a double bias, since *here* could refer both to the man—having no power—and to the film, in which the remark is made, that shows itself to be equally sterile.

Shot 17, of men, mirrored, at two sides of a switchboard, conveys the currents of both electricity and the wiring of synchronized voice. The self-referential placement of the figures cues a narrative bound to the association of electrical "lines" with a tissue—the metaphor of a story as a "weave" being the most classical and self-sustaining in the Western tradition—that is taking place in the binding of documentation and fiction. To a second degree the very figure at the basis of both is so strong that it serves as an entry into the theoretical frame of *Manpower*. The telephones report on the sound track what, on the image track, is flickering in the background. Redundancy is paramount once again, the film offering a multifarious duplication—hence an open-ended shape—that mirrors its own icons, its politics, and style of production. In this shot a crowd of men—but not women—are switchboard operators. The switching over of messages and sexual roles, the transfer of relays, and gappings of messages implied in the bustle, buzz, and crackle of machines and voices reinforce the erotic ambiguities of the first shots. Since men are playing women's roles, any spectator can momentarily fantasize engagement in another sexuality. Confusion at this point is identical to the unstable relation developed between fact and fiction, for the scene is *too* staged to continue in the documentary thread spinning off shots 1 and 2; yet it is also *too* typical in its pace and verisimilitude to ground the entry of the main characters listed in the credits. Voices bark about the break before a face enters into close-up and yells into the telephone receiver, an occasion for a match-cut to another figure at the other end of the line in a medium shot portraying the worker as an official who will distribute orders according to standard operating procedure.

But where is the order of the confusion? The montage quickly summarizes the narrative structure when, in shot 19, the camera pans left and dollies right in following the boss through a door to the right. He passes by a poster of a woman, exits *off* to the right, and in the quick dissolve is found behind a table where men play cards, smoke, and converse distractedly. Akin to a military barracks, a fire station, or a police precinct where time passes so slowly that its men must devise ways of killing it (through cards, jokes, coffee, or sleeping), the locker room protects men from the oedipal ravages of "Mother" Nature. It also defines an area of intermediate play that conveys the codes and behavior in the principal locale of the tale to follow. Raft, Robinson, Alan Hale, Ward Bond, Barton MacClane and others will retreat to the same kind of men's room. Since the documentary effect has not yet been dissolved, the space is not quite the privy area of intimacy and rivalry that will dominate the film. It documents a world of men (where their pubescent reveries can run free), and an archaic space of sexual division whose logic defines the symbolic and spatial boundaries of a greater social construct.[14] The situation resembles the problem of characters who stretch between life and fiction, Hollywood and the media: it can be said that we are not in the world of the film while, paradoxically, we are already there—and have always been there—and, all the more, since the film will later return to the same space in the guise of fiction. The film provides an anthropology of its narrative, in brief, an occasion to display the social fact of its division of labor long before its narrative unwinds.

One cinematic element of farce passes through these shots and binds shots 18 to shot 23. As the boss walks into the men's room and urges them to "look alive" (insisting again that they are dummies, reproducing the scene of the surgical operation of shot 10), the camera pans by a poster sporting a frontal view of a woman's face just before the lap dissolves overlay the figure, in profile, of a man smoking a cigar. For a brief moment the two are in literal congress. Man and woman, profile and front are linked by the oral mechanism of the cigar stuck between their two mouths. The camera takes the icon further by having the cigar point at the pinup picture and copulate with it. The cigar is both sadistic and farcical.[15] Either the cigar is shoved into the woman's face, or its iconically fecal properties make him suck his own turd in view of her gaze.

The shot owes its effectiveness to the fluid movement of editing. A noisy reveille from a dream, the din on the sound track is offset by the effect of amazingly supple movement of the camera dollying and panning, then cutting across the doorway to the men's parlor and the telephone, which allows a cut to the night-club and more languorous movement on the dance floor. The slippage from documentary to diegesis is rapid and economical. In this instant of sexual isolation,

farce and violence play on a broader cinematic motif of the perennial war between the sexes; battle can "take place" only in fluid movement, where difference of gender can be seen only as imaginary. Lounging in the doldrums of boredom, men become virtual *reflectors* of the audience that is being told to wake up
or be aroused in order to enter into the logic of the narrative, to "look alive," or
pay heed to the cinematic writing.[16] The call to work—the buzz of the sound
track and the overbearing music of apocalypse—interferes with the *otium*, lazy
play, and freedom from the symbolic conflict between the sexes or between man
and nature. The pinup at once disrupts and assures the continuity of the imaginary world of self-protecting males. With the impact both of nature and of her
image, the men quickly lead the half-documentary, half-fictional space into the
narrative that will seek to recover the historical space that is receding with the
progression of images.

Fiction finally begins in shots 20 to 23, where the "wiring" of the telephone
call leads to the sight of Edward G. Robinson mechanically turning in a bad mimicry of dance. A poorly wired magneto, his body is not in sync with the atmosphere, speed, quickened tempo, montage, or even the camera movement that
has dollied into the space. "Tell that poleclimber he's wanted on the phone,"
shouts the barman to a waiter. Shot 22 follows him into the center of the dance
floor before the camera rests on Raft, who stands over two B-girls. Raft's words
("I'll lay you three to one we've got to string up some wire tonight . . . ") are
addressed *both* to the B-girls and to the pinup at the edge of his nose. As in the
insistence of doubled indicatives that prevail in *Scarlet Street*, the discourse
arches back to himself, to the inert image, and to the world of men in the preceding shots. The film has wrought a circular and a very short circuit that binds
the tensions of its structure to self-reflexivity.

Some overriding historical dimensions of *Manpower* are written in the junctures of the filmic icons and narrative. They are enunciated in the documentary
part of the opening shots in order to recur—almost uncannily—in the middle of
the narrative. Reference to the "Los Angeles Bureau of Light and Power" makes
little sense beyond the identity of the movie industry in its creation of the electrical monstrosities of its characters. The outdoor scenes of *Manpower* are pre-
dominantly dark and of baroque cast in chiaroscuro. The saturnal aspect of Hollywood is obviously foregrounded so that the upside-down world will throw the
land of eternal sunshine into a mood of lusty obscurity—of doubt, disquiet, and
even apocalypse. Once the specific locale is dissolved into a play of light and
shadow, then, in the second place, the specificity of the dam and the unnamed
local airport are pasteled into fiction.

The men go on four missions: they repair the pylons in the rain (in the opening
sequence in which Robinson loses the use of his right leg); they try to fix the
frozen wires in the mountains ("Pop" is killed by a stray wire); they displace the
poles from the airport that is being widened to make room for the "big bombers"

(Raft falls and crushes his ribs); and they build the electrical circuits at the dam "up in the mountains" (where Robinson falls to his demise). Every time they venture out into the world they are maimed or killed. In the overall allegory of *Manpower*, it appears as if the men die when they confront reality. Women or history threatens the protective play of farce and flatulence of the men's world in the locker room and rooming house. Like a phallic object, reality is too much for the triad of leading characters. Yet, folded into the film, the theoretical discourse that erotically ciphers *Manpower* reveals more about an ideology used for the early war years when it was shot and distributed.

The studio is producing a simulacrum of the splendors and miseries of military service simultaneous to depicting an archaic world of undifferentiated sexuality on the verge of adolescence. The men brave the world in order to face the unknown that is either nature or female. They return, of course, to tell stories about their adventures, or to double on the sound track what has been offered previously on the image track. The context of recreation allows burlesque humor, practical gags, and farce to be identical to an invitation to war. Tendered to viewers of both sexes (for males to play the roles offered in the fiction by joining the armed forces; or, for females, to fill vacancies in the work force left by men going off to combat), the film shows us how *dummies* are recruited and wired for engagement in the cataclysms of nature, like the inexorable course of "History" that takes revenge on "man."[17]

A viewer can hardly fail to interpret the torrents of rain and flood as a figure of an impending war of the worlds, or a psychomachia of nature and man duplicating the Axis and Allies. The allegorical closure of *Manpower* indicates that the narrative is virtually producing both the reality of the Second World War and the ideal type of subject and mentality required for the loss of life that will have an international operation achieve full economic potential. The film blueprints American history by offering an alert analysis of its typology and sexual ethos.

The erotic design conveys some of the ideology. Robinson's toast to Marlene Dietrich at their wedding can explain the ambiguity of the body of desire and history. He calls her the most beautiful woman "in Los Angeles and the whole world, including Honolulu." Robinson has "the whole world in his hands." But, it can be asked, is hers the face that sank a thousand ships and burned the topless towers of Hawaii? Because of Robinson's topography that leads to a pun on " . . . lulu," the groom circumscribes the "whole world" between southern California and the islands to the west. Los Angeles is a microcosm of southern California and the rest of the world. As in the instance of American military policy, the map provides a center and a circumference of territories that defend the mainland. The remark takes account of a structure of defense and draws center and periphery through each other in the blazon of Dietrich. With her face set between the pylons on the wedding cake, Honolulu is aligned with Japan and the Far East, an area doubly connoted by the oriental singer, the array of flying chopsticks, and the *chinoiseries* painted on the bass drum of the Wing-Ling band. (Alan Hale even spots the slit-eyed enemy in two glass bottoms that he takes to be his binoculars.) And the other pole, the Axis (Nazi Germany), figures in the image of Marlene Dietrich. So where the two Americans surround the German figure—at once nemesis, attraction, object of an ambiguous mix of drives—the scene has the enemy surround the United States. In a global short-circuit of sorts, the allegory seems designed to elicit a double bind of broader scope.[18] The two components of manpower are politically inscribed at the border of the film, and the Axis at the center.

The foreign menace is both beyond the limits of the imaginary space of the film and right at the origin situated between the pylons. Yet, in another view—and here is where the plasticity of ideology and generic equivocation seems so powerful in *Manpower*, in the constantly present abstraction of the title in all of the episodes that inflect a problematic "manliness"—war is at the center of both the montage and narration. The adventures of Marshall and McHenry are exemplified by tender irritabilities. At the slightest provocation they jump "out of line" and throw their fists at themselves and their detractors. There are at least nine fights in the film, most of which are precipitated by offhand remarks mocking McHenry's demeanor or prowess.[19] Occasionally a brawl overwhelms a scene, but in general the instability leads to a temporary relation of exchange between moments of the war. The men pop off, explode, and either whack or punch each other when a gesture or a joke goes awry. The instability of characters, a typically regressive condition in its erotic coding, infuses the very genre of the film, fostering its use of a dialectical style in editing and composition. From the outset, the situation, like the toppling pylons of Malibu, is precarious. Ambiguity of space, of sexual functions, of ethics, and of other codes allows the film to develop both a tender and a hard-edged style. Its myriad fistfights appeal to its fast tempo of cuts and fluid motion of violent choreography initiated in the first twenty-three shots. Today the film's association with 1941 and Pearl Harbor seems obvious. But the relation of the "hard-fisted" editing, which lends an ambience of populism, of the carnivalesque, and of an uneasy relation with dialectical cinema, is not obvious. A studio style and the traits of an auteur's signature are being forged together. To explore how they are alloyed, the critic would have to see the film in the light of networks binding *The Roaring Twenties*, *Gentleman Jim*, *They Drive by Night*, and *Objective, Burma!* This begins another project that would have to go beyond the confines of Raoul Walsh the auteur and require broader study of what in filmic editing are farce, jokes, fisticuffs, and tenderness. It is Errol Flynn, Robinson's counterpart, who may share much with the inner eros projected through *Manpower*. The next chapter will venture to study one as an unlikely avatar of the other.

4

The Nether Eye
Objective, Burma!

In a comparative analysis of point of view in the cinema and novel, François Jost distinguishes between *focalization,* the ways the raw materials of a story are selected, and *ocularization,* the diegetic relation that unifies the camera and the expressions that hold narrative cinema together.[1] At certain times, he notes, the camera relays a character's point of view, in what he calls "secondary internal ocularization." At others it replaces the character, in a sort of free indirect discourse or "primary internal ocularization." The rest of the time the camera is "pure exteriority," and its position refers to no one in the narration. It simply reports pure fact. "That is what," Jost affirms, "I call zero-degree ocularization." In the novel the same exteriority amounts to the condition where "the narrator is everywhere and nowhere; he is omniscient."[2] An effect of truth prevails.

Jost locates the relations of immanence and transcendence or "interiority" and "exteriority" in cinema through narratology based largely on Gérard Genette's studies of figure and discourse. It informs a greater concern about the ways films and novels produce their ideology of history. They purport to represent truth where they proudly proclaim themselves to be false. Their visibly fake representation of historical time and space is now seen, thanks to narratology, not as a lie in a moral sense, but as a relay that crosses a gap of disbelief between present and past or what is deemed bogus or true. The model is almost too subtle to use in the treatment of erotic propaganda—Riefenstahl's *Triumph of the Will*— but seems to be especially appropriate for works that willfully sustain an allure of fake truth.

The preceding chapter explored an erotic scenario of violence underwriting a classical variant of tragedy and farce in *Manpower*. A confusion of sexual "codes" appeared both to collapse an ideology of sexual difference and to spur another of eros and conflict in world history.[3] One purpose of this chapter is to see if the principle of difference in filmic writing—again, the interface of word and image—can essay the problem of "ocularization" and history in works that parody their own effects of truth. It will intimate that "zero-degree ocularization" operates only because omniscience and exteriority, as good concepts, are impossible to use in any extended practice. The term works only in comparison with other terms that vary with it, and it always wavers in dialogue with specific films. Protracted application of the concept in a film with heterogeneous codes forcibly causes it to vanish. It will be seen that "ocularization zero" has, despite its scientific aura, an erotic charge that motivates "truth" to be a fetish of visibility.

Review need not be made of the historical convergence of sight as the privilege of veracity, nor of the ways that the first-handedness is used to accede to power, subjugate masses, or construct "ideological state apparatus." Its origins go back to Herodotus and are especially revived in the Renaissance with the birth of Cartesian perspective and Ptolemaic geography.[4] Since that time, it has been axiomatic that to see is to know, or as the great cosmographer and voyager André Thevet had pronounced at the end of his *Singularitez de la France antarctique* (1557), "Il est malaisé, voire impossible, de pouvoir justement representer les lieux et places notables, leurs situations et distances, sans les avoir veuës à l'oeil: qui est la plus certaine cognoissance de toutes, comme un chacun peut juger et bien entendre." (It is difficult, seemingly impossible even, to represent justly notable places and spaces, their situation and distances, without having seen them with one's own eyes: which are the most certain of all means of knowledge, as each and everyone can judge and understand).[5] Thevet can allow himself to represent the unknown because "he was there," or because he "saw and visited" the exotic and curious world of the South American jungles, islands, and indigenous peoples.

Thevet's tourism in the guise of verisimilitude of universal history combines the arts of travel and of representation. The problematic history of bringing home tales of strange peoples and places is highly cinematographic and, in its literary construction, not distant from Raoul Walsh's *Objective, Burma!* (1945). Both auteurs insist on giving unmediated "truth" through the exteriority of the "facts" of their accounts. For the purpose of filmed history, the director would have to establish a "degree-zero ocularization," or ungrounded omniscience, that conveys the lie of a discourse of truthfulness. Thus, *Objective, Burma!* begins with a roving eye that works as long as it is seen being undone by its inner divisions of language seen, written, and heard.

The film claims to tell the truth of the Americans in the torrid jungles of "Jap-infested Burma" with the same enthusiasm that Renaissance cosmographers reported of their encounters with cannibals. When *Objective, Burma!* begins, its voice asserts that the image is indeed something akin to "zero-degree ocularization." In fact, its ocularity is so ocular that the truth of the report is a bent reflection on the curvilinear lens, or *objective,* through which the truth is represented. The film seems to take joy in celebrating the goal, the "objective," of representing Burma far more than the place itself. The *telos* of the film, its finality, is contained in the scope of its lenticularity. The net effect is one of a carnival of visibility that ultimately challenges much of the ideology it seems to be mapping for its consumers.

At the same time, the history of the film interferes with its own portrayal of the facts of Burma. As a part of the film, Raoul Walsh typifies the fortunes of the Hollywood industry by virtue of his longevity as a top director. As of 1914 his work seems to evolve with the technology of American cinema, and to fit the Bazinian cast of the cinematic auteur, both in his preceding films and in the style and tempo established in *Objective, Burma!* In accord with André Bazin's conclusions to "The Evolution of Film Language," which argue that directors of the sound era were formed by silent film (for which the autonomy of the image track is so firm that it never plays a role secondary to the cues of sound), like Renoir and Welles, Walsh never makes the image a function of sound. Compositions of difficult and often complex or contradictory stamp result. The sound films depend on a silent frame that constantly informs its composition and narrative sequences.[6] As Walsh had begun his career with Griffith in New Jersey, he quickly came to know the force of deep focus, a plastic sense of reframing, and the power of writing in film as a mode of both hieroglyphic dynamism and narrative continuity. He was, in the words of many historians who write entries for encyclopedias of film, a "professional."

Objective, Burma! has a similar "professional" look in its editing and composition. It was ostensibly made to fill a gap in the history of American participation in the Second World War. Completed at the time of victory in the Pacific theater of operations, its allegory tells of a massively decisive presence of the United States in Burma when, in reality, a single battalion under the name of "Merrill's Marauders" gave sparse help to a valiantly and persistently fought, hard-gained British victory at the "back door" to China.[7] As it may have been conceived in the conscious domain of ideology, the film tells the American public of great victories where there were none. It assures the viewers that the United States had a global influence by the end of the war, not only in Europe, as was generally known, but also in Japan's East. In an indirect way, the film could ultimately influence American foreign policy by making a myth of its dominance in China. That the film was banned in Great Britain, or that it caused Errol Flynn unwanted controversy, would seem to confirm the bad faith of Walsh and Warner Brothers, for the English public could not be duped into having credit for a victory taken away from its soldiers. On the American side of opinion, *Objective,*

Burma! was hailed as a realistic masterpiece. For the first time atrocities were depicted in the margins of the frame, suggesting that U.S. Marines had been tortured and dismembered at the hands of the Japanese. As a pyrotechnical celebration of American ingenuity and endurance, the film perhaps led a next generation of male children of American soldiers to impatiently await their eighteenth birthdays in order to follow the blazing example of Errol Flynn and his squadron by parachuting into North Korea and, later, back into Indochina.

The first shots of the film require review. A long series of credits dissolves over a painting of either a setting or rising sun that casts its rays through the crags of a range of mountains. They are accompanied by music first of pursuit and then of martial tones. A scroll unrolls written discourse typical of the war film genre: one expects to read how the production is indebted to the U.S. forces, how the scenes are not intended to portray a real event, how the reproduction of the lives of real soldiers is merely coincidental, how thanks must be extended to the U.S. Signal Corps at Fort Bragg, and so on. But no: the credits cede to a disquieting silence that breaks the continuity viewers are asked—but hard put—to establish between the anthems of war and the painting that looks less like a chain of mountains at dawn (or dusk) than a flag emblematic of the Japanese army. The music is silenced, and the film lapses into an eeriness that favors a gaze and a silent, concentrated reading of words in white letters that emerge from the darkness of the lower edge of the screen into the crepuscule of the median area of the frame:

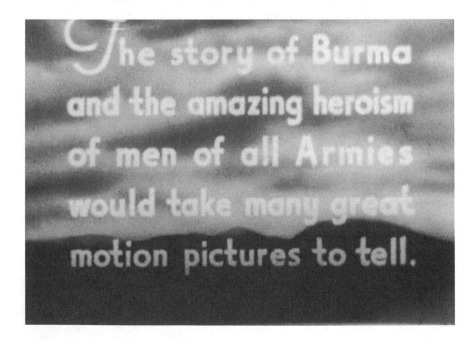

Because it is scripted over the background of the mountains, the last line is disengaged from the sentence. It tells in its paragrammar that films speak history, or that (it is up to) *motion pictures* (to) *tell* (that is, document what they decide has to be documented). The next paragraph moves up thus:

> This production covers a
> single, typical operation.

And then the next paragraph:

> The actors are American.
> But they enact experiences
> common to British, Indian
> and Chinese forces who
> victoriously fought the
> grim jungle war.

The text and image fade out and, next, after a half-second of an absence of image, a weird music accompanies an aerial shot of a forest and clouds below (no doubt of Orange County where the film was made) identified by a resonant voice asserting, "This is Burma . . . " A second shot, from a median aerial view, accompanies the words, " . . . the toughest battleground in the world, where the Japs had sealed off the Burma Road . . .," heard while there appears another aerial shot of a road on the crest of a hill, then dissolving to a seemingly official meeting of men gathered at a table. They face a commander adjacent to a globe on his left where hangs, behind his head, a map of India and China, whose outline of the Burmese peninsula drops onto his upper hairline, " . . . and closed the back door to China . . . a door that had to be reopened."

At this point the film inaugurates the type of schism that will code its realism for over one hundred minutes to follow: it splices to a highly theatrical decor a sort of photography that legitimizes its truth by its silence: it denotes that it is newsreel footage and therefore silent stock, hastily shot "on the spot" in the air and in conference rooms or on the site of Burma itself. The decisive split between theater and war is emphasized most in the next volley of shots (please see the Appendix for an explanation of the abbreviations used here):

VOICE	IMAGE

shot 1

This is Burma, the toughest battleground in the world, where the Japs had sealed off the Burma Road	*ls* of forest and cloud from plane flying toward the right frame.

<u>shot 2</u>

mls of forest seen from plane.

<u>shot 3</u>

and closed the back door to China, a door that had to be reopened.

Pan from forest to winding road on mountaintop.

<u>shot 4</u>

After months of secret preparations at Mountbatten's base headquarters in India

mls of men at table front of globe and map of Asia behind them.

<u>shot 5</u>

a plan of operations was about to begin.

mcu of same men at conference table.

<u>shot 6</u>

ls of 200 or so troops, outdoors, in line and at attention.

<u>shot 7</u>

British General Wingate conferred with his staff.

mcu of two men in pith helmets conferring with each other.

<u>shot 8</u>

General Stilwell speeded up his training of Chinese troops.

Tracking *ms* of soldier in doughboy hat who walks left and inspects men firing rifles in prone position.

<u>shot 9</u>

ls of 200 or so Asiatic troops stretching in front of building bearing Chinese flag in background.

<u>shot 10</u>

mcu of Asian troops exercising with rifles over their heads.

<u>shot 11</u>

A special force of American Army commandos was set up under Colonel Bill Cochrane.

mcu of six American officers consulting a map they hold unfolded among them, with central figure turning toward camera at the end of the shot.

shot 12

And, deep in the jungle, a forward command post of a

quick diagonal wipe to *mcu* of two seated men, both bespectacled, who consult a map.

shot 13

force called

Reframing, in *mcu*, of the same figures, now shot from the left, catching them observing the map. The figure on the right touches it with his hands.

shot 14

Merrill's Marauders got ready to push off. Only their top officers knew where to or what for.

cu, of the same two men, now framed from the right, who inspect the map even more closely. The left figure has a cigarette in his left hand.

shot 15

One hot afternoon, a reconnaissance plane from an advanced air base

ls from airplane, of the same forest, but now moving right (as opposed to left in the first shot of the film).

shot 16

near the border of the Jap-infested jungle,

Isolated *ms* of a P-38. Lightning seen from below.

[As the closure of these first sixteen shots represents a sequence because of the recurrence of the establishing shot that frames it, the second segment begins with the view of a single P-38 seen in the sky from the ground. A dazzling and, again, pyrotechnical sort of editing ensues, in which, in effect, the newsreel gives way to a global map of India on which we behold the plane literally landing.]

shot 17

the operation was about to begin. Its objective: Burma.

ls from airplane of the forest below.

<u>shot 18</u>

sound of airplane motors and martial music

ms of P-38 banking above and then spiraling downward.

<u>shot 19</u>

Silhouette of same plane in the sky, diving to artificial mountains drawn in relief above the photographic rendering of the clouds. Continued tilt down (with map coming up from below—in the fashion of the scroll in the titles) as the silhouette drops toward Burma in dark shading situated between India and China to the left and right and Tibet above. The plane spirals toward the script of ASSAM, which gives away to -SAM as the spiral continues in centering on names in lower case. *Dibrugah* takes precedence as a place-name in center, left of *Ledo,* above -SAM in diagonal. The frame is defined by a whitened portion above and a dark area of Burma below, as the silhouette of the P-38 now fades into white, then continues into the dark portion below. The map dissolves into a dark-and-light composition resembling the painting in the sequence of credits.

sound of motors decelerating

<u>shot 20</u>

squeak of tires hitting the runway

The P-38 emerges from the dark in *ls,* now approaching the viewer stationed at the far end of an airstrip.

<u>shot 21</u>

mcu of P-38 passing camera in landing to the left. Camera pans left in following its landing in a dark area

below the sky above in the same
field of contrasts.

shot 22

Dissolve into P-38, now immobile,
its propellers slowing down as a man
races from left to reach the plane.

shot 23

Dissolve to a man attending to
cockpit and nose next to left
propeller, his eyes drawn toward the
signature on the fuselage. He lifts the
canopy and gazes into dark as the
pilot, to the right, looks at a map.

shot 24

Cut to *cu* of camera or photographic
equipment (seemingly in plane or
under canopy of preceding shot).
Single objective of the camera is
aimed down at the viewer. Hands
disengage magazine and remove it
from the field of the frame.

shot 25

Dissolve to *ls* of trees and road on
which a jeep approaches to the left.
Camera pans left to follow the
aircraft. Jeep stops in the distance
next to a barracks among trees in the
background.

shot 26

sound synchronization of emergency
brake being cinched and engaged

cu of driver from right, hand pulling
emergency brake, steering wheel
jutting up, in profile, from groins of
the driver (whose head is out of
frame above). As the driver exits
with a box that he takes from the
spectator's position in the extreme
foreground, a sign is revealed in the

background: from the buttocks
covering the signboard, we read after
the body exits left: *United States Air
Force Aerial Photograph Section
Field Laboratory.* Camera dollies in
across seat of jeep to register its
lettering on the billboard.

shot 27

ominous notes of music connoting an
impending event of importance

ms from interior of building of a
soldier carrying the object while
another looks down and away to the
right. Shot pans left to follow the
soldier who goes into a darkroom,
switches on the lights, and
disappears.

shot 28

mcu of trooper developing film.
Hand moves up to the upper edge of
the frame as he closes the door that
is before the camera, which dissolves
into darkness, yet letting emerge
from the chiaroscuro of black and
some reflections off the corrugated
metal surface,

FILM
DEVELOPING

shot 29

ominous notes continue

sound of lightly splashing water

Dissolve of writing into a dish of
water in *cu,* where the words of
previous shot are "undeveloped" in
a clear liquid into which two hands
have inserted a sheet of paper. The
paper "develops" a picture of the
same forest we have seen in the
aerial shots above (except for a
clearing to the right of the center of
the picture). The paper is removed
from the dish and is drawn into

ecu by the forward movement of the camera.

shot 30

same music continues

sound of creaking leather shoes

Troop from right: "Major, photographs for the General."

Troop from left: "Wait here." Troop from right: "The photographs for"

"the General."

Paper dissolves in silhouettes of planes on the back wall of a briefing station in *ms*. During the long dissolve, his back to us, the soldier moves right with the paper in his hand. Another soldier enters from right, salutes are exchanged as a third man remains seated, tending to business on the desk before him. Pan left to door through which the first soldier moves. He enters another room where another man is seated at the right, this time busy on the telephone. Pan continues, soldier in profile moving toward back side of one troop looking at a map. Pan continues until it reveals a character seen in the former newsreel sequence: a gray-haired man with a doughboy hat and a cigarette holder in his fingers.

shot 31

"The photographs for the Red Robin operation have just come in, Sir."

"Good, good work! Fine!"

sound of paper crinkling

General: "Well, it's been a long time. This is where we start paying

Quick dissolve to a map seen frontally in *mcu* from behind four men scrutinizing it, backside of the soldier with round hat and cigarette holder in prominence. He turns 180°, faces both the viewer and the figure over whose left shoulder the shot is taken. He stares widely through round, wire-rimmed glasses. The shot pans right over his shoulders and follows the general ("Merrill"), who removes his hat and stares down as a map is revealed on the wall in the background. Two, back the Japs. Your parachutists will get the first crack.''

Major: ''That's okay with us. Rush these over to Colonel Carter.'' Troop: ''Yes, Sir.'' General: ''Get Colonel Carter on the phone.'' Troop: ''Yes, Sir.'' General: ''Take these to Colonel Carter, 503 Parachute Infantry Headquarters.''

then three men confer as they stare down at the map or pictures. Merrill picks up a magnifying glass to study the paper more closely. Through our eyes we see it magnifying a button on his shirt. He hands the paper to the troop on his right. The button stays in focus through the magnifying glass. Soldier to the right moves and picks up another map. Merrill puts his cigarette holder in his mouth.

shot 32

papers rustle

Reverse shot (*ms*) of the soldier carrying papers through a doorway: seated soldier to the right works at desk with airplane profiles above his head. Troops salute one another and turn away.

shot 33

Jeep is started and noise of buzzing phone and accelerating motor. Voice-off from phone: ''Colonel Carter.'' General: ''Carter? Feed your men some raw meat. We're going in. The Red Robin operation''

Quick dissolve to Merrill at his desk with a cigarette that he places in his mouth. In *mcu*, a soldier at our left peers down at the desk. A jeep is in profile in the background behind the window behind the desk. The man climbs into the jeep and drives away. Dolly-in to Merrill who telephones.

shot 34

''goes into effect immediately.''

undifferentiated noise of cheers

Dissolve to *ls* of men playing baseball, with two figures looking on the activity seated at the sideline, their backs to the camera. A jeep enters the frame from the far side of the field and comes close to the camera.

shot 35

sound of motor

Cut to jeep moving right, in *mcu*, the camera now panning right across more men whose backsides face the camera.

shot 36

sound of motor and creaking springs

ls of men playing horseshoes. Jeep enters frame in same way as in shot 33 and so forth. Camera pans left with jeep crossing the frame in *mcu*. Jeep stops at tent with the sign COLONEL CARTER stenciled on its surface to the left.

shot 37

Flynn: "Photographs??" Troop: "Yes, Sir, for Colonel Carter."

papers rustle

Flynn: "Okay, Ned, now you can go back to sleep." Troop: "Thank you, sir."

cu across jeep and shoulder of driver leaning toward Errol Flynn who, puffing on a cigarette, takes the paper in his hands. He signs a receipt, the jeep leaves by the sign to the left. Flynn walks to the tent, posterior to camera, as it dollies toward a man, his backside facing the camera again, his body arched over a map table.

shot 38

Carter: "Well, Nelson, here's your jump area. Jacobs, get a weather report."

mcu from right side of Nelson and Carter. They examine photos with a magnifying glass. A map is behind them. Carter looks left and speaks off frame. Flynn, with his cigarette pointing to the focal point on the magnifying glass (as if its tip were the burning focal point adjacent to that of the lights centering on his shirt and "burning" at the map under a spot there), looks down.

shot 39

Jacobs to phone: "Leopard, Five-One."

Reverse shot of soldier in foreground, in front of table, moving toward camera as Carter and Nelson, behind the desk in the background, continue to study the maps. Jacobs comes forward in making his telephone call next to the spot where a soldier is seated (in a typical composition so far in the film). Jacobs arches forward and finds the phone on the right edge of the frame. His face and shoulders shield the officers from view.

shot 40

Nelson (Flynn): "Looks pretty good to me, Colonel."

Return to *mcu* from right of Carter and Nelson as they continue to scrutinize the photographs.

shot 41

Nelson: "The edge of the trees ought to make good cover."

ecu of photo of the forest (same appearance as in first shot) with magnifying glass in front, enlarging forest and a clearing in the woods.

shot 42

Nelson: "With the wind blowing west, this ought to make a good go point."

Reverse shot from an unusual point of view, now over the shoulders of Nelson *(left)* and Carter *(right)*, in view of the backside of Jacobs, who is making the telephone call with the right leg bent and his body erect, as if the right foot were posed on a support. Sightline of Carter in the foreground goes directly toward the posterior of Jacobs in the medium field of the shot. In the background we see a jeep parked, several soldiers from the backside, and on a tree an arrow pointing right. Jacobs moves back and then faces the camera in looking at the spectator, then at Carter in one sweep of the eyes. He moves into medium *cu* and establishes

Jacobs: "The weather picture remains as before, Colonel, no changes expected."

eye contact with Nelson after having passed by the camera. He faces, as if to salute the camera, the spectator, and his superior.

shot 43

Carter: "Good. Report all changes as they occur."

"Well, Nelson, you're ready to go, I think." Nelson: "Yes, Sir." Carter again: "You take off at 3:45 and jump at dawn. Your landing will be covered by a"

Return to the position of the first shot of the sequence in *ms,* with Carter left, Nelson center, and now an Asiatic troop to the right. Carter turns to Nelson. Nelson has a circular reflection of the magnifying glass on his chest. He passes the glass to the Asiatic troop as Carter speaks to Lt. Jacobs off *(left).* Carter turns to speak to Nelson and points down.

shot 44

"diversionary bombing. The CG has assigned six bombers to drop a load here, at YAWE."

ecu of map with names of jump field—NAVAZUP, YAWE, KWETYIN, and YIAK—between ruler *(right)* and paperweight *(left)*; pencil moves from jump field to YAWE.

shot 45

"Once you get in, it's up to you and your boys to find the target and blow it. Well, Nelson, I don't have to pound on that thick skull of yours and make big speeches as to what this mission means to us. I think you know. If you do good, it means saving the lives of several thousand men. So do good."
Nelson: "Roger. Jacobs, you'll take the first platoon, eh? Briefing in an hour."
(music *off*)
Carter: "Here we go!"

Return to *mcu* of Carter and Nelson looking over their maps. They turn and look at each other. Nelson nods to Carter and checks his watch.

All of brief duration, the shots leave an effect of the rapid and efficient passage of orders from an upper echelon down to appropriately lower ranks. Jeeps drive by the camera quickly as a P-38 hits the runway and sails past the frame. Soldiers go about their business professionally, with skill and dedication; salutes are briskly exchanged; and troops scurry into formation. Everyone's attention is perpetually glued to maps and photographs. Yet the gaps between the sound track and the montage betray other impressions of standard operating procedure, especially in the crucial series comprising shots 41 to 44. Nelson and Carter scrutinize the picture of the area where they will land in the jungle and raid a Japanese radar station. In the single, *literally* reverse shot taken over their shoulders — which should logically catch the maps along the sightlines established by their eyes and noses, a point of view that shots 38 to 40 had taken care to establish — we are asked to contemplate them sighting the posterior of Jacobs as he bends over the telephone. All of a sudden, the concern about photographs and precise spots where the men will land turns into farce veiled only by the reverse order of the sound and image tracks. Will they land on his bottom? Where, in shot 40, Nelson remarks, "Looks pretty good to me, Colonel," the referent of "jump site" is located ambiguously between shots 41 and 42. Nelson can be seen alluding either to the spot on the photograph or Jacobs's buttocks at the end of the sightline. A comedy of satire is folded into what had been put forward as the

sanctimony of military procedure. The "objective" of the operation avers to be a desire to behold a rump or to capture farce within a dictature of rules and regulations. The sightlines of shots 40 to 43 recode what would be a purely narrative dimension on the sound track. The irony is increased in Nelson's assertion that the spot looks appealing, with his remark that, "With the wind blowing west, this ought to make a good go point," or Carter's "Your landing will be covered by a diversionary bombing. The CG has assigned six bombers to drop a load here at YAWE. Once you get in, it's up to you and your boys to find the target and blow it." The statements smack of flatulence and comedy of anal drive. Is the military life a serious business, or is it a question of "diversionary" farting and poop sucking, or what Marine jargon now calls "smoking White Owls"? Is this a proper display of the repressive eroticism of the orderliness of military procedure? The grim voice of Colonel Carter (John Archer) that barks to Jacobs, "Report all changes as they occur" (to have him keep his superiors posted about the weather), is also, in the context of the film, a sort of non sequitur.[8] It finds its most expressive—and incredible—moment in the obsessive scrutiny of the map and photo that are, thanks to the differential editing of the two tracks, identical to the nether hole of some imaginary, gigantic, anthropomorphic body of Burma. The sadism of the farce is of course confirmed in the characteristic manipulation of smoking materials that dominates the shots. While Flynn seems to puff and

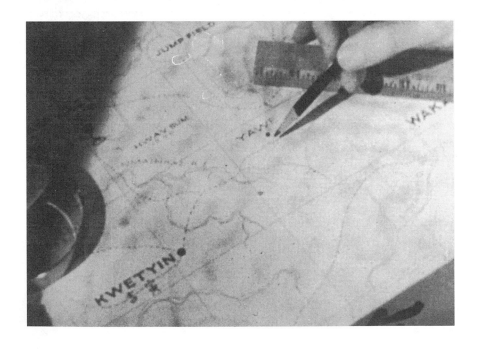

pucker his lips on the cigarette in shots 40 to 43, the image shows that its burning end is aimed at the map while, simultaneously, the light passing through the magnifying glass seemingly focalizes rays of light on his chest. The reversal turns the looking glass into a lenticular objective (Burma) constituted by the concomitant gaze of Nelson's eyes on the map and, in turn, ours on the buttons toward which rays of light converge on Nelson's shirt. The title of the film is constituted by the lens perched over the map, that is, as an *objective* contiguous to *Burma*. Military history recounted by the film is fabricated by an obvious play of scrutiny shared among actors and spectators. The process of viewing seen on screen merely doubles that of the viewer seeing the film in a theater.

The same dynamics hold true in the instances where the general toys with his cigarette holder in shots 30 to 33.[9] Soldiers' posteriors, maps, moments of silence and the noise of motors, the inscription of place-names or allusions to "back doors" of the world and the human body code the account told through the diegesis. The very elements composing realistic effects turn veracity into hilarity, and they also theorize the appeal of the military operation both as an agent of the political machine of the United States and as a basis for its own play with the body. The shooting style transcribes more than farce into the narrative. It can be argued that the director assumes an improperly satirical attitude in portraying the "Jap-infested jungle" as the anus of the Western world; that the Japanese, as regressive human forms, are conveyed to the American public of 1945 as objects worth little more than occasional homophobic aggression; or that a farcical view of the Axis' position in Burma makes the American job of victory — of "doing it right" — something of a comedy of *moeurs*.

Now it is clear why the P-38 had spiraled down to the area on the Burmese map next to Assam. The network of toponyms tells literally why men's buttocks tend to face the camera, and why all the photography of action in later sequences is tantamount to an illusion of murder — replete with exploding grenades, the *ratatat* of machine gun fire, and bellowing blasts of mortars — felt as the articulation, if a surrealistic metaphor can be advanced, of a great optical rectum. Ambivalence in the homoerotic drive that the film elicits could be seen producing an ideological urge that might, by the strategy of production and the reception of the film, be shunted onto a more simple condition in which repression, an act arousing regressive or sadistic drive, incites the viewer to engage in the patriotic murder of the Japanese.

Return to undifferentiated eros, if a Freudian tactic can be used in a fashion similar to what has been charted in *Scarlet Street* and *Manpower*, sends a constructive, socially redemptive channeling of energy into a masochistic urge that is rerouted, by virtue of the film, into a polymorphous kind of nationalism. In place of the unassuaged violence one enacts on one's own body, a neutral form — the enemy — can be the victim of violence otherwise directed toward oneself. The film retains a healthy ambivalence between sadism and farce in the sequences enumerated above and, further, in the whole film by representing the Japanese not as subhumans but as coequals. The Japanese do not reproduce the caricatures that contemporary comic strips had made of them. In the construction of the battles and representation of military life, both Americans and Japanese share the same orderliness, both have the same relation to their operating procedures, both follow the same kinds of commands, and both engage their work with equal professional dedication. It could even be argued that, unlike the effect of John Ford's patriotism, which favors superficial murder in the name of religion and country (*They Were Expendable* comes to mind), Walsh *literally analyzes* the military drive both in the Second World War and in the strategies of the media behind it. Where a viewer of John Ford's cinema is impelled to buy into ideologies that pervade the image, in contrast, *Objective, Burma!* puts forth a somewhat matte portrayal of the same materials.

One of the major consequences of the identity of scopic apparatus and anal drive of course concerns the paths that all the viewers' libidinal energies are ordered to follow throughout the film. If the production of a significant moment in American history involves writing a farce within its narrative, spectators of 1945 have to be figured as imaginary children taking glee at the sight of an Asiatic theater of operations conducing, in the final murder of the Japs in the nocturnal conflagration of the film's finale, to a cinematic fourth of July. American history celebrates American holidays: the orgiastic fireworks in the night at the end of *Objective, Burma!* follow the order of crescendo reaching a pyrotechnical display where, in the shadow theater of murder, soldiers' bodies are blasted to smithereens in the silhouettes produced by bombs exploding in darkness. Here the fine blade of interpretation must cut between two types of spectatorial fantasy. On the one hand, it must accord privilege to the film as a grandiose drama that, following Aristotelian poetics, arouses fear and then relieves it in a climax simulating collective death. Or, on the other, *Objective, Burma!* can be seen articulating an immense machinery of historical desire. It tells of American exploits exactly where it also marks that they are imaginary. This chapter of the Second World War proceeds to erase in farce the very facts that it asserts to be true.

Identical mechanisms of self-erasure (as opposed to self-authorization or the production of truth so common to many other films of the period) can be found in the redundancies of the overall narrative. The film redoes itself at every moment of its development. In this sense it is entirely dialectical both in its tale of repeated instances of *ruptured contact* and in its use of montage that splices the flyers in the air to the troops on the ground. In microstructure, in the opening shots of the film, the dialectics are evinced in the repeated scrutiny of maps at least eight times in the first two minutes. More broadly, the same goes for the three major battles, their foreplay, orgasm, and their after-effects. The troops take off in twilight, they land and sneak through the rain forest to the radar station upon which they gaze, mutely again, before opening fire. A massacre occurs without a single American casualty. The men return to the pickup point but are not met because the Japanese follow hot on their heels. They divide into two groups in order to converge at another locus indicated on their maps. A protracted sequence of chase in the jungle leads Nelson's troops to discover that the other party has been practically massacred. There they encounter a Khmer village adorned with opulent sculptures of lions, find the hacked remains of their comrades, and engage in battle again. They make a successful getaway and proceed to a new point on the map only to learn that once more, they will not be met. Provisions are dropped after they learn that they must go to an unknown place and wait for further orders. Arriving at a hill, they perch on the top with a new load of munitions and wait for an encounter with the Japanese by night. The final battle is the third in the series and reverses the givens of the first. At night they battle the Japs against insuperable odds. A bedraggled group of surviving heroes at dawn, they leap with glee when a massive invasion of parachutists comes to their aid. Soon the men are whisked away in apotheosis when a glider picks them up and ascends to the empyrean backgrounding the words THE END. Up, down, up, down, down, up: three battles of equal magnitude are initiated, explode, and then bring calm. It is so simple that it can be mapped congruently with every act of speech in Roman Jakobson's model of vocal enunciation in his work on general linguistics.[10] Tension, plosion, and *détente:* the first encounter is a success, however improbable the odds that bring victory to Merrill's Marauders; the second is a more graphic view of a skirmish in the jungle, and the third begins as defeat but is turned into victory by the *deus ex machina* of the arrival of the parachutists. In its effect and process the film is self-contained and virtually cannot end. It goes on and marks an "open" closure that allows additional episodes to be appended. Scenes can be scripted at will, but always according to the pattern of contact-rupture that keeps the narrative machinery going.

Circularity determines its cinematographic implications, as the history of Burma is produced less from an absent cause that the film cannot name than the libidinal interpretation *Objective, Burma!* assigns to itself. Once again, the initial moments are crucial. In shots 28 to 29 the film calls attention to its own process in an interior duplication. Up to this point the movie has been coded as a newsreel, its grainy texture of shots "taken" from the front (or, in the erotic scenario, from the back) accompanying a voice-off telling the rough truth of the Burmese campaign. Then, at the moment it shifts from the recording of history into a dramatic reenactment of it, at a crucial instant, the photographs taken from the plane claim to be those of *Objective, Burma!* in the preceding credits and shots 1 to 27! Redundancy is paramount for the continuity of the narrative. The film develops an image of the film at the very point it . . . develops into a film. The writing on the secret door concretizes the issue. In shot 28 the film "undevelops" the newsreel or past truth affirmed by the voice-off and historical footage in order, now, to "develop" into an area that is more true, that is, into one

where identity of anal drive, visual pleasure, regressive eroticism, and farce is the stuff of war.

The written sign and the still photograph of the forest and clearing in shot 29 are, together, the visible origin of the production of history. From the clearing where, as Nelson says, "the edge of the trees ought to make good cover," emerges the beginning of the dramatic narration. But what or who is being covered, and for what reason? From the arrested image of the photograph at the point between newsreel footage and studio stock a viewer deduces that the film connotes that the war is a tautological effect and cause of its own system of developing meaning, of continued self-production or authorization of violence. In the words of Colonel Carter, the filmic syntax reports to itself "all changes as they occur."

At the instant of the development of the recurring picture of the forest and the clearing—the object of everyone's repeated study throughout the rest of the film—suddenly the film moves from a silent mode and general sound synchronization to lip sync thus to engage itself more precisely in the field of dramatic illusion. Shots 1 to 16 appear to be a silent film (presumably of 16 mm, and taken from an aerial camera or a hand-held device shooting frames on the spot) with music and historical voice added to inform the viewer of its time and space of origin (the median voice implies: we are not at the Lucky Baldwin Santa Anita Ranch near Pasadena, but at the back door of China, that is, *Burma;* this is not

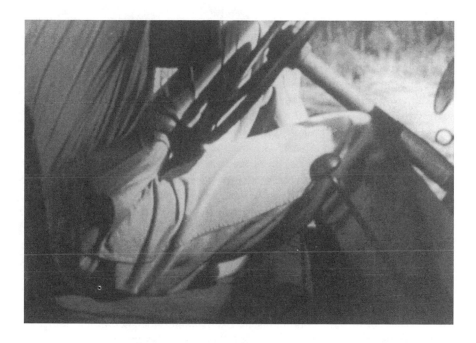

just anytime but 1944–45). Shots 17 to 28 are in undifferentiated, unlocalizable synchronization. The drone of the P-38 is heard as it lands, its engines cough and crank to a halt; the jeep sputters to the office, and, finally, the gurgling water in the developing room seems to have the first specific correlative on the image track in the sight of the hands agitating paper in the metal dish. It can be said that *Objective, Burma!* becomes a sound film when, in shot 28, it *develops* into itself.

Yet the passage from silence to sound and to a synchrony of silence and sound is marked libidinally in shot 26, which seems to function as a phatic marker announcing and explicating the dynamics that will come in shot 28. There we see, in close-up, a man's body at the steering wheel of the jeep that had been present in the two preceding long and medium shots. The camera draws the spectator into a progressive intimacy with the object designated by the motor's noise on the sound track. The jeep comes to a halt, and the driver's arm pulls the emergency brake with the accompanying sound of C-I-N-C-H, and the film begins to roll (it is carried into the laboratory and developed, and so we are under way with the Red Robin operation before it officially begins). When the motor stops the visible narrative begins. Or when a precise synchronization of the two tracks is firmly established, narrative can literally be seen developing or unwinding. If narrative owes its continuity to an imaginary linkage of the two unrelated elements that produce a "sign" because the spectator decides that they are not simply contiguous but a conflation of cause and effect, the precise location of a sound from a point on the screen—rather than a vague association of the whole frame or scene with a general sound—tends to ensure the verisimilitude of a story. Narrative is therefore scopic, both visible and graphic, and predicated upon the assurance that the eye can find an origin at a point in a specific space it unconsciously deems to be true. The issue can be made more compelling by affirming that in this view narrative becomes a libidinal, almost prurient agency of censorship, favoring the eye to seize on a detail rather than catch sight of things, all over, in a broader perspective, at the very moment it represses its agency of sight when it hears. The effect encourages our gaze to assure itself that it is apprehending an illusion of knowledge and history. Synchronization allows the viewer to invent the illusion of space as reality. As the work of Lang and Renoir also displays, such is the *modus operandi* of classical Hollywood film; it ventriloquizes in order to produce a lure of meaning and continuity that simply do not exist.

Because of the context of the preceding and following sequences, shot 26 puts in question the ideology of synchronization. The first extreme close-up in the film after a good volley of ten to fifteen long shots, it is the first really intimate view of a soldier's body. Since his head is out of frame, we can gaze at his corporal attributes without being distracted, undone, or caught in the act of looking by the return of his look. For an instant in an anamorphic slice in the frame, the steering wheel triumphantly bisects the right angle of his thighs and upper torso; his posterior is ensconced on the hard seat of the vehicle. But all of a sudden the C-I-N-C-H brakes our gaze at his midsection and calls us to attention. We are awoken from somnolence (shortly before Flynn tells the same driver, "Okay, Ned, now you can go back to sleep"). As the first analogue to lip-sync, an onscreen identification of a sound with its origin, the sound, in arresting the wish elicited to caress the body, leaves the impression of impugning both the narrative (as a realistic effect produced by synchronization of image and sound, a process of making the two tracks appear transparent) and the libidinal drive that must be established in order to "let go" and passively follow the sequence.[11]

Hence the brilliant overlay of planes in the same shot: the body contorted to conform to the jeep, in the seeming bondage of the vehicle within the cinematic frame, gives way to the visible writing of the photographic laboratory (or Hollywood's editing rooms and developing chambers), a sort of hidden intertitle of a silent film—which tells why the sound is so salient—in the background when the soldier's buttocks mediate the beginning (in *cu*) of the shot with its final position (in *mcu*), after it dollies across the inside of the jeep, to a signboard telling, finally, where we are. As it unfolds, the shot literally forces us to regress, to catch hold of the origins of the visible faculty, or move from an unconscious sense of sight to a conscious apprehension of it through a fugacious moment of *analysis*. It occurs when the sound of the brake is apprehended and associated with the grandiose figure, in medium close-up, of the soldier's buttocks.

From the point of view of the letter's relation to psychoanalytic process en-gaged in the second and third chapters, the film offers a kind of pictogrammar explicating how its machinery works in producing the invisibility of desire. Its visible wealth of detail scatters the "focalization" that the narrative encourages. And it does so in expressly erotic terms. The close-up of the soldier's body in the jeep obviously marks an evanescent instant where the order of meaning is re-versed, where the sound track that fits one shot anticipates what will confirm it in a following shot (or, vice versa, where an image on frame will give the clue to a line on the audio track that is only slightly delayed for a reason of censorship of the law of *doxa,* the specious truth of "common sense"). The procedure used here prepares our viewing of the next—and equally crucial—dissolve of the pho-tographic dissolution in the laboratory. It is as if the entire process, cast now in terms of anality and scopic drive, were contained twice in both shots.[12] Through this kind of redundancy the politics of the nascent drives in *Objective, Burma!* become clear. The film appeals to belligerence by having a viewer assume a vis-ibly violent and infantile condition; its jingoism depends on a classically Freud-ian energetic model of sadism equated with the structure of military behavior.[13] Yet just as Freud's own style undoes the order of his concepts, the obvious evi-dence of the same model in the film serves to interpret it, thus to neutralize it, or theorize the politics of its libidinal positioning.

If the logic of the auteur is followed, the information obtained from shots 16 to 18 may also tell more about both Raoul Walsh and why the film merits study today. First, in respect to Walsh and his relation to the silent film: the seasoned Hollywood director learned his lessons from the ideological machinery of Griffith at Biograph and then, in *The Birth of a Nation,* where he played the unheroic role of John Wilkes Booth, who assassinated the emblem of America. Through Griffith he learned the archaic art of *baiting* the spectator, or better, of giving to the audience at once simplified and contradictory messages in the shape of filmic ideology. But his training came through silent film and through, in the same tradition, its pregiven division of the image track from intertitles or writing that supplemented the visuals. The maker of silent films fashioned a rhetoric of narrative by appealing to objects localized within the frame and sequences of shots without having them cued through voice.

Now, from the standpoint of visual style, this kind of training might tell us why *Objective, Burma!* inscribes, at crucial junctures, modes of silent cinematography. Before the first raid on the radar station, the soldiers gather and gaze at their target through the trees and underbrush. Just prior to the massive volley of machine-gun fire, all sound is erased from the audio track. Its silence is synchronized with the medium shot of the radar screen, the emitter of *silent* electronic waves, turning about and scanning for the very residue of sound that has just been erased from the film. It searches on the frame for what has just twittered and crackled from the leaves and twigs in the breeze blowing through the nearby jungle. The Japanese are seen seeking what has just been cut away from the image in which they are seized. A simply dramatic explanation for momentary regression to a mute style of filming might argue that counterpoint of silence and din gives heightened effect to the image of the American destruction of the camp and its total slaughter of the Japanese battalion.

On a broader scale, the unconscious rhetoric seems to sally forth. The protagonists in Walsh's films are always in a frustrated relation with technical paraphernalia. Their walkie-talkies always break down; the men cannot coordinate their pickup points on the map with the voices heard; they are isolated by crackling flak or interference. Only when a shard of light reflected from Flynn's mirror — that is, an analogue of ideology — is seen by one of the flyers of the C-47, is the squadron saved. Flynn's instincts win over the predictable ways of technology. In *White Heat,* Cody Jarret (James Cagney) relies on his inner voice while his archenemy in a travesty of a kid brother, Hank Fallon (Edmund O'Brien), uses his radio transmitters to bring the hero to his demise; the same goes from the electric eye controlling the garage doors in *They Drive by Night;* an *ingenium* of silence and noise brings Wes McQueen (Joel McCrea) into the range of a gunsight aimed at his head from a promontory above a cave in the mountains in *Colorado Territory*, and so on, and so on. The moment of silence before the gunfire indicates, on the one hand, the appeal of a scopic moment, one of untarnished gaze that eroticizes the narrative prior to articulating it, where mutism and marvel are one, anticipating the regression — aroused by noise — that gives perspective and an analytical threshold to the scene. And, on the other, encapsulation is offered of the dramatic history of the slippage of silent film into a configuration of sound. A psychic interpretation of the "regressive moment" in the first battle reveals an equally productive historical side at the very points where the scene shows Hollywood fabricating its effects.

Such an optic tells—at least in the great sequence of murder and conflagration in the third encounter with the enemy just prior to the end of the film—why Walsh uses a close-up of a hand lighting firecrackers before a long shot places their explosions in a deeper perspective. One never knows who is lighting the fireworks in the distance, when the sound track *visibly amplifies* the noise, placing it near the American soldiers, and in having it echo as if the explosions were machine-gun fire in a chiaroscuro of night knowing no field of illusion (or depth). A voice-off of an American soldier explains, "They're trying to divert us." It is a "diversionary bombing" in miniature, with fireworks, now lit by the Japanese to trick the Americans. It mirrors in contrapuntal terms the bombing announced in shot 44. But the real trick is neither on the Japanese nor on Merrill's Marauders, since it perspectivizes the production of the war film in its overt appeal to fantasy of crackling, farting, and noise. Similar to vanguard experiment, the film tests the limits of reality by conflating the near and the far. More important, it covertly shifts a fantasy of heroism onto a regressive scene coded in a purely filmic production of effects. The same goes for many other strategies in *Objective, Burma!* but perhaps most notably the sequence by night when one of the men detonates a hand grenade under the belly of a Japanese marauder. "Hollis, are you okay?" whispers one soldier in the dark to another. The enemy guerrilla has just crawled over the foxhole after having stabbed Hollis to death. "Yeah, Joe, I'm okay," is the murmured reply—which only two shots later we ascertain to be from the throat of a Japanese soldier when, *off*, Hollis's (William Hudson's) friend whispers in a medium voice (implying to the spectator what is at stake with the effects of sound, sight and sync), "This is for you, sweetheart," as he rolls a grenade along the ground for a few seconds and all of a sudden a blast rocks the image. The American's final response, "By the way, my name ain't Joe," forces the spectator to deduce that the Japanese soldier had objectified the American as "G I Joe," but was lured into the ruse of silent film that scripted the components of the sound track from the film's virtual origin in comic books.

The overlay of two sorts of film reproduces other, paradoxically closed dialectical functions of *Objective, Burma!* The veracious part of the film had been couched in silent images of the seeming newsreel in the title, credits, scroll, and shots 1 to 26, and the dramatic remake of the rest of the film was its fictive counterpart, more imaginary than the first section that prepares its reenactment. Now if the division of silence and sound, which orchestrates the rudimentary psychology and dramatic effects of the three major battles of the film, can be folded back

over the beginning, the seeming truth of the Burma campaign turns out to be coded in terms of a cinema of its self-psychogenesis. It focalizes an intermediate stage in its erotic life. It is written in its own ocular fascination—degree zero—with itself. Attention is drawn to the literal anality of the war when we realize that General Stilwell (shot 8) "speeds up the training of his troops" by inspecting the rear ends of his soldiers who are in prone position; that the frenetic search for maps and photographic equipment bears the same, obvious, optical drive; that the war is precisely the return to the "back door," to *Assam* (*ass am, ass as am, s-m,* etc.); that the order to "drop a load and blow it" or keep one's nose glued to a weather report is part of a farce that contains all the elements that serve to undo it.

As an endnote, it can be asked why, in shot 44, Colonel Carter tells Nelson that his landing will be covered by a "diversionary bombing." "The CG has assigned us to drop a load here, at YAWE." Why is the unspeakable name of the old Jewish God, the stern deity of the volcanoes, indicated on the map by the amplified speech coming down from the unknown and unseen commander? Is the "CG," whom the spectator is lured into believing to be an abbreviation for the "commanding general," nothing more than a doublet of Yahweh? As in the image track, where the magnifying glass through which the two men look inverts the same image of authority, is Yahweh the printed identity of the CG voiced? Or

is the CG a code name for "see G," of the first initial of an absent commander or god? If so, it would confirm the fact that to be an authority, an authority must remain unutterable and untranscribable, and that its presence in the parody of military stenography (Jeep, WAC, SOP, KP, GI, etc.) is invested with problems of origin and law. An identity of Yahweh and CG would preempt Nelson's explanation of the mission, minutes later, when he tells his troops that they will start at point *W* on the topographic chart and proceed to point *B*. Will they go from *War*ner, through trials of violence and ritual tribulation in *War*, finally to arrive at and become *Br*others in order, as advertising reminds us, to become all they can *Be*? Is their secret code that of the Yahweh of the studio, affirmed in the subliminal writing of the film recounting the oldest of myths of ritual displacement? Is the film a document that proposes to "do it right" as the sign behind Flynn first indicates, or does it "rig" the same sign in a whisper next to Flynn's lips when he speaks to his troops?

If so, it must be asked why the CG has commanded its own destruction. Headquarters will be dropping a load on itself. *Yawe,* however, figures in a larger perspective of writing and history that can locate the contradiction. The name is one that must be confined to silence, and seen only in writing; it designates an earlier version of Jehovah, or an archaic, bloodthirsty god who belongs to epic fable. In Freud's analysis of the relation of myth and history, recounted in *Moses and*

Monotheism and published in the midst of the author's exodus from Vienna to London on the eve of the Second World War, Jahweh plays the role of a remote deity essential for the establishment of history-writing. His character is creatively distorted in order to be glorified by the nascent Jewish religion in its travel from Egypt to the Promised Land. His remoteness, or ineffable status, gives the imaginary past an epic allure. Freud notes that the illusory depth of the past, its own cover rather than its content, allows for the birth of history. An artist's distortion of the past is constitutive, indeed essential, for the granting of truth. "Incomplete and blurred memories" of the past, "which we call tradition," he notes corrosively about a highly cherished word of the critical lexicon, offer "a peculiar attraction" to the artist, who can caulk "gaps in memory according to the desires of his imagination."[14] Then, if in *Objective, Burma!* "Yahweh" is spotted as a sign of archaic violence that must be eradicated (does "Jahweh" equal "Japs"?), it nonetheless indicates that the film is both inaugurating and rewriting history in the same blow. It does so by its inner scripture, which, as it becomes increasingly detailed, also avers to be general and mythic. The production of a "history-myth" of psychogenesis that goes back to puerile origin, or an arrested eros, and elaborates an ideology that its hieroglyphic practices demolish, makes manifest a paradoxically dialectical cinema closed upon itself. To see how another version of highly graphic history-writing is made in Europe on the heels of the Second World War, it may be wise to appose *Objective, Burma!* to Roberto Rossellini's realistic epic, *Paisan*.

5

Facts and Figures of History
Paisan

A review of the opening montage of *Objective, Burma!* has shown that veracity is merely a pretext for strategic operations of ruptures of voice, image, and writing. The Hollywood film fractures the monument of epic history it simultaneously heralds. In *Scarlet Street* and *Manpower* as well, a break within written forms and montage seems to constitute a field of meaning. Close inspection shows how a film works heterogeneously. In this chapter I will argue that what the sacred and secret figure of YAWE revealed on the map of *Objective, Burma!* can now be seen, in Roberto Rossellini's cinema, as something staging the creation of a universal and sacred writing. *Paisan* (1946), also a war film of the same period, is situated in a vastly different context and made with far more restrictive means; but it also aims at manifesting an invisible scripture that "dissolves" and "develops," like the miraculous photograph of the reality of the Burmese landscape, right before our eyes.

The approach taken will again depart from a series of details or, specifically, shards of writing that seem to play only a decorative role in Rossellini's film. *Paisan* hardly makes erotic innuendo from the stenographic montage of jargon in the military genre of Hollywood. Rossellini paints a fresco from the stories of individuals affected by the Allied invasion of Italy during the German occupation. Six unrelated tales tell of the hard facts of the campaign. They are replete with particular human foibles and decant the essence of confusion and incertitude the Allies and Italians faced on the horizon of universal battle. The camera moves and cuts quickly, leaving penciled impressions of recent events whose trauma had not yet been softened by the passage of time. The pace is relentless and exhausting.

At one juncture, after four episodes of violence, a fifth sequence offers respite and calm. Three American chaplains visit a Dominican monastery that has been, thanks to good forture and to God, spared destruction at the hands of the Germans. The sequence appears to be an intermezzo inserted between two brutally graphic depictions of war. On the one side, a gratuitous murder of resistance fighters occurs in Florence and, on the other, in local activity having no influence on the outcome of the conflict, some desperate Nazi soldiers make reprisals by drowning partisan prisoners in the Po River. In the monastery a semblance of calm and grace is attained: Americans of three denominations engage the Dominicans, who welcome them cordially before they discover that one of the chaplains is Jewish and the other Protestant. They sense that the presence of the two infidels has sullied their sacred space. The monks fast to dispel the two malevolent forces in their midst. In the last shot of the sequence, the Catholic chaplain interrupts the meal by standing and giving thanks to the order. He waxes sentimentally over the lesson of faith and charity that the encounter has taught them.

Several pieces of writing fall into the episode. They are not documented in Stefano Roncoroni's quasi-definitive rendering of *Paisan* (with *Open City* and *Germany, Year Zero*)[1] but do appear crucial to what the sequence articulates in the median areas between word and image. It can be noted first, however, that the story figures as a variant of the "total social fact"[2] of exchange and obligation that marked *Boudu sauvé des eaux*. In chapter 1, we studied Renoir's film in part in terms of the encounter of one class or culture with another. Boudu, the tramp at the center, was an interpreter, a hermeneute, or a trickster, on the margins of an established social world. He forced its members to encounter their repressed other. And when they did, the conflict located the structure and history of given social contradictions. If the same terms are recalled from Renoir, *Paisan* takes up another first encounter of one culture with another but, unlike Boudu, without the benefit of any mediating agent. The three chaplains who have lived and toiled together in war now face the idiom and practice of an order and language they barely understand. They cannot escape the clutches of their hosts' goodwill and are imprisoned in relations of obligation. In order to tender signs of communication to the Italian monks, they offer first their kind words and then, more decisively, their objects and rations. The Italians reciprocate with gifts of speech and muster all they can, in a time of scarcity, to produce a ritual meal that will be worthy of the guests, full of symbolic charge, and especially nourishing. The monks aim to stage a sacred moment in which cultural differences will be literally alimented, digested, and dissolved.

The sequence clearly seems to essay what Marcel Mauss observes about the "instability" that looms in the gap "between festival and war" at the beginning of any communication. The first words the Americans utter are a macaronic mix of American, French, and Italian. After entering the monastery through the rounded arch of a portal that provides a fleeting image of a tabernacle over the chaplain's head, Captain Martin (Bill Tubbs) looks for sublime words to convey the impression of timelessness in what he sees. "You know, I can't help thinking that by the time this monastery was built, why, America hadn't been discovered yet . . . an immense wilderness! These walls, these olive trees, that church bell, were already here. This time—this time of the evening five hundred years ago— everything had the same soft color" (292, 29: 1226–5"2). The three men meet the Father Superior in a central corridor beneath the belfry. The soldiers remove their helmets, bow, embrace the monks (in a congress of bodies resembling a ringing bell that echoes the first images of men embracing at the matin hour [289, 15]). "Peace be with you, brothers! May Saint Francis bless you!" (293, 37: 1003–42"19).

Martin introduces the triad to the father and his brothers, in Italian ("Siamo tre capellani americani . . . "), in English ("Captain Jones . . . Captain Feldman . . . me, Captain Martin"), and then in a shift that appears to slip from Italian to French: "possiamo passare la nuit ici?" (294, same shot). The father welcomes them and introduces the other brothers to the Americans before ushering them all into their space. The Americans speak a pidgin-Italian, and the Italians cannot decipher a word of their English. Martin's maladroit Esperanto signals a verbal and visual condition that literally explodes the boundaries of the film from within itself, and precipitates conflict and war in the domestic regime of peace. His mixed discourse has the ring of an alloyed—or "allied"—tongue that translates the film's narrative into its own modes of contradiction; these invariably make up units of images and speech of figural or typological forms.[3] They appear as allegories inserted in the montage from a tradition of literature and painting. Two very different types of expressions are brought together, such that a didactic and unyielding order of image-signs, taken from Christian art, popular culture, and military heraldry, is set in motion and continually ruptured through the montage. But language inevitably releases the force of the image as it emerges *graphically* from its perpetual translation to and from English and Italian in most sequences and French, German, and regional dialects in other parts of the film. The break from one tongue to another both initiates and arrests movement, and places the characters in a world forever between familiar and foreign idioms, and between the vital effects of movement and the seizure of death.

Martin's hesitation expressed between one language and another indicates that the story is a redundant series of encounters, conflicts, and failed gestures of communication.[4] In *Objective, Burma!* narrative was woven around failed connections. "Baker One" could not reach "Baker Two," and the men could never blaze a trail linking point *W* to *B*. They knew one another intimately, in their social group, but they never met the "other." By contrast, *Paisan* takes up six attempts to make contact, but across different languages and traditions. One culture meets another and consistently affronts its own isolation. In the fifth sequence the trials of "meeting" and "comprehending" the other recur with the same outcome of total incomprehension: salutations are first offered, then cigarettes and candy; news of the outside world is mentioned before Fra' Raffaele accepts a bar of Hershey's chocolate and clasps it between his hands erected in prayer. In return, the monks offer the Americans apple liqueur that the Catholic and Protestant chaplains drink — Martin exclaiming in French, "A la santé" — but that the Jew refuses ("No, grazie, I never touch the stuff"). The monks offer their dormitory and remaining food ("broccoli") for the Americans, while Martin returns, as he heaps the objects in the arms of his brethren, "carne e vegetale, ciccolata, burro, ancora di carne, tutti boni per mangiare . . . ah, toothpicks!" (302, 67: 802–33″10). After food is exchanged, their ideologies are put on the block. Nonreception of the other's faith confirms the failure that has taken place in all of the initial attempts at exchange. Feldman and Jones, the Jew and the Protestant, are seen by the Italians as infidels, while Feldman and Jones view the monks as hopelessly anachronistic in the limits of their belief. The ultimate meal that they share, framed in the fashion of a tableau vivant somewhat reminiscent of Leonardo's *Last Supper*, turns out to be the celebration of a fast. A mute war culminates the episode that began with attempts at exchange. The dumb countenances of Jones and Feldman over their food, the perplexity about whether to eat or not to eat, and Martin's last words of grace in Italian and Latin — "a beautiful, moving lesson of humility, simplicity, and pure faith . . . *Pax hominibus bonae voluntatis*," peace and goodwill for all of humankind — seem to turn about in their own isolation, as speech offered to everyone but received, Italian monks and spectators alike, by no one.

The last words of Latin, a sort of emblematic legend to the episode, signal a visual cue that refers back to the first meeting. *Pax* indeed translates the brand name, PET, inscribed on the can of evaporated milk that Martin first gave to the priests. Its levels of meaning in the filmic allegory explode only through scansion across French, English, and Italian. A piece of manna, or a great gift that befalls the monks at a moment when they can offer no substantial food for their guests, the can of milk attracts the admiration of the two cooks, Fra' Pacifico and Fra' Felice. In shot 69 (302, 842–35″2), the monks gather around the can. Fra' Salvatore exclaims, and the intertitles translate: "These Americans! They think of everything! Give me this thingamajig." Fra' Felice tears from his brother's hands the "floating signifier," or piece of "manitou"[5] that the group interprets to be a gift from heaven. The camera cuts to close-ups recording the brothers' expressions of amazement at the potentiated energy contained in the can being placed at the vanishing point in the perspective of the establishing shot. Seven quick shots (70 to 76) record their discovery of the miraculous substance.

Crucial, however, is the area the can occupies between the onlookers, and its inverted position that reads P-E-T upside down, over the well-known emblem of

the cow's head emerging from a Pet Milk can, within a Pet Milk can, within a Pet Milk can, and so forth, into infinite *mise-en-abyme*. Thus read, PET alludes not only to a fabricated and self-authenticating brand name but also to the infinity and zero degree of meaning, or the essence of manna. But *Pet,* glossed in French, becomes a visual homonym, a rebus of a contained explosion (a *pet,* a blast or a fart) welding signs of violence and peace *(paix)* on its surface. It concretizes Martin's last words—*pax*—of the last shot, so as to conflate the memory of war, the noise of machine guns (recorded in the shots of newsreel stock that open the sequence, 288, 3–4), within the overriding silence of the monastery. Further, when read inverted, the writing on the can of milk can be scanned only through an optical inversion that pulls God, a supreme reader of Scripture, into the proximity of the frame. The deity looks over the scene from above, over the upper edge of the frame, to see the writing below that the faithful display to honor it.[6]

Hence the Pet Milk can becomes an ideograph, or interior duplication to a second degree, that pulls the outer frame of the scene into the configuration of writing. The sequence that in fact ends here is taken up again (312, 100–2) when the narrative crosscuts from the discussion that Martin, the friars, and the Father Superior are holding on conscience back to the kitchen. The camera moves emblematically from the "soul" to the "body" of the narrative, from words of faith to food. It tracks and pans to follow Fra' Felice taking a sausage tied in the shape of an oval from the oven to the table where he sets it under Fra' Pacifico's eyes. In its passage the sausage, hanging from the brother's fork, resembles a mandorla that for an instant frames at its center the Pet Milk can, seen in the background, that now serves as the base for a votive candle. Posed rightside up, the can is now a token of appreciation for the miraculous gift that it was, and it now turns topsy-turvy from its initial presence as a piece of medieval writing to a figure that has been lending visual and scriptural perspective to the drama. A focal inversion takes place, in miniature, that seems to motivate both the visual rhetoric and the structure of the six tales.

The writing of Pet Milk inflects the dialogue that the sound track engages about war, peace, infinity, and transcendence. Its mute, objectal status shows how other shards of writing and allusions to pictures form part of a carefully wrought, at once didactic and ironic surface of signifiers. The Pet Milk figures as an industrial essence of goodness. But what of the bar of chocolate that Captain Jones (297, 43: 475–18"19) gives to Fra' Raffaele? The friar is overwhelmed with gratitude ("I'll say a special prayer to the Holy Mother for you, for spiritual and temporal aid throughout . . . ") before his Father Superior coaxes him into silence and into a mutely devout stance in slight genuflection. Fra' Raffaele is seen in profile, clasping the bar that reads HERSHEY, as if the brand name, which recalls the chocolate manufacturing town in Pennsylvania as well as refers to the secular and familiar forms of everyday life in America, were now transformed into another piece of manna. What is invisible or meaningless to one group—the

...thank you with all my heart!

American spectators—becomes precious to another.[7] The Hershey bar is placed in the frame in order to establish a corner of an imaginary triangle with the faces of the two figures who affront each other in profile. It becomes part of a configuration connoting a hidden, half-visible law, as well as a legible shape that forces the spectator's eye to scan the visible surface of the frame and to discern the legibility of the drama in all of its matteness.

H-E-R-S-H-E-Y, seen as a glyph, becomes another manna of Scripture, a piece of writing falling into the drama from without and, literally, both spelling and resolving the enigma that folds failed communication into the narrative. Later in the sequence, after Jones and Feldman are remarked failing to pray at vespers (306, 76: 149–6″5), news circulates that infidels are in the brothers' midst. "Father Claudio, one of the chaplains is a Jew! . . . The short one's a Protestant," gasps Fra' Pacifico. To which Fra' Raffaele responds, exclaiming, "The heresy of Luther, the worst Protestant" (307–8). The indirect accusation of heresy comes from the mouth of the very brother, Fra' Raffaele, who held the *Hershey* bar in the ecstatic pose of an early Christian orant. Now, in the shift from the brand name as image to the word-sound of *heresy* in Italian (and its doubling in English in the white letters of the subtitles) emerges an explosively translinguistic rebus-pun: *Hershey* in the introductory sequence typologically anticipates the coming of *heresy*. The identity of the two names, like that of Pet, pet, pace, and pax, unbridles acceptance and rejection of the other's culture. Stamped into the icon are universal Augustinian antinomies.

If Italian, English, Latin, and French idioms appear to be working in and through the discourse of the sequence, then the trademark of the chocolate bar can be seen as a perspectival object toward and through which they move in order to make meaning disseminate within the visual discourse. A sort of joke-object, the chocolate bar virtually reflects the social and erotic configuration of the story. The word connotes HER, HE, and SHE. It effectively divides and unifies the sexual isolation of the monks by hinting that all the brothers and chaplains are reconstructing the orders of a greater social world through the division of labor — another "total social fact" — assigned by sexual difference. "She" will perform certain duties, whereas "he" will do others. "Her" duties involve one set of tasks; "his" take up another. Hence the extraordinary attention that the camera pays to domesticity yields the imprint of men "playing" at being men and women in the tasks they assign of sweeping the corridors, cooking in the kitchen, and serving plates of food to one another.

Reenactments are made up of an ever-given division representing order to a group by the way it codes gender and social function.[8] The necessary labors of life that various societies distribute to their members are taken up, but in such an originary fashion that the timelessness and ostensively innate goodness of the scene that Martin describes as he approaches the camera in the opening shots ("This time — this time of the evening five hundred years ago — everything had the same soft color" [292, 29]) or to his companions ("No need to ask any questions. You'll find everything very clear and simple here" [304, 77]) reenact the invention of beginnings. These go back, on the one hand, to a moment of miracles that inaugurates a gap, a break, or a change celebrating an origin and a continuity.[9] Each is a "trademark" for a common form, but both "Pet" and "Hershey" figure as manna that "miraculizes" its product by virtue of the name that has come to be welded to it. Like the paradox of "Kleenex," which reads between word and image as a "clean spot," a clean-x or a miracle of an act of dirt cleaned that must be redone with each purchase — or pull of the paper tissue from its pop-top box — to clean and maculate at once, to *clean* an *x* that leaves an *x* . . . to *clean* . . . an *x*, etc., "Pet Milk" and "Hershey" mime the self-engendering and self-canceling aspect of authenticity at the basis of religious aura. A bogus — but also, it will be seen below, a very real — miracle comes with the names when they are placed in an unfamiliar context. They come from nowhere at the same time their perfection brings discontinuity to the nameless and timeless labors of the monastery. Now, unlike most practices of cinema, in which brand-name products are inserted contractually in order to be advertised covertly,[10] these two products seem to come from nowhere but also to determine how and why the filmic writing at that moment is so sacred.

They embody the process and contradictions in miniature across a national idiom in both legible and visible registers. They are writing that is a gift of God, that is, a redundant evidence of the miracles that "fall" into the plot of the sequence, and thus establish a network of figures that allow all objects of the entire film to correspond to one another in similar figural analogies. The milk and chocolate are "dropped," like the miracle of the chickens that comes as repayment of the debt incurred when the priests saved the townspeople's animals from the Germans (301, 63–64). They bring peace, violence, accord, and heresy; they mark the system of originary violence that comes with the rupture of change or the advent of a foreign element inserted into a communal space. In turn, they point to the way that their writing, placed at virtual vanishing points in the frame, indicates the sign of an absolute figure and, because of the inconsequence or incongruity of the objects themselves, its absence.

They are placed between the view of the two cultures and become an inner subtitle within a film that makes subtitles an essential part of its visual and lexical form. They can be likened to a cultural signifier of difference, what Guy Rosolato has called a *signifiant de démarcation*.[11] In either an American or an Italian version subtitles have to play a prominent role in both the image and the narration. In the medium shots or *plans américains* that set the interlocutors on opposite sides of the frame, the subtitle has a tendency to bind one figure to the other. The two are attached by what is exterior to them, yet the exteriority of the writing binding them is an intrinsic part of the composition. The discourse of the other links the Americans and Italians, indicating that the white line of characters on the lower edge of the frame becomes an imaginary scriptural bond that is visual, in conflict. What is usually a necessary supplement to the genre of the "foreign-language film" happens, in *Paisan,* to be drawn into its overall configuration of forces. Thanks to the subtitles, a spectator can see how the film accomplishes in its visual patterns and rhythms what the players cannot attain in the narrative. In a fashion that merits comparison with *Scarlet Street,* the writing avers to be both in and out of the film at once, to be both a part of a visual scheme and an element outside and beyond the film. The speech of the characters is cast in figural movement that goes toward the entire plastic vision of the film. Like the meaning of "paisan," when *read* as a common human measure, the subtitles, when *seen,* offer exactly what the title of the film seeks to find. At the same time, violence is sealed in the contradiction of the duplicitous role that the subtitles play throughout this and the other five sequences.

The same function is assumed by objects that literally "write" the themes of bonding and breakage. The chaplains' helmets complement the tonsured heads of their hosts. In fact, the vicar touches a helmet and refrains from donning it early in the narrative (298, 50). The opposition is almost structural in essence, for the bald head contrasts the artificial skin of metal that connotes religious force no less than does the Catholic chaplain who fondles his helmet. An utter identity of difference underscores the ironies of the narratives in each of the six tales. In this respect the problem of writing and objects in the fifth sequence is tied to a broader motif that, likewise, breaks and unifies the disparate qualities of each episode.

The details of the fifth sequence ramify through *Paisan*. They can be followed in the ways that the film portrays images of heads without bodies or bodies without heads. Each chapter establishes a visual plan that varies on attachment and severance of head and body. In the first sequence in Sicily, the infantry gropes along the abandoned cavities of a great geographical skeleton. They follow abandoned paths in the dark of night, climb into a tower, and seek passage through a space that will be free of land mines. A translation of the early cantos of Dante's *Inferno* in terms of the American disembarkment, the opening sequence plays on the fantasy of the national body dismembered by an explosion going from the feet to the head. The soldiers confide in their topographical interpretor, Carmela (Carmela Sazio), in order to find a way free of the bombs under their legs. When the chapter ends, both Germans and Americans look down, their heads bowed, at their respective victims below them (201, 158–60).

The story of Joe (Dots Johnson), the black military policeman, ends with reverse shots of the two protagonists in close-up, one of Joe looking around without meeting Pasquale's (Alphonsino Pasca's) eyes, another of Pasquale looking up at Joe (224–25, 130–31). Joe's white helmet over his dark complexion anticipates the irony of the tonsured heads next to the chaplains' accoutrements, but with the typological innuendo of the initials MP (surrounding the emblem of an American star held aloft by two wings) that concretize *exactly* what the Italian street urchin has lost—his parents. As Joe explains the rebus of himself in fractured Italian, "Dove Mama e Papa?" (224, 130), in a way that he is both M(ama) and P(apa) and no longer a member of the military police. Head and body inflect the writing of the two shots that finalize the pathos of the nonmeeting of the boy and the adult from such different yet common origins. Joe had walked into a cave filled with a throng of homeless Italians only to discover what the boy had just expressed in a language of animism, a tongue more real than English or Italian, that conflates cause and effect of war and murder: "Boom, boom! Capiche? Gli bombi! Boom! Boom!" (225, 130).

In the third sequence, which appears to correspond to the stock shots of a tank in the foreground, below a view of Mount Vesuvius (where a touristic view is seen across the filter of newsreel footage; 206, 2), Fred (Gar Moore), a tank driver, relates to a prostitute what it was like to emerge from the depths of his enclosure. He embodies the experience of war, fatigue, and history. The story flashes back to a moment that appears to be both a continuation of the stock shots, but in a way melding news footage and personal vignette (239–40, 77–79). The driver pulls himself out of the metallic turret, head first, then back, shoulders, arms, torso, and legs. He comes out of a vacuity, from darkness into light

("The sun was spread out all over the place. Everything was just like summer air—and for four hours I was shut up in the dirt of that tank!" [239, 76]), as he relates, in the chiaroscuro of the brothel, what the spectator sees in the illumination of the flashback. The fourth sequence follows Harriet's (Harriet White's) and Massimo's (Renzo Avanzo's) quest through the rubble of Florence in search of a foyer and of a painter named Lupo. They run through holes in a maze of debris (269, 71–72; 271, 85) and shadows (274, 92) before finding themselves in a battle between partisans and Fascists. Massimo is murdered as he seeks his family. Harriet's astonishment and grief at the sight of the brutality respond to the pathos that had marked the first episode.

The movement of bodies dropping in and out of closed spaces of rubble, light, and darkness is taken up in stock shots (288, 3–4) counterpointing the calm of the monastery. All five episodes seem to anticipate the highly graphic rendering of head and torso in the landscape of the sixth story. Its visual and scriptural configuration seems to summarize the five preceding it and to denote exactly how a hieroglyphic motif binds the six tales in a loosely visual and legible order. It takes as its point of departure the figure of the head and helmet that were studied in terms of obligation, war, and cultural blindness just before. An extreme long shot follows an object, floating downstream, in what the voice-off designates to be the Po River. When the flotsam turns and floats into closer view, it is named by an intertitle within the film. A sign that reads PARTIGIANO is placed over a man's

head buoyed by a circular life preserver (316, 1). The first element of the narrative concerns the double reaction that the form elicits in the way it is named. A
shot taken from the water (316, 3), ostensibly marking the viewpoint of the dead
body, shows Italians and Germans following and gazing at what the preceding
two shots have shown. The Germans have apparently placed the sign over the
body in order to deter the partisans from continuing their warfare.

Like the film as a whole, the figure exacerbates violence: the Germans are
showing what they have done for the sake of promoting its opposite, but all the
while the partisans become murderously enraged at the sight of their dead comrade. Thus Cigolani (Cigolani), who wears a woolen hood over his head,
emerges from the reeds in the marshes and attempts to retrieve the dead body that
has floated into the river's alluvial delta (318, 10–12). He rows a skiff through
the stalks and out into the open waters while Dale, an American OSS troop col-
laborating with the partisans, diverts enemy attention by blowing up a great,
globelike water mine washed up on a beach.

At no point in the sequence of retrieval does the spectator ever see the partisan's dead body in its entirety. A first a *head* was glimpsed above the water, Now,
in six shots (320, 25, 26, 27, 33, 34; 321, 36) the viewer sees only the *body* as
it is recovered; its head is flopped over the gunwales or out of sight. Then, when
other partisans lift the corpse out of Cigolani's skiff and carry it to its burial site
(322–23, 40–42), only the limbs and torso are visible before the camera pans

(shot 41) to the Americans, Dale (Dale Edmundo), Dan, and Alan, who confer in medium close-up in the foreground. The dialogue synthesizes the rupture of head and body articulated in the adjacent visual montage. The three soldiers walk and talk as the camera pans right:

DALE, *to Alan:* What've you heard from Fifth Army . . .

DALE *(off screen):* . . . Headquarters?

ALAN: General Alexander's headquarters says to cease all operations and for all partisans to return immediately to their homes.

DALE: There's another partisan in the Po.

The music fades out in the sound of the wind, which is heard in the following shots along with the sounds of water. The three Americans stop to watch the partisans carrying the corpse.

DAN: These people aren't fighting for the British Empire. They're fighting for their lives.

The Americans start walking again (camera pans right after them).

DALE: What else did Headquarters have to say?

ALAN: I told them we were completely cut off, and that any minute now . . . (322, 40–41)

The movement of the camera all but erases the rupture of figures on the sound track, in which the Americans, asking about word from a hidden God — "Headquarters" — respond with a metaphor that is matched in visual terms on the image track. "I told them we were completely *cut off* . . . ," retorts Alan, bonding the sign of decapitation to the figure first glimpsed in the portrayal of the corpse in the first shots of the sequence, anticipating the next shot (322, 42), which registers the partisans carrying their dead comrade, his head in half figure, before his face is shown isolated in close-up (324, 44). The body will be immediately buried in the dirt that the mourners are piling over him. They place the sign PARTIGIANO at the head of the grave. On the sound track, Dale's speech ("Headquarters?") simultaneously indicates how the plot will merely be working out the more literal expression being shown on the image track in extreme depth of field.

Alan tells of the plan to light fires in the oncoming darkness as a signal as to where to drop a load of manna, now in the form of food and ammo. Following

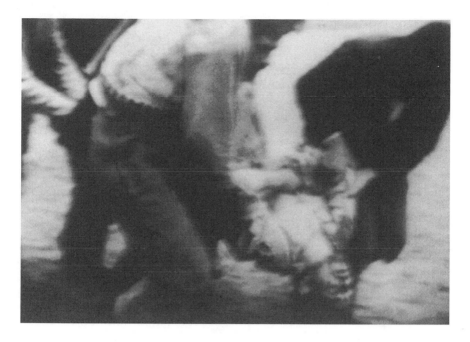

the logic of miracles retained in the recent memory of the fifth story, Dale is seeking salvation that will be parachuted from the sky to the beach:

DALE: But don't you understand? If we light those fires, the whole German army'll be *down our necks!*

DAN: Well, we'll all die one way or another—but that's *a small matter for Headquarters.* (324, 42, stress added)

The men's heads will be cut off, and seen no less graphically than that of the first partisan floating down the river, whose severed body and head were represented with such care in the exposition.

The relation of icon, word, and image in terms of body and head is developed through the rest of the narrative, but with connotations that touch on primal spaces delimited by danger and fear. Dale and Cigolani run to the Casal Madalena to obtain food and respite and to exchange news with their compatriots. A double entry is staged. The first "announces" or rehearses the coming of Dale. It appears as a phatic moment in the ritual process of exchange, and the second, which indeed is the coming itself, avers to be real because it has been announced. In the first, Cigolani comes on screen in full profile from the right, holding up a sickle in his right hand and carrying a pistol in his left. The sickle seems incongruous. A sign of the paucity of means that the partisans have at their

disposal in the war with the Nazis? A hidden allusion to the Soviet flag and the Communist party? Or a piece of local scenery, a "realistic effect" that binds the men to the canebrake that gives so much natural texture to the locale? Probably all and none of them, for when Cigolani enters the home (330, 72) for the *second* time, the camera, inside, records him entering from the left and then placing his sickle on the table in full frontal view. He puts the curved blade on the left side of a table behind which stands a child, his head the only visible part of his body. Cigolani's sickle is set exactly along the eyeline that puts its cutting edge around the boy's neck.

Here a "phatic" murder is performed almost so quickly and adroitly that it passes almost imperceptibly. When Dale sits down to the right in the same shot, a peasant is visible behind the table, his head obscured by a kerosene lantern that hangs from the ceiling. Dale eats as if he were attended by a headless *paisan,* or uncanny return of the figure of Saint Denis. Then, Dale sits down and eats his bowl of polenta just as one peasant, who has fetched a mass of small eels from the basket anchored in the water just outside, begins to prepare them by cutting their heads off. On and about the table three imaginary decapitations are staged. Like the viewer, Dale has been blind to what the spectator has just seen. He looks upon the scene from the right but, his head arched over the bowl of polenta, he cannot glimpse three beheadings visible from the spectator's point of view.

In the preceding episode, the moment of respite and symbolic binding, the meal crowns the meeting of the two cultures and three religions, but also hides the same figures of separation and amputation. We recall that the chaplains in the monastery had to eat under the stern approbation of the monks who were fasting before them; in the last tale, Dale accedes to intimacy with the other culture where the chaplains had not: he arrives second, only after Cigolani had announced his coming, and only through the promise of universal decapitation that will bind the Americans and the Italians. The instant of the meal may be the most intensely visual point in the film, at once summarizing and prefiguring the closure of the signs that link the beginning and the end of the entire narrative.

The ensuing battles in the canebrake and along the beaches are staged according to the figures articulated in Magdalena's house. At night, in a shot of a curvilinear surface of the globe under the stars, shown in a perspective that could be taken from either near or far, the arc of the horizon recalls the sphere of the globelike mine that Dale had ignited to divert the Germans from shooting at Cigolani on his mission to retrieve his dead comrade. Now the viewer hears disembodied voices expressing confusion about where they are and what is happening (331–33, 80–92). We find ourselves in a space reminiscent of *Objective, Burma!* At the end of Walsh's film, the survivors were lost in the night, facing battalions of Japanese soldiers creeping upon them from all sides. The men were obliged to make foxholes and burrow into what seemed to be self-dug graves "on top of the world," at the summit of the hillock. The night sequence disembodied the men in the same way. No one knew where or who the other was. The men became voices of silence: when the Japanese inched into close-up, their helmets seemed to be globes seen through the filter of a lunar eclipse. Nelson's men paradoxically went *up* to go *down* and were seen on a miniature sphere of a hill that confused all sense of distance and proportion. When one of the troops catches sight of the plane coming to drop provisions, he brandishes his shovel skyward to display the caked dirt and grime on its surface as if it were a topographical relief map. In *Paisan* the return of the map folds the space of the film onto itself, especially when the night, erasing markers of distance, suggests that the men are slogging through a universal swamp.

So closed and totalizing is the last episode of *Paisan* that little perspective of time and space can be gained. Its beginning and ending are both everywhere and nowhere. The sequence appears to terminate when the camera glimpses a child (the same child of shot 73, whose head was on the verge of being amputated by Cigolani's sickle) shrieking and weeping, wandering among the corpses, looking for its mother and father.[12] Dale and Alan are seen seeing what is happening (334, 94). The filmic disembodiment of the preceding shots now has its figural counterpart in the severing of the child from its family, but in an instantaneous identification with the infant's point of view. In total solitude, the boy is aghast at the sight of the coming day.

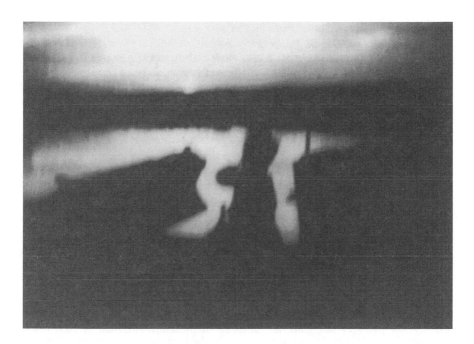

The shot has since become famous in the critical canon of Italian neorealism. In his intensive study of Rossellini, André Bazin stated that *Paisan* "yields the most aesthetic secrets" of the movement of Italian neorealism in general.[13] To illustrate his point Bazin chooses this shot, "in the twilight," where "a half-naked baby cries endlessly," to reveal how an *image-fact* (35–36) is seen independently of any causal logic that most montage would invest into the scene. Without narrative attachment, it embodies more suggestively and completely the entire sensibility of the film. Noting that "a baby cries beside its dead parents" (35), and that nothing more can be made of the moment, Bazin is impelled to argue that the "shot" is less "an abstract view of a reality which is being analyzed" by Rossellini than a "fact" (37) acquiring "a special density within the framework" (38). Seeking to use the "fact" as a literal trait or pencil stroke of a cinematic sketch, Bazin is obliged to repress momentarily the figural typology informing the relation of word and image in the given "facts." When the child weeps over the dead bodies, not only is an affinity with an earlier fact confirmed typologically, but so also is the presence of an ideological revolution: the child's silhouette is aligned with the sunrise in the extreme depth of field; he walks and wails; in the movement his cries are disembodied because he is seen in silhouette before the rising sun and thus heard without lip synchrony. The shrieks seem to come from everywhere and nowhere: Is the world, seen and felt from the eyes of a child, witnessing its pains of growth?[14] Is the sun, as the narrative would suggest, rising? With the deaths that the allegory has fashioned to depict universal time through the identity of decapitation and the second coming, the viewer observes a crepuscule that describes a time both ending and beginning. We can now ask if the film imagines a moment of life and history beyond the realm of time measured by nocturnal and diurnal rhythms. Whatever the answer, agencies of cinema, typology, and iconic figuration make the scene an implicit sequel to all of the earlier episodes. Universal time is glimpsed figurally, and by dint of an image-fact that not only sketches a trait of common time but also univeralizes its fragmentary character in view of history.

Through a severing of the body from the world the characters "see" where they figured in the rhythms of global time. The ensuing battle plays on ruptures of continuity that follow the pattern established by bodily parts and speech. Gathering the last remnants of their squadrons, the partisans row to the delta to lift a soldier out of a Dantesque cylinder immersed in the water. The watery foxhole seems to be a reminder of the dead partisan in the lifesaver in the first shots. In the melee of battle with the two German gunboats, one partisan crouches by a dead comrade, reloads his double-barreled shotgun, and places its muzzle under his chin. Viewed from the standpoint of a young German soldier pursuing him, the shot (343, 154) consummates another of the many ritual murders that have been taking place. The cut to the close-up of the German soldier's face (343, 155)—aghast at the sight—associates the suicidal gunshot with the filmic *cut* itself, the bodily dismemberment that had inaugurated the sequence. Next to the partisan who places the shotgun barrel against his throat is a dead soldier, lying face down, whose head, clearly obscured by a tuft of reeds in the foreground, is invisible. The resistance fighter is about to blow his own head off, next to his friend. The soldier becomes the inverse of the first partisan of the film, head buoyed in the water without a corpse. The body next to the soldier presages what he will become in the infinitesimal gap that comes with the pull of the trigger. Two decisive moments in time, the past and the future, are sealed into an inexorably totalizing present that responds to the figure of the coming and going of worlds that just seconds ago had been set in the coextensive dawning and setting of the sun. The absolute nature of life-as-death in the present is cast into an image that sums up the filmic icon articulating *Paisan,* correlating the cinematic process with the sight of death, in which decapitation becomes the basis for a relation of framing and narrative.

Like so many others, shot 154 is carefully composed; it lasts no longer than a glimpse, but nonetheless translates its static allegorical pose into movement. Effects of passage are obtained when actions occur at once in the center and along the edge of the frame. In shot 157, in a moment just following the partisan's suicide, in the foreground and to the left, Dale attempts to reload his gun but discovers his ammunition is exhausted. He flings the rifle into the pool of water behind him. With the trajectory of the rifle in the air, action now goes from the

foreground to the back, where a head floats on the calm surface of the pool. Dale's gesture of defeat points to the bodiless head, a figure of the dead partisan at the vanishing point of the composition.

The suicide announces even more violence. The graphic configurations of the last shot leave an imprint no less traumatic than newsreel footage of war. In the images preparing the end of the tale, in shot 164 (344), to the upper right of the darkened image, Cigolani figures below a headless body hanging from a make-shift gallows. Below, illuminated in small circles of light, are the heads of parti-sans huddled beneath his pendant feet. Their faces and heads complement the body above as they await their execution. One partisan whispers that he has uri-nated in his pants (which suggests, in the allegory, that he is returning to the home of the waters from which the first partisan was lifted). In shot 175 (347), six partisans, hands tied behind their backs, stand by the gunwales of a German patrol boat. They face the water and look away from the camera. Four shots are crosscut to depict the passage of orders from the German captain to his assistants on the boat. He signals with his hand, indicating silently to his men that they are to push the partisans overboard one by one. The two foreign prisoners, Dale and a captured English flier, observe the scene in astonishment. Yelling ''Stop!'' Dale runs left, in the foreground, while his comrade goes in the same direction in the background.

They appear to be running to see what remains invisible in the twilight. The

Germans gun them down in the back, Dale falling into the water just below his feet (348, 178). Dead, he *literally* glimpses what is seen in the next shot: the horror of the wanton reprisal and the invidious drowning (348, 179) of the Italian survivors. The camera shoots the last living instant of each partisan from the standpoint of the one who will die in turn. In the last shot of the sequence, the calm surface of the water is seen in medium depth just before it is broken with the bodies falling and causing concentric ripples. Out of the water, however, emerge the letters FINE that dissolve into the center of the frame. The four characters seemingly come from the vanishing point marked by the bodies dropping into the water. The voice-off of the narrator dispassionately remarks, clinching the Italian FINE that soon appears on the image track, with some liminary words on the sound track:

> This happened in the winter of 1944. A few weeks later, spring came to Italy, and the war was declared over.[15]

The conventional end credit appears to sprout from the water in which the bodies were thrown, in an instantaneous transubstantiation, in which men are sacrificed in order to become writing. FINE, which grips the tragic finale, turns the gratuitous and loathsome murder that had been portrayed as a senseless reprisal, into a broader issue of filmic process: the men are cast into the water, like seeds, so

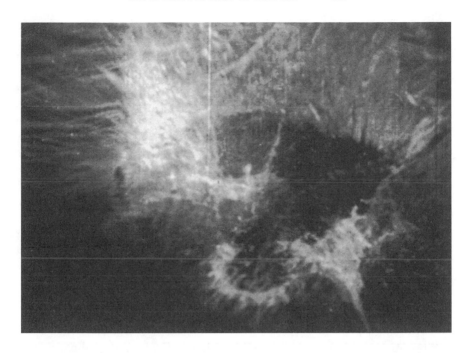

that a more permanent dialectic of life and death of writing and action can be born. The partisans are jettisoned into the Po, the voice-off specifies, in the winter of 1944. FINE seems to dissolve out of the water after the narrator states that spring came to Italy. The film implies that bodies are planted so as later to burgeon into scripture. In the crosscut shots depicting the drowning (347–48, 175–80), the spectator hears one splash (in shot 179) and then sees and hears three others (in shot 180). The four splashes match the four letters of *Fine,* which in the resulting rebus are confirmed by the date of 1944 heard *off* or out of time.

The fleeting impression of violence is crafted with exactitude. Not only do the bodies fall into the water in accord with the writing that comes out of it, with *Fine* matching *1944,* but in an instant the viewer witnesses a passage of time recalling larger and longer revolutions of the planet that turn not from shot to shot or second to second but from season to season. The figures of the globe from earlier moments of the sequence are recalled (the water mine and the world under the starry night), but the aural texture has a recursive, almost medieval trait that equates the conflict of the war with medieval poetic motifs that portray violence in seasonal change that comes with the passage from winter to spring. Din is indeed what was seen emitted from the shock of contrary forces in conflict.[16] The poet, whose speech in an archaic culture entails the singing and writing of a productive noise to promote and retard seasonal change, has a vital function in maintaining rhythms that generate the world's renewal. The same task of renaissance appears to be taken up in Rossellini's film. Historical change is now aligned with the revolutions of seasons, but with the difference that a hieroglyphic writing elicits and promotes a broader transformation of life and time. In this way the utterance, "the war was declared over," becomes multifariously plastic in respect to the end credits. In most copies of *Paisan,* the words fall so abruptly that "over" is cut off before the sentence is completed. The film ends so quickly that the voice appears to be cut by an effect of editing, hinting that the statement is cut away ("the war was declared ove(/r)"). The narrator's *r* seems to be abbreviated by the onslaught of the End. An instance of decapitation appears to be imposed upon the last word of the film. The epic ends so tersely, it implies, that real action must begin here and now, over and over, beyond the film's visible duration.[17]

The voice-off is really stating that the war is *not* over, and that being merely "declared" over, its finality is indeed far from complete. In fact, in the dialogue of the sound and image tracks, when the film is over, a new war begins. Ciphered thus, the ending resembles Sartre's dilemma of "liberation" articulated in his famous "La République du silence," an editorial that appeared in *Les lettres françaises* on August 26, 1944, the day following the freeing of Paris.[18] For Sartre freedom could be declared over. The imponderable question he asked was where and how to begin again, and how to assume the new, more difficult, more *real* freedom of building a new society from the rubble of the war. For him and, no doubt, for Rossellini as well, the task of reconstructing civilization was more frightening and overwhelming than battling against a single and visible oppressor. Rossellini's final emblem shares affinities with Sartre's vision. The bizarre figure of a *declaration of war over* assumes a dialectical pose. War is declared on war in order to precipitate peace. Rarely in the performatives of diplomacy or even the official tenor of speech in everyday life is peace ever "declared." The act of declaration, like that of instancing or naming, carries within it a violence of interpellation. The narration seems to respond to the memory of the beginnings of the Second World War, but through the filter of five calamitous years, the reminder "the war was declared over" is stated to prompt a new social battle that has no easy representation in view of the future.[19] The sacrificial and dialectical attributes of social action seem to be embodied in the discursive traits welded in the images ending *Paisan*.

Yet more emerges from the relation of the voice-off and end credits. In the allegory of seasonal change, the bodies are planted into the Po with the hope that they will bring a FINE to the conflict and a return of springtime, generally viewed as at once the most peaceful *and* most violent of all seasons. Immersion and death by drowning arch back to the very first image of the film, a stock shot that records the explosion of a depth bomb on the high seas. The beginning responds to the end: newsreel gives way to a staged rendition of reality; the South cedes to the North; the opening of the invasion of Italy corresponds to its bitter end, and the bleak time of the present to the perhaps — but only perhaps — brighter vision of the future. These conflicts are threaded through the six episodes of the film and acquire special urgency in the filmic icons that inform the network of objectal facts, such as the Pet Milk can that becomes a bomb of peace and war, an avatar of the empty tins that the black MP kicks around when he and Pasquale recline on the rubble of Naples, or the sight of the shell of a Sherman tank and Vesuvius on the same landscape.

From the configurations of images and writing a typology of history is crafted, and at least two consequences seem evident. First, the end credits bring the film "home" to its violent conclusion by establishing a complex of figures that determine the entire narrative. The network always reiterates what it means to "come home." Second, it raises numerous ideological issues that bind the film's political ambiguities to its editing. Coextensive, both forge the tenets of what has been used to describe the aesthetics of neoreal cinema. The actual ambivalence or undecidability of its politics may indeed be responsible for the violence of rupture that is located between writing and image or mix of discourses and idioms.

More than one critic has noted that *Paisan* thematizes problems of home and country.[20] Various individuals and groups of the Italian countryside see their homes invaded; in universal conflagration, everyone is uprooted; in the midst of war, combatants seek the illusion of finding family and home. Dots Johnson pants in miming an accelerating locomotive chugging south from New York that he is "Goin' home! Goin' home! Goin' home! Goin' home! Goin' home! Goin' home! Goin' home!'' (216, 89) before he discovers that the urchin Pasquale, who has stolen his boots, has, like himself, neither family nor home. Home seems to be whatever is broken, sundered, or irretrievable in contemporary history. But, even if it is inaccessible, throughout the six sequences it marks a presence as a vanishing point between language and image. The most limpid representation of the coincidence takes place in the first meeting of an American GI, "Joe from Jersey" (Robert Van Loon), and Carmela (Carmela Sazio), a young Sicilian woman who is appointed to lead the invading Americans through the German mine fields. Taking pause in an abandoned tower, the couple acts out the "total social fact" of encountering each other as embodiments of the unknown. Over and across their incomprehension of each other—unlike the bumbling chaplains in the monastery—they understand one another through the mediation of the film folded into, but also outside of, their own drama. They seem to be bound by the horizontal bar of the subtitles that represent each other's words through ourselves as viewing interpretors. Joe is afraid. His fright may be attributed to many causes, at once to the war, to the foreigner, to the woman in his presence, and to the language he cannot fathom. He utters: "Say something! You may be more scared than I am, but I doubt it! I don't mind telling you, sweetheart, I wish I were home!" (186, 94). But Carmela hears *home* as *come*, or "what," to which Joe responds, in clairvoyant ignorance, "What?" His question poses an expression of doubt or incomprehension and is the perfect translation of his utterance, which Carmela retranslates back into her own idiom: "You said *come*." The icon of speech identical in script and voice is confirmed when Joe, hearing Carmela (a brunette) note that he is *biondo*, exclaims, as if hearing in the word for his blondeness a vision of an American Italian "beyond," or a "beyondo," in all fear and anxiety. "*Biondo?* You know, I can almost imagine I'm home—it's quiet at night like this where I come from. I'm sorry, just thinking about home" (187, 94). Carmela once again mistakes "home" as *come*. The languages co-respond to each other as identities and as images. *Come* turns into the English "come," just as "home" is somehow heard as *come*, with the effect of leading to absolution when the characters, in death, can translate and transubstantiate their words and desires into "come home," into the fear of the future in " . . . what come?" or into a fundamental doubt of origins in the statement, "What? Home." They "come" home only by migrating across a barrier of meaning, all the while "what?" seems to be the enigma of the identity of a character's home.

Joe retorts, "Home! Yeah! In America I was truck driver for a milk company . . . " (187), before he shows Carmela some wallet-size photographs of his family. The flame from his cigarette lighter precipitates his demise. At the other end of the valley, a German soldier fires at the speck of light in the distance from his trench. In a play of perspective anticipating the night sequence on the Po River, in which far and near are set along an extended axis that concretizes apprehension of a cosmos beyond visible bounds, the sight of the home occasions the on-slaught of death; when Joe from Jersey grasps the vision of home, he is irreme-diably ripped away from it. But in an infinitesimal instant, in the glimpse of a shooting star *(stella cadenza)*, the two are together, at home, in a moment of tran-scending metaphor, where one term is identical to another, before both are extin-guished into each other.[21] Once a difference is overcome, in the dialectical sys-tem of word and image, a breakage and disappearance ensue.

The end of the film welds that very gap in place. When the partisans are dropped into the River Po in the gruesome finale, they are literally planted back into their homeland. They go "home" across the trial of death that comes with the representation of cinema,[22] whose simulation in turn, in the closed dialectical scheme, intends to bring the viewer to action. Home figures as an enigma or a perspectival object toward which languages and figures converge. In ideological terms, within and at the edge of the film, the translinguistic pun appears to mo-tivate a portrayal of Italy that melds history, literature, cinema, and current events. Obviously the first sequence, which shows the soldiers crawling down pathways amidst rubble in chiaroscuro, cannot fail to allude to Dante and Virgil's descent into Hell in the opening cantos of the *Inferno;* nor can the compartmental structure of six unrelated but contiguous stories not suggest a cornice structure characteristic of Boccaccio's *Decameron.* An Italian *literary* tradition is brought forward, and the life of its form is renewed through projection onto contempo-rary history. And the recurring intertitle of a map of blackened Italy slowly whit-ened by invasion can only arch back to truism about its national history in the nineteenth century. The nation, it is known, was virtually born not of itself but from a reaction to the Napoleonic invasion or, further back, to that of the Vandals and Goths of late Roman times. The German occupation and the Fascist govern-ment under Mussolini appear as variants on the same order of dispersion and uni-fication. The film appears to be asking, beyond the violence of the murder of the partisans in the Po, if the passing of the war will bring the nation together again.

In this sense the filmic writing appears to forge a paradox that might be called a typology of history or a contingently political biblical vision. The motif of de-capitation inscribed into the sixth sequence entails a medieval figure of the po-litical body bereft of its *chef* or head. It would not be impossible to see in the profile of so many headless forms continued allusion to the figure of Italy under the rule of the Acephalus, or the monstrous political body that lacks the intellect it needs for adequate direction.[23] The current state of the world, where the film ends, embodies chaos, confusion, and wanton murder; the men who are pushed into the Po are honored as sacrificial victims for a future state through the medi-ation of film that turns a *fait divers* into something of greater import.

How to attach a head to the body of Italy seems to be the problem envisaged just beyond the border of the final sequence, and all the while the dilemma of unification seems to retain its powerful ambivalence as the partisans and the

American OSS troops row their skiffs through a landscape of canebrake bending under the harsh winter winds over a low horizon of dark clouds. The stalks that waver under the wind and clouds appear to be disbanded reeds that could be tied together and reformed in the sign of *fasces*. In the biblical range of Rossellini's camera, the Fascist emblem can be seen everywhere in the landscape. It is only up to the viewers, who detect the multiple configurations of the allegory of the film's writing, to see that the coming of the unification of the Italian nation may — as it may not — be born of the elements before their eyes. Such seems to be the typological wager that *Paisan* puts forward in its configurations of facts and figures of history.

This chapter began its study of *Paisan* in the failed communication that transmutes into successful filmic writing. It first studied how gaps between one language and another open onto a figural view of cinema and history. The abyss between the two cultures is framed as a noncommunication producing the dialectics of film and montage. A merely pragmatic view of language or art as vehicles of "communication," or as veracious expressions of reality, would have insulated the film from its more urgent task. It is clear that effective works of art, if they do "communicate," always communicate incommunicably, through channels of interference and conflict. They are, as Roland Barthes said of Balzac, masterpieces of *cacography,* of camouflaged, self-contradictory writings split and united between image and writing. The success of *Paisan* resides still in its multiple portrayals of relations failed and then regained in the arcane, hieroglyphic aspect of scriptural language.

It is more than forty years since the film's first showing, and its heritage may be telling. In 1990 we are witnessing a blitzkrieg of monolingual films produced to appeal to an international market. "Europe is entering its Berlitz era of moviemaking," notes Vincent Canby,[24] but not because its films are mirroring or anticipating the coming of the European community of 1992, but because they seek returns on their investments. Producers are now promoting English-language films that have audiences in North and Latin America, the Far East, and in distribution provided by television and videocassettes. The consequence is that language is relegated to "oral signals necessary to keep the plot moving. Important national distinctions go unrecorded. Subtleties are eroded." The same could be said of subtitles and writing: French, German, and Italian films now convey a pabulum of cost-effective English that eradicates idiomatic boundaries. *Paisan* stands as a monument that prods a spectator's passage into unknown lands and not, in what is being witnessed today, toward a blandly reassuring regnum of unthwarted or monolingual "communication."

The babel of *Paisan* signals universal confusion, but also a system of rupture and relay that works with the graphic traits of language in the field of the image. It appears that the film does have important affinities with conventions that are hidden or veiled in other films of the same period. In order to vary on the evidence of writing in other conventions, it may be wise to turn back to the Renoir of the immediate prewar years and then move forward, in the remaining two chapters, into the mute presence of global conflict in film noir.

6

The Human Alphabet
La bête humaine

In chapter 5 we saw how Rossellini envisions a universal history through a figural cinema. His "image-facts" appear to fracture its experience of war and disperse its historical intensities across a surface of images and scripture. If Rossellini aims at creating a myth from current events, he faces the paradox of making a film transcend the history that it is writing at the same time; or failing that, he must reduce to a minimum all distance in time and space between the recent events he transcribes and the time and space of the film. Rossellini's work is grounded in a reality of imaginary events so close to the historical calamities of 1940–45 that their violence makes his cinema approach what language cannot touch, that is, the *real*.[1] Bazin coined the concept of the image-fact to resolve an aspect of the same paradox. Our earlier analysis has shown that they devolve from broken concatenations of writing, tableaux vivants, and rebuses that focalize language into pictures, and vice versa. They both respect and transgress various idioms and styles; they tend to elevate local history into a typological cinema, in which the *real* seems to be at the end of history and of cinema.

If Rossellini's vision is unique, what happens in other contemporary cinema that does not deal so directly with the present? What about films that veer toward entertainment and refuse to ponder these questions? The problem might be approached first through Rossellini's films: both *Roma, città aperta* (1945) and *Paisan* use traits of Hollywood icons. In *Roma, città aperta*, Manfredi (Marcello Pagliero) is led into an inferno of cabarets and nightlife. His friend, Francesca (Maria Michi), impersonates Lauren Bacall by smoking cigarettes *à l'américaine* and listening to big-band jazz. In the third sequence in *Paisan*, the same actress mimes the first meeting of Bacall and Bogart recorded in *To Have and Have Not*. The beginning of a failed romance culminates in a pun playing on cigarettes and Howard Hawks, in the actress's question posed in a heavy Italian accent that all but destroys its referent, "Hey, boy, you got a cigarette? . . . You got a match?" (234, 69). There she and Fred (Gar Moore) are obviously not up to the snuff of the professionals whom they mime. Their relation with Hollywood dehistoricizes fact but remains crucial for the figural and iconic force of Rossellini's work.

Rossellini appears to draw on American traditions in order to turn them against themselves and thus interpret and rehistoricize them. Their presence in the neoreal ideolect broadens the discursive range of his films. Elements of a dominant system are reformulated for the purpose of writing a popular epic that embraces the 1940s and projects its allegory toward time immemorial. Hollywood, like the Nazis, appears as a term charged with specious values. It partakes of representation to a second degree, and not to the urgent abstraction of things that are real.[2] In both films, Maria Michi looks at herself as a false value when she stares into the mirror and discovers that she is a victim of substance abuse (that is, an abuse of images or, the film implies, of "Hollywood") when under the influence of the cocaine the SS uses to bribe her in exchange for information. It might be that the sheer intensity of the allegorical "image-facts" that Rossellini constructs from Hollywood styles owes much to the allegory and the ritual murder of the "good" forces in the paradigm he inherits from medieval icons.

This chapter will therefore assign itself the task of seeing how and why the iconic systems of Rossellini's style may also be located in a contemporary context of French cinema and also have impact on American film noir. The relations of history, allegory, and filmic writing seem to prevail in all three areas; in turn, they can be used to study the grounding of representation in terms of the "real" that their styles cannot put into any palpable shape. I will begin with *La bête humaine* (1938) with the working hypothesis that Renoir's film blueprints film noir, and will work toward Walsh's *White Heat* (1949), a feature (because it cannot conform to the principles of noir that it uses) that appears to mark the end of the convention. Analysis will move from issues of writing in Renoir to its presence in Robert Siodmak's *The Killers* (1946) before arching back to a paradigmatic film that began much of film noir, *High Sierra* (1941). The trajectory will lead forward to the threshold of the 1950s, but in view of the figural process Rossellini had developed in his war trilogy.

In chapter 1, I demonstrated that Renoir builds filmic icons from recurring scenes that engage relations of writing, film, and painting. In *Une partie de campagne* (1936), a Rousseauesque view of the world and writing is projected over a lush and protean landscape. It is so transient that de Maupassant's novella seems to be not an origin but an alibi for the filmmaker and his troupe to leave the grime of Paris and spend "a day in the country."[3] Not so with *La bête humaine*, which was completed just two years later. Renewing and implementing Zola's novel for spectators living through the tribulations of the Popular Front involved careful preparation. Renoir and his crew assiduously studied the railways and the world of the *cheminot* before completing a project intended not to leave a public indifferent to its interpretation of the nineteenth-century classic.

Zola offers an ideal plot for a scenario in the tradition of film noir. Jacques Lantier, an engineer for the national French railroad and a victim of the hereditary blemish of alcholism, faces some idle hours when the locomotive he loves (he has nicknamed it "La Lison") is sidelined to have its hot box repaired. He visits some family relations one afternoon at La Bréauté and meets Flore, with whom he spends a passionate moment by the railway—at once embracing and strangling the young woman who loves him—before returning to Le Havre. En route to work on the evening train, he encounters Séverine in the corridor. She and her husband, the conductor Roubaud, have just murdered Grandmorin in his first-class compartment. The plot has led to this meeting after depicting the way Roubaud's honesty in dealing with the wealthy sugar magnate, Turlot, has led the couple into evil: Séverine has known the highly influential Grandmorin since her childhood (one never knows how or with what implications, however, perhaps as either daughter, lover, or both), and offers her husband the chance to use her wit and charm to settle business over the squabble with Turlot. She visits Grandmorin, only with the effect of enraging Roubaud. The latter, victim of his worst suspicions, beats Séverine and forces her to write a note that will arrange a meeting with Grandmorin on the train, where they will murder him. After he meets Séverine on the train, Lantier, who is inevitably attracted to her, tells the police that he has seen no one in the vicinity of the murder. An imbroglio begins in which Cabuche (played by Renoir), a reputed skirtchaser who had disliked Grandmorin and the only other railway worker in the area, is inculpated. (He in fact acts out the very destiny of Dédé in *La chienne,* and with the same dialogue.) Séverine and Lantier become lovers while Roubaud disintegrates. Enraged and unable to club Roubaud upon Séverine's entreaty, Lantier succumbs to a second fit of madness during the railworkers' ball. He strangles Séverine to death in an adjacent bedroom, leaves the scene of the crime, and arrives late for work the next morning. His helper, Pecqueux, operates the locomotive while Lantier tells of the crime he has just committed. Unable to sustain himself, Lantier (like a modern Oedipus) takes his own life by jumping from the speeding locomotive. Even though Renoir slightly alters the original plot of the novel, the grim and unyielding tenor of Zola is maintained. The novelist had seen fate cast for a whole generation—*un bétail humain*—that Renoir transposes onto the stage of history in 1937–38. By 1936, Zola was a cherished author sustaining a national readership. How would Renoir handle the sequence of the "runaway" train that does not stop at the end of the novel? How would he interpret issues common to the Second Empire in the prewar climate of 1938? What would be the result of

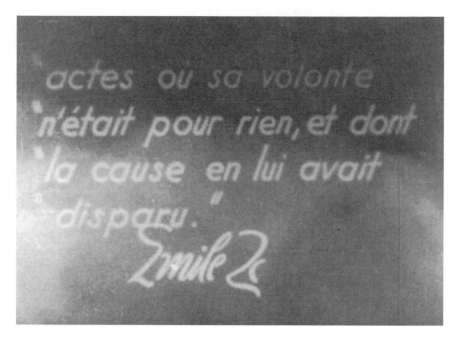

applying Zola's semantic wealth and exactitude to a system of representation that, ideally, knows not words but the priority of the image?

The questions can be approached only if we imagine how Renoir's investment of contemporary events into nineteenth-century literature could serve as a sort of detour without delay, or the presentation of a past that is simultaneously present and that runs endlessly over a depthless surface of history. Seen from this angle, writing serves to caulk the gap of forty-eight years between the publication of the novel and the release of the film. Its dramatic, social, and aesthetic aspects have been studied in depth, but its dialogue remains to be treated.[4]

Few of Renoir's films since *Boudu* seem so fraught with questions of writing and naming. The relation of the credits to the first sequence signals the divided mode that will follow. The names of the film's stars stand in uppercase art deco characters over a chiaroscuro of steam, darkness, and ominousness emphasized by brooding notes of music. Gabin's and Simon's names acquire tragic tenor as mute figures set over swirls of steam and smoke. The credits terminate with a signature that signs itself below the scrolled quotation from Zola, the autograph seemingly confirming the truth of the writer's words apropos the Rougon-Macquart family's hereditary alcoholism and Jacques Lantier. Apposed to the signature, the final sentence declares, "La cause en lui avait disparu" (the cause in him had disappeared). But the real cause of the effect, the novelist—not alcoholism, the grounding cause and overall structural component of the epic of the

Rougon-Macquart family—has *not* disappeared, simply because Zola's signature appears right where the origin is said to disappear. Once reminded of the greater lines—the *grandes lignes*—of the novelist's project, the viewer beholds a portrait of the bearded author in three-quarter profile looking at the world through pince-nez. The still photo that seems to sanctify Zola is endorsed by the self-written effect of a mechanically produced autograph. Like a serialized relic (not unlike a baseball card), the document obtains an effect of truth by placing a signature on a photo. Zola's picture is *still* while his signature *writes,* the script therefore inaugurating an ambiguous relation between moving pictures, still photography, and cursive letters. Movement, which at that time had been debated as the cause and effect of cinema,[5] seems to be invested into the play of the signature that signs *Emile Zola,* exactly where Zola is immobilized. A gap opens between one form of nomination and another, but through an inversion by which the image remains while writing, a practice satirized for its inertia in most of Renoir's other films, now traces a cinematic effect.[6]

Contradiction between the meaning and the relation of image and text has Zola's declaration about the genealogy of evil refer to the stigma the signature is branding on the photograph it simultaneously subscribes and falsely authenticates. Zola is divided by his own name in the paradox that his portrait signs his autograph. Because the autograph is written, a plurality of transcriptive possibilities is offered. A sort of "*stylo-caméra,*" or inverse of the *caméra-stylo,* the

writing moves, cursively, from letter to letter, so quickly that the pen could be likened to the movement of a train on its tracks. By the time the collapse of the metaphor of writing and cinema is noticed, the credits are discerned as going not from beginning to end, *A* to *Z*, but from end to beginning, from *Z* . . . to *a*, in a movement that puts in question linearity, progress or progression usually going hand in hand with cursive writing. The double bind that is set in miniature concretizes the comic and tragic dimensions of *La bête humaine* in general. It cues the viewer to see the film engaging a set of problems concerning writing and visibility that supersede the novel.

The dazzling initial sequence of the film, the thirty-one shots that register the movement of the train and its entry into the station at Le Havre, appears to abandon writing for action and movement. An experiment is made in filming a landscape. The camera is attached to the front of the locomotive so as to guzzle the oncoming horizon. After Zola's signature ends, the film comes to life with the first shot of the flames in the shadow of a boiler. The camera pulls back to include the working space of the cab. Dramatic and informational shots tell how the train is run. The viewer is placed in a scene of toyish regress that entails the fantasy-desire of a child living the dream of being a fireman or an engineer. In the cab Lantier (Jean Gabin) and Pecqueux (Julien Carette) appear to be in an ideal state, playing at their work, or doing what children would hope they could do in the fantasy of adult lives.

The stuffiness of Zola's project now set aside, practical, narrative, and perspectival elements combine in the first sequence. The spectator is told how the speed is controlled: the locomotive goes full tilt on the straight stretches of track, slows down and then accelerates after following curves. Because of its tremendous mass and speed, the train must decelerate over a long stretch before approaching Le Havre (its "haven" or heaven), which is written into the geography and doubled in the shots of sky over the Normandy countryside. The thermodynamic system of locomotion is shown from the standpoint of those feeding the boiler and giving the mechanical animal to drink without stopping.[7] The system of hydration is explained. The engineer and his assistant drop a pipe into a long gutter filled with water, set in the interval between the rails and nestled in the ballast of the road. Lantier whistles and signals with his thumb that the machine is ready to imbibe, indicating "bottoms up" with a flick of his wrist, his finger pointing at his eye, a clichéd gesture in the world of French taverns by which Lantier tells the viewer that his tragic flaw is present in the world of work he loves. Pecqueux lets the cylinder fall at the appointed second and retracts it just after the train has rolled over the trough. With the technical information relayed, the filmic allegory is already set in place, for the viewer has connected the relation of drinking, sight, and locomotion in the figure of the great beast of unslakable thirst.

Narrative is only insinuated in the operation. As the symbolic dimension of the beast, the man, and the train is established, the two men eroticize their activities in the cab. Lantier presses his body against the levers and dials of the control panel as if copulating with the engine, while Pecqueux moves about with the gait of a vaudeville performer.[8] The intimacy of the two partners at work — one more instance of male bonding that Renoir emphasizes — reveals that two laborers who are familiar with each other's world seem to have a more stable contact and sublimated erotic life with each other than with members of the opposite sex. The "drive" that Lantier and Pecqueux share with toys, goggles, and gadgets in the locomotive takes place *before* they encounter others. The dramatic cutaways that record the train rolling down the line and in and out of the tunnel are studies in perspective that refuses to vanish. The converging lines of the tracks hint that they will meet at a vanishing point, like the dot of light at the end of the tunnel, down and beyond the frame. Momentarily illusory stereoscopy is figured, but the advancing train pushes the promise of visual resolution further and further back. In doing so, the shots maintain a two-dimensional and hence scriptural definition of the frame. The first shot in profile that contrasts the dominant view of the train rolling into space takes place as the camera approaches the station. All of a sudden, the camera registers a frieze of majuscules,

L E   H A V R E

that move from right to left and follow the course that traced Zola's signature in the credits.

A critical inscription of writing takes place in the second sequence, which tells of Roubaud's character, his pride, and of the first (and fatal) mistake in his life. He disallows Turlot, a sugar magnate, from carrying his dog onto the train. As in *Boudu,* where the dog was part of a complex of filmic icons, the sequence opens with the close-up of a canine on a leash that the camera, trucking back, then places on the platform among the passengers walking toward the station. A viewer of 1938, familiar with Renoir's films, would immediately see the dog as an avatar of Boudu's mutt and a sign alluding to a long French convention of animals in paintings, reaching from Auguste Renoir back to Watteau and Oudry.[9] In the visual tradition, the dog had offered painterly "freedom" to the artist who had been commissioned to render faithful portraits of their patrons. Like clouds in the background of landscapes, dogs gave artists areas of indeterminate play and variation. Now Renoir uses the dog to typify the opposite, since it figures as the motive of fate that will determine the outcome of the human players.[10] The iconic rapport of the "human beast" with the dog is made through allusion to paintings and earlier films of Renoir's signature.

The dog is attached to Turlot, the figure who sets the narrative in motion. When he notices Turlot committing a misdemeanor, by having the dog on the train, Roubaud calls for order. A shift in perspective, from the tracking shot taken along the platform to one of a "frontal-profile" view on the platform, codes the

problems of destiny and closure. In medium depth, in a two-shot sequence, Roubaud (Fernand Ledoux) looks left and directly at Turlot, who looks directly back at him and threatens to send a letter of complaint about the incident to the SNCF. A billboard figures between Roubaud and his supercilious passenger as a third point of reference. It pulls the viewer into the dialogue of surfaces and jostles the code of superiority and obeisance that usually employs the relation of frontal instead of profile views of human subjects.[11] People and writing are at the same level, but the billboard on the other side of the spectator's eyeline, a remainder of the tradition of silent cinema and ostensively added for a realistic effect that avoids recourse to speech, further locates the provenance and destination of the train. Letters read

VENANT

de

PARIS

and tend to confuse and disperse Zola's narrative. Attention is divided between the dialogue that casts the fate of Roubaud, on the one hand, and the innocuous sign, on the other, which remarks both much more and much less than it seems. Who or what is "venant de Paris"? Is it Turlot, an urban aristocrat? Is it Roubaud, a commoner and everyman, a reminder of the Popular Front and the collective of humanity of *La vie est à nous*, who is on the visible right? Is it both

men, out of their urban context near the mouth of the Seine? Is it *we,* as a collectivity that is "coming from Paris" to see *La bête humaine?*[12] Is it the film and its production? No matter how the signboard is glossed, it inscribes an aesthetic and political distance that turns the speech of the antagonist's bitter words into a rebus. Turlot asks Roubaud what his name is. And with the naîveté of a Charles Bovary that draws attention to the scriptural components of his signature, Roubaud utters in a deadpan flourish, "Je m'appelle Roubaud, et je ne rougis pas de mon nom" (My name is Roubaud, and I'm not ashamed of it, that is, I don't "blush" or "redden" at it). The presence of both the signboard and the words that turn to the graphic element of the speech makes Roubaud's statement almost *spell* and *color* his character with comic innuendo. The name fits the context of a train movie so obviously that it fails to carry any allegorical force. Is he a handsome wheel (*Roue-beau*)? Less likely, a red-haired or pretty baud (*roux baud*)? A mechanical man, or a variant on a *robot?* He can be none of them, but the verbal and visual coincidence nonetheless prompts the questions.

At this point, confirming the credits, the film dismantles its field of illusion through gaps of speech and writing. It shunts narrative onto a field of interpellation. Turlot gives himself the right to ask about—therefore, to establish—Roubaud's identity. He produces him as a subject who, because he, Turlot, is naming him, is putting Roubaud "in his place." His act of extorting Roubaud's name translates the way that a simple instance of power defines a greater representation of French society of 1938. The relation of the quadrant of characters, billboard, and spectator reveals how the figure arrogating the right to say "Who are you?" acquires authority. Turlot's instance of discourse requires Roubaud to respond the way he does.[13] The act that instances speech calls the other into question. It tends to constitute the subject's essence in view of the instancing agent. Whatever force of *self* the interpellated figure musters in response to the question belongs neither to one nor to the other. Like the name, the title has already been conferred upon Roubaud (or Turlot, a quasi-identical sobriquet) by another, pregiven interpellator that is aligned with writing, or the laws that one inherits simply by living in a given symbolic order. An absent power is marked as being not in Zola but in the texture of exchange in contemporary life.

Clearly Roubaud counterinterpellates Turlot when he remarks that he does not blush at the sign of his name. Roubaud denies his discursive and symbolic "place" by indicating that he remains only at the level of his interlocutor, a fact that the billboard—which addresses everyone at all social strata—adduces. He tampers with the intersubjective relations of speech and space that produce signs of authority. But on another level, his manner of drawing attention to the innocuously funny side of his name collapses the mimetic fabric of the narrative.

The film literally invokes a toyland of political implication. If Roubaud is Roubaud, then who are the other characters in the film? Jacques Lantier? Séverine? Cabuche? Philomène? Grandmorin? Pecqueux? Are they all interpellated by the drama in which they act out the rhythms of work and play, as in the marionette theater of the prologue of *La chienne?* Placed thus in the space of the image, all the names lose their allegorical charge. In lieu of an opposition of values is a field of tension that opens between the semantic fields that the first and last of the characters occupy. First, of course, is Lantier, who has to be Lantier because Zola's novel places the character at the center of its structure. Lantier functions according to what makes him go, the locomotive that he nicknames (and thus motivates, so as to defuse in the imagination all effects of interpellation that come with a given proper name) "La Lison." The sobriquet is a perfect homonym of the imperative of the first-person plural that imposes an order of reading: *La lison(s)*, or, "Let's read it." Read thus, *La* can refer to the article of *La bête humaine*. The locomotive thus "reads" the film—as in the action of the opening sequence—that it figures in the form of a mechanical beast. Or, when it is voiced in the film, "La Lison" can be counterinterpellated as *Là* (or *la*) *lit son*: "There *sound* is read," "*la* [a musical note] reads sound," "sound *reads* it," or in the field of desire, "*there is her* [or *his*] *bed*." The problematic nature of the signature recurs.[14] In the same fashion, it can be seen that Renoir puts himself in the role of the poacher, Cabuche, so that perhaps he can be a mimetic victim of his own movie. The director becomes the character unjustly convicted for the murder of Grandmorin. He confers upon himself the name of the tail or caboose (or the coda of a filmic allegory).

The other characters fall into the imaginary space between the head and tail of the train, between Lantier the engineer and Renoir the cabooselike paraph, with traits that the visual register uses to subvert the narrative. Flore first appears as the "good" woman opposed to the "bad" Séverine, the blonde, sunny figure of nature who recalls the presence of a medieval Flora. She is located in a Flaubertian landscape of Normandy, of rolling hill and vale, by mottled cows and gently flowing waters. Séverine, the urban force, has dark hair and lives only in the city. The doublet that she forms with Flore heightens her presence as an archetypic noir female — but she is anything but a Joan Crawford or a Barbara Stanwyck. In Zola she is the cutting, *severe,* relentless force of destruction that goes with the innuendo of the castrative edge of her name. But in Renoir, she is a toylike doll with mechanical gestures and a voice that undoes the tragic essence that the novel puts forward.[15] Pecqueux, avatar of Marceau in *La règle du jeu,* recalls something of a rodent, a rat, or a totally Parisian worker striving to make ends meet (his wife, he says to Lantier where they wash and eat, works in the lavatory at the Gare Saint-Lazare — a station that, because of the saint's myth, stinks more than any other). He is redolent of mixed odors — of urine, food, and disinfectant — and is something of a *Pet–queue*, a little end, or even "fart–tail." And until being murdered, Grandmorin looks over the drama from above because he is seen in the distance in space, scarcely visible and thus eminent in absence. In Zola's novel all the names are invested in a scenario that reflects the traits associated with their names. Beyond their onomastic virtue, in Renoir's film the names acquire a graphic range of association that turns them into rebuses of visual and political charge that orient the film toward a broader study of the relation of the powers of sight and speech to class, position, and subjectivity.

Thus, because the proper names figure as filmic icons, the narrative can be followed in ways other than Zola's plot suggests. The story blueprints a noir structure by having a deracinated character fall in love with the "bad" component of a doublet. Lantier's unrequited love, and Séverine's propensity to double-cross, inevitably brings about their demise as well as that of the man to whom she is married. The same type of plot informs *Double Indemnity, The Postman Always Rings Twice, Scarlet Street,* and most trenchantly, *The Killers* and *Criss Cross.*[16] *La bête humaine* appears precocious both in its structure and in its prevalent use of chiaoscuro, its neutral point of view, and its appeal to visibility. Beyond the narrative, the film continually asks: who sees? who speaks? who reads? who doesn't? These questions are all raised in the sequence depicting Grandmorin's murder on the train.

Roubaud has let jealousy overtake him.[17] He stages a theater of cruelty that thrusts the viewer into the role of a compliant agent. Like Rossellini's model of Nazi ideology in the spatial articulation of the antechamber between the officer's club and the torture room in *Roma, città aperta,* cruelty in *La bête humaine* is made to be seen *across* the threshold of a doorway. The latter isolates and assigns a position to the spectator so as to insist on the relation of power that comes with the placement of the spectacle at a distance. In the train, the establishing shot takes the form of another "frontal-profile" view of the first-class compartment, reproducing the framing used in Roubaud's first meeting with Turlot at the moment of his interpellation and remaining characteristic of Renoir's treatment of windows and doors in general. The director shoots across a jamb or a sill so that the world before and beyond it will be framed twice by the rectangle of the screen on the outer periphery and the smaller frame within it. The camera uses deep focus and tends to indicate its position at a recognizably distant point in the frame.[18] The style marks *Boudu* and *La chienne* and is used with powerful effect across windows looking out on the courtyard in *Le crime de M. Lange*. But the extent of its force in *La bête humaine* depends on how the illusion of space is collapsed with the frame cued by a 180-degree reversal and the doorway or window through which it is seen. It is all the more powerful when the camera is perceived to be located in an impossible, totally illusory space that lacks any realistic ground.

In this sequence of *La bête humaine,* the effect is first anticipated in Roubaud's flat with a view giving over the railway station. At first we see the window from within the apartment, through the doorway, when Roubaud is captivated by the sight of his wife sitting on the window ledge, stroking a fluffy angora cat in her arms. Later the camera looks down over the sill to the trains, far below, that seem distantly real (in the smoke and steam of the station below) and near (as if they were toy trains because the depth of field, as in *Boudu,* is flattened where it is most extended but seen through the window). At times the shot is taken from outside the window in order to discern the characters looking outside, as they survey the world of partial objects on the horizon below. In these instances the camera is spotted in an absolutely impossible position: it cannot float three floors above the station; if it does, it must be on a scaffold that anyone can visualize through the realistic effect of the shot. Wherever it is placed, the camera disturbs the convention of the shot-reverse shot sequence through its countershot along the 180-degree sightline. The illusion necessary for the narrative is put into question all the while the story is told. Conflict is so minimal that an effect is held of two simultaneous discourses being developed in the same space.

In the sequence narrating Séverine and Roubaud's excursion in the train prior to their murder of Grandmorin, a new set of figural problems juxtaposes a frieze of actors with clichéd views of their faces.[19] When they are riding in their compartment, awaiting the moment to perform the murder, Roubaud and Séverine fidget about in their seats. Roubaud is armed with the pocket knife that Séverine had given him to deflect Turlot's complaint away from superior officials of the SNCF. Roubaud's mad jealousy and suspicion about incest in the relation be-

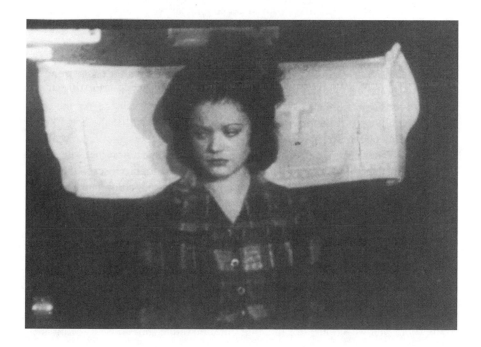

tween Grandmorin and Séverine has turned his character from that of a dazzled child to melancholic psychopath. Each is seen in close-up, both together and in isolation from each other, their faces nervous and looking forward into the void before them as they rest their heads on the cushions bearing doilies on which is printed the title of the train: *ETAT*. Thus named, the liner that goes back and forth between Le Havre and Paris is immediately associated with the age-old allegory of the "ship of state," or the vessel of the nation, like the emblem of Paris with its craft that "floats but never sinks" (*fluctuat nec mergitur*) on the waters of history, an idealized timeless picture of French society. But when the characters move their heads, the state is severed into single alphabetic units, such that E-TAT, ET-AT, ETA-T, TA, and TAT emerge as Roubaud and Séverine nod toward and away from each other. The priority of the national body and its course on the rails of history seems to be relegated to a role that is secondary to the bestial human relations of the two murderers. Séverine's face is adjacent to TAT, thus implying that she is what she is, a doll, "fondled" or touched (*tâté*) gingerly; or that she is *ta*—your, our—Séverine and, as she will later remark "tragically" to Lantier with the allure of a Barbie doll, a person loved by everyone and no one, a thing or fetish of beauty that simply acquires definition by the other's desire to touch and fondle it.

The murder is performed in view of the rift between the individual couple and the state that is printed in the background. In the episode detailing Grandmorin's demise, the camera is set in a position perpendicular to the aisle of the train. It can either be outside of the aisle and windows that overlook the countryside whizzing by in the night, on the liminal edge of the wall of the train car, or somewhere in between. The camera is not at a vantage point that Lantier, the passenger en route to work, could ever share. Nor does a reverse shot taken from the compartment indicate where the camera has established its view. The improbable setting of the camera enhances the visibility of the narrative since, like the characters themselves, it fails to witness the murder. Implied is that the act, like all violence, may be too invisible, or too real, to merit any representation or realistic camera placement. But the position also makes the spectator the sole agent needed to keep the illusion of violence intact, since the film proposes that torture, murder, or atrocity of any kind depends on the presence of a compliant spectator-agent.[20]

The viewer has a privileged view of a drama made manifest by the theatrical decor of a proscenium space of the compartment with its curtains drawn shut and with Roubaud's hand pulling the shades down; with back lighting providing the effect of a limelight; and above all, with a strip of paper glued on the outside window, with the word RESERVE indicating that the first-class booth is reserved, but also rebounding the theatrical dimension of a spectacle *reserved* for the viewer. As the spectators we are virtually pulled into the scenario at this point in the film. That we agonize for the long duration of the shot without seeing any-

thing between the moment Roubaud and Séverine enter the compartment and exit underscores the gratuity of our role in the act. The style repeats the manner of Legrandin's killing of Dédé in *La chienne* and now anticipates Lantier's murder of Séverine during the firemen's ball. Here Grandmorin's death sets the scene for the way that Lantier glimpses the invisibility of the murder. He is seen unable to see what we have not seen. In the famous shots that portray Lantier looking list-lessly out of the window of the train as he kills some time during the ride,[21] vague allusion is made to the emptiness of the same act of staring out of windows that had marked *Boudu* and *Madame Bovary*.[22]

Réservé has the effect of neutralizing the drama of Grandmorin's murder. Now, as Lantier loses his stereoscopic vision when a cinder lodges in his right eye, the camera moves from a medium close-up that establishes his action of bringing a handerkchief to his eye with his right hand, to a close-up of his face. To the right of his left cheek, on the very level of his eyeline and on a horizontal axis held between the medium close-up and the close-up that follows, is located a common sign in the world of trains: FUMEURS (Smoking Permitted). The word offers a view of the kind of "moving writing" that complements the automatic signature in the credit shot of Emile Zola. Lantier's head moves back and forth such that FUMEURS, adjacent to his left cheekbone, loses an F, yielding UMEURS. Then, at the moment of the greatest pain, his head moves further left, erasing the U and displaying MEURS.[23] Conflicting meanings emerge from the two shots:

meurs, of course, is the imperative interpellation ''to die,'' but it lacks any spec-
ification as to who is being asked to die, by whom, or by what authority. The
graphemes inscribe a turning point in the narrative—the story changes its
course—but they become an autonomous movement of scriptural vision.
Lantier's squinting left eye is placed next to and oblivious of the command that
the letters seem, by contiguity, to be imposing on him. But, since he is Lantier,
he suffers from the genealogical failure, the fêlure engraved in his blood, or his
complexion of (*h*)*umeurs*. And of course, the smokiness of the film makes it just
what the word says, the writing conflating the cause of the narrative, Emile Zola,
in the effect of the film's essay on its own properties. Because the writing draws
attention to the protagonist's closed eyelid, it anticipates a corollary problem at
the end of the film. The murder in the train appears to be reduced to a problem of
visual perception couched in the differences of image and writing.

These alphabetical moments in which ETAT, RESERVE, and FUMEURS are
glimpsed also trigger a play of visibility, writing, and allegory. In the latter sense,
as *Paisan* has shown, allegory and history inform each other through the agency
of scriptural, even diagrammatical patterns that combine image and picture. The
historical spectrum of *La bête humaine* appears to be couched in graphic elements no less pervasive than the myriad allusions to contemporary time made
throughout this film and its sequel, *La règle du jeu* (1939). Their presence in the
latter may have prompted its negative and violent reception. The allegory of a

closure of a "play" in the château of Solognes was perceived as based on the metaphor linking the representation of the impure French aristocracy's antics with the *Sitzkrieg* and a general decadence of French social mores.[24] The film of 1939 has often been remembered as a study of a prerevolutionary moment, à la Beaumarchais and Marivaux, of a debacle to come.[25] It prompts comparison with the coming of the Second World War and a populace gone crazy in its frenzy to love and kill in the same blow. The same figure is embedded in the depiction of the train in *La bête humaine*. After Lantier jumps to his death from the speeding locomotive, the train-of-state rolls toward disaster, out of control, until Pecqueux averts disaster by pulling the emergency brake.

Nonetheless, the train that would bind the allegory of history of *La bête humaine* to that of *La règle du jeu* is not located in abstraction. The premonition of international calamity is shared between the two films in literal ways. In *La bête humaine* the fresco of state turmoil is cast into ciphers. Lantier's monocular view of the world is determined by an awareness of violence that comes from the past. In Zola's novel, the determining agent is alcoholism, whereas for Renoir, remembrance of the First World War is enough to imply a return of the repressed in a coming apocalpyse of history. In the sequence just studied, Lantier was wiping his eye, unable to perceive what the spectator apprehends graphically in the adjacent letters of FUMEURS. His eyelids were almost closed. Paradoxically, they seemed to block the entry of light from the surrounding darkness onto his retina. An eye was closed; he could not see clearly anymore. Only at the end of the film do they open and accede to stereoscopy. Thus, he who was bonded to "La Lison" could not *read* the nature of his relation to the world until he ripped himself asunder from it. When the speeding train is stopped, and when the chorus of Pecqueux and the *cheminots* run along the ballast by the tracks before retrieving his dead body, they come to the very space where he and Flore had embraced in a scene of love and murder. Now Lantier is viewed in calm, as if he has found solace in death. Pecqueux, his closest friend, puts his hand over Lantier's eyes in order to shut them and offer terse words of sympathy.

In the close-up of Lantier's face, a tranquil countenance is betrayed by mellow and creamy patches of skin around his eyes. For the first time in the work sequences of the film Lantier is viewed with his goggles removed. A softness imbues the flesh the goggles had protected from wind, sand, and cinders, suggesting that a figure from a tradition of medieval representations of terror is invested into the depiction. His eyes no longer have the squinting, protective fold of the lid that shields the eyes from being blinded by excess light, experience, or history. Rather, in death the eye has now turned into an oculus that appears open, aghast at the vision of what it sees. His eye, which had been in a correct or rational distance with the world, is now almost exorbitantly childish, and morbidly open to it. Lantier's face registers a teratological view of oncoming apocalypse.

The same figure of the "exorbitant" eye reaches back to Romanesque art, but it no doubt had been current in contemporary circles in the 1930s that were comparing the relation of evolutions of art to universal history. In the 1920s Elie Faure's *L'esprit des formes* had called into question the relation of cinema, the future of European culture, and the organic process of life. Henri Focillon composed his work of theory, *Vie des formes,* on the basis of his study of the styles of architecture and sculpture from the early Christian period to the end of the Middle Ages. In the same vein, in 1938 André Malraux had just returned from the debacle of the Spanish Civil War, after fighting and flying for the Republican cause, with a ciné-novel, *L'espoir,* and a film, *Sierra de Teruel.* Both were, as one of his characters remarked, "lyrical illusions" of the battle for just causes but, despite their failure to stem the tide of fascism, they were "creations of style" that mixed contemporary media with what were felt to be timeless monuments of art. The descent of wounded flyers from the Sierra de Teruel was imagined in the novel as a tableau vivant mixing a war scene with memories of Rembrandt's etchings and Goya's *Disasters of War.*[26] No doubt Malraux's vision of politics, history, and aesthetics was taking shape in the work that would result in *Les voix du silence,* a filmic montage of image and texts recounting, in a flash of illustrated pages, evolutions of human representation of invisible forms.

At one point in the epic Malraux distinguishes between the Romanesque and Gothic visions. A remarkable intuition contrasts the apocalpytic eye of the Romanesque style of sculpture on capitals and tympana with that of thirteenth-century portal figures. A close-up of the visionary eye is placed next to that of the Gothic counterpart. The former is bulbous and round, staring as if astounded and in eternal gaze at the sight of remote and violent gods. Its stylized character conveys the impression of a body that is seeing *too* much or that glimpses an eternity of death that a stern deity imposes upon it with a silent order from above. The body of the sculpture is reduced to stiff conformity with the exiguous confines of the capital or tympanum. But the Gothic eye is alive, squinting, and almost smiling because it has a highly practical sense of knowing that light blinds and that to live and work in the three dimensions of the world, the human body must adjust its sight to the light that illuminates it. The Gothic eye has effectively recognized the world for what it is and has mediated the violence from without by screening its pupil with the wall of its eyelid. For this same reason the portal sculpture is disengaged from the colonnettes and shafting to which Romanesque forms were more firmly attached. Gothic sculpture, thanks to the pragmatic eye that *knows how to see,* moves away from the church and wills to live practically in this world.[27] The Romanesque eye is born of millenarian vision and has a childlike view, at once irritable, sensitive, and uncompromising. It reflects the terror of the Christian subject under the power of gods that are about to bring fire and brimstone to the world. The Gothic eye tells the viewer that the sculpture has come of age and is a subject in a universe whose symbolic shapes are accessible to human sight, a universe that celebrates male and female alike and is free of the terror imposed by the real.

In his death pose, Lantier's eye, seen with its goggles removed, is something of a great white O that reproduces a Romanesque vision of terror. His death appears to stage a regression from a practical sense of the world of work to a puerile, visionary, even infantile fear of impending doom. At the end of *La bête humaine* the depiction of the dead Lantier clearly parallels Malraux's vision of the Romanesque and Gothic cultures. The character sees beyond life and death, and in the context of the later 1930s, he beholds a vision of history at the same time that his demise is comparable to a fantasized return to a child's sensuous, violent, irrational apprehension of the world.[28] Such is the tragic, but overriding, vision of the protagonist, who has gone beyond the visual limits of those around him. At another level in Renoir's oeuvre, and in a way that recalls the concept of the filmic icon, Lantier's death purports to be an uncanny birth, or a labor that gives life, through his own death, which enables spectators to articulate a collective view of History. The cost of the vision, like that imposed on Rossellini's peasants and common folk, is of course Lantier's life, but it comes visibly with his regression to a state of the unconscious, in which the subject cannot understand any contradiction or law that would bar its will from attaching the entire world to its body. Lantier's suicide suscitates a return to what can be ascertained as a condition—a primary narcissism—that allows the vision of the film, namely, to be the premonition of Fate that will see the advent of the Stalin-Hitler pact of 1939.

In the last shot of Lantier, the arm that comes from the right side of the frame to seal his eyes recalls the initial scene of interpellation. For an instant narrative is broken. The hand that comes from out of frame, even if it appears to be Pecqueux's, is nonetheless detached from its body *off*. In the iconic tradition of painting that inspires Renoir, it is the hand of an absence, of a god, that comes from without and once again calls into question the drama and its players. Like the detached hand coming from above to point at Peter Lorre in the trial at the end of *M,* Renoir's hand seems to be that of an authority marked as being without origin or cause—that is, both a reassuringly imaginary being who has organized the world and keeps its order, like a god, as well as a power that democratic action cannot influence. The hand partakes of authority but is represented as immanent, detached, and lacking prescience. The hand coming from *off* reproduces the initial, vocal interpellation of the film (Turlot's encounter with Roubaud) in manifestly visible terms, as a "voice of silence" whose iconic tradition reaches back to the time-held law, in the Romanesque period, that interdicts any representation of God other than by a hand.[29] Both the syntax of the film and the icon imply that the authority that has ordained Lantier's death is not a genealogical fault or a hereditary imbalance precipitated by alcoholism. It is, more frighteningly, simply *nothing* and of no cause, at the same time it figures in a typology arching back to the years 1914–18.

If Lantier's corpse has Romanesque trappings, in psychogenetic terms it confirms the status of Renoir as an auteur. Almost all of his would-be heroes of the 1930s tend to personify infantility at the moment of their deaths. In *Toni* (1934), the protagonist of the same name (Charles Blavette), in an identical place between a railroad bed and a Cézanne-like landscape beyond in the distance, dies like a baby in the arms of his old friend when leveled by a double-barreled shotgun blast.[30] And when Amédée Lange (René Lefèvre, a child by dint of his name, which recalls an angel and an infant's diaper, as well as *M* and Fritz Lang) shoots the evil Batala (Jules Berry) in *Le crime de M. Lange* (1935), the antagonist utters not a shriek, a sigh, or a death-gurgle, but a baby's bleat. André Jurieu (Roland Toutain) runs to the greenhouse with the glee of a little boy before Schumacher (Gaston Modot) guns him down with buckshot, "comme une *bête*" (like a beast, stress added), as Marceau, avatar of Pecqueux, reports in *La règle du jeu*. Heroes regress to infantile stages when they die, reproducing the drama of their first sight of the world. Vision, therefore, comes with death, or at the moment its figure is deprived of sight. To see means something tantamount to being in a condition of impossibility that can be read as either tragic (if the viewer has a penchant for myth and history, in a good deal of French cinema of the 1930s) or conceptual and dialectical. In the latter sense, it appears seminal for the experiment of the relation of visibility to ideology that acquires such powerful charge in all of Renoir's work and exerts influence on both neoreal cinema and American film noir.

The overall impact of the film might be summarized in the first view that locates Flore in the Normandy countryside. In a long shot taken from the shore of a river flowing under a brick railroad bridge of neo-Romanesque style in the background, the maiden cools her legs over the gunwale of a skiff on which she is alluringly perched. The boat points toward the two dark shadows cast under the rounded arches behind. An image of luxuriant, exotic "nature" seemingly unbounded by culture, the scene in the foreground offers to the voyeuristic spectator the delight of taking undisturbed visual pleasure at the sight of Flore (Blanchette Brunoy) pulling up her dress and baring her thighs over the shimmering water. The skiff that aims at the imaginary, ambiguous receptacle of the cave (or literally, the *antre* or lair) under the bridge (like Courbet's paintings of the source of the Loue) brings a tremor of risk and danger. The background seems to eroticize doubly the sight of Flore. Her sex is close to the prow of the vessel. The desire elicited by the scene is blemished by the din and smoke of a locomotive and its train passing right and spewing black fumes on the picture below. But since Renoir attributes almost all of his shots to an origin seeing the scene within the film, the spectator, having glimpsed Flore as Actaeon sights Diana, is associated with two bumpkins whom she then approaches (in the course of a tracking shot

pulling backward) and upbraids for having watched her in a privy moment. But in the historical and millenary network of the film, articulation of the point of view is redundant. It can be seen that the two arches of the railroad bridge are two gigantic *eyes* that look over the spectacle and hence mirror the viewer's stare that maculates the scene. Their look matches the inscriptive power of the train that imposes itself upon the landscape that for a moment had the allure of being self-contained and bereft of either industrial revolution or history.

A double view has been gained, by which ocular forms point at an exceptionally intimate relation between the individual subject and the collective force of history. History seems to be a force of writing that moves forward. Inexorably, it is like the train that blemishes nature, confines all of the travelers, and carries them along the implacable course that they have chosen to take. As Céline had recently written at the beginning of *Voyage au bout de la nuit,* "Once you're in, you're in." Everyone is in the machinery. When we happen to see ourselves in it, myriad problems of visibility and of its genesis arise. In this way the characters of *La bête humaine* seem to be units of a collective human alphabet that inscribes them, like Romanesque figures, in a world of confinement. Along with backlit decors, chiaoscuro, and a pattern-plot of destiny, this inhuman area of incarceration and seriality is what Renoir bequeathes to film noir. It remains to see how and why in the final chapter.

7

Decoding Film Noir
The Killers, High Sierra, and *White Heat*

In chapter 6 the human will was seen squinched into the frame of destiny announcing the coming of the Second World War. *La bête humaine* appears to be a vital, even precocious study of a convention that would soon develop on both sides of the Atlantic during and after the debacle. Did Renoir indeed offer a blueprint for the coding of destiny in the postwar years? The risk one runs in posing the question inheres, it seems, in the convention of film noir itself. It shares much with the plot and texture of *La bête humaine,* but it is neither a commanding style nor a genre. It may be a convention, or it may not. Its origins reach back to Lang's *M,* to the gangster film, and poetic realism in France of the 1930s, and these origins remain so pervasive that any point of departure would no doubt be erased in the search for beginnings.

Another approach, one that puts historical affinities aside in favor of common political and aesthetic concerns, may be warranted. In the view of the tensions generating the filmic writing of Rossellini or Renoir, the current chapter will see if, on the one hand, film noir shares much with relations of figures and ground crafted in the European tradition. On the other, it will examine how history is inscribed multifariously in the literal play of characters and scripture set in the frame of the image. Three films will be studied. The first, *The Killers* (Robert Siodmak, 1946), figures centrally in most histories of film noir and seems to be located at a center defined by two films that mark beginnings and endings of the convention,[1] but that also reflect the ideologies studied in chapters 3 and 4: Raoul Walsh's *High Sierra* (1941), a beginning, and *White Heat* (1949), an end that revives a vision of apocalpyse and history through the syntax of his earlier work at Warner Brothers studio.

The Killers appears to use writing to locate and disseminate its relations with history. Its first ten minutes recount Ernest Hemingway's story of an encounter in a café before it unwinds a long imbroglio in an entirely different style. A baroque complication, the tale is based loosely on the structure of inquest that informs *Citizen Kane*. A common man, a filling station attendant, is murdered for no apparent reason. He has left a modest insurance policy that a company investigator assigns to the rightful, but unlikely, beneficiary. Intrigued by the case—why would a nobody be so brutally murdered?—the sleuth interviews witnesses to solve the enigma posed by the victim's last words, "I . . . I did something wrong . . . once," and by his sole effect, a green scarf printed with figures of golden harps. Fade-outs and dissolves generally distinguish one sequence from another.[2] The first, which recounts Hemingway's story, is located in the here and now established in the credits superimposed on the image of a café seen across a street after dusk. The remaining thirty-five units begin in the present, but then arch back into the past—sometimes dissolving into a past within the past—before the story "catches up" with the present and unties its knots. A familiar agent of the noir convention, Edmund O'Brien, is the intrepid agent and double-crosser driven to solve the riddle.[3]

The writing betrays much more than the convention. It figures prominently in the first and third sequences, and appears to extend the film's range of connotation. The first glimpse of scripted material in frame indeed occurs *before* the credits, in the first shot, taken from behind the front seat of a car speeding down a road at night. An instance of the convention of the 1950s and 1960s that rolls back the credits after pulling the spectator into the visual field, the scene summarizes all of the problems of visibility taken up in the film. Headlamps illuminate the road ahead as the car advances toward a vanishing point defined by the converging lines of the median and border stripes of the highway, pointing to an imaginary intersection in the darkness beyond the scope of the two cones of light. As it rolls forward, in a narrative stratagem inherited from silent film (and because the music is amplified on the sound track, the film appears especially silent), the lights move by a road sign that displays, before it disappears into the dark that engulfs it from the left:

The billboard moves into view from the left and then disappears into the penumbra after the lights have scanned them in movement down the road. Since the headlamps are an icon of the cinema being projected over the head of the viewer, they can only be likened to eyes that *read*. The filmic conventions in the shot occasion a simultaneously tabular and linear decipherment that moves along paradigmatic and syntagmatic axes at once.[4] The last strands of writing seen in the frame are glimpsed in passage, when the lights pass over the sign, and leave in brief retinal suspension,

The sign that asks the public to drive carefully (i.e., *safely*) gives way to *sey . . . fully,* while *sey,* a homonym of *say,* murmurs in the silence of the hieroglyph, "say fully," that is, to utter visually what speech is masking so carefully. But as *sey fully* is a scintilla of the unconscious, *sey* becomes a rebus combining *say* and *see,* in other words, the very riddle posed by the film itself. Before it reaches its credits, the film is asking the viewers not only to see what it says so carefully but also to decipher its inner speech adroitly.

The two vestiges of script, below the proper name of Brentwood, seem to be an emblematic legend to the inscription of the toponym, such that the -OOD of Brentwood looms out (almost as a reminder of the spectacles of Doctor Eckleberg along the Long Island road in Fitzgerald's *Great Gatsby*) as two eyes that look over the drama that will follow. If the relation of the double O of Brentwood is persistently phantasmatic, the name cannot fail to nag the spectator's memory.

The toponym is reported to belong to the tristate area of New Jersey. If located in the region of Matamoras and Port Jervis, or the Delaware River and the Kittatinny Mountains, it is a downright illusion: the nearest "Brentwood" in the area, many spectators know, is a suburb of Pittsburgh at the opposite end of the state. Brentwood appears to be a signifier floating between the tristate area and a better-known town adjacent to Hollywood — Brentwood, which is next to Beverly Hills. The origin of the film is situated by tertiary reference to the very place, like the time, in which the film is being made.

In the credits and second shot the name of the filling station opposite the café is tipped into view anamorphically. On a marquee the title arches into the space over the street and provides an entry into the depth (and concurrent matteness) of the overall chiaroscuro in extreme deep focus. For a moment the letters TRI-ST are in view, but they do not yet spell the "Tri-State Station," a name that will be seen in daytime shots in the minutes to follow. The graphics translate the homonym, *tryst,* into the frame before it can be stabilized as a place-name. "The Killers," seen contiguously in the title credits, is thus not the Hemingway tale announced but the story of a tryst. Duplicity prevails: Whose tryst is it? Can it be the noir standard of the triangular relation of a "bad" woman, a self-victimizing lover, and a double-dealing husband and his unlikely, double-dealing wife in collusion with him? Or that of the complicitous relation, established by the film, of both the spectator and the production? If so, the inner speech of the film is both graphic and ocular in its manifestation and arcane in its composition.

The writing becomes iconic in the first shots that follow the credits. A street is placed in light that cuts through the center of the frame, with the station (next to an *x* that seems to mark a spot) to the left, and the café to the right. The shot includes the graphics of the credits and lasts about two minutes, in deep focus, immobile, before it pans left with the entry of the two killers (Charles McGraw and William Conrad), rescans the gasoline station sign above, registers its emblem of a triangle below, and follows the two characters ambling to the right toward the café. *Tri-State* and the triangle are glimpsed on the pumps as the camera shows Al (McGraw) putting his hand to his jacket (apparently to verify the presence of his revolver beneath his overcoat). As he does, a shadow is cast onto his face from the brim of Conrad's hat. All of a sudden, a black triangle is seen in the place of McGraw's mouth. Given the adjacent icons, the *tri* of the Tri-State, the tri-angle, and try-st are reproduced in place of the origins of his voice, right where the "mouth" of the film would otherwise enunciate the dialogue of its narrative. The tale is shown thus to "sey carefully" its structure in the relation of graphics to shadows, bodies, and space.

The first shot taken in the café inversely confirms the effect of the triangle just seen over McGraw's lips. It locates a young man, in profile and in extreme close-up, at one end of the longitude of the counter, looking down at a plate of food that is before him. The two killers enter from the screen door located just *off* and be-

hind, pass by him, and then sit at the opposite end. They stare down the length of the counter, as if the total movement of their bodies and their eyes were both defining the extreme deep focus photography and the narrow aisle indicating the depth.[5] But as the two men move down the space past the young man, he blurts out, "Catch up." The remark would seem to be indicating to the waiter that he is asking for a bottle of tomato *ketchup* to give color and taste to his bland sandwich. Yet the film does not signal any destination toward which the utterance is directed. The young man does not look up at the waiter. "Ketchup" can therefore refer to the tomato sauce but also spell *catch up,* or make an implicit sign telling viewers that we must now, in the identity and the gap of sight and sound, "catch up" in the narrative where feedback or relay is no longer possible. No enigma lurks beneath what is seen and heard immediately; only the illusion of an imbroglio will force spectators to believe they must "catch up" with the narrative machine that is moving ahead of them. The illusion puts the spectator both in and out of the film; it serves as an agent of interpellation that arrests the viewer and displaces all security of an uninvolved viewpoint.

The entire sequence in the café entails an almost calligrammatical rendition of Hemingway's text, the short story being reproduced at the foot of the letter. The montage literally translates the absence of decor in the author's liminal style into a rebus of angled shapes and speech. Latent visibility of Hemingway's diction is made manifest to the degree that the film locates how an almost aestheticizing, even thematizing mode of "hard-boiled" essence operates in the writing.

Siodmak's camera works, as it were, like a lie detector in its reproduction of the realistic effects obtained in the aura of the narrative.[6] It collapses coherent space through contrapuntally defined reverse shots placed at both ends of the counter and by disjoining the speech from the image. What is seen *on* on the image track is indicated *off* on the sound track. Redundant articulation of words becomes a poetry of focal reversals that match the shooting of the space. The apparently invisible, commonplace decor of the café is turned into a miniature maze of interior frames and acute angles seen from strange points of view in extreme tilts. But, contrary to Welles, in *Citizen Kane* or *The Lady from Shanghai,* the deep focus and expressionistic views are not primary objects of attention superseding the narrative. The writing of Hemingway is distorted and doubled—ventriloquized—through the montage and framing that intensify it.

When, in a deep-view shot, after Max (Conrad) has asked the young man for his name, the killer's interpellation is represented by the gruff voice, *off,* so as also to ask spectators what our names are. When the youth (Phil Brown) responds, "Nick Adams," an authenticating moment locates the proper name of Hemingway's narrator. Just as the narrative space is motivated, an act of violence occurs. Adams, whom the killers nickname "Bright Boy," wonders what is happening. He looks down the counter at the killers and asks, "What's the idea?" He receives a response, *off,* that in the style of framing could virtually become the viewer's mouth. Only the timbre of the voice associates it with Conrad, unseen, who utters in a pellucid tone, "There isn't any idea." Because the laconic speech of the tale is seen *off,* the original literary model is utterly changed. A more realistic locution would require Nick the narrator to respond, with fidelity to oral English, "What's the *big* idea?" And Conrad would be more believable as a dumb killer if he retorted, "There ain't no idea." By having the killer respond to the narrator's fearful question in perfect syntax, the film puts in question the platonic aura of the "Idea" idealized in the speech of Hemingway. Although Conrad replicates Hemingway to the letter, he speaks *off,* to the spectator, in proposing an entirely *material* discourse in which articulation does not disappear in favor of essence or abstraction. "There isn't any idea": as in the sight of the signboard in the first shot of the film, the speech aims at concretizing its own literal, visible quiddity. The film turns the classical text into a hieroglyphic surface.

Similarly, the instance of writing returns in the representation of the story when Al is seen reading the menu and pondering over what he will order. A moral viewing, faithful to the story, would elicit disquiet at the fact that two murderers can eat hot food prior to killing a man in cold blood. But the doubling of the words in speech (Conrad: "Whaddaya wanna eat?" McGraw: "I dunno what I wanna eat," etc.) and the scansion of liver "on the dinner menu" that is unavailable for the next ten minutes turn voice into a rhythmic montage that follows exactly the articulation of visual signs on the image track.

It might be said that Hemingway's "The Killers" is put to an extreme test of film writing because, when subjected to the limits of the image, the laconic story loses all of its evocative force. Yet readers cannot fail to see in memory Siodmak's aural and visual interpretation, *off,* through the spoken writing. Hemingway's narration is now filtered through the actors' voices and Elwood Bredell's camera. It stages the enigma placed at the center of the film noir that will follow. Siodmak, often remembered as a filmmaker of memorable fragments, structures the convention according to the difference in style made manifest between the opening sequence and the narrative that follows.[7] The second sequence reconstructs the past that was visible only seconds ago. A fade-in leads to a close-up of the objects left by the late "Swede" (Burt Lancaster), a prizefighter who had gone into hiding as an attendant at the Tri-State Station in Brentwood. The triangular patch, the emblem seen only anamorphically in the first sequences, now returns to view; the voice *off* of the insurance investigator remarks a scarf—he calls it green—before emerging into view. He goes to the morgue, studies Swede's body, and notices his huge and battered hand. Under a triangular shade over a hanging lamp in the center of the frame that projects light below, Reardon (Edmund O'Brien) asks Nick Adams for his impressions of Swede's last days. The first of twenty-four dissolves and eleven flashbacks, marking a shift between past and present or two layers of the past, leads back to the Tri-State Station in daylight. The signboard of the gas station is seen above and behind the gas pumps. Nick's voice, now *off* in the new scene, states before the dissolve is completed, "I dunno. It was something a long time ago . . . ," before the image track seems to appropriate his point of view. A black, prewar Cadillac enters the station. The dumb, mute Swede attends to it after he has been questioned by the voice (*off*) of the driver who notices him, in extended depth of field, a tire iron in his right hand as he tends to the back of an old coupé. The x-like iron seems to cast a stigma of death on his body, in the style of the fatal writing of Howard Hawks's *Scarface.* The Swede drops the iron, comes forward, and encounters the body that has just spoken: the strange figure has come "out of the past" to catch up with him. A shot and a reverse-shot record him cleaning the windshield, such that its transparent surface is almost likened to a movie screen and a Freudian "screen-memory." As the Swede sprays the glass surface, the driver, whom viewers will later identify in memory as "Big Jim Colfax" (Albert Dekker) follows his gestures. The eyes that fix upon the Swede are his own past; the cleaning liquid that drips down the windshield seems to be a tear—of a crocodile— dripping from the driver's eyes but reflecting the Swede's onset of sadness. The reflective surface of the windshield becomes the ground of a writing that places the past, present, and future on the same plane, hence establishing a surface of multiple "reflections" imbued with an allusive reminder of the movie screen recalling the first shot prior to the credits.

Nick, image-on and voice-off, has been recording his first memories of the Swede being unsettled. The presence of the car and driver, he asserts, left the Swede uneasy. In the continuity of the shooting, the two characters look off to the right when the car drives off. They are seen below the marquee of the station, its last digit, *n,* removed, and the right half of its *o* cut away. To the left and in vertical writing, *Tires* extends another strip of writing perpendicular to the marquee:

On the horizontal axis above, we read STATE STATIC, while in acrostic, on the vertical axis to the left, is scripted TIRES. The Swede registers his uneasiness by appearing disquieted. Nick's voice confirms, "And he walked off, rubbing his stomach, and he didn't come to work the next day." Lancaster's body scans and rewrites the letters behind him. As he places his hands — just remarked by Reardon in the former shots in the morgue, and now a center of visual attention — on his midsection, all of a sudden, because his head blocks the first two letters of the marquee (ST), ATE STATIC *reads* his gesture and translates it into an intertitle explaining the cause and effect of the discomfort that his hands make manifest. The abstract cause of his plight, the sight of Colfax, is collapsed in a self-contained play of gesture and figures. Does the character have an upset stomach because he "ate static," or because, as his head wavers, the letters read "tate static," that is, that he tastes the immobility of destiny? Or, in the aspirant configuration that might translate his inner speech into visual form, is he the one

who can only ''(h)ate'' the ''static'' fate in which he is placed? The play of the
head and the writing also reveals a political dimension, of *state static,* or of a
steady, unchanging state of things. Exhaustion and fatigue imbue the scene, and

inflect the acrostic *tires* from reference to wheels and rubber or benevolent force ("Firestone," "Goodrich," or "Goodyear") to the state of being that characterizes both the Swede and the dream of Nick's flashback. The Swede *tires* when he realizes, at the sight of his nemesis, that his days are numbered.

All of a sudden the billboard and the sign appear to comment furtively on the conditions, the politics, and the history of the noir convention being articulated. The dissolve leads into the recent past, which the film marks as 1946, but the car that enters the station dates to prewar years. A current continuum of stasis frames an absence. The unnamed period, marked between 1941 and 1946, the Second World War, becomes an ineffable, remote, and unnameable event that the film can only encircle in its temporal scheme. The present "state" appears to be one of an uneasy, unmoving *being*. Thus the crucial enigmas that are posed at the outset, particularly in the Swede's cryptic remark, his last words in which he said to Nick, the present narrator, "I . . . I did something wrong . . . once," taken from Hemingway, are not merely a signboard that encodes a mistake, but a framing allegory that encrypts the Second World War. The protagonist becomes the subject of history but now is seen as a pawn in an ideological configuration beyond his ken. Filmic writing shunts the convention of an inquest onto a more commanding problem of the existential dimension of viewing and living in current history. Though set in the past, the sequence is scripted as absolutely present. Its historical moment, now the cold war, offsets the muted, imaginary violence the narrative is casting out of frame. The character is *written* by the past destiny that any spectator can read in the world history surrounding the film.

No less, the gesture signaling the dubious hero's upset stomach opens a dialogue with other conventions of literature and film. The omnipresence of nauseously greasy food in the first sequence—deep-fried croquettes, liver, ham sandwiches—goes with a speech decrying abstraction outside of the sensory present. There is no *idea* put forward to calm the physical disgust of the murder. The Swede's heartburn appears to be an aftereffect not just of the greasy spoon but also of the sight of a world consisting only of material shapes. All of a sudden the film seems to tap into a graphic tradition of European origin and of existential intensity more common to Renoir, Sartre, and Rossellini than Universal Studios or Hollywood. The code word of humans facing their destiny had been, just prior to the Second World War, *nausea* felt by the narrator of Sartre's novel of that name. Roquentin experienced "nausea" when he passed beyond an intellectual sense of absurdity and into an immediately physical apprehension of his destiny. Disgust is motivated by figures of food consumed for no purpose. Sartre's alimentary figures generally evoke the relation of helplessness that subjects have with history and that reaches back to his lifelong study of Flaubert's novels. His characters also draw much from an exalted sense of moral lubricity, of viscous conscience that had been conventionalized in Marcel Carné's existential films, such as *Le jour se lève* (1937). The malaise evinced in prewar film and literature can only, because of the history of the name of the effect, be related to "noise," to interference in a communicational context, or to a prevailing *static* that occludes and impedes any passage of information.[8] Nausea, noise, and static: by describing failed passage and biological immobility in a figure of indigestion, the film refers to its own existential failure. The representation of a noir scenario extracts from history the sap and force that would redirect collective energies into changing it. Unlike Rossellini's war trilogy, in which disgust at the sight of inhuman events prompts a drive to change the world, *The Killers* offers a nauseous conscience of a past that determines an unsettling and unchanging state of things blocking all dialectics of change. When Burt Lancaster looks away and puts his palms to his upset stomach below the sign of the Tri-State Static, he makes us see an unconscious configuration scripted as an unyielding historical destiny.

The film, like its simultaneous representation of nausea, has no remedy for its effects. In fact, the gastric upset shown between the sign and the character signals one of the many actions that are identified as the unique mistake the protagonist made when he "did something wrong . . . once." In the thirteenth sequence the Swede protects Kitty (Ava Gardner) from the police by falsely assuming the guilt for a petty theft of jewelry. She is spotted by the camera that takes the point of view of the police lieutenant Lubinsky (Sam Levene). She is seen out of earshot, in the noise of a busy Italian-American restaurant—hence silently amidst more bad food and bad taste, in a sort of flashback in the very fabric of the present—clasping a brooch on her breast and then removing it with her left hand. Seconds later Lubinsky extracts the pin from a bowl containing a half-eaten portion of minestrone a waiter is taking to the kitchen on a platter of dirty dishes. Like a crab or a spider, the brooch is fished out of the slop and drips of broth. Existential undercurrents are clear: those who eat and drink are morally obese, like Max the killer, saturated with the cholesterol of crime. Those who fight the racketeers are svelte and have no time to eat. Reardon orders a beer and a sandwich at the Green Cat Club (in the thirty-third sequence), while Kitty takes a glass of milk. The food he munches is only a front to attract the fat killer and his henchman.

Food and drink evoke a world of illusion and depth that the visual order strives to flatten. The "bad" money of the gangsters' network is on the side of consumption, and is hence coded as "static," immobilizing, and morally suspect. Reardon, in contrast, is a reader and a writer. He sees the world's texture as it is, and he passes through the labyrinth of information he reads as he nears his goal. Thought, seen as gastric and mental stasis, is contrasted to passage, as total action. The binomial commands much of film noir, but in *The Killers* it shows how the medium itself is an inculpating agent. The film mirrors its own reflection. In the twenty-first sequence, which recounts the payroll heist from the Prentiss Hat Company in Hackensack, a crucial instance of disjoined writing marks the presence of the camera in the imbroglio. It begins in the insurance office, where Reardon's cynical boss occupies a place of authority behind the desk; like a recalcitrant son, the investigator enters to bargain for more time to solve the case. He brings a news clipping, dating from 1941, that describes the theft. The boss begins to read the column, voice *on*, before the scene of the crime dissolves into view from a crane shot taken over the outer barrier of the factory. The boss's voice continues to transcribe the text, now *off*, while the image track offers a silent representation that doubles the verbal description. Upon first view the spoken words seem to divert the spectator's eyes from what they designate on the image track; but the objects are so distant and confused with others that the two tracks unwind without any concession being made for visual or narrative synchrony. One of the robbers—Lancaster—is described as wearing a green scarf (but is seen on a field of black and white). The extreme depth of field allows the action to scatter as the camera, in a shot of over a minute's duration, tilts up to record the safebreaking operation behind the second-story window in the payroll office, and then down to the car that drives down the main thoroughfare in the factory and out, under, and beyond the gate that has the name of the company erected in open-work iron lettering. The eeriness of the sequence is enhanced by the exchange of mute gunfire whose noise is only reported in the verbal description, *off*, that the insurance boss reads aloud. Obviously close to the art of Joseph Mankiewicz's flashbacks, the robbery engages a silence that impugns any synchrony that might provide an illusion of the passage of historical or rational time. The viewer cannot—except for the oral report of the date of the larceny (1941), and its place (Hackensack, New Jersey)—tell when and where it took place. The violence is unmoored and floats adrift in the history surrounding the Second World War.

The writing that would provide veracity makes the sequence a mirrored illusion. In the tracking shot that arches over the gate (whose presence seems to function as a hidden intertitle confirming in space what the voice reports *off*) the letters spelling PRENTISS HAT COMPANY pass below the camera and disappear as the crane turns right to follow the workers entering the factory. But, as the camera exits the space along the track it entered, following the bandits' car (from which they exchange gunfire with the officers in pursuit), it catches the name of the company passing furtively over the windshield, in a *double reflection* by which the mirrored writing is turned right because of the script projected backward when seen behind the gate. The glass is a perfect frame for the reflection of the Prentiss Hat Company scrolled fugaciously from top to bottom. The windshield seems to be a moving screen within the movie. Just adjacent to the writing, the crane, the camera, and the operator are also visible. The spectator beholds the mode of production brought into the film where it is cued by a double mirroring of script.

It would be easy to conclude with a historical coda that *The Killers* is providing self-reflexivity for the New Wave to take from the general convention of noir, or that it is offering a quasi-Brechtian view of itself, as an illusion undone by the attention it brings to its system of fabrication. The shot seems paradoxically either too obvious or too subtle to allow for an aesthetic and historical interpretation of this type. The proximity of the multiply reverse writing to the inscription of the camera codes the "unconscious" of the film, by which the time and space of New Jersey in 1941, narrated in the flashback, are pulled across the war years into Universal Studios, in Los Angeles, in 1946. One historical sign is the identity and the reverse of the other. The moving writing reiterates the effects of the first shot of the film, which defined the retinal qualities of the narrative. As in *Objective, Burma!* the filmic agency seems to be the motor of history. The gap of almost six years that the flashback is filling is flattened by the windshield, the camera, and the play of graphics. The resulting existential stasis—of characters regressing to times past to fill a void in the present—seems to be what the film is producing and, no less, displaying as its very force of interpellation.

In the moving shot of the robbery, spectators are led to gaze in literal suspension of disbelief at the instant the mode of illusion passes before our eyes. The camera appears to be casting the viewers into a mute condition, into a "static state" that the patently disjoined discourse of image and word underscores. The gritty voice of the insurance company president is seen detached from the event even though simultaneous with it. The film insists time and again on breaking synchrony by having interpellations heard, *off*, bruising the conscience of a character *on*. When Burt Lancaster holds the x-like tire iron by his side in the first shots of the third sequence, a disembodied voice, *off* (only later identified with Colfax), calls out, "Hey, you!" The same speech recurs elsewhere.[9] Because it is detached from any synchronous origin on the image track, the speech can be seen aimed at a destination both everywhere and nowhere. "Hey, you!" is also directed toward the spectator, for it is *we* who are interpellated through the division of tracks; as the agents who make the law of the film by producing continuity where there is none, *we* are put in question for being the self-made victims of our illusions. The inner writing, when it becomes visible in the existential frame, undoes not only its own illusion but the very marks of interpellation coming from oblivion or from tradition, which we impose to make continuity of time, space, objects, and surfaces.

It can be added that the frequent interpellations in *The Killers* perhaps owe their effectiveness to the scenario, whose intricacies are seen, in turn, casting a spell on everyone who is tempted to "figure out" the enigma of the double-cross.[10] The writing seems to run along a line of rupture that it opens and closes along the image and sound tracks. For the same reason the paradox of a concomitant suture and gap also yields a temporality of the "absolute" present. When the past is pushed upon the screen (or windshield), it seals all gaps between viewing and narrative time. Once again, a rebus is fashioned by the two tracks in order to lend a sense of absolution and immediacy to the film. In the end credits that capture the boss and Reardon making amends after their stormy relation in which each bargained with the other for time off, the president ends by telling his employee that we are in 1946, the moment in which the representation shows no gap between fictive and real time.[11]

That the present tense is written on the two sides of a windshield is not surprising. The writing, the history, and the politics of film noir seem to have origin and finality in relations that characters have with screens that flatten an illusory depth of field they otherwise underscore. *High Sierra* (1941) blueprints the problem, but also offers contrasting articulation. In Raoul Walsh's film, all sense of past time is momentarily expunged from the drama. W. R. Burnett's novel (published by Alfred A. Knopf in 1940) includes flashbacks in which the ill-fated hero, Roy Earle, is cast as a victim of fate that reaches back to the worst years of the Depression. An allure of prehistorical and presexual innocence in former time sets the backdrop for an unnamed power to pardon the aging criminal from life imprisonment. He is set free to direct a holdup at a ritzy hotel in Palm Springs. The protagonist gains a last chance to change his ways once the job is done. Burnett's potboiler narrative uses veracious names and places to give the text a sense of immediacy. Where Hemingway quoted toponyms (which the narrator of *A Farewell to Arms* found more "real" than psychological abstraction or current events in history), Burnett allegorizes them: the "Last Chance" gas station is depicted in the novel exactly as it is in the film—as the signboard, as in Edward Hopper's paintings, of just another filling station. But the discursive mode cannot fail to invest fate and doom in the allegory of the title, where the film makes it so evident that fate is a form of writing. The film places the billboard next to the vista of the southern Sierras, diverting it from abstraction and toward a skein of figures that includes the postcard scene of the mountain, the title the credits had recently scrolled up over the peaks and into the sky. The allegory of destiny seems to be other than where it is in the novel, thus betraying Burnett's tale.

A shot that recurs in *High Sierra* catches Roy Earle (Humphrey Bogart) behind the steering wheel of a coupé assigned to him to perform the heist. He often looks forward, directly at the viewer, who in turn sees him in front of the back window and behind a small rearview mirror just above. Today the shot would be emblematic of "Bogart," of the "gangster" film, or of a cinematic "intensity" that has the criminal stare down the viewer in an expression of internalized anger and frustration. In the context that binds writing, history, and filmic transposition, the classic shot collapses depth and time onto a single surface. Earle looks ahead, at time and space approaching him; but we see them receding backward in the frame of the rear window. The imaginary depth ahead is canceled by the identical volume that pulls away in the back. The rearview mirror becomes a rebus (but not a symbol) of Blind Fate because, as Earle looks up at it—or at the police cars in hot pursuit behind in the final chase—*he is penetrated from the back.*

Space and time become an absolutely liminary surface identical to the movie screen on which the image is taken.

Articulation of the screen in *High Sierra* seems to prompt the figure exploited so adroitly at the outset of *The Killers*. Both films ground a sense of depthless space and time. The hero, immobilized in the moving vehicle, as the victim of the illusion of a moving vehicle (i.e., a metaphor),[12] typifies one of the many filmic icons of destiny in *High Sierra*. These generally associate issues of visibility, writing, and historical time. Throughout *High Sierra* fate is designated as an eye. It is perhaps identical to the spectator who engages in the voyeurism of seeing Earle trapped in his coupé, a sight affording the viewer's pleasure at once of not being seen looking at him. It can be summed up in the way circular and cyclopean forms offer ocular homologies to the figure of destiny: the eight ball, like a detached eye, that Earle encounters on the ground in the park; the round "Circle Auto Court" signboard that designates where Earle and Marie (Ida Lupino) spend their only night together; Algernon's (Willie Best's) parody of a black person's expression of astonishment, his widely opened eyes blazing round and white against the dark skin of his cheekbones. Or, in a tenor close to what has been studied in *Objective, Burma!* above, the sight of Earle looking at the buttocks of the stool pigeon who pets Pard, the mutt of Fate. The motel keeper literally bends over to moon a one-eyed view in the direction of Earle, who looks at him.

The most elaborate icon, a hidden sign in Walsh's oeuvre, inaugurates much of the narrative. Driving westward, Earle happens upon a slow-moving jalopy. He comes up from behind and passes it, but then encounters a jackrabbit that is crossing the road. He swerves to avoid collision with either the car or the rabbit. After the mishap, at the "Last Chance" station where he refuels, Earle meets the other car and notices the young Velma (Dorothy Malone), who will envelop him in the proto-noir love story. Yet the narrative reverts allusively to a primal scene, of enucleation, that marked the director's career since the time when he was filming *In Old Arizona* (1929) near Bryce Canyon. A jackrabbit, frightened by the headlights of Walsh's car driving from the location in the night, jumped and crashed into the windshield. It shattered and left slivers of glass in the director's right eye. The event, absent from both Burnett's novel and John Huston's adaptation, is tipped into the film in the mode of an enigma or perspectival object.[13] The scene scripts an optical obsession that comes forward in transfilmic terms. The event runs through other features that vary on the same trauma — *The Cock-eyed World, They Drive by Night, Gentleman Jim* — at the same time the figure fits in the overall narrative of fate.

Henceforth the film cannot fail to be seen ciphered with hidden characters.[14] Genre and myth seem to converge, but in personal terms that have the unsettling effect of theorizing the conditions of the film and visibility in general. If Walsh has inserted allusion to the trauma of the loss of sight into an event that constitutes the narrative, he is also defining the screen, like the windshield of a car, as a sort of paginal surface that receives impressions of writing on a single plane and that must be seen, both within and bereft of depth of field, from a monocular, "cockeyed" view. A personal event, like a signature, both explains and decodes the rhetoric that produces the unconscious dimension of the many films that *High Sierra* will soon inspire.

How writing is tantamount to the visual autograph of the rabbit is also seen in the opening sequence. The famous credits scroll the title and names up over the horizon of Mount Whitney—the high sierra of *High Sierra*—as the landscape dissolves from a view of the cloudy peak to valleys before, finally, the name of the director is imposed upon the craggy mountainscape. In a first moment the image doubles the title that is laid upon it; the movement of the leading characters, upward and into dissolution above, anticipates and resumes that of the protagonist at the film's denouement. Already the humans are preempted by the movement of scripture on a landscape. When the end credits return to the same image, the allegory is doubled over.[15] The scenario, which depends on the enigma of the expression "to crash out" (Earle wants to "crash out" of the shackles of destiny, but his friend Marie never understands what he means), has its iconic—and ironic—tension placed in the interface of the postcard view of the mountain and the rustic letters that designate the title of the film.

The rest of *High Sierra* runs along the same divide. Six dissolves in the first fifteen seconds of the narrative use montage to lead from the view of an unmarked capitol—the "law" of a state that follows the order of Washington, as in the first shot of *The Roaring Twenties* (1939)—to a close-up of a hand signing an official document that awards a pardon to a person inscribed as "Roy Earle." The dome of the building gives way to the portico and entablature on which is written STATE CAPITOL, which then dissolves to a door engraved with OFFICE OF THE GOVERNOR, under a series of net-like shadows that give a sense of confinement, before the camera holds on the backside of a figure—ostensively but never named as "the governor"—putting his signature to a document. Seen from the back, the figure characterizes *authority* in a way typical of most of Walsh's films. It is posed so that what is being written or spoken has no effective origin. The character is bent over and attending to business that comes from elsewhere. Because of the shot-cut, the editing, and the unspecified origin of voice or image, the edicts of the "law" originate from a space that only the viewer is led to assume as "authoritative."[16] The act of pardoning is broken from the authority when the camera cuts to a shot that moves into a close-up of the official paper that is implied to be on the desk.

The words of the pardon are no less gratuitous than the figure of the law. The name of the hero, Roy Earle, is adjacent to the majuscules spelling PARDON. The play of letters invokes a magical operation, an inner gloss of the relation of the proper name to the act of pardoning. For the dog of fate in the film, an-

nounced in the credits as "Pard" (played by the canine "Zero"), is embodied in
Pard-on. Zero, the figure of the eye in the same obsessive network, happens to be
an oculus of destiny. Always behind the eight ball or eyeball, Earle is joined to

Pard, and is thus unpardoned, or irrecuperably confined to Fate. The figures enchain the hero in a network resembling the webbing of ironlike forms cast over the document bearing Earle's name.

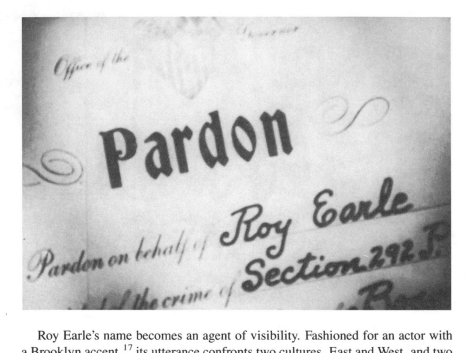

Roy Earle's name becomes an agent of visibility. Fashioned for an actor with a Brooklyn accent,[17] its utterance confronts two cultures, East and West, and two technologies, one based on analogy and instinct and the other on Cartesian logic. On the one hand, spoken in his own Brooklyn accent, "Earle" is "Oil," as in "Roy Oil," an urban streetwalker, while on the other he is an "Earl," a country gentleman. In either case he is "royal," or of a past aristocracy of criminals, a holdover who is very real by being early. Crucial is the identity of *oil* and *Earl* in order for the scansion to designate unbounded, precious energy. He fuels the narrative in name and deed, but also, in the political unconscious of the 1941 film, in view of European and Pacific conflicts, he reflects everything that the social world is lacking: the contemporary picture is one of an energy wasted, a force spent poorly in a self-enclosed spectacle that shuns current events, transcoded perhaps in the relation that Roy Earle keeps with a King Lear.

When being pursued, in one dissolve Earle is seen as a function of his fuel tank. Letters of the gauge are superimposed on his face, the gas and oil becoming synonymous with his character of energy. Its loss near the end of the film (when its 100 minutes, like the fuel tank, will be spent) is marked immediately (237, 164), just after he turns on the radio and hears a broadcasters's voice, "turning away from world news," to report on the whereabouts of the notorious "Roy Earle." The viewer is obliquely inculpated for following the fiction of Earle instead of contemporary reality. Allegory and history collide: the mythic and erotic dimension of Earle as Orpheus or as a world-historical personality is gauged against his uneasy relation — like the film itself — with the elements of history that the voice-off is tipping into the image. Yet in a broad manner, Earle becomes the agent that *writes* the film and becomes its agent of historical revelation. A figure of apocalypse, he marks the world by passing through it and, as he does so, he historicizes it. When, at the Circle Auto Court, he telephones his agent to obtain the money due to him, the camera places Earle behind a glass window frame next to a telephone (218, 154). Between the receiver and his mouth are the letters PUBLIC TEL. The rebus is designed to mask his speech in the narrative (which is known and hence redundant if spoken) but, in the scripture that is visible, the sight suggests that he will *tell* the *public* of itself and its bad faith. In the ill-fated trip that leads him up the mountainside, when he robs a drug store, Earle is seen displaying an emblem of the film's economy. In typical shot-reverse-shot editing that places a cash register between the pharmacist (Harry Hayden, also the waiter behind the counter in the first sequence of *The Killers*) and Earle, who faces him with his gun in his hand (271, 173), the letters CASH are seen on both sides of its glass panel. The two shots are an equation and an analysis of filmic exchange. The outlaw, Earle, is a function integral to the law, and the median term, or money, is in turn a means or a mediation in a spectatorial transaction.[18] Money, like writing, is a shifter that defines the very system of illusion before the spectator's eyes. One pays for the delight or fear of the other, just as a viewer pays a given sum to be entertained by an eros and a violence that cannot be practiced except in the conditions of illusion.

The wipe-dissolves that punctuate the episodes mix the arrested form of letters with the movement of cars and bodies. Just as Earle is a function of an arrow on a fuel gauge between E and F, so are other characters insinuated into a writing that comes from nowhere — the shapes of the media of everyday life — to determine their fate. In a narrative dissolve that moves from Marie's head twisting in close-up to the signboard of the *bus stop* from which she will leave to meet Earle in Los Angeles (not elaborated in the script, but located by shot 228, 162), her head scans the letters: B gives way to U, U to S, S to T, T to O, and O to P. In the fraction of an instant an allegory of scripture emerges before the sign is fixed as a narrative item in the scenario. The two characters are ready to crash into freedom: Be US on TOP, on the "top of the world." But they are caught in a mechanism of fate, and really are in a B U S (S) T. And the Depression marks the atmosphere, in which throngs are unemployed in a world theater that places America in a marginal position, the secret, silent voice of history. Stasis can only be titled with either movies or war or both. Yet the hidden script impels the characters and viewers to Be U.S. (on) T O P of international affairs where they are not. All of a sudden the film is shaken out of its torpor as entertainment and now scripts its multifarious ambivalences in the wink of an eye.

If this capital dissolve of *High Sierra* can be said to write the Second World War into an already established genre of heroes on the run (dating to *You Only*

Live Once, 1937), it tells how the historical moment excluded from the illusion nonetheless pervades. In *The Killers* the war was the ineffable vanishing point between image and writing. Here the same holds true, except that finality is *always* yet to come but, like the Depression and the years 1914–18, has already been experienced. An apocalypse is signaled as an absence both past and coming, like Armageddon, with Roy Earle. For this purpose *High Sierra* seems to use the finale and end credits to repress and reveal a scriptural relation to history. The film seems to advise viewers duplicitously about how to live, doing so at the conclusion by combining elements of myth, ocularity, self-reflexivity, and feminism. After a Vorkapich montage sequence overlays a map onto the figures of the police barking into telephones and troopers straddling their motorcycles (the sequence replacing the episode 251B–252, 168–70)—the place-names "Independence," "Alone," and so on functioning like the toponyms on the maps of *Objective, Burma!*—a chase follows Earle up the side of Mount Whitney. One shot verbally writes the figure of the film: perched at the edge of a hairpin turn, the camera watches the speck of the coupé below, in the distance, driving up the slope, approaching the camera, before a pan moves left, registering the car skidding around the sharp bend, then accelerating up the next slope. In the invisible style the camera would cut to the police in pursuit, but in the finished version a straight cut is not used. The camera tilts down to where it had begun its career, catches the dusty trail of a motorcade of cars and cycles blaring their sirens into

the silence of the landscape, in a sort of cinematic Doppler effect that evokes the aural depth of the scene,[19] and follows the same course upward to the pivot and then beyond along the slope. In a breath the camera has described a 720-degree panoramic, drawing the O of the point about which it turns, therefore writing the fate of the character in respect to the ocular shape it describes in its career.

The enclosing movement coincides, of course, with the ending that stages a rupture of voice and image. A newscaster is summoned to the site to relay radio reports of what is being seen ("Hot dogs and peanuts are being sold," relates the script, 273, 174, not in Walsh's version). A limelight is cast on the mountain to make the face of Mount Whitney a Broadway stage. The lack of synchrony between the description uttered and the silence of the decor outlines the protean figure of the law. The name of the director appears to be engraved into the silence of the natural decor, as the ultimate mediation between man and nature, since the memory of the signature of *Raoul Walsh* on the rocks of the credits returns to align the director—the hidden law—with the mute decor.

For this reason the film no doubt appeals to the myth of Orpheus and Eurydice to heighten the arbitrary beauty of nature that humiliates "man" who desecrates the world. Earle is murdered when, during his ascent, he turns his back. He is penetrated from behind, betrayed not by his love but by Pard. In the murder sequence (292, 180), shot in a fashion quite different from the script (which puts his body in the reticle of the gunsight), he becomes a vanishing point in the

skewed perspective. A sniper armed with a telescopic rifle shoots the speck from above, just as it moves onto a ledge to catch sight of the barking dog that runs up from below. Earle is shot in the back in an ocular scenario that celebrates the technical paraphernalia at the hands of the police.

Rejecting a bargain to be set ''free'' at the cost of betraying him, Marie had refused to encourage him to turn back. Up to this point the film has aligned writing with the law. An officer has decided to use the high-powered rifle to ambush the hero but has really prepared a media event around the stratagem. When the sheriff begs for her collaboration, Marie is seated under a promontory and crouches, pressed on all sides by the police, portrayed as gun-toting thugs whose adipose genitals press into her face (289, 178). Law, a phallic privilege, is displaced when the twist of the Orphic myth becomes evident. Pard betrays, but Marie does not. Effectively the female is on the side of pathos, while the technocratic world is marked as sadistic and masculine. The final shots, in which Marie cries over Earle's dead body, underscore the relation that binocular vision holds with authority: blinded, and in fear and terror, she walks away from the scene just as a detached hand—the law or authority as it had also been represented in *M* and *La bête humaine*—enters the frame and comes to rest on her left shoulder. The hand locates her in an otherwise indistinct space (not elaborated in the script, 180ff.). The film literally ''crashes out'' when the woman implies that stereoscopic vision belongs to the scientific world. A feminine optic that cre-

atively confuses objects and forms in space is glimpsed where Marie's face finally fills the screen in order to have the narrative end with a totalizing feel or
texture. Her face actualizes what the oblique reference to enucleation had indicated earlier, to the effect that a monocular or one-eyed view of the world de-
differentiates depth and surface or image and writing. In doing so, it sees the
world *all over,* in continuous flow of forms but not according to Cartesian categories that subjugate one figure in space at the expense of another. Laws of spatial proportion and sexual difference seem to be dissolved at the endpoint in *High
Sierra.*

Seen historically, the film can arguably be situated on the cusp between the
end of the gangster film and the beginning of noir. Some of its interiors are
bathed in backlit chiaroscuro that anticipates *Double Indemnity* and *The Killers.*
Its prevailing structure of doubles, of a bad "good" woman and a good "bad"
reciprocal, set within a mythic plot, seems to share much with the typology. But
the awesome landscape of Mount Whitney in 1941 behind the Orphic finale does
not seem to concur with noir conventions. Even though the dominant films use
the outdoors to offset dark interiors,[20] the touristic reality of the Sierras would
seem to include a time too specific for a more brooding ambience of war and
stasis. What, then, happens to the protoconventional film when seen through the
lens of writing and the auteur? If *High Sierra* is shot at the beginning of noir, it
might be worthwhile to look at another film of the same stamp, *White Heat*
(1949), also by Walsh, a companion piece that stands at the very end of the convention.

White Heat tells the story of a psychopath, Cody Jarrett (James Cagney), who stages a daring train robbery at the exit of a tunnel in the California mountains. The leader kills the engineer but is hampered by the accident—a blast of steam from the boiler of the locomotive—that burns a rookie criminal in the gang. After the group takes refuge in the hills, Jarrett and his mother decide to leave the bandaged victim to die in the cold. The group divides, Jarrett, his wife, and mother going in one direction and Big Ed (Steve Cochran) and lesser members of the gang in another. After the police learn of Cody's whereabouts by molding a death mask from the frozen body left behind, the killer is pursued through Los Angeles. He escapes from a drive-in movie, later pleads guilty to a charge of theft in the Midwest, and serves a term in prison. A stool pigeon named Fallon, alias Vic Pardo, is sent to befriend and follow him. Pardo saves Jarrett from being murdered and literally plays the role of his mother. Meanwhile, Big Ed murders Jarrett's mother and takes up with his wife. Jarrett escapes from the prison, settles accounts with Big Ed, and engineers the robbery of a payroll office at a refinery. He is tricked by Pardo. Jarrett flees to the top of a Hortonsphere where he reigns alone before blasting the globe (and, by implication, the world) to smithereens.

The connections between *High Sierra* and *White Heat* are obvious: both films place an ambiguous force of evil at their center; cast "good" and "bad" women in orbit around it; engage multiple fraternal rivalries; oppose an instinctual, empirical, and poetic logic of the villain to the alphabetic, technical reason of the police; contrast the breathtaking view of a nature devoid of man to an urban world reeking of his dirty effects; end with a chase up respective "hillsides," one the Sierras and the other a Hortonsphere at the gasoline refinery near Manhattan Beach in southwest Los Angeles; and have the central figure caught or killed in the sights of a telescopic rifle.

But a stronger tie can be seen in the hieroglyphics binding the two films that effectively show how a collective technique of film is virtually underwritten by filmic icons or signature-effects. These traits articulate an unconscious discussion, at odds with the narrative, that produces ambivalence as well as a more problematic shape of ideology. These are evinced when *High Sierra* is compared to *White Heat,* and where the convention of the inner writing of noir, as seen in *The Killers,* is held in view. We know that Roy Earle, the sign of energy, is Orpheus tricked by a dog of destiny named Pard. He moves helplessly against the fixity of the pardon on which his name is inscribed. In *White Heat,* the enemy of the psychopathic killer-hero, Cody Jarrett (Edmund O'Brien), is named Vic Pardo. He is a double-crossing informer whose real (fake) name is "Hank Fallon." In *White Heat* Pardo betrays Jarrett by attaching himself, like a dog, a brother or a male lover (even, figuratively, like the magnetic device he sticks to the axle of the truck that leads Cody to his demise) to Jarrett while he is in prison.[21]

At one moment, after Pardo has gained the intimacy of Jarrett in prison and in the course of the getaway, Vic meets the head of the laundering operation in which the gang is engaged. The "hidden" boss, nicknamed "the Trader" (Fred Clark), visits the gang in the mountains. Sporting the gear of a trout fisherman on vacation, he encounters Vic, who then asks if him if he enjoys fishing, and what species he prefers to catch. The scenario and final version read as follows:

296. INT. LODGE HOUSE   CODY AND TRADER

VIC: What're ya after, mister?

TRADER: Bass.

VIC *(slams door shut)*: Get his gun, Cody! He's a phony!

TRADER: *I beg your pardon.*

VIC: This is trout country. There ain't bass for a hundred miles. (*Trader looks to Cody, who chuckles heartily.*) What's so funny?

CODY: Ya're right on your toes, kid. (196, 165, stress added)

At the moment Vic tells Cody that the Trader is a phony (or a *phonè*), he is identified doubly by the Trader—a name betraying itself—in his proper name in common expression. The traitor, when *seen* written, unwittingly identifies the doubly fake. The trader begs Vic's *pardon*, that is, his name as it percolated from *High Sierra*, to Pard, to Pardo, the traitor of *White Heat*. The name acquires a graphic resonance by being placed between the plot and the overall unification of forces at play.

The exchange between the Trader and Vic is set to prepare the moment of hubris. When Jarrett discovers that Pardo has been a double agent (that is, in the theological field of the film, that Fallon has been an actor, a filmmaker, or a demonic agent of mimicry), Pardo aims a gun at Jarrett and his two henchmen. Bo Creel (Ian MacDonald), whose name arches back to the many allusions to fishing and the arts of baiting that the film uses everywhere, barks, "I tell ya he's a copper! He's a T-man. His name's Fallon" (346, 186).

The crucially iconic moment of revelation is detailed in the script:

348. FULL SHOT

Cody merely stares, his mind momentarily refusing to assimilate the actuality of the betrayal. His eyes are glassy. The rest of the gang, gaping in consternation, look to Cody for orders. Then Cody starts to laugh, softly at first but becoming a hysterical outburst.

CODY (*through laughter*): A T-man . . . How d'ya like that, boys? . . . A T-man . . . His name's Fallon . . . And we bought it . . . *I* bought it . . . Treated him like my kid brother . . . They must be waitin' to pin a medal on him . . . (*Cannot stop laughing.*) (187)

In the filmed version Cody does not laugh in a "hysterical outburst" but snickers with bestial lucidity. The dupery that turned fraternal and erotic relations into a commodity has scriptural innuendo: *Fallon* is the proper name that Jarret *fell for.* The name manifests a nuclear residue, or *fallout,* that comes with the technology he champions. *Pard* and *Pardon* are transmuted from canine Fate into atomic catastrophe. Given the feminist resonance at the end of *High Sierra,* a moment that reveals Fallon also unveils *phallon,* the phallus (or fall-us) of the law that is associated with prostheses of murder — including the telescopic rifle he will aim at Jarrett, the bulging genitals of the police, thick leather belts, pistols, and handcuffs — everything that turns eros into sadism or that substitutes violence and murder for exchange.

Archaic and conventionalized — or technological — sensibilities of language are contrasted. Cody twice calls Pardo a "T-man" while laughing over his tragic flaw as he bides time enough to murder him. The moment is linked to the first sequence of the film, which took up analogies of proper names and letters. In the twenty-fourth shot, which shows Cody aiming his gun at the engineer of the mail train the gang is robbing, an explosion is heard *off.* Zuckie (Ford Rainey), an inexperienced crook, speaks.

25. MED. IN ENGINE CAB

Cody's gun still menaces engine crew. Shots are heard.

ZUCKIE: Sounds bad, Cody.

The exchange of looks between fireman and engineer at the name is not lost on Cody, who snarls at Zuckie.

CODY: Why don't ya give'em my address, too?

Here, as elsewhere, the exchange must be heard and seen as a hieroglyph. The narrative element of Zuckie's speech refers to the explosion, but graphically, "Sounds bad, Cody," is also "Cody sounds bad," that is, exactly what the image track develops within the narrative. All of a sudden the visual aspect of the memory of names inflects the filmic writing with the effect of concatenating associations that motivate proper names and common interests. Cody happens to be *cold*, a reflection of the alphabetical configuration of his name:

25B. MED. IN ENGINE CAB

ENGINEER: You won't get away with it, Cody.

CODY: Cody, eh? (*To Zuckie.*) Go get the car started. (*Coldly, to engineer.*) You got a good memory for names. Too good. (*He cocks his .45 as Zuckie starts to descend.*)

26. CLOSE FIREMAN

his face fixed with horror. Cody's gun explodes off-screen, sending death into the body of the engineer. As he crumples, his arm trails lifelessly, without strength, along the fireman's sleeve, drops from sight. The fireman stares down, then back at Cody. In Cody's face he sees mirrored his own death, *and is afraid. (62, stress added)*

The scenario often makes the sight and sound congeal in the hero's name, and it scripts, almost unconsciously, the analogical and anagrammatical relation that holds between *Cody*, death, and *cold*-bloodedness.[22] Cody kills whoever "names" him, and in doing so, he draws the viewer's eye to what constitutes the law's acts of interpellation. He thus becomes, like Roy Earle, the embodiment of law. Cody kills Zuckie by a quirk of fate. His murder of the engineer (Murray Leonard) precipitates that of the partner who made the mistake of naming him. Jarrett *stops* or "unwrites" those who assign him a social space, but also draws attention to the archaic tactility of the letters that seem to determine his character.[23]

As an inversion of the T-man, Cody is the D-man, or Code-D, the Code of *D*eath, the letter that supplants the police when they use three cars, A, B, and C, in pursuit of his mother in Los Angeles (shots 65–92). Evans (John Archer) barks, "We'll use the ABC method. I'm B" (65, 79). The cops coordinate three unmarked cars until they reach the place — and the letter — that follows C: "Come in A. Any trace? (A harsh crackling.) Come in C. Come in C. (Crackling persists.)" (92, 82), when Evans's driver responds over the radio, "D[ea]d spot, Phil" (92, 82). The reiteration, like that of "Baker one, Baker two," in *Objective, Burma!* makes voice visible, since "Come in C" is also *come ('n') see,* or

come and see, that leads to a blind spot, an ocular absence that marks both Cody's whereabouts and his essence.[24]

If Cody is D, the cipher of Death, as the description of shot 26 (62) implies, he is part of an alphabet of forces linked to the credits and all other pieces of writing seen all over frame. Here the unconscious of the film makes image and language indifferent and, hence, no less violent than the narrative. The credits place a script of the majuscules of the film's title in large, squat letters that seem to wilt under the heat of their own form. They are rebus-characters that concretize their own referent[25] and are seen on the screen when, from a vanishing point in a dark recess, a small ball of light grows larger and is ascertained to be a locomotive chugging out of a tunnel. The head lamp moves toward the majuscule O of the name of Virginia MAYO adjacent to that of James Cagney. The phallic drive of the train approaches the name, as if seeking to penetrate the *O* of Mayo. When it almost touches the circle, the locomotive thrusts out of the tunnel, blasts a jet of steam upward, and suddenly WHITE HEAT replaces the names of the two leads. An act of visibility is scripted into the erotic relation of the image of the train moving toward the scripture with which it is about to fornicate, but which is exploded at the instant of contact.

The scene takes place by a great cliffside to the left of the tunnel. The rocks have a strangely humanoid appearance and acquire the look of a dummy-sculpture, reminiscent of the group of bandaged heads of *Manpower,* that doubles the spectator's view of the erotic play of the train and Mayo's name. The figure on

the left appears both dead and alive, like a sleeping spectator, looking at the event. Its aspect poses the relation of the film being seen in the film, and of the scripture of the film being read as the credits are scrolled. The figure of the cliff-side as spectator suggests that there is present a blind, diseased, or mutilated victim of a nuclear holocaust, its face reminiscent of the horrible appearances of the victims of the bombings of Nagasaki and Hiroshima. The association is confirmed when the locomotive, emerging from the tunnel, spouts a blast of steam that mushrooms upward in the manner of an atomic explosion. All of a sudden, before the narrative is begun, a *nuclear* genre begins to inflect both the gangster film and noir. The unclear face of the landscape on the left, almost matching the viewer's position, also resembles Zuckie when his head is wrapped in gauze after being brutally burned and left to die in the California mountains. Zuckie relays the uncanny figure of death back to its initial inscription in the credits, just as, too, in the robbery sequence the train rolls out of the tunnel (19, 60) over which Cody is perched before he jumps down onto the tender. For an instant Cody's body blends in the space of the mushroom cloud, identifies him with the force of nuclear power.

The relation of the credits to the background spells out the broader tensions and violence of the film. The mushroom blast sets into *abyme* the conflagration of the Hortonspheres, implied to burn Hollywood and the world in the end credits (out of whose flames, nonetheless, as if it were made of asbestos, zooms the Warner Brothers emblem). The monocularity of the signature is obvious in the relations of the white dot to Virginia Mayo's O. The camera, however, also articulates an unconscious webbing of transfilmic forms. When it pans right, from the initial scene of the tunnel, to frame into an extreme long shot of the rocky California hillside descending to the fertile valley below, the director's name dissolves in and out of the landscape. The land is bright, rocky, and of an absolute, almost Mediterranean texture, but hardly the "mountainous terrain, bleak, ominous" (1, 57) the script describes. For a moment, before the camera continues its pan to a sign, "California State Line," a division that inaugurates the narrative, the name of Raoul Walsh *is* the landscape. Name and decor prompt recall of the scenes of *High Sierra* and *Colorado Territory,* and become synonymous with the kind of nature into which Earle or Wes McQueen (Joel McCrea) had tried to escape. Walsh in fact becomes the vanishing point of the narrative, and the presence of his name is coded across other ciphers — such as the radio report that reiterates on the sound track the robbery just seen. A man's mouth presses against a microphone in a broadcasting booth:

32. INT. BROADCASTING BOOTH CLOSE ON ANNOUNCER DAY

RADIO ANNOUNCER (*into microphone*): A week has passed since bandits jumped a
    mail train coming out of the High Sierra tunnel and fled with three hundred
    thousand dollars in federal currency, leaving four dead. Treasury authori-
    ties now believe. . . . (63–64)

Reference to the earlier film of 1941 is clear, but in view of contemporary history in which *White Heat* is placed, *High Sierra* is now, in the freezing mountainscape, transformed into an icy era, a sign of a cold war that presages total annihilation.

The announcer's tale would be innocuous if the memory of Bogart were not clear, and if the slight drift on the sound track had not confused the "mail" or "male" train with the visible residue of the female lead, with the "mayo" train. The spectator hears both articulations, such that the erotic drive of the mail train is both male and, as "mayo," female. The oral dissolve overlays connotations that are ultimately linked to the association of Earle with oil or energy both potentiated and wasted. Sexuality is at best androgynous or knows little distinction between male and female. When Cody suffers his first migraine headache in the cold mountain cabin, he exits into an adjoining room where Ma follows to caress him — "she clutches his hand tightly, rubs his back, croons over him — the tigress suddenly becomes gentle with her cub" (42, 68); he takes a shot of whiskey she pours for him, and she remarks in tendering the glass, "Top of the world, son" (44, 69). Analogy of libido and energy gathered from the film of 1941 now grows more complicated: Cody is brought back to life at once by an oedipal essence (his mother's caresses), by fuel or potable gasoline (whiskey), and by iconic actions that associate him with serials and cartoons, such as Popeye and Superman (Cody having gone to a chamber to change his clothes or to eat mannalike spinach and exit brimming with force). Ma's words prepare his famous line at the moment Cody launches a worldwide cataclysm ("Top of the world!" 390, 197),[26] and they also link the writings of the film to a substructure that runs from Walsh's oeuvre through the ideology of the Hollywood industry.

Two episodes are key and respond almost subliminally to the visible articulations. One is a transition from the night sequence in the drive-in theater, where the gang has taken sanctuary to watch another Warner Brothers film (which, at the inquest in Evans's office seconds later, Ma identifies as [Delmer Daves's] *Task Force* [115, 90], but which is in reality a set of stock Pacific battle footage from the Second World War, an unconscious past that arches to the bombing of Japan). In the transition from the space of the theater to the office, a stock shot locates a Los Angeles boulevard busy with traffic. Above and to the left of center frame, a sign on a building advertises *Seagram's 7*. The allusion to blended whiskey falls into the shot for the effect of the city, but as an icon of film writing, it also locates the motif of energy between the jigger that Ma administered to Cody, the gasoline propelling the cars below, the motif of nuclear force, and the very power of cinema itself. Even the most inconspicuous views of the contemporary world are marked with a hidden but pervasively obvious writing. Evidence of Cody's identity is everywhere, like nature itself, scripted into every sign.

The dynamics of the inscription become obvious in two similar stock shots that frame the sequence detailing Evans's discovery of the identity of Zuckie, the crook who was left to freeze in the icy Sierras. A sequence in the morgue has just detailed Zuckie's effects (54, 74–75) A dissolve leads into Evans's office (55, 75) that shows the skyscrapers of downtown Los Angeles, between which an American flag is seen waving in the wind. Emphatic music connotes that the camera has left the world of death in the morgue and is now moving into the triumphant order of life, the law, and American ideals. In the scenario, the first shot is close on "Willie Rolph, a weasellike informer" (Milton Parsons, 75), and then is supposed to pull back onto Evans's desk and keep in view a portrait of President Truman on the wall behind. It was removed in the final version in favor, no doubt, of the flag in the dissolve, so as to dissociate Warner Brothers from an unpopular leader, but retain patriotic ideology required for the scene. In the film version, the shot carefully includes the sight of Zuckie's death mask. When photographs arrive and are studied, revealing that identical "dust particles" prove the identity of the face of the mask to be one of a member of the Jarrett gang, Evans is seen reading aloud what he sees on the teletype machine before he returns to the sculpture, takes it up in his hands, and shakes it:

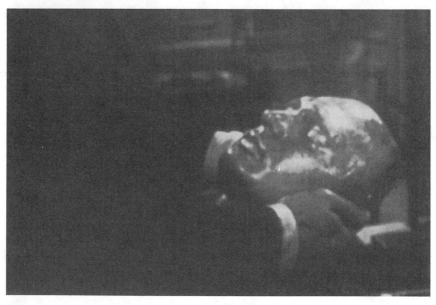

57. BACK TO SCENE

Evans returns photos to Ernie with grim satisfaction.

EVANS: Looks like we're in business. (*Teletype starts. Evans moves to it eagerly, reads heading.*) From Washington . . . (*slowly.*) Have — no — fingerprint — record — dead — man . . . (*Teletype pauses; glumly.*) That's one I never expected. Dead man. Dead end. (*Teletype resumes; reads slowly but with mounting excitement.*) But — prints — on — cellophane — of — cigarette — package — belong — Giovanni — Cotton — Valetti — known — member — Jarrett — gang . . . (*Picks up Zuckie's death mask.*) I thought you were never going to talk . . .

DISSOLVE TO

58. EXT. AUTO COURT SIGN   **NIGHT**

reading: Milbanke Motels — All Over Los Angeles. Pan down as a dark coupé drives in entrance, skirts around the back line of auto courts, stops. (76–77)

The remark that accompanies the close-up of Evans's hands shaking the mask leads into a dissolve of the same decor of downtown Los Angeles that had opened the sequence. Closure is obtained, but a problematic sign of indication emerges: when Evans sighs, with relief, "I thought you were never going to talk," *you* refers (a) to the technology of the teletype machine that has just spoken robotically in its clickety-click; (b) to the mask itself, that is, a voice of silence almost doubling the machine; or, crucially, (c) to the landscape in the dissolve, equivocating on America itself, in other words, the collectivity of viewers that the filmic "Law" and the studio are shaking into submission. The violence of the act directed against the spectator is confirmed by the fact that the opening dissolve, which displayed the American flag fluttering in the wind, is not identical to the closing dissolve, which substitutes a still photograph — or a dummy view — of the same scene with a flag *not* waving in the breeze. Evans agitates not only the immobile death mask but also, in the dissolve, the now-dead icon of America that had been welcomed at the beginning so triumphally with movement and Max Steiner's musical score. Evans imposes a guilt and then makes the public own up to it in silence; an unconscious is produced in the emission of stenographic blurbs of meaning coming from nowhere. He shakes a "truth" out of an American image by his violence enacted against its icons. The dissolve further aligns the spectator with the dumb shape of the death mask by analogy with the mutilated figure in the credits peering at the moving train. The pristine aspect of the burned face contrasts the leperlike figure of the imaginary viewer on the landscape who stages a viewing of the film.

A system of inculpation is set in place through an overlay of still and moving forms. A scene of terror is inscribed along the edges of the narrative. The system prevails in other written shards, such as the many visual allusions to gasoline and steam, two ciphers of "old" and "new" forms of energy; the motif in the final robbery of the Trojan Horse as a cistern-truck, on whose exterior is marked, "Capacity: 10,000 GALS, referring not just to a finite quantity but also to 10,000 women who are equated with fuel; the Hortonsphere that resembles at once an eye and a globe on which the delirious hero is perched when he explodes in apotheosis; the many shots that enucleate Cagney—the shadow of a chain cast over his right eye in the prison cell 206, (126–28)—in order to liken him to a one-eyed monster whose instinctual savvy is owed to his ability to see the world creatively, as Raoul Walsh with his proto-Hathaway eye patch, without depth or illusion.[27]

Most important, the "secret" forms that are displaced into the film share much with the texture of the noir tradition and reach back to filmic codes of the 1930s in Europe and America. The scriptural discourse of *White Heat* appears fraught with fear, pleasure, and paranoia. The not so despicable hero effectively crosses the threshold of an oedipal drama upon the death of "Ma," and he accedes to a lucidity that likens his character to that of a writer, an agon and a trickster, like "Roy Earle," who in name and deed decodes the devious forces about him. Before his eyes the law is a gang of technocratic double-crossers, mimetic spies, and spineless killers, blessed and sanctified by the American flag. Cagney's cyclopean view shares an affinity with Renoir's instinctual feel for nature, and it is finally blinded in pyrotechnical spectacle. Its inner speech, subversive of the order it celebrates, does not allow *White Heat* to vary quite exactly on the tradition begun in part with *High Sierra* and developed through *The Killers*. It remains an auteur's film that celebrates a surface of characters that work through and across their narration, in ways that require the spectator to read a hieroglyph of space, of letters, of movement, and of silence.

White Heat is said to owe much to Cagney's interpretation of the central figure. At the same time, however, in the context of the writing of film that has been studied between the screenplay and the finished version, Jarrett functions as a *decoder* of the patent ideologies of American film. He performs a role similar to the writing in the field of the image or in the montage: he remarks where the world about him is lying, or where its illusions are produced. The lucidity of his vision, like the hieroglyph fashioned from the movement of writing and the film, sums up the forces of film noir that evoke a world of fate inscribed implacably on all human activity. It also explodes the infinite closure of noir by orienting the convention toward nuclear fear that follows in the wake of the Second World War. The same apocalypse is manifested in the scriptural effects of *White Heat* that share much with New Wave cinema in the decade that follows. Detailed study of these investigations goes beyond the scope of this essay. At this point it may be time to leave *White Heat* at the end of the classical tradition taken up in the preceding chapters and sketch the lines of a tentative conclusion.

Epilogue

This study began with *Boudu sauvé des eaux* (1932), in which the central character was seen as an instrument inaugurating a movement of film writing. An antagonist, Boudu passes through a world of books, lithographs, and tableaux for which he has little concern. He can read nothing more than "fat letters" *(grosses lettres),* but his good fate is sealed when, by chance, he asks a pedestrian on the quay Conti how to decipher the numerals 3—4—6 on the lottery ticket left in the waistcoat Lestingois bequeathed to him. The gentleman asks the tramp if the stub belongs to him and, if it does, then he has won the lottery, for the winning number, 346, had just been heralded, *off*, in the street, by a cyclist. Letter, image, and sound converge: a winner, Boudu can give the money away, dispense with his bourgeois trappings and its system of obligation and reciprocity, and finally return to the wilds.

It was argued that Boudu is thus a hermeneute, a trickster, or a sort of daimonic figure, a modern Panurge, who lives on the margins of culture, but who also mediates its various modes of exchange. In this sense he cuts a path between speech and writing, sight and sound, and letter and image. He moves indiscriminately from one to the other, and in his artful passage he traces and reveals the gaps that produce illusions of meaning in cinema. Like Chaplin, who defines space and identity in *The Pilgrim* by moving endlessly along the edge of one territory and another, Boudu crosses through the world of nineteenth-century letters—Balzac, Hugo, Baudelaire, and Flaubert—that the film represents; as an icon of the medium of cinema, he articulates its traits through his inscription of passage. He leaves in his tracks something of a film hieroglyph.

In the archaic role he performs, Boudu is a film writer of sorts, a *caméra-stylo* within his own film. He partakes of a tradition that links the act and art of movement with writing, that conceives of errancy and venture as a scriptural activity. He need not know how to read or write because his movement writes what we read. He thus is an avatar of the vagabond narrator of Montaigne's *Essais*— especially "Vanity (III, 9)"—who finds his style in the rapport of writing and the craft of displacement. "Mon style et mon esprit vont vagabondant de mesmes [my mind and my wit go errantly together]," he said, leaving his reader to ponder his tracks of printed words. Like Montaigne's demon, Boudu is a mystic, a cipher in whose trace the spectator finds the living matter of his life. The mystic writer is one who moves from the past into the present along a path his or her body frays in passage, and whose signs become the link between the time of life, here and now, and time immemorial, in memory or oblivion. A version of the wandering Jew, of Freud, of Marguerite Duras, and a host of other literary names, Boudu marks the essence of mystical writing crucial for the expansively infinite imagination concretized in film. and like any mystic worth his salt, he both seduces and frightens. He is the *salê,* the dirty idiot, the passerby and passenger, who wanders through kitchens, has an unutterable name, and speaks less than he makes others speak and discover themselves.[1]

The figures in all of the films studied in the preceding chapters share common concerns with the passage of writing. Each articulates its form and its limits both through their filmic acts of writing and their inscriptive agencies that transform the world through which they move. Boudu, we have seen, initiates the model for Renoir's creatures of passage. Like Legrand, Lantier, Jurieu, Toni, Lange, Boëldieu, or other famous characters who find themselves caught in and expelled from the film that portrays them, Boudu defines the optical limits of his social and historical condition when he floats off and turns into a reed, a sylvan stylus growing by a bridge from which he could have jumped to his death. In *Scarlet Street,* Christopher Cross—whose name scripts his fate—also walks through the film that imprisons him for all time. He is reincarnated in *Manpower,* as a man, like Lantier of *La bête humaine,* who must die. His relation to the title of the film cues the special fragility and delicacy of his presence in the culture he defines through his difference. And the fabled "Captain Nelson" of *Objective, Burma!* is also a writer who traces the lines of the map that the film unfolds between fable and history. He is present in the space that is lost in the failed connection of the sky with the earth or of one of the squadrons with the other. "Baker One, Baker One, can you *read* me?" exhorts a troop into his walkie-talkie: "Baker One, Baker One, can you read me? Please come in, Baker One, this is Baker Two." Flynn sees and reads a way through the nameless forest that puts them "on top of the world," on a hill in which they bury themselves in a ceremonial ritual that combines fox-hole digging with the rite of self-inhumation. His men burrow into unknown worlds where the partisans of the Po were dropped at the end of *Paisan.*

Where they find their rebirth at the world's nadir, Roy Earle finds his demise at the other end, not far from where Cody Jarrett is reborn at a zenith on a California Hortonsphere. The figures are all inscribed into the world left vacant by the bombing of Jahweh or a holocaust. Chris Cross and Hank McHenry return and are redeemed in a new life; Nelson "wires" the mystical circuitry that assures the passage of forms through and across a body of films in ways so graphic that the auteur Raoul Walsh who directed them also becomes an instrument of writing.

The writers of the films studied here are therefore their very *characters,* but characters apprehended in the most literal sense of the term. They define the space of their narrative by climbing to its upper reaches, like McHenry. Or they are rolling full-tilt across it, like Lantier. They may parachute into its folds, like Merrill's Marauders, or lose themselves in its maze, like the melancholy artist in Greenwich Village. They can be severed from within it in the fashion of the decapitated heroes of *Paisan.* Or they can be hapless and silent victims of its writing, like the dumb Swede of *The Killers* or the noble badman Roy Earle of *High Sierra.* In a common way, the characters of all the films we have studied are objects of perspective, ciphers of visibility that afford collective glimpses of passage.

All of them seem to share much with one of their recent reincarnations, another wanderer, a young woman named Mona Bergeron, the itinerant tramp, an agon, a new Boudu at the crux of Agnès Varda's *Sans toit ni loi* (*Vagabond,* 1984). In that film Mona Bergeron (Sandrine Bonnaire) seems to be something of a mystic: she is a bum, she is irrational, whimsical, she is filthy, and she stinks. *Elle a les mains sales:* she has dirty hands, but none of the Sartrian conviction of commitment that goes with the close-ups of her greasy fingers. She hitchhikes, catches rides, holes up in a trailer, squats in a flat, and lounges in a railway station. She meets a human comedy of individual types, is oblivious to all of them because, being no doubt always hungry, she has her mind in the kitchen. She is another *salê.* In her passage she changes the lives of everyone who meets her. Numerous reviews of the film have shown convincingly that Varda's film reenacts *Citizen Kane:* like Kane's, her body is found before an inquest is launched.[2] The film reconstructs a past filtered through the quasi-documentary look of reports and interviews that lead into flashbacks that, in sum, reconstitute Mona's dead body.

Yet the relation she shares with films other than *Citizen Kane* is extensive and complex. The same wandering woman moves through the world of the writing and film of Marguerite Duras: Mona seems to be an avatar of the mystic "elle" of *Le camion* (*The Truck,* 1978), an *auto-stoppeuse,* or hitchhiker, who cues the intimate relation of contact and rupture in the rapport of her being to her passage. As an *auto-stoppeuse* she is a "self-stopping" figure, a commutator who turns the world "on" and "off" by dismantling the illusion of continuity that would otherwise be thought to pertain in life and cinema. Her passage makes language and image highly problematic and in turn calls into question all modes of representation that hold currency in most symbolic activity. Likewise, Mona is seen in movement begun and arrested by her body posed, on highways and bridges, adjacent to stop signs, gas-station marquees (BP, Fina, Esso: mettez un tigre dans votre bidon, etc.), and billboards that make up the unconscious of the graffiti field of the French winterscape of the Midi. Like Duras's heroines, Mona is born of the sea—*la mer, la mère*—is thus gratuitous, and has no reason for being where she is or where she goes.

But the spectator cannot fail to ask why the woman carries a purse on which is sewn an uppercase M, which seems to be taken from some anterior travels, to Midwestern America perhaps, where she might have been, in another life, in *translatio studii*. Is M a memento, a heraldic letter taken from the University of Michigan at Ann Arbor? As the M travels with her, American viewers cannot fail to persist in seeing the memory of the "wolverines," the totemic beasts that accompany the letter and its color field of blue and gold. It may be that "M" signals Mona coming to the Midi, if not from Middle America or Michigan, then from other continents, other languages, other beings, and other media. Is she an avatar of the totem of the North Woods that the legend of Bo Schembechler has consigned to oblivion? Perhaps. She is no doubt a migrant slouch—but neither immigrant, emigrant, nor *émigrée*—who figurally, on her back and in frontal view, embodies her M.

Hovering between a figure and the world the M flattens all about it, Mona is named as an unintelligible sign. She almost defies interpellation when she is first born of the sea, seen by male motorcyclists. Her appearance on the blue water recalls Botticelli's *Birth of Venus*. Her face is likened to what the M of her name forces the spectator to read into it, through the Mona he or she once saw and read in painting, or *lisa*, in La Gioconda of the Louvre. Like Leonardo's painting, her M calls into question her eros, her place, her role, and her aspect. It names and unnames her, but because it is identical to her first initial, the letter comes before her name. *Prénom: M*. Her first initial displaces her from the world, as it also flattens Varda's film into a screen of image and writing that are distinguished with difficulty. A sign that has no referent, and a figure of the world not yet marked by symbols, the M brings a wealth of reverie to the space and time that precede her name. Doubling and undoing it, M makes of Mona an M-ona, or an M on a . . . M on a what? On a ground? On a field? On a figure? She is set against walls and barriers that her passage inscribes by force of her moving M. Before *Vagabond,* Varda had recently finished a film entitled *Mur Murs* about graffiti in California. The title, as an unconscious shard of voice literally seen, a "murmur," takes up an age-old pun that goes back to Rabelais, in the Abbaye de Thélème sequence in *Gargantua*, and forward to Kafka, and then Maurice Blanchot, in *Celui qui ne m'accompagnait pas,* in which printed *murmure* is an effect of incarceration for those in prison, behind doubled walls, and whose words are confined to the redounding echo of *mur-mur*. The title of *Mur Murs* whispers through the composition of Mona's passage, along stone walls and signboards, on the highways and over the windshields, all through *Vagabond*.

The affinities of the letters common to each film disengage the writing. The paradox of Mona's letter entails the M in relation, on the one hand, to cinematic movement and montage and, on the other, to icons that inflect both writing and film. M is an arcane cipher that has long been coded as a diabolical sign that divides the alphabet in half.[3] The thirteenth letter, the M settles close to the middle. Its form, too, is allegorically median, in that it cuts itself into congruent halves. Mirrored, M remains M. It is, as it were, a *prime* letter that sundry authors have used to evoke the traits of things unique. In this way Mona is a sort of nomadic monad, self-contained yet dispersed, one and other, attached to and detached from all the ciphers that brand her. It refers also to memory of a world of film, for the sight of M can only call forth memory of the blind balloon seller, in *M,* who hears the Düsseldorf murderer's whistle and who chalks the letter M on his shoulder. The killer (Peter Lorre) is finally marked and mirrored by the undecidable form he sees in his reflection on a mirror. He is M, a character now named, and assigned a status in a world that presses upon him from the right or above (Lohmann and the Weimar police) or the lower depths from the left (Schreker and the thieves, who reproduce the very ways of their law-abiding enemies). Between, his impossible, untenable position calls into question the entire ground of the world in which he lives at the same time, as a case, as an avatar of Chris Cross, he stands to be incarcerated and murdered by it.

As a character-letter, a form between a body and an abstract shape, like the shadings of the mountainside of Cézanne's *Mont Saint-Victoire,* Mona writes and paints not only a narrative picture, but the forms that figure the world. She displays the laws of its traits to those who are marked by their memory of her, and she transforms the universe of shapes and colors into a mystical writing. In this sense, Mona Bergeron's passage sums up the work I have attempted in these pages.

Appendix

The synopses that follow accompany analyses in chapters 1 and 7. Elsewhere reference is made either to published scripts or to summaries in each chapter. Abbreviations used here are as follows: *cu* = close-up; *ecu* = extreme close-up; *ms* = medium shot; *mls* = medium long shot; *ls* = long shot; *els* = extreme long shot.

I. Two Sequences of *Boudu sauvé des eaux* (1932)

Boudu sauvé des eaux (Boudu saved from drowning). Société Sirius, 1932. 83 minutes. Adapted from the play by René Fauchois. Directed by Jean Renoir. Photography: Marcel Lucien. Music: Raphael and Johann Strauss; flute, Jean Boulze; choir, Edouard Dumoulin; song "Sur les bords de la rivière," by Léo Daniderff. (See also André Bazin, *Jean Renoir* [New York: Simon & Schuster, 1973], 233–34).

With: Michel Simon, Charles Granval, Marcelle Hainia, Séverine Lerczinska, Jean Dasté, Max Dalban, Jean Gehret, Jacques Becker, Jane Pierson, Georges Darnoux.

A. From the First Intertitle to Lestingois's Discovery of Boudu

shot 1

Intertitle: BOUDU. It is seen over dappled light on water to the music of Pan's flute. (8 sec.)

shot 2
Cut to black (loss of image and of writing). (2 sec.)

shot 3
Fade-in, beginning with left side, of a theatrical proscenium in *ms* with a vertical column to the left of center of the stage, in front of a painted backdrop of a seventeenth-century French garden (in the style of André le Nôtre) whose lines recede toward a vanishing point in the center. Anne-Marie, dressed as a nymph, prances across the stage right and out of frame; she is followed by Lestingois, dressed as a siren, pursuing her from left to right and out of frame; Anne-Marie enters in frame from left, followed by Lestingois, who turns about the column, then jumps from the left; Anne-Marie leans against the column, as does Lestingois, who bumps into it and causes it to sway; he throws his flute down in frustration and arches back to embrace Anne-Marie in center frame. (25 sec.)

shot 4
cu of embrace and dolly-back. (2 sec.)

shot 5
Dissolve to a *mcu* of a bust of Voltaire on right of frame, above a pile of books, the ensemble apposed to a characteristic nineteenth-century iron column left (which seems to correspond to the bogus column in shot 3) and, in the center, the two figures from shot 3, tightly embraced in a ball. Music-off carries chords of the leitmotif of film and continues into the following shot that emerges from the dissolve. (2 sec.)

shot 6
Dolly-back from the bust and books below to the column of a spiral staircase behind them. The camera moves (7 sec.), stops, and then pans left across the flat space of a window and a shot interior to Lestingois, now dressed in a suit, looking left and out of frame (11 sec.). Shot ends when cued with the voice of Lestingois, ostensively *off*, calling, "Anne-Marie!" (26 sec.)

shot 7
cu of Lestingois petting the head of Anne-Marie, whom he holds in his arms while he recites to her alexandrines that parody romantic and bucolic traditions (specifically, Hugo's "Le syrène"). (21 sec.)

shot 8
Cut to *ms,* in countertilt, of Vigour playing his flute out of the win-

dow seen diagonally from below. The music-*off* in the first seven shots is now located in the space of the film. (8 sec.)

shot 9

Cut to frontal, establishing *ms* of the bookstore seen across a street with writing below the shop windows, in slightly mannered capital letters: ANCIENNE MAISON LEMASLE. Flute music continues. (5 sec.)

shot 10

Cut to *mls* of the store seen from further across the street. One car drives across the frame from the left; a tram enters from the right, crosses left, and is followed by a third car. The opposite directions of the movement leave the effect of the cars crisscrossing or erasing each other. LEMASLE seen above a vitrine that displays the name of Lestingois's bookstore. (5 sec.)

shot 11

Cut back to the cadre of shot 8 of Vigour, who finishes his melody, takes the flute from his lips, and moves by the window sill to the right as the noise of moving cars (seen in shot 10) is now heard, *off*. The disjunction is remarked as he closes the French window. (10 sec.)

shot 12

Cut to Lestingois in *ms*, who continues to hold Anne-Marie and recite bucolic lines (''Mes pippeaux jusqu'au dernier instant chanteront'' [my pipes will sing up to the last moment], etc.). Anne-Marie exits right (moving toward the camera as Lestingois turns and follows her with his eyes); she reenters frame from the right, in an area near the camera, as he ogles her and then holds her in his arms, fondles, and kisses her (''Je vous aime, Monsieur Lestingois,'' she says, as if psalmodizing his lines), before he commands, ''Va, va, préparer la soupe . . . et n'oublie pas le sel sur le bouillon'' (Come now, go prepare the soup, and don't forget to put salt in the broth). (46 sec.)

shot 13

Cut to Anne-Marie in *ms*, turning about, but adjacent to two pictures—lithographs—to her left on the wall behind her right arm, which moves up. (2 sec.)

shot 14

Cut to Anne-Marie, seen from a slight countertilt, looking down the spiral staircase; the shot then begins to pan right and up as it follows Anne-Marie behind a white cloth placed in *ecu* on the balustrade in the foreground before panning left and up as it follows her looking down, her body posed in front of a background of floral wallpaper immediately behind her. (4 sec.)

shot 15

Cut to window in *mls* (its bright texture seems to oppose the dark wall in the preceding shot), and a pan left to Lestingois looking right from the left side of the frame; he moves to the center in *ms* as he quotes French proverbs about life and then waves. (6 sec.)

shot 16

Cut back to Anne-Marie in *ms* in position she assumes in shot 14. She turns about and comes forward to the left. A pan left follows her as the camera registers the wall in the foreground—the camera seems almost blocked in the narrow space—and then the doorway giving onto a kitchen in the depth of a *ls* within the shot, as if a frame were within the frame. She enters the space, her back to the spectators. She ambles into the back of the kitchen and picks a pot hanging on the wall, turns about, and spins it around on its handle. (10 sec.)

shot 17

Cut to *ms* of Lestingois before the window, now in silhouette and looking left, as he pushes the right-hand shade aside to the right, and then the left shade to the left, the opening of which (as in a puppet theater) opens onto a view of another frame of a window over a courtyard, on the same horizontal axis, that displays a woman at work. The woman in the window is in the background while Lestingois stands in the foreground; they almost match each other's movements as both look left; then he turns back, around, moves right (toward the camera)—while the woman's head in the background appears for an instant to be placed on his shoulder—in *mcu* and smiles (murmuring, ''Elle est charmante,'' but not specifying if he refers to the woman we are seeing or to Anne-Marie who is *off*). He sits down to the right (''J'ai vieilli . . . mes pippeaux sont fatigués,'' [I've gotten old . . . my pipes are tired], etc.) as the woman in the frame behind continues to work while standing. (23 sec.)

shot 18

Cut to a window and door in frame in *mcu,* with scene of the street in soft focus in the background, while the door handle in the medium ground points left. Emma comes from the left, walks toward the door (as city noise is heard), looks right as her head is blocked by the column formed by the door, turns back, opens the door with her head down, enters the space indicated by the rod of the door handle. She

moves directly toward the camera, into *cu,* and turns left and closes
the door with her left hand, holding the handle for a long moment as
she begins to move ahead; she finally releases the handle of the
closed door and exits in *cu,* left, as the camera offers a divided image
of the curtain to the left and the background of the street (as in shot
10) in soft focus. The camera pans left slightly. (8 sec.)

shot 19

Cut to Lestingois, seated, in *ms,* from a view 180 degrees opposite
that of shot 17, looking right over a table. Emma enters from the
right, stops before the spiral staircase, removes her gloves as she
looks at Lestingois (who mutters, "Te voilà déjà . . . " [You're back
already . . .]). They exchange words about the funeral she has attended before she turns about, up the spiral staircase; a fade-out in
black ends the shot. (10 sec.)

shot 20

Fade-in to a shimmering surface in *mcu,* of water, before the camera
follows a large toy sailboat floating laterally, left, in a long pan that
ends with the boy (back to the camera) pulling it out of the water as
he is being yanked back by a woman with a wide-brimmed straw hat
and a dark long dress. They struggle ("Allons, viens!" [Come now])
as they exit left off frame while the camera holds on the trees in the
background over the water on the right side of the frame and the
white surface of the ground to the left. (20 sec.)

shot 21

Cut to *cu* of Boudu embracing a curly-haired, black dog in front of a
tree trunk. Noise of the city is heard *off*; he breathes with heavy gut-
tural sighs. (4 sec.)

shot 22

Cut to deep-view shot, Boudu in *ms* and landscape in *els,* of receding
space perpendicular to Boudu's left where he remains seated at the
bottom of the tree, which now is parallel to the right side of the
frame. The woman and her child with the sailboat walk by from right
to left in medium depth. They turn to look at the bum, and hasten
away, exiting left. Boudu continues to embrace the dog. (9 sec.)

shot 23

Cut to position of Boudu in shot 21. He guffaws, pushes dog away
left ("Va me laisser . . . " [Leave me alone]), looks right as the tree
trunk forms a background to him in *mcu,* he moves left, utters
"Chien" to beckon it, then looks down at his hands. (8 sec.)

shot 24

Cut to water in *ms;* lilies float in the background. A black dog moves toward the water from left, its feet making ripples on the surface; camera pans right with an airy effect of chiaroscuro and dappling. Located in the left of the frame, the dog stops, then moves; the camera divides the image into the dog and the shimmering water; it pans left with the dog moving left, abruptly, into *cu* by the left edge of the frame. A bar of light reflected on the water recedes in the background. The dog moves right, looks toward the viewer and then right; camera tilts vertically, reframing the scene with the single "shot sequence" that it is; camera holds on dog, then a horn gurgles, and dog runs right, in *cu,* with camera following its tracks. (15 sec.)

shot 25

Cut to Boudu nibbling bread, putting his hand to his mouth, and gnawing on the crust, as he slurs a tune (" . . . par la rivière" [. . . down by the riverside]) camera holds in *mcu* as he budges, turning left and right while he is slumped under the tree; he eats out of his hand and continues to chant ("au murmure des eaux . . . " [in the murmur of the waters . . .]); he stops, turns left, calls out "Chien, chien," as he looks left and right twice, the camera panning left and right, reframing as he moves about. He pulls himself up, his buttocks facing the camera, and exits right and up, as the tree trunk, left, frames a block of light between Boudu and its right side. He exits right. The camera holds on the scene, Boudu's legs moving left back into frame and then behind the tree (voice *off,* he utters, "Chien, chien!"). (33 sec.)

shot 26

Cut to *ms* of Boudu against the background of the park. He moves left toward a man seated on a park bench, dressed in an overcoat in the sunshine. Bending over, Boudu asks if the man has seen his dog. In background continuity is held by the water and lilies shimmering. The seated man rises theatrically, the camera reframing laterally, and says, "Ouah" (Yeah), spouts verse ("Donne un baiser . . . " [give a kiss]), gesticulates, and prompts Boudu to turn and exit right. Camera holds as the man holds a book in his left hand and cites a romantic phrase before sitting down again with renewed resolve. (19 sec.)

shot 27

Cut to *ls* in which a lady pushes a perambulator past where the figure in the former shot had been seated. View of neatly aligned trees in the dark background with light of the walkway foregrounded as the

woman and her carriage enter in the medium field diagonally; another woman enters from right and moves toward the woman and carriage left. At the instant they cross in the background left, Boudu enters from left, running, catching up with the woman pushing the
perambulator, and addresses her. She fails to respond, and he then
turns left toward the other who has just exited left; he turns about
under a shadow while a figure—a policeman—enters from the left
and moves into the center foreground while he puts his right hand to
his ear and removes a cigarette lodged between it and his temple.
Three fields are established: (1) trees in the extreme background; (2)
Boudu in the center, blocked by the policeman (3) in the extreme
foreground. The policeman turns about and right (allowing Boudu to
be seen in the middle area) with his back to the camera. Boudu
moves directly forward, along the sightline that moves toward a vanishing point through the trees. Boudu addresses the cop childishly
("Eh, type, vous n'aurez pas vu un chien?" [Hey buddy, you
wouldn't have seen a dog, would you?]). This question prompts the
response, doubling the cue word ("Un chien?"), which Boudu underscores again ("Un chien, au poil noir" [A dog, with black hair]);
the policeman compares his description of the hair to Boudu himself,
and tells him to scram (débiner) as a man on a mounted horse moves
right in the background. The camera holds on the officer smoking
(looking right, listlessly), as Boudu recedes into the background
along the sightline leading to the vanishing point, his head seeming
to roll in isolation along the line of the policeman's left shoulder.
Boudu exits in background left. The cop remains immobile, while in
extreme background a woman enters where the horse had exited (the
last image being that of its buttocks and erect tail), crying not
"Chien, chien!" as in earlier shots, but a slur that resembles "Black,
black!" (43 sec.)

shot 28

Cut to *mcu* that puts the background in soft focus, as the woman
moves along the same axis toward the officer who moves right
slightly. She clenches her broad-brimmed hat, uttering, "Monsieur,
est-ce que vous n'aurez pas vu un chien?" (Sir, would you not have
seen a dog?) and establishes a foreground of dialogue against the
background, in soft focus. She notes that the dog she lost was worth
10,000 francs. He turns right, signals for his men, off screen ("Eh,
mes amis, écoutez!" [Now, my friends, listen!]). A mustached policeman with a bicycle enters from the right, laterally again, coming into

frame center, saluting the woman, while the officer repeats that the dog was worth "dix mille balles" as he turns left. (13 sec.)

shot 29

Cut to *ls,* of sun in background, behind the grove of trees planted in parallel rows that imply a vanishing point in the background. Boudu enters from right, looking toward the trees, walks deep left, then right, toward the vanishing point, then left in the distance, yelling for his dog; a sense of depth is obtained by the echo of the voice in the distance. (13 sec.)

shot 30

Cut to *mcu* of policeman and woman. They exit to underscore the depth of the scene in the background. A man in a car (whose motor seems to gurgle) enters from left; he looks over at the woman ("Comme vous avez l'air triste, Mademoiselle" [Oh Miss, how sad you look]). He picks her up, inviting her to look for the dog with him, as she moves left and around the convertible, stepping in on opposite side. The car then moves right and out of frame. Camera holds for an instant. (25 sec.)

shot 31

Cut to *ms* of a park bench located in a slightly diagonal relation to the depth of field. The ground below is illuminated below a dark clump of bushes and trees in the background. Boudu enters from the right (his body not contained in the frame) and turns to sit on the bench. He slumps down, sits where the man of shot 26 had been, and expresses sadness by looking back to the bushes, his legs crossed. A woman and a child enter from right. She bends forward and down to give money to the child, who takes it and moves gingerly toward Boudu on the bench. (19 sec.)

shot 32

Cut on opposite axis in *cu,* in tilt downward, to the child tendering the money to Boudu right. Floral design of the woman's dress is visible in immediate background. Boudu asks why she is giving him the money, and the child responds, "Pour acheter du pain" (So you can buy some bread). (5 sec.)

shot 33

Cut back to location of shot 31, as the woman and the child exit frontally right, toward the camera. (3 sec.)

shot 34

Cut to *ls* of the park into which another convertible immediately enters laterally, from the right, in the foreground. Camera pans left to hold on the young man driving, and stops when he stops. He stretches, as if tired and bored, in medium field. (8 sec.)

shot 35

Cut to a *ls* resembling a painting (reminiscent of Seurat's compositions of outdoor space), of white ground before a dark depth of trees, as a small group of children is perched over the water to the right. A large tree is illuminated on the left. Boudu, reframed on the bench by the lower corner of the frame, gets up in the medium ground from the bench and takes two steps right. (4 sec.)

shot 36

Cut to the scene of shot 34, as the driver in profile searches his pockets to find a match to light his cigarette. Boudu enters from left, as if dazed, and disjointedly opens the door. The man lights his cigarette and slowly descends, steps up, his head grazing the upper edge of the frame, as he searches in his pockets again, facing Boudu left. He puffs on his cigarette before Boudu donates five francs to the rich driver. He responds, "Eh, vous êtes fou? Vous vous fichez de moi?" (What, are you crazy, are you putting me on?). To which he responds, "C'est pour acheter du pain" (So you can buy some bread), turns, and exits right. (21 sec.)

shot 37

Cut on the perpendicular axis to the back side of the man in his suit next to the left side of the car (facing the space of shot 35), while Boudu walks left into the depth of field defined in *mcu* by the trees, shadow, and bright spots of light on the surface—an "all over" shot, where the two figures become ciphers defining the depth of field. The man's shadow below seems to aim at Boudu who shuffles into the distance. City noises are pronounced while the shot fades out in black and loses image for almost 5 seconds. (16 sec.)

shot 38

Fade-in to *mcu* of Emma inside the store, looking down, and counting dryly ("eighty, eighty-one, eighty-two, eighty-three, eighty-four, eighty-five . . . "). (6 sec.)

shot 39

Cut to *mcu* of a student (Jean Dasté), head moving up, while Emma's voice is heard counting, *off*. He inquires about the price of a book with the discount. (3 sec.)

shot 40

Cut to *ms* that establishes the placement of Emma and the student in the two preceding shots, as Emma, barely looking up at the student, head down, quips, "Sixty francs, Monsieur," before quickly looking down again. The student, left, in front of a row of books and lithographs on the wall, looks frontally, and then left, while the iron pole divides the frame in the center, with Emma counting, right, behind the desk. A comic-strip configuration is obtained. She moves and exits left, walking behind the pole and by the student. He moves a bit, displaying the open book he holds in his hands. Voice *off* of Lestingois entering from the right, asking if the price is too dear. Yes, he answers, for his scholarship money. Lestingois asks if he is a student, which prompts an affirmative response. Lestingois, in profile on the right, asks, "Do you like Voltaire?" "Oui, Monsieur!" Yes, you're right, says Lestingois, tapping his spectacles on the books, as the student answers, "It is he who is right." Then looking frontally and furtively (for the absence of Emma), Lestingois impels the student to take it. He refuses, but Lestingois insists that it is for his pleasure, while he turns around the pole and goes behind the desk, looks up right to search for a book. A lithograph is behind the desk, and the student moves right, leaving both men on the right division of the frame. Lestingois finds a book, dusts it off, and begs him to take it. The student notes that the bookseller doesn't even know him, and Lestingois responds by saying that he knows the student better than he thinks, for "Your name is Youth," he adds, crossing the bar—a visual transgression enacted right where he tells the student not to say anything to his wife. The men exit left, as the camera holds on the scene for a second, displaying the divided screen with the speech of Lestingois and the student, *off*. The bar, the desk, the lithographs behind, and pictures cut off above, and the row of books are remarked. (52 sec.)

shot 41

Cut to an *ls,* outdoors, of a tugboat chugging up the Seine, its high smokestack belching black fumes. The vertical shape of the smokestack corresponds visually to the bar in the room in the former shot. A vague outline of the Louvre can be seen in the distance in the upper background to the right of a bridge—no doubt the Pont-Royal—in the distance. (14 sec.)

shot 42

ls in telephoto perspective that pans left as Boudu walks by the *bouquinistes* along the quay Conti. Cars with writing on their sides pass by from right to left. The long shot ends with Boudu exiting left after the camera holds on the spare tire on the back of one of the many vehicles seen in frame.

shot 43

ms of the interior of Lestingois's house. Anne-Marie, looking left and out of the window aligned with the left of the frame, is polishing a telescope and singing lyrics of "Springtime in the Forest." She extends the telescope, looks through it backward, and then forward. The song asks, "Who is the magician" just before Lestingois enters from right and takes the instrument from her. He assumes her place, tells her to go and dust the piano for fear of Madame Lestingois. He looks out to the left into the telescope.

shot 44

Cut to *mcu* of the artificial leaves of the wreath placed over the piano. Looking right, Anne-Marie dusts as she bangs the keys of the piano. Slight reframing downward. She hits the bars of the song on the piano keys.

shot 45

Cut to *mcu* of Lestingois, from behind, as he looks out of the window. It appears that a matte shot is reproducing the scene of Parisian life in the street below.

shot 46

Iris of two women seen in telephoto perspective—through the instrument—as the camera pans right and descends to the women's bare ankles. Cars pass by, interrupt the view, and display writing moving left.

shot 47

Cut to *ms* of Anne-Marie pouting and looking left, complaining that Lestingois is ogling women. "I'm jealous," she utters in deadpan tone.

shot 48

Cut to *mcu* of Lestingois looking back and noting that jealousy is a frightful condition unworthy of her spirit and beauty.

shot 49

Cut to Anne-Marie (as in shot 47) who dusts the wreath and sings.

shot 50

cu of wreath being dusted.

shot 51

ecu of the same.

shot 52

Cut back to the scene of shot 45, of Lestingois peering out of the window.

shot 53

Iris of Boudu seen on the quay, walking left. the camera follows as the song sings of the smile of spring. Boudu ambles up on the bridge.

shot 54

Cut back to *mcu* of Lestingois looking through the telescope. He tells Anne-Marie to wait as he looks at this great specimen (''Oh! Oh!'' he grunts in exclamation).

B. Boudu's Seduction of Emma

shot 1

Frontal *ms,* foreshortened, of Emma on bed as she files her nails with an emery board. ''Oh! Je suis épuisée, moi,'' she sighs (Oh, I'm really tired) before hurdy-gurdy music is heard, *off.*

shot 2

Cut to *ms* of the hurdy-gurdy. The player turns the crank with his back to the viewer; as a man on the left looks at the scene as he leans over his bicycle. Cars pass in front of the scene.

shot 3

Back to shot 1, with Emma covering her head with her elbow as if being murdered. She uncovers her eyes and gets up.

shot 4

Cut to *cu* of the window looking onto the street below (in matte perspective). Emma enters the frame and looks left.

shot 5

Establishing *ms,* now of Emma looking right, from reverse angle. She assumes the pose of a dryad.

shot 6

Cut to hurdy-gurdy player as in shot 2 (music continues to play since shot 1).

shot 7

ms in countertilt that shows the window of the barbershop (with "antiseptic service" written to lower right).

shot 8

ls of Boudu walking brusquely down the quay, from left to right and from extreme depth to the foreground (hurdy-gurdy music continues).

shot 9

Cut to scene of shot 5. Emma rises, leaves, and shuts the door behind her.

shot 10

mcu of space into which Emma enters from right. She turns, sits down, and assumes the pose of a water nymph.

shot 11

ms of Boudu opening the door as had Emma previously (in shot 19 above). He lets it close and moves forward.

shot 12

ms of Lestingois huddled behind his books, under the bust of Voltaire and next to the stairwell. Boudu now enters from the left. Lestingois tells him to go upstairs and report to Emma. Lestingois looks up, muttering, "L'homme qui a craché dans *La physiologie du mariage* de Balzac n'est plus rien pour moi" (For me the man who spit in Balzac's *Physiology of Marriage* is worthless).

shot 13

mcu of Boudu in stairwell (as if in jail because the bars of the balustrade enclose him) who looks down and wonders who that man is.

shot 14

Cut back to scene of shot 12, Lestingois telling Boudu to find out by asking his wife. He continues to puff on his cigar.

shot 15

cu in tilt down of stairwell. Boudu comes up, the camera tilts up into *ls* and catches the sprinkling can to the left and a door at the extreme end of the hall in deep focus. Boudu goes down the hall and opens the door.

shot 16
Cut to the other side of the door, in *ms*, of Boudu opening and holding his left hand on the knob. He closes it and asks for Madame Lestingois.

shot 17
mcu of Emma seated. She gets up, moves forward by the camera, and leaves the seat vacant.

shot 18
Cut to the space of the scene of shot 16. Pan right with Boudu opening the door to the bedroom and encountering Emma, who pushes him back with her right hand. They move out after Boudu remarks, "Il paraît qu'il y a un homme qui crache" (It seems a man who spits is around here).

shot 19
Cut to *cu* of Boudu sniffing Emma by the mantelpiece. They flirt. He speaks to her in familiar terms. She exits left and speaks, *off*, redressing him.

shot 20
ms of Emma's backside, Boudu to the left, as she continues to scold him. They flirt. He repeats her words in mimicry.

shot 21
cu of mantelpiece below the lower edge of the two prints on the wall. Emma enters and adjusts the dress on her shoulders. Camera reframes the scene, tilting up as he looks at her "beauty spot" above one of her breasts. More of the prints comes into view. They tussle and turn. She shows fear before she succumbs to Boudu's embrace. Both drop below the frame as the camera dollies toward the prints over the two embracing plaster *putti*. She cackles, the camera continues to move toward the Bugle Boy print. Brass music starts as the camera comes close to the boy's mouth.

shot 22
Cut to *ls* of children in parade, in the street, prancing to the marching music of victory. Vigour leads a small band of uniformed musicians down the street.

shot 23
ms of inside, Lestingois seated left, by the open window in the cen-

ter. He looks left, apparently perturbed by the music, *off,* that interrupts his reading. He continues to smoke.

shot 24
ls of outside, seen through the doors of the shop on the inside, of the parade converging on Lestingois's apartment. Music continues.

shot 25
Cut back to the scene of shot 23. Lestingois looks up from his paper.

shot 26
mcu, outdoors, of Vigour and Godin leading the band.

shot 27
Cut to *mcu* of the Bugle Boy picture, the camera now pulling back to show it in full view. Victory music continues, the couple Boudu and Emma rising into the frame, in *cu* of their faces expressing delight. They exit left one by one, Boudu raising his finger to twirl a sign of victory.

shot 28
Cut back to the scene of shot 24. Vigour and his neighbor come to the doors, open them, as Vigour exclaims, "Victoire, mon cher voisin, victoire!" (Victory, my dear neighbor, victory).

shot 29
Cut to *ls* of the room from the opposite axis. Vigour enters into frame, followed by Godin. Vigour: "Vous l'êtes! Vous l'êtes!" (You're it, you're it!) Lestingois wonders and mutters. Vigour: "Décoré!" (Pinned!) Vigour explains that he obtained the documents and forged them with the help of Emma's signature. Boudu and Emma enter from the right, and Anne-Marie from the left.

II. Synopsis of *The Killers* (1946)

The Killers, Universal Studios, 1946. 105 minutes. Written by Anthony Veiller from a story by Ernest Hemingway. Directed by Robert Siodmak. Photography: Elwood Bredell. Music: Miklos Rozsa.

With: Burt Lancaster, Edmund O'Brien, Ava Gardner, Albert Dekker, Sam Levene, John Miljan, Virginia Christine, Vince Barnett, Charles D. Brown, Donald MacBride, Phil Brown, Charles McGraw, William Conrad.

1st Sequence
Shot of road from behind windshield of car speeding down a road at night. Sign indicating "Brentwood" comes into view in headlights

at left and slides by. Credits follow, placed over street scene at night, backlit, with killers' entry into diner, exchange with Nick Adams, the waiter, and the cook. First word of the film: Nick Adams mutters at the counter, "Catch up." Killers mutter over menu and bait the waiter. Identification of "the Swede" as "Pete Lund." Establishment of atmosphere and killing in rooming house across street from diner next to Tri-State Gasoline Station. Murder takes place in shadows after Swede murmurs to Nick Adams, "I . . . I did something wrong . . . once." Fade-out in black after murder.

2nd Sequence
Fade-in to details of Swede's effects on table in police station (including insurance policy), investigation by Reardon (Edmund O'Brien) in company of Nick Adams and the black cook ("Sam"). Dissolve to Brentwood morgue where Reardon notices size of the corpse's hand; first exchange with Nick.

3rd Sequence
Dissolve back to Nick's impressions of Swede's (Burt Lancaster's) troubled days at the Tri-State Station ("I dunno. It was something a long time ago. . . . And he walked off, rubbing his stomach, and he didn't come to work the next day").

4th Sequence
Dissolve back to present where Nick and Reardon speak. From telephone booth Reardon calls (in *cu*) his insurance office. Information obtained on beneficiary of dead man's life insurance policy worth $2500. Fade-out and dissolve.

5th Sequence
Dissolve to room in Atlantic City where Reardon looks (from behind, in *plan américain)* out of window before him. Superintendent (Mrs. Grimes) exits as Queenie, the beneficiary, learns with astonishment of the money. Reardon queries her about her knowledge of Swede: "That was long ago, in 1940, the year of the hurricane."

6th Sequence
Dissolve back as Queenie (or Mrs. Doherty) reconstructs memory of chaos one evening in Swede's room (1212) and attempted suicide by plunging through the window. ("She's gone, she's gone! . . . Charleston was right, he was right!") Fade-out.

7th Sequence
Fade-in to insurance office. Reardon enters and raps with secretary: "Good morning, Stella." "Good morning, Green Boy," she ri-

postes. Entry into boss's office. Disgruntled, boss scowls, "One of those $2500 death cases." Reardon: "Try and see if you can get a pinch on that guy Charleston. By the way, who made the pinch on [Ollie] Anderson," asks Reardon of secretary: "Lieutenant Lubinsky, Philadelphia, 5th Precinct."

8th Sequence

Dissolve to Lieutenant Lubinsky on rooftop terrace before his blonde wife (Lily) enters from right. Asks Reardon from left of frame: "I dunno if you remember but you arrested a guy named Ollie Anderson [the Swede]."

9th Sequence

Dissolve back—from Lubinsky's point of view—to Swede's fight with Tiger Lewis. Lily watches fight intently. Swede is TKO'd before attendants discover his right hand has been broken. His promoter decries losing "10 G's" over him and considers backing a kid named Callahan. Dissolve to street outside. Lily, Lubinsky, and Swede exit from locker room into street. ("You know," Swede says apropos the $10,000 just lost, "some months I made that much in one fight.")

10th Sequence

Cut back to Lubinsky and spouse on terrace. Lily adds her reflections on Swede's past.

11th Sequence

Dissolve back—now in Lily's eyes—to nine years back, to Swede's first date with Lily. Entry into club where Blinky is seen. Swede is captivated by Kitty Collins (Ava Gardner) crooning by piano—"The more I love life, the less I know . . . The more I give to life, the more I owe." He falls in love. Seeing that her date has fallen for Colfax, Lily has her ginger ale laced with rum. Blinky notes that Big Jim Colfax is out of town.

12th Sequence

Cut with voice-off to present as Lily ends her narrative. "He'd never been in love before." Reardon asks, "Who was Big Jim Colfax?"

13th Sequence

Lubinsky dissolves back to the time he arrested the Swede in a jewelry heist. Scene is set at a table in a café where Kitty entertains friends; Kitty hides a spider-shaped brooch she takes from her breast (in a very quick close-up). Lubinsky notices from another table and recovers the jewelry from a bowl of minestrone. Swede enters and takes the rap for Kitty: "I swiped that stuff myself!" He hits Lubinsky and runs off.

14th Sequence

Cut to present and Lubinsky who notes (rubbing his cheekbone) that Swede broke his right hand at that moment in their past.

15th Sequence

Dissolve to present: Swede's funeral in twilight. Shots of mourners: Packy the promoter and Smalley the trainer as well as the "old time hoodlum Charleston."

16th Sequence

Dissolve to present: a poolhall and bar where Charleston drinks. Reardon queries him from frame right in medium shot.

17th Sequence

Charleston dissolves back to his two years in "stir" with Swede. Swede is on his bed, caressing his green silk scarf. Charleston studies constellations in sky above the prison windows. Swede asks Charleston, who will leave "stir" in two weeks, to look up Kitty on his behalf. Charleston murmurs gnomically about Kitty's ways.

18th Sequence

Dissolve to present: Charleston continues as he drinks with Reardon. He tells Reardon that he knew Swede very well.

19th Sequence

Charleston dissolves to past immediately after release from prison: a meeting and card game where hoodlums deal beyond the supine figure of Kitty reposing in boredom on a bed. First noteworthy shot of Colfax. Swede enters, meets Kitty, who begins to captivate him again. The hoodlums' "job" is reviewed. Charleston refuses to play and leaves the quarters. Swede stays in. Charleston waits outside, but Swede does not exit to join him. Dissolve to present.

20th Sequence

End of interview with Charleston. Fade to office and secretary. "See if you can get a line on a girl named Kitty Collins." Reardon passes into office where his boss begins to read an old newspaper account about a robbery from a hat factory payroll office.

21st Sequence

Dissolve to scene of robbery (seen in silence) as boss's voice *(off)* quotes newspaper report that describes in words the scene before our eyes. Description ends by remarking that one gangster who got away was wearing a green scarf.

22nd Sequence

Dissolve to present as Reardon and boss discuss the status of the scarf. Reardon pieces together the 1940 holdup with Swede and Kitty's check-in at the Atlantic City Hotel. The year 1946 is mentioned as the present time. Telephone call from Lubinsky interrupts and promises news.

23rd Sequence

Dissolve to Lubinsky and Reardon entering the corridor of a hospital in *els* (as in first shots of film). As they walk toward frame, Lubinsky describes the details of the most recent murder. Close-up of Blinky, who confesses in throes of death following a shooting. He babbles of the night before the robbery at the hat factory.

24th Sequence

Blinky dissolves to the rainy night before the robbery. Kitty looks vapidly out of the window. She turns to observe Dumdum, Blinky, and Colfax playing cards. Swede enters. An argument over Kitty ensues. The stakes increase ("Up you a hundred," etc.). Swede accuses Colfax of cheating at cards (turning down his hand too early) and punches him in the face. Blinky quips to Colfax: "Swede shouldn'a hit ya."

25th Sequence

Dissolve to present. Blinky expires in hospital. "He's dead now but keeps breathing," admits doctor. Bus ticket to Brentwood and newspaper clipping are reported found in Blinky's clothing. Blinky blathers words about a bus ticket to Brentwood.

26th Sequence

Blinky dissolves back to the getaway after the robbery. Scene takes place at a farmer's house. Money is counted among the thieves. Swede watches the scene from the outside, stealthily enters with gun and holds them up. Swede makes off with the money after shooting the tires of two getaway cars.

27th Sequence

Cut to death of Blinky. "At least we know why Blinky was on his way to Brentwood."

28th Sequence

Dissolve to Reardon in abandoned hotel room in Brentwood. A door-bell rings: Colfax's henchman Dumdum enters — Reardon hides be-hind door — and searches for hidden money. With his gun Reardon confronts Dumdum, sits him down, and interrogates him: "Did you kill the Swede?" "Not me!" Dumdum killed Blinky to get to the room ahead of time. Dumdum lunges forward and grabs Reardon's gun. He begins interrogating Reardon before sound of police sends Dumdum onto roof. He confronts police gunfire outside.

29th Sequence

Fade to Reardon, who meets Lubinsky on train. Train is going to Pittsburgh where they will seek Colfax. Messenger enters scene with telegram from fire department (with a report about the chronology of the burning of the halfway house, the alternate meeting point estab-lished in respect to the farm).

30th Sequence

Cut to Colfax Iron Works. Colfax cleans a shotgun in his office. Reardon queries Colfax about the hat robbery and the death of all its witnesses — the farmer, Dumdum, Blinky, and Swede. He wonders about Kitty Collins. Reardon double-crosses Colfax into believing Kitty knows where the money is.

31st Sequence

Dissolve to hotel room where Lubinsky and Reardon confer about the history of the events until now. "You know what I think?" "I think we're dumb," says Lubinsky, "to wait for Kitty to call." Kitty calls. Meeting is arranged to take place outside of a movie theater. Reardon says a friend will be there wearing a bow tie as he dons a bow tie.

32nd Sequence

Cut to street and space under the marquee of the Adelphi movie the-ater. Kitty and Reardon meet. "Got a match?" says Kitty. Man with a cane follows the two as they exit. The two original killers (McGraw and Conrad) enter and follow. In car Kitty says, "A voice from the past, Jake the Rake, called me." They are driven to the Green Cat Bar on Sultan Street. Reardon interrogates Kitty: "How about it? Where's the $254,000?" He double-crosses her by putting the green neckerchief before her eyes. Arrival at the Green Cat Club.

33rd Sequence

Dissolve to Kitty's story about the moments following the robbery. "They're planning to double-cross you," she says to Swede about Dumdum and Big Jim Colfax. "I'm poison, Swede, to myself and everybody around me. I'd be afraid to go around with anyone I love for the harm I do 'em." She mentions the rendezvous point at the halfway house.

34th Sequence

Dissolve from past to present with Kitty's words, "That's the whole story, Mr. Reardon." "Too bad it had to *catch up* with you," quips Reardon [stress added]. She exits to powder her nose. The two killers enter bar from back during the track following her in deep focus across the tables, spot Reardon isolated behind a table in the background. Lubinsky, who stalks by the bar on the left, is warned and kills the killers as they shoot at Reardon (who defends himself by turning the table into a shield). Reardon runs into the ladies' room to discover that Kitty has left through the back window.

35th Sequence

Fade to cars on the wet streets. Chase to a mansion outside of town. A deep shot locates the scene from the inside. Shots are heard *off* as police enter through door in background. Dumdum falls downstairs and dies. Colfax is discovered on the stairs. Kitty appears upstairs. In his last moments, in *cu* on the stairs, Colfax recalls that he is married to Kitty, and that he had the Swede knocked off. Colfax and Kitty kept the money from the others through the ploy of the halfway house. Kitty is shown to be guilty. She panics as the dying Colfax refuses to assume responsibility for her.

36th Sequence

Dissolve to the present, in insurance office, of the boss reading the final report. "Do I have it all straight?" "The double-cross to end all double-crosses," replies Reardon. Reardon is awarded the weekend off. Date of 1947 is noted in speech as END overlays the last shot in the office.

Notes

Introduction

1. Gérard Genette, *Figures III* (Paris: Seuil, 1972).

2. In *Power and Paranoia: History, Narrative, and the American Cinema, 1940–50* (New York: Columbia University Press, 1986), Dana Polan has shown how the American film industry built its institution on such grounds. He studies how narratives were fashioned to impose perplexity on an international community of spectators. I intend here to orient some of the same issues in the direction of compositional strategies that inform film of all genres.

3. Alexandre Astruc, "La caméra-stylo," translated and reprinted in Peter Graham, ed., *The New Wave* (London: Secker & Warburg, 1968), 17–24.

4. The term belongs to Jean-François Lyotard, in a book of that title (Paris: Minuit, 1984), which argues that a politics of aesthetics can be engaged through the recognition that difference is at work in every human praxis. Yet the concept of the *différend* seems to be casting into political terms what was latent in the difference Lyotard studied between discourse and figure in *Discours, figure* (Paris: Klincksieck, 1972). The concept finds effective practice in Marie-Claire Ropars-Wuilleumier, *Ecraniques* (Lille: Presses Universitaires de Lille, 1990).

5. Michel Butor has shown how a tension "fans out" from a signature or a title and its image-field in *Les mots dans la peinture* (Geneva: Skira, 1971). Lyotard arrives at similar conclusions in *Discours, figure*.

6. Critical writing on the emblematic tradition is legion. In *La forme et l'intelligible*, Robert Klein spells out the principal tenets of the theory as it developed in Renaissance Italy (Paris: Gallimard, 1970), 125–50. His work thresholds a growing body of research on word and image in, for example, the journal *Emblematica* that elucidates emblem work in both theory and history.

7. See, among others, Michael Riffaterre, in *Semiotics of Poetry* (Indiana: Indiana University Press, 1982), 90–100, in which he studies how the units composing a name are subject to recombination in the reader's wit. This common practice among surrealist poets and film makers was, as François Rigolot has demonstrated in *Poésie et onomastie* (Geneva: Droz, 1978), a licit activity pro-

217

ductive of knowledge throughout the European Renaissance. Roger Dragonetti reminds us of the wealth of the tradition in the first two chapters of *La vie de la lettre au Moyen Age* (Paris: Seuil, 1980), 13–83. It is clear that film study depends on the tradition of writing that Etienne Gilson has shown to be at work in our literary tradition, in *Les idées et les lettres* (Paris: Vrin, 1942), and that Ernst Curtius has traced through the Christian tradition, in *European Literature and the Latin Middle Ages* (New York: Harper, 1963), 303–42.

8. A case in point: Ermanno Olmi's *Tree of Wooden Clogs* appeared to be a fitting title for a richly human, albeit nostalgic, portrayal of life on an Italian farm in the nineteenth century. Yet its title proposed an enigma that required two hours of viewing to solve, for the significance of "clog," a term familiar only to a given area of fashion or to those who can translate *sabot* into English, was revealed when a principal character found himself expelled from the patron's order after he had sacrificed a tree to make clogs for his family. The narrative could be taken seriously, as an element of a Christian-democratic point of view that sought to find real values in a representation of the past for an urban and decadent present, or it could be seen, in the mid-1970s, to be rife with an unrealistic and impractical humanism. In this sense a spectator would be led to rewrite the title in a spoonerism as "a clog of wooden trees," effectively sabotaging—because in question were sabots, the etymological origin of "sabotage"—its ideology.

9. The term is coined from the title by Doris-Louise Haineault and Jean-Yves Roy, *L'inconscient qu'on affiche, essai psychanalytique sur la fascination publicitaire* (Paris: Aubier, 1984), in which the authors argue that the media generate Freudian "drives" in the imaginary relations they produce between images and writing strategies. The study is exceptionally productive in hypothesizing that the unconscious force of ambivalence and contradiction, which are elements of subjectivity in general, do not spring from the fathoms of an individual consciousness: they are all surface effects, seen on television, in magazines, on posters, newspapers, virtually everywhere. Mark Crispin Miller has studied the economy of the process in "The Hollywood Ad," *Atlantic,* 264 (April, 1990).

10. The way a poster baits and summarizes a film or a text is taken up in "A Message without a Code?" *Studies in Twentieth Century Literature,* 5 (Spring 1981), 147–55, a study of Roland Barthes's work on images and the media. It posits that the field of "desire," which the media inaugurate, establishes an implicit law of difference that tells a reader to read words and to see images, but all the while it mixes the two and breaks the very law it puts forward. This is how a feeling of subjectivity is produced. Its effects in the contemporary world of politics and the arts are taken up in my "The King's Effects," the foreword to Louis Marin, *Portrait of the King* (Minneapolis: University of Minnesota Press, 1988), xix.

11. Kevin Brownlow remarks: "Eliminating titles from a silent film was about as simple, and desirable, as eliminating dialogue from a sound film. It could be done . . . and it was done. . . . Tortuously explanatory visual passages were needed to dispense with one simple title, and the effect, far from being a satisfying artistic achievement, was frequently irritating and gimmicky." Quoting Gerald Dufy apropos *The Old Swimming Hole* (in *Picture Play,* August 1922, 22), he notes, " 'That picture without titles was the strongest argument possible for the picture with titles,' " in *The Parade's Gone By* (Berkeley: University of California Press, 1968), 294.

12. Brownlow notes that the lipreading public could note whether a title had anything to do with what characters were saying. Yet, when producers aimed films at a public of immigrants, they had to be more explicit in informing them of American traditions through their appeal to titles. At the same time, a seasoned director like Raoul Walsh could use the close-up to record raucous speech that would never have passed a censor in titles, such as in *Sadie Thompson* and *What Price Glory?* (Brownlow, *The Parade's Gone By,* 295–98). In the latter respect the spectator and producer engaged in a complicity that made censorship a necessary part of the illusion of interpretation.

13. These affiliations are developed in Richard Macksey, "The Expatriate Art: European Directors in Hollywood," *MLN,* 98 (1983), 1063–70. Annotations about the checkered careers of Lubitsch, Lang, Ophuls, and Hitchcock are added on 1187–96.

14. Marie-Claire Ropars offers a more complete analysis in "The Graphic in Filmic Writing: *A bout de souffle,* or the Erratic Alphabet," *Enclitic,* 5–6 (1982), 147–61. Her reading of the close-up of Maurice Sachs's novel does not engage the translinguistic dimension of the rebus, which is also at work in the title, *A bout de souffle* (About a [visual] whisper, or About D souffl[é], where the almost mute D, detached from both the English and the French scansions of the title, is tantamount to the figure of Death).

15. The point supplements T. Jefferson Kline's telling study of the "signboard" ambiguities of the shot in "The Unconforming Conformist," in *Bertolucci's Dream Loom: A Psychoanalytical Study of Cinema* (Amherst: University of Massachusetts Press, 1987), 91.

16. Angus Fletcher, *Allegory: Theory of a Symbolic Mode* (Ithaca: Cornell University Press, 1964), 19.

17. Her raised skirt confirms what Joel McCrea said of his vision as a hypothetical movie director in Preston Sturges's *Sullivan's Travels:* that a good realistic film committed to a social cause should also be sprinkled "with a little sex." That Leisen and Sturges worked together is evident from the common style and dates of *Arise, My Love* and *Sullivan's Travels*.

18. Through different means Paul Virilio argues that the relation of erotic fantasy and the production of twentieth-century war are intimately bonded. The film and media have keenly invested interests in representing a spectacle that they both reflect and promulgate. His arguments, in *Logistique de la perception* (Paris: Editions de l'Etoile, 1984), will be taken up in chapter 4 in a study of Raoul Walsh's war films.

19. This is what, apropos Sade, Roland Barthes called a "pornogrammar" in *Sade, Loyola, Fourier* (Paris: Seuil, 1972), to designate the alphabetic positions of deviation and excess, which, because they are orthogonal (and hence, because of etymology, grammatical), neutralize any remainders of prurience in the *120 Days of Sodom*.

20. André Bazin was first to note how Bogart literalized his body in the later films of his career. His "Mort de Humphrey Bogart" is translated in Jim Hillier, ed., *Cahiers du cinéma: The 1950s* (Cambridge, Mass.: Harvard University Press, 1985), 98–103.

21. The practice that sustains ambivalence is varied. It usually entails inscription of an enigma, into the film, or an articulation of discourses that, by covertly failing to indicate their referents, multiply their possibilities and appeal to the "lurid" imagination they concomitantly construct in the spectator. See Michèle Lagny, Marie-Claire Ropars, and Pierre Sorlin, *Générique des années 30* (Paris: PUV, 1988), 87–88, apropos a theory of "generalized camouflage."

22. As Jacques Derrida summed it up in an emblem-pun in *Marges de la philosophie* (Paris: Minuit, 1972): "Signature, événement, contexte." Read discursively, the title contrasts, in parataxis, the signature with the concept of an "event" and a "context" to the degree that each gives rise to the other in a speech act. But in a "writing act" or a "film act," where no oral interlocution is possible, the title can be read according to a visual frame, yielding, by way of homonymy, "Signature, événement qu'on texte," or "The signature, an event that is written," in other words, an event that gains its name only in the place of both voice and the graphics of writing (or cinema).

23. See the late Richard Roud's introduction to *Rediscovering the French Cinema* (New York: Museum of Modern Art, 1982). He argues that the plastics of the French film and its reception have always tilted the concept of cinema in favor of aesthetics instead of entertainment.

24. In Guy Rosolato, *Eléments de l'interprétation* (Paris: Gallimard, 1985), 17 and 123–32, and especially 305–16. It acquires visual emphasis in "L'objet de perspective dans ses assises visulles," *Nouvelle Revue de Psychanalyse,* no. 33 (Spring 1987), 151ff.

25. Maurice Merleau-Ponty, "On ne voit que ce qu'on regarde," *L'oeil et l'esprit* (Paris: Gallimard, 1964), 17.

26. In his entry in the chapter, "The Far Side of Paradise," in Sarris, *The American Cinema* (Chicago: University of Chicago Press, 1985), 120.

27. Pamela Cook and Claire Johnston, "The Place of Women in the Cinema of Raoul Walsh," reprinted in Bill Nichols, ed., *Movies and Methods* (Berkeley: University of California Press, 1985), vol. 2, 381 and 387.

28. Walsh's hard-boiled answer to the growing genre of self-estrangement (which would go from *High Noon* to *Shane*) is, of course, *Pursued* (1947), a Freudian film combining Oedipus, the return of the repressed, and rough-and-tumble action. It applies the conceptual machinery of Fritz Lang's *The Return of Frank James*, that is, the return of the other who is the traumatized self, to the imposing figure of Robert Mitchum. (Mitchum succeeds in *Pursued*, it can be added, where he fails in Jacques Tourneur's contemporaneous *Out of the Past*.)

29. Walsh had begun his career with D. W. Griffith at Biograph in Fort Lee, New Jersey. He went to Hollywood, worked with Griffith, shot a film (now lost) of Pancho Villa in Mexico, and returned to direct one- and two-reelers after having played John Wilkes Booth in Griffith's *Birth of a Nation*. The origins of Walsh's career synchronize with those of the Hollywood industry. See Walter Conley, "The Silent Films of Raoul Walsh," *Silent Picture*, 9 (Winter 1971), 9–20, and Walsh's own account of his career in the mythomaniacal autobiography, *Each Man in His Time* (New York: Farrar, Strauss and Giroux, 1974).

30. In a still-unpublished manuscript on recent narratives set in Los Angeles, Sharon Willis has shown how an economy of gratuitous sadism structures the two films through quickly framed, subliminal references to the art named—allusively—as that of Julian Schnabel. They point to an overall "posturing" of modernity, of a contemporary and fast-paced "art scene" rather than a critical positioning in respect to it. Her work effectively determines where inscriptive effects are marketed. Similarly, in "The Graphic Unconscious," in M. Charney and J. Reppen, eds., *The Psychoanalytical Study of Literature* (New York: Psychoanalytical Books, 1985), I have argued that a useful criterion for separating the force of art from aesthetic rubbish (hence Schnabel, David Salle, and others) is the "strategic" use of image-texts that keep a subliminal grasp on the buying viewer or reader as opposed to a "tactical" mode of analysis and creation that uses and distorts illusions for broader ends. Strategy refers to what, in *L'invention du quotidien* (Paris: UGE, 1980), 75–80, Michel de Certeau calls an ideological agency that wills to control large numbers of subjects by virtue of designs that coax or seduce subjects into behavior that will bring profit to it. A tactic is a local measure that, like bricolage, subjects invent for locally collective benefit within but despite the globalizing strategies what would otherwise contain them. A film viewer who "reads" figures outside of narrative and who evaluates their effects in order to use them in a critical practice would be a "tactical" spectator.

31. In *Le texte divisé* (Paris: PUF, 1981), part I, Marie-Claire Ropars coins the term *hiéroglyphe* in order to dispense with the semiotic illusion of controlling a film's "meaning" through segmental analysis or scientific pretensions of an *explication de texte*. She demonstrates how the filmic hieroglyph, a concept she obtains from superimposed readings of Freud, Benveniste, Eisenstein, and Jacques Derrida, scatters meaning and subverts the aims of any critical mastery.

32. It can be added that Lulu's "Johnny," or pimp, is named Dédé. Renoir makes the piece of "realism" or *tranche de vie* of the style of the film turn into a child's play of baby names. But Dédé also cues, as "Dumb-dumb," or "Dead-dead," which contrasts his whore, Mlle. "Read Read," and therefore points, iconically and indexically, to the sound and image tracks that produce their poverty of character (each having but two letters as their final essence), but inspire a graphic view of the medium.

33. See Denis Rouart, *Renoir* (New York: Skira/Rizzoli, 1985). In 1870 Renoir portrayed a nude bather covering her pudenda with her left hand above a seated black terrier (p. 12). The year before, in *La grenouillère*, he pictured a boating party beyond a dog sleeping in the median ground (p. 17). Madame Georges Charpentier was painted next to her daughters, one of whom sits next to a somewhat disgruntled-looking dog, in 1878 (p. 46). An 1880 painting of Aline Charigot pictures a maiden sitting in a luxuriant field next to a spaniel (p. 54), as if to imply a freedom for the child that is absent from the portraiture of the children who are immobilized in stiff dress, like Proust's Marcel, in *Com-*

bray, who is stuck next to the hawthorns for the image of adults who know nothing of his sense of movement and time. Renoir's *Apple Vendor* of 1880 (p. 90) puts a dog in the company of four women. Freudian analogies motivating the aspect of the dog and female attributes are clear.

34. See Andrew Horton and Joan Magretta, *Modern European Filmmakers and the Art of Adaptation* (New York: Frederick Ungar, 1981) and its bibliography (369–71).

35. Robert Ray studies the mix and its effects in *A Certain Tendency of Hollywood Cinema, 1930–1980* (Princeton: Princeton University Press, 1984), 288–95, and insists on the ways that the American industry co-opts and controls the European tradition. The force of the filmic icons at work, it can be argued, disenfranchises the historical or merely sociological stance that grants Hollywood such privilege.

1. The Filmic Icon: *Boudu sauvé des eaux*

1. The appendix includes the shot sequence detailing Boudu's entry. The shot numbers in this chapter correspond to the descriptions given there.

2. In *Le texte divisé* (Paris: PUF, 1981), 77–87, Marie-Claire Ropars notes that *fil* is a charged word in Renoir's work. At the beginning of *La règle du jeu* (The rules of the game), the radio broadcaster warns spectators to stay free of the wire *(le fil):* her words — "Attention au fil!" — might also be evidence of a third voice that beckons the viewer to stand clear of the story. The same innuendo holds at the end of *Boudu.*

3. Psychoanalytic readings depend on dismantling these oppositions. They are ideologically weighty, for they code moral norms of behavior in highly reductive terms. In *L'invention du quotidien* (translated as *The Practice of Everyday Life* [Berkeley: University of California Press, 1984]), Michel de Certeau observes that unreflexive oppositional thinking ranks at the lowest order of mental activity and is thus most ideologically charged in the sphere of everyday life. His view inaugurates a way to work through thematic oppositions that make up so many of the plot structures of narrative cinema. Freudian and other means are needed. Some are developed in Robert A. Paul, "Lina Wertmüller's 'Seven Beauties': An Analysis and Reevaluation," *Journal of Psychoanalytic Anthropology,* 9 (Fall 1986), 447–92, especially 481, where the spectator is seen as unable to reconcile opposition of sexuality and maternity between one kind of mother and another. Marc Vernet sketches a structural history of the Freudian mechanism in the industry in his "Freud: Effets spéciaux — mise en scène. USA," *Communications,* 23 (1975), 223–34.

4. The literature is ample, from Paul Radin's classic *Trickster* (New York: Schocken, 1972), to Roger Bastide, "Le rire," in *Echanges et communications* (The Hague: Mouton, 1970). In a path-breaking essay on communication, passage, and metamorphosis, Jean Pépin shows that the trickster is a character always somewhere between, and has as a principal function the mediation and double transmission of information. Boudu seems to be an avatar of the same pre-Socratic figures studied in "L'herméneutique ancienne: Les mots et les idées," *Poétique,* no. 23 (1975), 291–300.

5. Citing *Playboy,* October 1965, 43, in Lévi-Strauss, *Mythologiques 4: L'homme nu* (Paris: Plon, 1971), 21.

6. In *Boudu,* the bourgeois are bourgeois "despite themselves," whereas in *Toni* the workers have gained a sense of a common earth because they are transients. In *La règle du jeu,* nobody seems to belong at all in the space he or she purports to inhabit. Now, in *Le crime de M. Lange,* the communal identity is established only because the agon, Batala, becomes the man everyone loves to hate. Comparisons can be extended.

7. The threads of this classic essay seem to run through Boudu's character. Mauss's original subtitle, "Forme et raison de l'échange dans les sociétés archaïques," shows that the film and the essay share a common concern with "origins," "beginnings," or "total social conditions" that are approached through a common attempt to depict primal scenes of communication. When confronted with societies that "waste" what they produce, as in the Northwest Amerindian potlatch, Mauss is

forced to rationalize their behavior under the formal definition of a "prestation totale de type ago-nistique" (total prestation of agonistic type); see *Sociologie et anthropologie* (Paris: PUF, 1973), 152–53. Renoir, too, seems obsessed with local social groups that paradoxically work where they are not supposed to, and with larger hierarchies that cannot promise any adequate representation of what really happens in the chaos of human behavior.

8. In *Jean Renoir and His Films* (New York: Doubleday, 1972), 168 and 202, Leo Braudy re-calls that Fauchois, upon seeing Renoir's alteration that accords Boudu a central role in the film, threatened to sue the director.

9. Renoir noted in *Ma vie et mes films* (Paris: Flammarion, 1974), in the chapter devoted to *La règle du jeu,* that the worst of all of mankind's productions is progress. The kernel of his archaic view is shown in the image-figure of the bust of Voltaire, which, like the artificial flowers in the apartment, is only good for gathering dust.

10. Roland Barthes's discussion of objects and space in Flaubert pertains to *Boudu.* In "L'effet de réel," he shows how the denotation of objects gives meaning to movement or passage by syntax that momentarily arrests single elements in the descriptive field. Thus the writing can claim lenticular truth or "objectivity" that seems to exclude novelistic fantasy. See *Communications,* no. 11 (1968), 84–89, translated by Gerald Mead in *Film Reader,* 3 (1978), 131–35.

11. In "L'albatros," the inaugural poem of the "Tableaux parisiens" that make up a significant segment in the architecture of the *Fleurs du mal.* The poem appears apropos because the noise in the film, along with the images of traffic jams and crowds of people on the image track, is a literal ref-erent, an icon corresponding to what the poem had initiated. Two vastly different cultural "speeds" are apposed. It is as if Renoir were seeking a filmic picture, another "tableau parisien," almost light years away from Baudelaire, in the outdoor scenes of the modern city.

12. Some of these were cigar-lyrics, which have the smoker's body drawn through the burning tobacco of the cigar and wafted away in smoke. It is akin to the vision of having letters "disappear" into spirit, or breath, that Mallarmé suggests in "La musique et les lettres," in *Oeuvres complètes* (Paris: Gallimard-Pléiade, 1945), 635–54, especially 649.

13. The spiral staircase becomes a figure of social flow and excitement of communal activity. It figures in the printing sequence of *Le crime de M. Lange* and seems to have its initial expression of political drive in *Boudu.* In *Lange,* it objectifies the panoramic movement of the camera in the court-yard, and in *Boudu* it prefigures the dazzling circular shots taken on the river in the last sequence. In both films the object and the camera appear to motivate each other.

14. The middle career of the pan contrasts tonal qualities and, for a fugacious instant, recalls the form and texture of Mark Rothko's paintings. Characters above are no longer in frame as their music plays, and the camera has not yet reached the nuptial skiff below. For an eternal moment, free of humans, the riverscape appears to be one shade of gray and the background another. Each forms a block of tone or haze that contrasts the other.

15. The political investment of the 360-degree shot is more obvious in *Le crime de M. Lange,* but has its first expression here. It appears that Renoir's use of the extended pan exerts influence on Ber-tolucci's reflections on cinematic and political revolution in the discussions about circular shots in *Prima della rivoluzione,* and in the double 360-degree shots in *A bout de souffle* that seem to be made in homage to *Boudu* and Walsh in *High Sierra.* Its infrequent but decisive political presence in Hol-lywood film will be taken up in chapter 6.

16. See, for example, "The Reeds and the Wind," in the *Lux Claustri,* a series of emblems of monastic life, reprinted in Howard Daniel, *Callot's Etchings* (New York: Dover, 1974), no. 219.

17. Emblem is used in a historical sense, in which pictures and words are mediated by the view-ing reader, who looks at a superscription, or motto, an image or inscription in a frame, and an allusive explanation or subscription below. It is part of a literature of enigmas that plays on the traditional difference of word and picture and soul and body. As Henri Zerner notes in his introduction to Robert

Klein, *Form and Meaning* ([New York: Viking, 1979], a translation of *La forme et l'intelligible* [Paris: Gallimard, 1970]), commenting on the author's study of figurative expression of the Renaissance, "The motto does not explain the image, nor the image illustrate the words, but their juxtaposition both reveals and hides the underlying impulse" (xi).

18. These terms are taken from Rosolato, *Eléments de l'interprétation* (Paris: Gallimard, 1985), which melds perspectival questions with those of forces that move forward (as visual desire) and backward (as memory and fantasy of childlike, unbridled eros in a subject's past) in his or her relation to language. Piera Aulagnier (see chapter 2, note 16) coins the term "pictogram" to study a similar relation between image and language.

19. See the appendix, part I, section B.

20. The organ grinder is a crucial icon that both Renoir and Fritz Lang share. The mechanical production of music that "turns on" everyone in earshot has a definite analogy with the calliope in *La règle du jeu*. In a pan that André Bazin called one of the greatest in Renoir's oeuvre, a very mechanical movement goes left, across a gallery of spring-driven youths, who hold drums and lift swords by their midsections, before it reaches La Chesnaye, in close-up, who wipes his grinning mouth with a black handkerchief. The toys are, like the human, "turned on" by the mechanical jangle. The depiction of the "human machine" in *La règle du jeu* has its early analogue here in *Boudu*. Now Lang no doubt used the *orgue de barbarie*—the "barbarian organ"–to liken cinematic and human drive in *Scarlet Street*. See below, chapter 2, and André Bazin, *Jean Renoir* (New York: Simon & Schuster, 1973), 79ff.

21. Alexander Sesonske adroitly associates the "variety of suggestions, all activated at some point in the film," among *boue, boueur, boudeur,* and *boudoir* (mud, scavenger, sulky, and powder room), in *Jean Renoir: The French Films, 1924–39* (Cambridge, Mass.: Harvard University Press, 1980), 115. That Renoir renews an archaic process ordering names and space by combining language and volume must be emphasized. It has much to do with what Frank Lestringant—drawing his concept from Jacques Derrida's *logique de la marque*—calls a spatial metonymy. It occurs when one names a space, marking it with a rod, a gesture, or a word, so as to appropriate its extension for oneself. In *Boudu* it merely "takes place" when Boudu arrives in the boudoir, and is hence not arrogated because the pun both names and explodes its appropriative instant. See Frank Lestringant, "Rhétorique et dispositif d'autorité," *Littérature*, no. 32 (December 1978), 21ff.

22. The poet had punned on dryad by associating it with an oak tree, but in such a way that his readers could recall that the word actually meant an oak through its etymology (the Latin *dryas* going back to the Greek *druas,* from *drus,* or oak): the contemporary world is "L'époque où, faute de dryades, on embrasse, sans dégoût, le tronc des chênes" (The period when, for lack of dryads, without distaste we make love with oak trees). In shots 21 and 25 in the first part of the film, Boudu had been associated with the tree trunk and hence is in verbal and visual identity with Emma.

23. In *Apollon et Dionysos ou la science incertain des signes: Montaigne, Stendhal, Robbe-Grillet* (Marburg: Hitzroth, 1989), 374–76, Michael Nerlich traces the verbal and visual relation of the woman shielding her eyes with her forearm from drawing and poem into film (Robbe-Grillet's *Eden et après*). The surrealistic figure seems to inflect the gesture that Emma seems to be miming from Lulu in *La chienne*.

24. The difference that Renoir's film writing inaugurates with his critics can be shown here. Apropos the last forty-five shots of *Boudu*, Alexander Sesonske notes that water becomes the "dominant image," and thus "a symbol of another transformation performed within the film," of Lestingois by Boudu as the principal figure of the work (123). That is, transformation, which moves continually to and about images and icons, cannot be arrested into a metaphor or a "symbol." It can be said that the concept of symbol must be desymbolized in order to make the movement of its terms supersede the terms themselves. Sesonske, no doubt unwilling to abide by his own formulation, writes two extraordinary pages (138–39) about the innovations of Renoir's camera style in *Boudu*. They in turn exceed

his own concepts of "character," "treatment," and other descriptive criteria he uses to organize his keen observations.

2. The Law of the Letter: *Scarlet Street*

1. The filmic icon shares something with what Michel Foucault has written of the calligram, in its playful ways of erasing the oldest oppositions of our "alphabetical civilization" in terms of showing and naming, of figuring and speaking, of reproducing and articulating, imitating and signifying, and of seeing and reading; see Foucault, *Ceci n'est pas une pipe* (Montpellier: Fata Morgana, 1973), 20ff.

2. See the account Lang makes of the film in Richard Koszarski, ed., *Hollywood Directors: 1941–1976* (New York: Oxford University Press, 1977), 141. *Scarlet Street* had originally been banned in New York State, Milwaukee, and Memphis.

3. Noel Burch, "Fritz Lang," in Richard Roud, ed., *Film: A Critical Dictionary* (London: Secker & Warburg, 1980), vol. 2, 583–609.

4. Godard and Lang develop this debate further in a series of interviews, since recorded on videotape under the title *Le bébé et le dinosaure*. See also Raymond Bellour, "Sur Fritz Lang," *Critique*, no. 226 (March 1966), reprinted in *L'analyse du film* (Paris: Editions del l'Abatros, 1982); Jean Douchet, "Dix-sept plans (of *Fury*)," in Raymond Bellour, ed., *Le cinéma américain: Analyses des films* (Paris: Flammarion, 1981), vol. 2, 200–232; and Reynold Humphries, *Fritz Lang, cinéaste américain* (Paris: Editions de l'Albatros, 1982), revised and substantially rewritten in English as *Fritz Lang: Genre and Representation in His Films* (Baltimore: Johns Hopkins University Press, 1988).

5. Examples of author-centered monographs are Peter Bogdanovich, *Fritz Lang in America* (London: Studio Vista, 1967), and Andrew Sarris's typically incisive pages in *The American Cinema* Chicago: University of Chicago Press, 1985). On Lang, film noir, and feminism, see E. Ann Kaplan, "The Place of Women in Fritz Lang's *The Blue Gardenia*," in *Women in Film Noir* (London: British Film Institute, 1978), 83–90.

6. "The Uncanny," in *The Standard Edition of the Complete Psychological Works of Sigmund Freud*, ed. and trans. James Strachey, vol. 17 (reprint, London: Hogarth Press: 1986), 217–52 (hereafter referred to as *SE*). The Freudian immediately notes the relation of the Hogarth Press to J.J.'s firm in *Scarlet Street*.

7. The scene complements Edward G. Robinson's meeting with Joan Bennett in *The Woman in the Window*, where, instead of saying "Make mine the same," he says to her as she pours him yet another glass of champagne, "I should say no, I know, but haven't the slightest intention of saying so." It can be said that *Scarlet Street* and *Woman in the Window* tend to double each other. On the affinities, see Humphries, *Fritz Lang*, 100–119, and *passim*.

8. Alexander Sesonske locates what may be Lang's reason for Duryea's interpretation of the character. In *La chienne*, he observes, the actor Flamant seems to overplay "in a way which emphasizes the obnoxious traits of this young scoundrel. But then one sees how the overplaying comes from within his character himself and that Dédé is both performer and audience" (*Jean Renoir: The French Films 1924–39* [Cambridge, Mass.: Harvard University Press, 1980], 86). Lang will take up the same problem in his use of image-signs that Duryea heralds.

9. See the appendix, part I, section A, shot 36, which seems to invert the moment in *La chienne*.

10. The French term *emprise* seems apropos. It is characterized by a state of immobility so great and devastating that the subject cannot even find fantasy enough to dream. A narcotic state of seizure, it is a state of death-in-life that reduces patients to their most pitiful condition of existence. Roger Dorey details it in "La relation d'emprise," in *Nouvelle Revue de Psychanalyse*, 28 (1985), 116–39, a special issue devoted to the topic.

11. The identity with Buñuel's film of the same title (1952) does not seem gratuitous. Both interpret a pathological case, inner anguish, and manifest violence through different styles.

12. See Piera Aulagnier, *La violence et l'interprétation* (Paris: PUF, Série "Le fil rouge," 1981): "The pictogram will represent a same unity of 'object-zone' as a space of a double desire of destruction, a place where a deadly and endless conflict unwinds" (62 and *passim*).

13. Gabriele Schwab comes to this conclusion in her comparison of Lacan, Bakhtin, and Winnicott in "The Subject, Imaginary Functions, and Poetic Language," *New Literary History*, 15 (Spring 1984), 469ff. The work concurs with Claude Abraham's observation that any authentic work of art is thus endowed with an unconscious dimension; see *L'écorce et le noyau* (Paris: Aubier-Flammarion, 1978), 118.

14. Tactic and strategy are used in accord with Michel de Certeau, *L'invention du quotidien* (Paris: UGE, 1980), 75–94, in which the first term amounts to a creative and collective activity that shunts away from massified strategies of subjectivity. It must be added that division into a "dominant" and "dominated" ideology is erroneous. All ideology is, by definition, dominant.

15. See the Introduction regarding Huston's *African Queen*. Clearly Hollywood created "subliminal" effects, like those of advertising today, that attempted to program the unconscious for its own ends. Walker Key's popular studies of "media sexploitation" and "subliminal seduction" contend that a writing, and not an absence, is at the basis of the practice of desire. Words and letters are grafted into pictures and clips to be seen in their evanescence. See also Doris-Louise Haineault and Jean-Yves Roy, *L'inconscient qu'on affiche* (Paris: Aubier, 1984), and Bill Nichols, *Ideology and the Image* (Bloomington: Indiana University Press, 1981), 61 and 129.

16. He is a function of anamorphosis and anagrammar. The archaic, magical, even Freudian gloss of the surface of names throughout *Scarlet Street* has its theory elaborated in Ferdinand de Saussure's notes on Latin poetry in the posthumous *Les mots sous les mots*, ed. Jean Starobinski (Paris: Gallimard, 1974). The longstanding logic of the anagram is the subject of Etienne Gilson, *Les idées et les lettres* (Paris: Vrin, 1932), or Claude-Gilbert Dubois, *L'imaginaire de la Renaissance* (Paris: PUF, 1985), 49–76.

17. That Hell was associated with the camps, that they were the first, living, graphic scene of what medieval painters could only imagine, is adduced in the title of a book that was widely read in Germany and America in the early postwar years: Eugen Kogon, *The Theory and Practice of Hell* (New York: Farrar, Straus and Cudahy, 1950), originally appearing under the name *Der SS Staat*.

18. The letters I and J play out a more radically defined role than that of simple shifters which, in the matrix of Benveniste's *Essais de linguistique générale*, still retain existential and referential functions. Here, however, I, a figure that is not quite a pronoun, is in contrast to a curvilinear J. In the relations of spectatorship it is we who constitute the difference between the two characters in order to make sense of the film.

19. The mark is complemented (or identified) by Chris's description of the act of painting. He remarks to Kitty that he draws a circle around what he sees. His art does in its imaginary way what J.J.'s monogram effects in a practical world of exchange.

20. In an unpublished study of *King Kong* (1933), Roger Dadoun writes that the king who is the monster in the jungles is dethroned and displaced, utterly transformed when subjected to a culture of writing, when he becomes kong. King, a noun and a verb in the present, becomes a past participle in kong. The same holds for Criss . . . Cross.

21. This recoups the concept of the "logic of the mark" studied above and the problem of interpellation taken up in "The Human Alphabet" below.

22. Orson Welles uses the same effect with reinforcement to portray Hank Quinlan's murder of his accomplice (Akim Tamiroff) in *Touch of Evil* (1958).

23. Implicit reference goes back to *Citizen Kane*, in the zigzag stairwell below Suzy's apartment, when Kane yells down to Boss Jim Geddes, "I'm going to send you to Sing-Sing," just prior to the

montage of Suzy in her failed singing career. The same montage-rebus is at work in *Scarlet Street* as in this crucial moment in Welles's film.

24. It would be easy to thematize the safe as a "Freudian" element in Lang's work: thus it would symbolize what is "locked up" in the unconscious, or prefigure the motif of incarceration and guilt that pervades the film. But the safe is also a figure of the auteur. In *Rancho Notorious* (1952), Marlene Dietrich is shot next to the "safe" at Chuck-a-Luck where she feigns an act of inventory in front of the local sheriff. Here and elsewhere the vault becomes an object-surface of sorts that works both intra- and transfilmically in Lang's oeuvre.

25. The social inversion by which the black person momentarily controls the destiny of the white man replies to the reversals of power that are coded in the characters. The black plays at being the tamer of the lion, Chris, in the cage. "Kitty" calls Chris a "lion," and one of the paintings portrays a lion tamer. The setting of the vault next to which Chris "spends" his life is likened to a three-ring circus in a world upside down.

26. When the voice-off says *time,* it also literalizes the bong of one o'clock that sounds when Chris seeks intimacy on his lunch hour with Kitty, and refers back to the first words of J.J. addressed both to the spectator and to Chris, in the lead-in, "Speaking of time . . . " The word is concretized in objects and figures throughout the film. Time seems to be one of its principal filmic icons.

27. He is enclosed in a box, on display like an animal in a zoo. The image of Chris in his prison, as a specimen in the cashier's office, has definite Freudian innuendo if one remembers that the Dora history (1905), was a "clinical picture," rendered in English from the German, "*Bruchstück einer Hysterie-Analyse,* Fragment of an Analysis of a Case of Hysteria" (*SE,* vol. 7, 3–122), which translates well the obsessions in the narrative with "reticules," purses, and other containers. Dora is likened to Pandora's box in the drama of countertransference. Like Chris, she was a literal box, a vault of illness that Freud incarcerated into his case-novel.

28. The letter A has always been the sign of a beginning, but not just in an alphabetic sense. Its shape, on which the film insists at this point, is that of an angle opened, as a sign of the origin of an apprehension of space and extension. The figure, according to Lucette Finas in her reading of Georges Bataille, is a mark of angst and anguish that comes with a subject's accession to sight; see *La crue* (Paris: Gallimard, 1972), 20.

29. The history of reversible writing is embedded in the Western poetic and arcane tradition. See Michel de Certeau, *L'écriture de l'histoire* (Paris: Gallimard, 1982), and J. M. Lévy, "L'écriture en miroir des petits écoliers," *Journal de psychologie normale et pathologique,* 32 (1935), 443–54. Mirror writing is historically, according to de Certeau, "like a cryptography in children's games or in counterfeit money . . . a fiction fabricating dupery and secrets, tracing the cipher of a silence through the inversion of a normal practice and its social codification" (102).

30. Lang is literal in the same way elsewhere. In *Rancho Notorious,* just before being raped, Beth Haskell (Gloria Henry) steps out of a door that has the sign ASSAYER'S OFFICE above. She points her arm upward, as if waving good-bye to Vern (Arthur Kennedy), but also, in putting her hand below the middle of the word, she scands it such that "Ass here" can be connoted. And that it is: Kinch, the villain, arrives (but not yet announced) and soon violates her brutally. The invitation to rape is scripted "subliminally," and passed onto the spectator by the duplicitous reference to the writing above the indicative hand.

31. Fat men have a similar function of self-reference in Lang's films. "Cherokee" (Dan Seymour) was the Fatty Arbuckle-like Indian in *Rancho Notorious* who lived at Alter's (Dietrich's) dinner table. He is the same character who turns up in *The Big Heat.* His gigantic buttocks flowing over the stool on which he sits in the decrepit office of an auto junkyard, he sucks a bottle of Coca-Cola through a straw. He tells Glenn Ford ("Dave Bannion") about a certain "Slim" who fell victim to a heart attack ("bad ticker," in other words, another timepiece). If we code the heart in terms of the pocket watch given to Chris Cross, then the notion of wasted potentiation binds all the obese figures in Lang's films. The initial manifestation is seen in *M*. Viewing fat Lohmann in close-up from a

countertilt that emphasizes his Goering-like aspect—his bulbous balls pushing against his pants—draws the letter M in the tradition of a grotesque *Menschenalphabet*.

32. Pipedreams circulate everywhere in Lang's American oeuvre. "Alter Keene" in *Rancho Notorious* was first seen at Chuck-a-Luck as Vern Haskell's "pipedream." Dressed in jeans and with splotches of grease on her arms, she literalizes the metaphor. Dana Andrews ("Ed Mobley") in *While the City Sleeps* speaks of the same illusions in front of a decor with plumbing and pipes along the walls and ceilings of the newspaper office.

33. In the "other" dimension of the film, Dan Duryea's own name is incorporated in the circulation of closure. Like his beckoning gesture of the curved palm that recuperates what it has not yet semiotized, Duryea points to the cliché he embodies, a tough, sleazy gigolo (DURyea) and his fluid excrement of himself (dURyEA).

34. Reynold Humphries notes alertly that in *The Woman in the Window* the straw hats "function as signifiers in the fullest Lacanian sense: they structure the spectator's unconscious whose reading of the text is an effect of their place in it, a place that determines the spectator's"; see Humphries, *Fritz Lang* (1988), 106. In this sense they are identical to the doubled and reversible signs of indication noted earlier.

35. Rick Altman, "Moving Lips: Cinema as Ventriloquist," *Yale French Studies*, no. 60 (1980), 76.

36. The imagination that sees aural language has a long tradition that is studied in the "regressive moment" in psychoanalysis, but it can be more immediately recalled, perhaps, if a viewer compares the art of seeing film to the study of a second or third language. The "foreign language" that is spoken is "seen" in grammar held in the memory of the speaker as he or she utters it. The retention of the sight of language constitutes a moment moving back to an initial apprehension of words laden with visual investment. It may be that a subject's penchant to forget initial contact with language assures a greater oral use; but the structure of a visible grammar subtending the order of discourse is embedded in the production of language. Walter J. Ong, S.J., opens a discussion along these lines in *The Presence of the Word* (Minneapolis: University of Minnesota Press, 1981), 111–38.

37. The girl-talk and love talk are seen as literal "soap opera" when the camera cuts, in the sequence in Kitty and Millie's flat, to a close-up of the kitchen sink (the other of Chris's sink) filled with unwashed dishes, behind which is seen a box of detergent named LUX.

38. Lang's work is generally rich in the art of verbal and visual delay. The doubly bound relation of title and work, a "contract" of sorts, as Jacques Derrida has argued in *Parages* (Paris: Galilée, 1985), is abused. One of the enigmas of *Le rouge et le noir* is that Stendhal's title does not find any exact explanation in the narrative. Its underdetermined status resembles *Scarlet Street* insofar as it does not quite summarize or represent the contents. Elsewhere, however, Lang puts his titles into the narrative. In *The Big Heat*, Dave Bannion (Glenn Ford) shakes and almost strangles Tom Duncan's widow (Jeanette Nolan), warning her that when her hidden letter is revealed, "The Big Heat will fall." By contrast, *Rancho Notorious* seems to be a mock title that puns on Hitchcock's *Notorious* and uses a macaronic structure to undo its illusion of authority.

39. In his precocious essay "Art of cinéplastics" (in *Film: An Anthology* [New York, 1970]), Elie Faure notes that a viewer often sees color through black and white. And perhaps Merleau-Ponty was among the first to articulate the unconscious in terms of color, in *L'oeil et l'esprit* (Paris: Gallimard, 1964), when he takes Descartes to task for his failure to reckon with "things without a concept," or "le murmure indécis des couleurs" (the indecisive murmur of colors) (43). Color can be seen, if ineffably and mystically, in black and white.

40. Here dialogue can be opened with Reynold Humphries's impeccable reading of *Scarlet Street*, in which he sees the ending as being much more "conventional" than that of *La chienne* since it does not have Renoir's "amoral and anarchistic" savor (*Fritz Lang* [1988], 196). Punishment, he notes, must be emphasized. Yet the theme is only a lure in view of the more effractive play of the

narrative and visual borders that twist together in the end credits. Lang always plays with confinement within the illusion of film.

3. Dummies Revived: *Manpower*

1. The film seems to follow Paul Virilio's often repeated hypothesis that Hollywood actually mapped the reality of history in our century. Time and again he has shown that the industrial production of classical cinema shapes policy and logistics, both in *Esthétique de la disparition* (Paris: Balland, 1980), and in many articles in *Traverses,* from 1986 to the present.

2. It is legible if Roland Barthes's concept of "pornogrammar" is recalled. Drawn from a study of the Marquis de Sade, the concept designates the tension obtained from humans who literalize alphabetic shapes in erotic syntagmas—letters that copulate each other—that display the type of sexual congress also being described *through* the novelist's words. This type of catachresis grounds all the analyses included in *Sade, Loyola, Fourier* (Paris: Seuil, 1972).

3. Following Lacan, it can be said that the film tells the tale of the *objet petit-m,* or the "male" inaugurated by an originary castration. For Lacan, castration amounts to truth, but for Hollywood it appears to institute a mode of production.

4. In fact, the history of the film has become the same myth. The contributor to *The Motion Picture Guide, 1927–83* (Chicago: Cinebooks, 1986) seems blind to the congruence of events on and off screen. It is reported that Robinson and Raft "were quite taken with Dietrich," and that the latter refused to be a "weakling" in front of her: "There was no joy on the set between the two tough guys. Robinson was very patronizing to Raft, telling him how to deliver his lines, and Raft responded by loudly telling Robinson to keep his advice to himself. Both men began shouting at each other and, before director Walsh could step in, several punches were thrown, with Robinson getting the worst of it." (1872). Myth, history, and archive purport to be the same.

5. Sergei Eisenstein, *The Film Form* (New York: Harcourt Jovanovich, 1949 and 1977), 26.

6. Guy Rosolato explores the same problem in terms of an exchange between patient and analyst: "Through exchange in the analytical scene, sexual phantasms and repressed desires are exposed." This is exactly what seems to be staged in the viewer's relation to *Manpower,* especially in the ambiguity of Robinson's character, which both attracts and repels. In Rosolato's words, "What comes from what can be expected of the potential force vital to anguish and seduction." See "L'hystérie, névrose d'inconnu," *Topique,* no. 31 (1988), 45. Thus anguish can be a vitally productive energy in the dialogic world, a world that must include the activity of analysis.

7. Leo Bersani and Ulysse Dutoit capture the flow of ambiguity in the eros at play in "The Shifting Line of Sensual Experience"; see their *Forms of Violence* (New York: Schocken, 1985), 104–9.

8. When movement, the basis of metaphor, is literalized, healthy obscenity takes over. In the film, "to blow a fuse" means to overload a circuit and break a connection; but it also implies to suck a phallus. The figure also denotes the film celebrating itself making figures of itself, its narrative, and the history of its position in the media—exactly homologously to the way *Life* had projected its still of Raft and Robinson.

9. "But from the great waters of Versailles to modern dams, a decision intervened that went not only in the direction of the collectivity pitted against the nobles: essentially, this decision opposed the growth of productive forces to unproductive bliss," notes Bataille in *La littérature et le mal,* in *Oeuvres complètes,* vol. 9 (Paris: Gallimard, 1979), 205–6 (my translation).

10. Mikhail Bakhtin, *L'oeuvre de François Rabelais et la culture populaire au Moyen Age et sous la Renaissance* (Paris: Gallimard, 1970), 38. Baltrusaitis's remarkable *Moyen âge fantastique* (Paris: Colin, 1955) offers a valuable compendium of many of the same orificial figures.

11. Natalie Z. Davis, *Society and Culture in Early Modern France* (Stanford: Stanford University Press, 1975), studies the topos through the optic of Roger Bastide and Victor Turner. So does Mikhail

Baraz, *Rabelais et la joie de la liberté* (Paris: Corti, 1983), 42–75, and Michel Rousse, *"Le mariage Rutebeuf* et la fête des fous," *Le Moyen Age*, nos. 3–4 (1982), 435–49.

12. Jean Céard traces a history of the monster as "de-monstration" in his critical edition of Ambroic Paré, *Des monstres et des prodiges* (Geneva: Droz, 1971); see also Jean-Louis Schefer, *L'homme ordinaire du cinéma* (Paris: Gallimard/Cahiers du cinéma, 1980), 31.

13. The celebration of the unlikely rite of marriage shares much with Gustave Flaubert's *Madame Bovary* and arches back to problems of composition and montage. A wedding cake figures at the center of Charles and Emma's festivities and marks, as Jean Ricardou has noted with algebraic brio, a form of the novel's inner duplication (in *Pour une histoire du nouveau roman* [Paris: Seuil, 1971], 33–38). Here too the decor of the cake mobilizes the allegory of icons at work in the film.

14. The sexual isolation might be compared to what Lévi-Strauss notes about "Dual Organizations," of societies, in which men and women willfully isolate themselves from each other in order to define the imaginary space of a social compact. Apropos the Bororo tribes, he notes: "We are dealing here with a concentric structure of which the natives are fully aware, where the relationships between center and periphery express two kinds of oppositions, that which we have just noted between male and female and another between sacred and profane. The central area containing the man's house or the dancing place serves as a stage for the ceremonial life, while the periphery is reserved for the domestic activities of women, who are by definition excluded." See "Do Dual Organizations Exist?" in *Structural Anthropology* (New York: Doubleday, 1958), 37–38. The sexual isolation in *Manpower* and other films by Walsh seems to celebrate the principle, from *Sadie Thompson* all the way to *Marines, Let's Go.*

15. The cigar's use bears comparison with *Scarlet Street*, in which J.J. indicates his status and power with the dot-like form stashed between his lips. Static editing makes cigars figure at once what marks and is marked. In the sequence in which J.J. "fires" Chris Cross, a first shot portrays J.J. standing behind his desk. The second cuts to Chris looking guiltily at his boss. The third cuts back to J.J. in the same pose, but all of a sudden the boss has a cigar in the corner of his mouth. Only a second viewing shows the minuscule detail of the cigar in the ashtray in the first shot; no visual sign is given of a gesture that picks up the stogie. In a word, Lang goes without transition from an "unmarked" to a "marked" world, without making any concession to continuity or transition. He does the same in *The Big Heat* (1953), in which a lieutenant, facing Dave Bannion (Glenn Ford), tells the enraged ex-officer to consider seeing a priest (whose Freudian name is symptomatic of all of Lang's work: *"Father* Master*son"*). One moment the lieutenant speaks directly to Bannion, and the next he has a cigar stuffed in his jowls. Walsh does not break synchrony so insistently. He and Renoir both use the cigar in a comically perverse fashion through use of extensive depth of field.

16. As will be seen in chapter 4, Errol Flynn tells his subaltern, as soon as he receives the "photographs from the general," "Okay Ned, now you can go back to sleep" (shot 38).

17. History is clearly the "repressed" in the film, the unmarked agent that arouses fear. Its erotic cast shares much with Fredric Jameson's sense of its allure in *The Political Unconscious* (Ithaca: Cornell University Press, 1981), described, in terms of desire, as "what hurts," "what refuses desire and sets inexorable limits to individual as well as collective praxis, which its 'ruses' turn into grisly and ironic reversals of their overt intention" (102).

18. The ambiguity here resembles, perhaps, the system of paranoia that, according to Dana Polan, Hollywood puts forward in its massive ideological campaigns in the 1940s, a point at the center of *Power and Pananoia: History, Narrative, and the American Cinema, 1940–50* (New York: Columbia University Press, 1989), especially 1–21.

19. In the following order: (1) McHenry attacks the dance hall bouncer after the latter corrects him for his indecent behavior; (2) McHenry punches a cohort (Ward Bond) in Mrs. Lynn's rooming house when provoked about his impotence; (3) McHenry brutally pummels one of Faye's suitors in her apartment on an afternoon visit; (4) Johnny slugs everybody in the Midnight Club when he argues about the cost of a beer and a champagne cocktail he has shared with Faye; (5) McHenry beats his

cohort (again Ward Bond) in the locker room when he is ridiculed about his marriage; (6) Johnny hits the same cohort who has insulted McHenry ("A new groom always sweeps clean") after he has left a café to "wire Faye and have her come up"; (7) the women and police brawl in the Midnight Club when Faye returns to get a tip for future employment in Chicago; (8) Johnny slaps and shoves Faye down the stairwell in the police station ("Don't turn on the waterworks for me," he slurs in response to her tears; (9) McHenry swings at Johnny on the pylon before falling to his death.

4. The Nether Eye: *Objective, Burma!*

1. François Jost, "Propositions pour une narratologie comparée," in *Mana* 7 (1987), 255, which summarizes much of his *L'oeil-caméra: Entre film et roman* (Lyon: Presses Universitaires de Lyon, 1987), 105–39, also taken up in "La narratologie: Point de vue sur l'énonciation," *Cinémaction*, no. 47 (1988), 63–66.

2. Jost, "Propositions," 255, and *L'oeil-caméra*, 119.

3. It is fitting that in the early 1970s Raoul Walsh became a topic of analysis of feminist orientation. Claire Johnston and Pamela Cook initiated a study of the ways Walsh tends to erode the male-centered system from within Hollywood codes (see introduction, n. 27). Their work centers on the later Walsh, which tends to parody his earlier years. *The Revolt of Mamie Stover* clearly takes up what had been done in *Sadie Thompson, Klondike Annie, High Sierra,* and other films, with the difference that the historical relation of sexual conflict and the immediate history of conflict (World War I or World War II) are not taken in account in the context of postwar America. In *The Revolt of Mamie Stover* the writing in frame locates the field of parody. At one moment Jane Russell is seen reading a paper that headlines the "Battle of Midway" that locates a time in the Pacific theater of operations in 1942, but also a battleground between the two sexes. No doubt either Walsh or the Hayes code did not have the actress seen reading an account of the Battle of the Bulge.

4. François Hartog, *Le miroir d'Hérodote: Essai sur la représentation de l'autre* (Paris: Gallimard, 1980), 271ff., an analysis that follows Michel de Certeau, *L'écriture de l'histoire,* 241ff.

5. I quote from the French at length because, however much Thevet praises pure sight, it is given to us, indeed *(voire)* as knowledge that comes through the ear *(entendre)*. Where he distinguishes different modes of perception, his graphic style also conflates them. He is thus at his most truthful where his visual discourse betrays him. The cosmographer is a prototypical cinematographer.

6. See Walter Conley, "The Silent Films of Raoul Walsh," *Silent Picture,* no. 9 (Winter 1970–71), 2–18. Jean-Paul Torok is correct in asserting that Walsh's *In Old Arizona* and *The Big Trail* (1929–30) are the most important early sound films, far more complex than either *The Jazz Singer* or *Hallelujah,* because, amidst the sound, "the screen is endlessly filled with actions and gestures over a backdrop of events and adventures"; see *Le scénario* (Paris: Henri Veyrier, 1988), 38.

7. The veracity of the history is still being contested. The author of the entry in *The Motion Picture Guide, 1927–83* (Chicago: Cinebooks, 1983) takes a patriotic view by revising the narrative that the British had made of the Burmese affair. The United Kingdom was angered at the misrepresentation of its valiant efforts to free Indochina from the Japanese, "despite the fact that thousands of American soldiers were dying in Burma while heroically performing their duties" (2215). The contributor writes of "xenophobic" British critics "niggardly" attacking the film in order to recoup the glory lost through the representation. The film was banned in Britain between 1945 and 1952. It is ironic that the American captain and hero of the film, Errol Flynn, has a patently British accent (at least for most American viewers). It may be that Flynn's voice, and not history, may have been the cause for the furor over the film in the British Isles.

8. John Archer appears to have been a crucial figure in Walsh's work at Warner. With Arthur Kennedy, he plays the loud-mouthed coward, one of the two "saps and punks" in *High Sierra,* in which his voice is too resonant to be an adequate report for his actions. In *White Heat* he plays Lt. Phil Evans, the police chief who broadcasts to Edmund O'Brien his plans to get the "Jarrett Gang." At

the end of that film, he is an amplification of an amplification when he speaks through an electronic megaphone to Cody Jarrett (James Cagney). The cone is aimed at the villain, perched on a Horton-sphere far above. Archer speaks, voice-off, in echoes that reverberate about the entire refinery, "You might as well come down, Jarrett. There's no one left but you" (196, shot 388; as noted in the edition cited in chapter 7, n. 21). Archer's voice is coded in all of these films as that of the *Law*. In *Objective, Burma!* he also speaks as if he had an amplifier in his throat.

9. The same play of sadistic burning is used in *White Heat*, where the end of John Archer's cigarette is applied to the skin of Edmund O'Brien; Walsh reiterates the same gestures throughout his oeuvre. The trait does merit comparison with Renoir's treatment; for him smoking is both a common denominator of communication and an expression of intense frustration or unvarnished resentment (George Darnoux flicks his cigarette into the Marne in the confusion of pathos and undirected aggression at the end of *Une partie de campagne* [1937]). Furthermore, the way Nelson "burns" in looking at the truth of the photo contrasts the view of Boëldieu, in *La grande illusion* (1937) who sees—with his monocle—that nobody can figure out what is represented on the freshly developed aerial photograph. Walsh and Renoir appear to have uncanny affinities here and elsewhere.

10. Put to work, for example, in the essays collected in Jakobson's *Questions de poétique* (Paris: Seuil, 1973), especially on Shakespeare's verbal art (356–77).

11. This remark is made to complicate Jean-Louis Comolli's interpretation that argues for a passage from action to spirit, in which an "epic of the body" portrays a battle "against the invisible." Clearly the battle is optical, but wherever optics are in play, so is eros. His "L'esprit d'aventure" still stands as a high point in Walsh criticism; see *Cahiers du cinéma*, 24 (April 1964), 11–14.

12. Raymond Bellour's notion of *symbolic blockage* and Guy Rosolato's *projective identification*, elaborated in their interview in *Hors Cadre*, 1 (1983), 132–44, pertain here. Desire and scopic drive center on a vanishing object.

13. The dynamics of sadism are studied at length in Claude Sylvestre, "Le moment régressif," *Topique*, no. 25 (1980), 27–30.

14. Sigmund Freud, *Moses and Monotheism*, the last part of I(B), "Latency Period and Tradition," in the *Standard Edition*, vol. 23, 71.

5. Facts and Figures of History: *Paisan*

1. Stefano Roncoroni, *Roberto Rossellini: The War Trilogy* (New York: Grossman, 1973). All subsequent references to *Paisan* will be made to this edition and cited with page numbers followed by the shot numbers, and where appropriate, footage noted in parentheses.

2. In *Les structures élémentaires de la parenté*, 2nd ed. (Paris: Mouton, 1967), Claude Lévi-Strauss takes up a concept Marcel Mauss had encountered in the famous "Essai sur le don." Mauss ends his study, noting, "On voit comment on peut étudier, dans certains cas, le comportement humain total, la vie sociale toute entière" (It can be seen how, in certain cases, total human behavior, entire social life can be studied). See *Sociologie et anthropologie* (Paris: PUF, 1973), 279. Following Mauss, apropos exchanges among strangers who meet in workers' restaurants in the French Midi, Lévi-Strauss notes that "we are surely, at a microscopic level, in the presence of a 'total social fact,' " of a fundamental situation in which individuals "enter in contact for the first time with the unknown" (70–71, my translation). Rossellini appears to be taking up the same problem throughout *Paisan* and in terms of common people.

3. As understood in the sense of Erich Auerbach's study of Dante, in which "the idea that earthly life is thoroughly real, with the reality of the flesh into which the Logos entered, but that with all its reality it is only *umbra* and *figura* of the authentic, future, ultimate truth, the real reality that will unveil and preserve the *figura*. In this way the individual earthly event is not regarded as a definitive self-sufficient reality, nor as a link in a chain of development in which single events or combinations of events perpetually give rise to new events, but viewed primarily in immediate vertical

connection with a divine order which encompasses it, which on some future day will itself be concrete reality; so that the earthly event is a prophecy or *figura* of a part of a wholly divine reality that will be enacted in the future. But this reality is not only future; it is always present in the eye of God and in the other world, which is to say that in transcendence the revealed and true reality is present at all times, or timelessly." See *"Figura,"* in *Scenes from the Drama of European Literature* (Minneapolis: University of Minnesota Press, 1984), 72. The passage is quoted at length to show how much this concept informs Rossellini's cinematography. It also explains why allegory can be a productive form in his work; it follows Angus Fletcher's still forceful interpretation in *Allegory: Theory of a Symbolic Mode* (Ithaca: Cornell University Press, 1964).

4. Robert Warshow, *The Immediate Experience* (New York: Atheneum, 1971), 252 ff., has underscored the theme of failed communication as an element basic to *Paisan*. He notes that the title underscores a common humanity that is sought across cultural differences. The latter impede any attainment of a collective ideal. Warshow does not, however, take up the ultimately religious basis of the gap between tongues, like that which exists between past and future in the typological vision of figural reality.

5. Claude Lévi-Strauss chooses *manitou* to relate the notion of "thingamajig," "truc," "machin," or "manna" to explain what cannot be named but conveys force in a society, in "Introduction à l'oeuvre de Marcel Mauss," in Mauss, *Sociologie et Anthropologie* (Paris: PUF, 1973), xlix.

6. The practice is common in medieval literature: here it immediately recalls Van Eyck's upside-down writing on the outer panels of the Ghent altarpiece, where the phylacteries are inverted in order to make manifest the presence of God as a reading spectator looking down from the sky over the panels below. Erwin Panofsky develops the problem in *Early Netherlandish Painting* (Cambridge, Mass.: Harvard University Press, 1953).

7. The word-object proves the validity of what Michael Thompson calls "rubbish theory," that is, the study of the fortunes of visibility and value that culture assigns to objects over time. What is invisible to a group at one moment or place will acquire value in another. Judith Schlanger takes up the problem in terms of a productive metamorphosis of images and objects in "Les aventures de la valeur cognitive," *Littérature,* no. 73 (February 1989), 3–18.

8. Again, Lévi-Strauss studies social and sexual positions in the concept of the "culinary triangle," developed at the conclusion of *Les origines des manières de table* (Paris: Plon, 1968), 406ff.

9. A point Marcel Détienne studies in "Qu'est-ce qu'un site," *Critique,* no. 503 (April 1989), 211–27. He notes that a "pensée du pr[i]mordial sans rupture" (215) in given civilizations must be renewed "through contact with living forces from beyond. At regular intervals, temples are rebuilt, domestic sanctuaries are redone, limits are redrawn" (216, my translation). This is a work in the dimension of miracle that brings the other into each other's world in *Paisan*.

10. Stuart Ewen provides a history of the channels of the advertising industry that, it can be implied, leads into cinema in *All-Consuming Images* (New York: Basic Books, 1988). He quotes Raymond Loewy: " 'I'm looking for a very high index of visual memory retention. In other words, we want everyone who has seen the logotype, even fleetingly, to never forget it, or at least to forget it slowly' " (244). Montage of narrative and brand names in the plot can be the only consequence of the advertising executive's remark. For years films have been a testing ground for the ineffable names of products marketed by industry. In this light Eric Rohmer's recent *Les amis de mes amis (Boy Friend, Girl Friend)* is a love story constructed to sell Perrier water; Claude Lelouch's *Un homme et une femme (A Man and a Woman)* markets Marlboro cigarettes and *Time* magazine. And so forth.

11. In Rosolato, "l'hystérie, névrose d'inconnu," *Topique,* no. 31 (1988), 20. See also chapter 3, note 6.

12. Hence recalling the scriptural rebus of Pasquale and Dots Johnson in the second sequence, who look for an absent mother and father (244, 130).

13. In André Bazin, *What Is Cinema* (Berkeley: University of California Press, 1971), vol. 2, 30.

14. Emphasis need not be placed on Rossellini's penchant to align the camera with the point of view of children in the films of neorealism. He thus obtains an urgently sensitive, inquisitive, and forcefully naive view that matches the style of editing.

15. The Roncoroni edition's wording—"This happened in the winter of 1944. At the beginning of spring, the war was over" (348, 180)—differs crucially from the English version on most American copies and, it will be suggested, does not reproduce the overall violence of the gapping of image, writing, and voice.

16. See Terence Cave, *The Cornucopian Text* (Oxford: Oxford University Press, 1979), apropos Ronsard's *Hymnes;* Lévi-Strauss again, in *Le cru et le cuit* (Paris: Plon, 1962), 302–5; see also my "Jargon d'Orléans," *New Orleans Review,* 11 (1984), 22–27.

17. The presence of the translinguistic element establishes the possibility of another reading. Since the film is inherently polyglot, the viewer has the liberty of hearing through alliteration that the "war was declared . . . *dove*[/]"; that is, that it was declared and in being declared *over,* it was begun—but also begun in the quandary of an atopical place. Where *(dove)* is it declared (over)?

18. Reprinted in Sartre, *Situations, III* (Paris: Gallimard, 1949), 11–14.

19. Rossellini appears to be taking up a Catholic and Hegelian wager that the poet and statesman Paul Claudel had also signaled, in the aftermath of the First World War, in his intention to "declare war on war," to introduce to the world the concept of the "outlawry of war," in other words, a homeopathic relation of language and event, in which the mimetic violence brought forth through the experience of poetry would inspire the world to work toward peace. Claudel is cited in the "Discours prononcé au dîner offert par l'Association France-Amérique, February 6, 1928," cited in Rev. Francis J. Murphy, "The Poet and the Pact: Paul Claudel and the Kellogg-Briand Pacts," *Mid-America: An Historical Review,* 60 (1978), 50.

20. In Richard Roud's *Film: A Critical Dictionary* (London: Secker & Warburg, 1980), vol. 2, Robin Wood's entry on Rossellini and *Paisan* (888–89) notes that the theme of a displaced home marks the second and last sequences, but he does not take up its cinematic inscription across the film. He in fact calls the fifth sequence "the Fellini-dominated and quite undistinguished anecdote about American chaplains in a monastery."

21. Peter Brunette aptly describes the sequence in terms borrowed from Renoir, where "one can work one's way back to the basic, primitive level of cooperation" (in *Roberto Rossellini* [New York: Oxford University Press, 1987], 65) of community that is the ground for the manifestation of the "total social facts" that align Rossellini with a tradition of anthropological cinema.

22. In this sense Rossellini appears to reproduce a classical ideology that evinces in the photographic image a fear of being caught in death or of being deprived of love and movement. The double bind of using a film to explore that ideology informs the violence of the discourse. Here it is clear that Bazin's affinity for Rossellini has its affective and philosophical grounding in "The Ontology of the Photographic Image" and other essays.

23. The term is adumbrated in Georges Bataille, "La structure psychologique du fascisme," in *Oeuvres complètes,* vol. 1 (Paris: Gallimard, 1970), 339–75, especially 357–58.

24. Canby, "European Films: Entering the Berlitz Era?" *International Herald Tribune,* June 9, 1989, 9.

6. The Human Alphabet: *La bête humaine*

1. The *real* is used here in allusion to Lacan, as a concept that even the psychoanalyst's own language cannot clarify. His statements about the real are fraught with as much creative tension as the concept itself. As the real defies language, even Lacan's lapidary formulation of it makes it skitter from grasp. American scholarship has often tended to approach it diacritically, through juxtaposition

with Lacan's equally problematic notions of the symbolic and the imaginary. It must be recalled that the real, especially insofar as it might touch on the "neoreal," tends to be whatever cannot be mediated by language or image. Or, in a more classic frame, a study of "reality" would amount to no more than a "semiology of the real." Lacan's approach to the world of things is not far from that of Sartre's Roquentin, in *Nausea*, who cannot account for the objects before his eyes because they are not tagged with words in the way an illustrated dictionary—a *Larousse* or a *Britannica*—would have us believe. They are there, like the physical mass of a stone or a briar root, as if to defy our rational will. Yet Roquentin, who sees the nagging quiddity of a pebble before his eyes, never happens to realize that a pebble is focalized in his name, in the echo of "Ro(ck)entin," of the language that confers the essence of stoneness upon him. The alluring—but only alluring—sense of the real as a drive to motivate language and things seems to dominate Renoir's cinema and in turn has decisive influence on its legacy.

2. In this sense Rossellini's rapport with Pasolini in respect to "reality" pertains here. For Pasolini, following Renoir, cinema is the *written* language of reality. The cineast makes incursions into the real but never represents it. The influence of one director on the other may warrant extended study. Teresa de Lauretis summarizes Pasolini's views incisively in *Alice Doesn't: Feminism, Semiotics, Cinema* (Indiana: Indiana University Press, 1984), 48–50.

3. "Rousseauesque" is used from the standpoint of Lévi-Strauss, for whom the philosopher is an ethnographer who sees the Golden Age of prehistory as an exemplary world in which society does not expand at the expense of the natural world. The idea of the past serves as a practical corrective for the future. He sees in Rousseau a figure whose almost Manichaean view grounds the invention of the opposition of nature and culture, an antinomy useful for investigation of the beginnings and ends of humankind. The Rousseau of Lévi-Strauss would concur with Renoir's argument, expressed in *Ma vie et mes films*, that *progress*—despite Ronald Reagan's televised pronouncements on Sunday evenings in the 1950s—may well be the worst of human achievements. The relation is developed in Lévi-Strauss's "Jean-Jacques Rousseau, fondateur des sciences de l'homme," in *Anthropologie structurale II* (Paris: Plon, 1973), 45–62.

4. The difference is at the crux of the drama not only of the film but also of the contradictions among genres and "styles" that Renoir had been essaying throughout the 1930s. Some critics have developed analyses along these lines: Dudley Andrew, "Jean Renoir and the Pathos of the Thirties," in "Textes et Médialités," special number of *Mana (Mannheimer Analytica)*, no. 7 (1987), 325–52. Also Juan M. Company, "El enunciado naturalista: paradojas de lo visible," *Estudios Semióticos/ Estudis Semiòtics* (Barcelona), 10 (1987), 79–94, some of whose conclusions concur with the discussions in this chapter.

5. Among others, in André Malraux's famous "Esquisse d'une psychologie du cinéma," and the "cineplastics" of Elie Faure.

6. "We're not here to write our memoirs," quips the old general in *La règle du jeu*, as if telling the Marquis de la Chesnaye to partake of the movement that is Renoir's film and to wait until later—as did the director, prior to completing his own memoirs, entitled *Ma vie et mes films*—before taking up such static occupations. Boudu, we remember, was only good for deciphering "big letters" *(les grosses lettres)*, while, in *Une partie de campagne*, M. Dufour (Gabriello) tells his hapless and bumbling future son-in-law, Anatole (Paul Temps), that nature is a closed book in front of human eyes. He also informs his deaf mother-in-law of what they are ordering to eat. Yelling in her ears, he "will write her" *(on vous écrira)*. An ironic view of the technology of writing prevails in the oeuvre.

7. The title of the film offers the classical metaphor of the mechanical and human beast, or the paradox, reaching back to the origins of Cartesian thinking, of the man-machine, robot, or automaton. When Pecqueux casts spadefuls of coal into the boiler of "La Lison," a prolonged metaphorical aftereffect encourages the viewer to recall the depth of the tradition that Renoir is extending, beyond the *Discourse on Method*, to carnivalesque figures of voracity, or to the gentle giant, in *Gargantua*, into whose mouth pages shovel tons of mustard to give savor to the sausages he consumes. Renoir,

whose films insist over and again on the irrational basis of all human activity, cannot fail to work within a *popular* tradition that is ostensibly more lithographic and caricatural than tragic.

8. The inscription of eros in advanced technology is almost axiomatic in the aesthetics of cinema. The machine offers the lure of human perfection to pique desire and frustration in terms of visual pleasure. In Flaherty's *The Louisiana Story,* in an extraordinarily erotic moment—no doubt because the viewer identifies with the prepubescent child who looks at the spectacle through the optic of an entirely latent sexuality—an oil-rig worker copulates with a drill that is wound and unwound by heavy chains. This kind of eros will be given more lugubrious shading in noir conventions, such as in the network of pulleys, winches, and levers seen adjacent to Robert Mitchum's neck in the gas-station sequence of Tourneur's *Out of the Past.*

9. See Albert Châtelet, *French Painting from Le Nain to Fragonard* (Geneva: Skira, 1964), 151–56.

10. See chapter 7 on the role of the dog as fate and writing in *High Sierra.* The parallel between the films seems far-fetched but indeed works. In both Renoir and Walsh the dog initiates the movement of tragedy. The connection is studied in my "Auteur enucléé," in *Hors cadre,* 8 (1990), 77–95.

11. The human who looks face-to-face at the viewer often gains power while those seen from the side are subject to the authority of the person looking down upon them. The opposition is current in art since the Carolingian period. See Meyer Schapiro, *Words and Pictures* (The Hague: Mouton, 1973), apropos the sight of the Pantocrator and of kneeling disciples.

12. As noted earlier, it must be added that the image or speech of Renoir's characters always displaces this drama into a tradition—a moment of transmission—of literary metamorphosis. A French viewer would not fail to associate *venant de Paris* with a world of urban poetry and art, such as Villon's bitter ballad of arsenic and hate that keys the populist refrain about tipplers and tricksters, in the ballad Clément Marot entitled "La ballade des femmes de Paris": "Il n'est bon bec que de Paris" *(Le grant testament,* ll. 1515–42). Villon, as his name indicates, heralds an urban writing that is part of a highly local manifestation across literary history, that is, a *Parisian* mode known for its cosmopolitan provincialism. Renoir uses Julien Carette's Parisian accent to insist on its presence in *La grande illusion, la bête humaine,* and *La règle du jeu.* A distinctively "Parisian" locale already pervades the diptych of *La chienne* and *Boudu.*

13. The scene enacts Louis Althusser's conclusions about the relation of paranoia and power that dictates how some elementary structures of ideology operate in everyday life. It has similar resonance in Emile Benveniste's study of existential basis of exchange, in which interlocutors engage to define positions of subjectivity through relations of shifters. Benveniste's famous essay "Les instances du discours" appeared in *Problèmes de linguistique générale* (Paris: Gallimard, 1966), 243–52. Althusser's studies were first published in the Marxian journal *La Pensée* in the 1960s, before being collected in *Pour Marx* (English translation, London: Verso, 1977). In *Discerning the Subject* (Minneapolis: University of Minnesota Press, 1988), especially 21–22, Paul Smith unfolds the concept and shows how it can be put against itself for tactical ends—by subjects themselves—against the force of interpellation.

14. This gloss is an instance of what Marie-Claire Ropars calls "the film, reader of the text," in which inversions of intellection, due to the heterogeneous nature of the medium, are basic to filmic dissemination of meaning. The point is elaborated in her article of the same title, *Hors Cadre,* 1 (1980), 70ff. Réda Bensmaïa explicates the point in "Marie-Claire Ropars-Wuilleumier ou le texte retrouvé," in *Cinémaction,* no. 47 (1988), 90–94.

15. Renoir apparently wanted Simone Simon to flatten the narrative's tragic dimension. She was precisely not a vamp, nor was she a figure that would draw the spectator's eyes to her. Renoir praised her for striking a balance of modesty and force; see *Ecrits* (Paris: Belfond, 1975), 268–69, quoted in part by Alexander Sesonske, *Jean Renoir: The French Films, 1924–39* (Cambridge, Mass.: Harvard University Press, 1980), 367–68.

16. Using principles taken from Northrop Frye *(Anatomy of Literature)* and Wellek and Warren's *Theory of Literature,* James Monaco sketches a working structure of the *Ur*-noir plot in *"Film noir: A Modest Proposal," Film Reader,* 3 (1978), 54ff. Other studies of the convention include Paul Kerr, "Out of What Past? Notes on B Film Noir," *Screen Education,* 2 (Winter 1979–80), 33; and Amir Karimi, *Toward a Definition of American Film Noir* (New York: Arno Press, 1976). In terms that link *La bête humaine* to film noir, Paul Schrader's emphasis on the rapport of the underworld and the attraction of both visual and psychological chiaroscuro is productive; see his "Notes on Film Noir," an essay of 1974, reprinted in Barry Keith Grant, ed., *Film Genre Reader* (Austin: University of Texas Press, 1986), 169–82.

17. Roubaud's problem, an enthusiast of auteur theory would remark, is that he never knew Lestingois's statement, originating in Balzac's *Physiologie du mariage,* to the effect that jealousy is the most inappropriate of passions in a bourgeois household. Because Renoir plays Cabuche, the spectator can muse that Roubaud's tragic flaw was simply due to his inability to see other films by Renoir.

18. Noël Burch uses its principle to explain Renoir's unusual sense of spatial dilation—through the opening and closing of doors and entry of characters into filmic space—in the pages devoted to *Nana* in *Theory of Film Practice* (reprint, Princeton: Princeton University Press, 1981), 17–25: "As soon as a character has actually entered the frame, his entry retrospectively calls to mind the existence of the spatial segment from which he emerged" (19), that is, it can be added, the very space that the camera was seen occupying.

19. I use the word "cliché" because, in *La grande illusion,* the same penchant for framing is used so much that it thematizes the gaps of class, culture, and language that the characters cannot assail. The famous geranium on the window sill between Rauffenstein and Boëldieu calls so much attention to the motif that the camera is almost complicitous with von Stroheim's nostalgia for frames of social difference. But the viewer welcomes Pierre Fresnay's ironic, monocular view that refuses nostalgia. "Ca se démocratise" (Things are democratizing), he says of the populations of Europe as if, too, he were commenting on the collapse of spatial barriers. Again, where language reads the image—as in the *Germanic* association seen in the "germanium" of *geranium,* the cliché is undone.

20. See Elaine Scarry, *The Body in Pain* (New York: Oxford University Press, 1985), chapter 1.

21. Again, Renoir's travelers never make use of the free time they have by reading (as they might in the tradition of impressionism, in which time is often spent by figures reading). Gustave Caillebotte and others of the same generation explored the ways writing could be slipped into an image without recourse to having printed characters disturb the overall impression.

22. Emma's sight of death was equated with her apprehension of *nothing* outside of the window frame. Renoir had used the motif in his rendition of the novel in 1934. In his film the heroine falls victim to the toxic effects of writing (she gobbles arsenic from a pharmacist's jar whose written label is posed near her mouth), and the relation of the void beyond the murder mirrors the flatness of the frame afforded by letters placed on the image field.

23. Richard Blakely has noticed the effect and drawn a productive conclusion from the episode. *Fumeurs* gives way to *meurs.* The critic turns his observation back into the allegory of the film's plot in order, it appears, not to study the scope of the visual disruption caused by the erasure of letters. "The word behind him has been cut in half, leaving only the second syllable. Of course that syllable sums up the true impact of Séverine's casual remarks and indicates the outcome of their stormy relationship, through which she takes the first step here"; see Blakely, "Teaching Film with Blinders On: The Importance of Knowing the Language," *ADFL Bulletin,* 16 (September 1984), 47. In a narrative sense, the statement shows how a scriptural effect contributes to the abstraction of the melodrama, but it does not aim at the more commanding and disruptive issue of the filmic rebus. Blakely's remarks nonetheless lead to a percussive conclusion quoting *Hiroshima mon amour:* "Bien regarder," says Emmanuelle Riva in the sunlight on the porch, "je crois que ça s'apprend" (I think that seeing well is something you've got to learn). Blakely affirms compellingly that the faculties of

Renoir's language and his literary tradition must be known if patient study of his visual work is to be undertaken.

24. See Georges Sadoul, *Histoire du cinéma mondial des origines à nos jours* (Paris: Flammarion, 1949), 286.

25. But in Renoir's oeuvre it falls *after* his own study of the Revolution, *La Marseillaise* (1938), thus throwing all sense of progress out of sync.

26. The relation of Renoir to Malraux may need much greater study. Malraux appears to embody the paradox of a writer and artist, like Victor Hugo, aiming at a niche both within and above the history of his time. Renoir is also both a reflector and an agent. Juan Miguel Company and Vincente Sanchez-Biosca, in *"Sierra de Teruel:* El compromiso, el texto," *Revista de Occidente,* no. 53 (October 1985), 14–20, offer a view of Malraux and visibility that recoups the work of "El enunciado naturalista," cited this chapter, note 4.

27. It should be added that Malraux's observation was part of a currency in the late 1930s. Henri Focillon may have inspired it, in *L'art d'occident* (Paris: Colin/Poche, reprint of 1938 ed.), published the same year as the release of *La bête humaine,* at the beginning of his discussion of Gothic sculpture (495): "Tandis que la sculpture romane nous fait pénétrer dans un règne inconnu, dans un dédale de métamorphoses, dans les régions les plus secrètes de la vie spirituelle, la sculpture gothique nous ramène à nous-mêmes et à ce que la nature nous offre de familier" (Whereas Romanesque sculpture throws us into an unknown kingdom, into a dedalus of metamorphoses, into the most concealed regions of spiritual life, gothic sculpture brings us back to ourselves and to what nature offers in her most familiar shapes). A common obsession seems to motivate different and complementary visions.

28. Lantier's "fêlure" that makes him skitter from passion to murder is not simply drawn from Zola. It marks the tensional configuration of the characters in dialogue — such as the relation of Batala and Lange in *Le crime de M. Lange* — and is a trait common to single figures as well, such as Jurieu, who is almost a double of Lantier. Perhaps Freud captures the traits of this suicidal sensitivity in *Beyond the Pleasure Principle* (1921), in his comparison of sensibility to the utter "irritability" of protoplasm (*SE,* vol. 18, 26–27).

29. One recalls the fresco of the martyrdom of Saint Stephen (ninth century) in the crypt of Saint-Germain d'Auxerre, in which a Romansque body, in profile, is being stoned and looks up to an azure sky, where it beholds nothing more than a detached hand in the cerulean field. Other examples abound.

30. In fact, Toni's murder is also one of writing. An X is marked at the end of the bridge where he was standing before his murderer, on the other side of the tracks, aimed his gun at the target.

7. Decoding Film Noir: *The Killers, High Sierra,* and *White Heat*

1. Here the pattern established by La Borde and Chaumeton, in their *Panorama du film noir américain* (Paris: Minuit, 1957), is followed. The authors make an impressive inventory of film noir according to a model of evolution, roughly following Focillon's *Vie des formes,* in which experiment of the early 1940s leads to a classical, early postwar phase that becomes refined to the point of self-reflectivity, when it is "à bout de souffle" (74) by the mid-1950s.

2. See the rough description of sequences in Part II of the Appendix. References to the story will follow the units of that synopsis.

3. O'Brien also plays the foiler in *White Heat* (1949), as well as Frank Bigelow, the insurance salesman who solves his own murder in Rudolph Maté's *D.O.A.* (1949). The relation of the insurance business to film noir is welded, of course, in *Double Indemnity* (1944), in which Fred MacMurray has a role somewhat homologous to O'Brien's and to Lancaster's in *The Killers*.

4. The problem has been taken up in studies on the comic strip (as in *Communications,* 24 [1978]) and illustrated writing. Jacqueline Cerquiglini has shown how the double operations reach

back to late-medieval literature in her "Histoire, image, raccord et désaccord du sens à la fin du Moyen Age," *Littérature*, no. 79 (May 1989), 124.

5. The takes characterize the director's visual style. A viewer of 1946 would recall the deep focus views and contrapuntal reverse shots of the bar at the end of which Ella Raines is first seen in Siodmak's *Phantom Lady* (1944). See also Hervé Dumont, *Robert Siodmak: Le maître du film noir* (Lausanne: L'Age d'homme, 1981), 155-63.

6. Youssef Ishaghpour's words about Godard's *Prénom: Carmen* are apropos: "Through its realistic effect, the camera is a lie detector, an instrument of disenchantment"; *Cinéma contemporain: De ce côté du miroir* (Paris: Editions de la Différence, 1986), 128.

7. In fact, Siodmak has been labeled a director less of films than of merely memorable scenes, such as that of Cliff (Elisha Cook, Jr.) in his masturbatory drum solo performed in view of Kansas (Ella Raines) in *The Phantom Lady;* the writing and Rorschach tests that Lew Ayres administers in the double script of *The Dark Mirror,* or the uncanny view of the stairwell in *The Suspect.* This view is advanced in John Russell Taylor's entry for Siodmak in Richard Roud, ed., *Film: A Critical Dictionary* (London: Secker and Warburg, 1980), vol. 2, 924.

8. Lévi Strauss opens an oblique dialogue with Sartre about the ideology of "noise" in *Le cru et le cuit* (Paris: Plon, 1962), 345ff., reminding us that the word goes back to a medieval tradition in which language does not necessarily "mean" what it says, but that its performance exceeds its semantics. Among shamans its interferential effects play a crucial symbolic role that promotes or retards seasonal and biological change. Hence, in *Paisan* the "noise" of senseless gunfire promises, perhaps, a new beginning for Italy; but in *The Killers* its muteness projects eternal stasis.

9. It recurs identically in *The Phantom Lady,* but from the side of the law rather than that of the outlaw. Thomas Gomez, a police detective (who is generally cast as a bulky heavy, as in John Huston's *Key Largo,* 1948), asks for information from a mechanic working on a car suspended on the hydraulic lift in a garage. The greasemonkey (named "Al Alp") is seen going about his business until a voice—Gomez's—utters *off,* "Hey! You!" Not only does the same interpellation recur: *The Phantom Lady* follows a plot about strange hats, and *The Killers* tells the tale of the robbery of a millinery factory.

10. Marc Vernet posits this as a contractual agency between title, enigma, and film in "Le transaction filmique," in Raymond Bellour, ed., *Le cinéma américain* (Paris: Flammarion, 1980), vol. 2, 129ff. But Dana Polan effectively works through the historical drive of paranoia at work in the implied absence as authority in both this film and *Objective, Burma!* in *Power and Paranoia* (New York: Columbia University Press, 1986), 210.

11. The effect is tantamount to a shot, in Siodmak's *Criss Cross* (1949), that captures Burt Lancaster driving a Brink's truck down the California freeway, en route to another payroll robbery that he is performing with a sleazy mobster, the analogue of "Big Jim Colfax," in the person of Slim Dundee (Dan Duryea). Lancaster, who had been seen in three-quarter profile behind the steering wheel flashing back as the van moved forward, seemed to cue the irruption of the past into the present. The story of his ill-fated marriage with Anna (Yvonne de Carlo), his tribulations in gaining employment at the Brink's office after an absence (was it the war? or merely existential peregrination that fled the wreck of wedlock?), and his involvement with the underworld are detailed. Only when, in a frontal shot that has the windshield of the truck in medium close-up framed by an ironwork bridge, at the moment the past is used up and the film is narrating in the present, does the spectator see a registration sticker, bearing the numerals 1949, stuck to the inside of the window. The film accedes to a depthless existential present: image and writing conspire to note that the narration is literally here and now; the time in the film is that of the time seen in the theater. For the spectator there is no possibility other than being mirrored by the events, like the truck, that are rushing ahead and, like Zola's train, out of control.

12. It might be said that the 1940s Hollywood convention of men in cars is the rebus of the figure of fate, in the European literary tradition, embodied in Valéry's line, "Achille, immobile à grands pas,"

which illustrates Zeno's paradox of the hare and the turtle in *Le cimetière marin*. Clearly the generation of film writers of the 1950s, weaned on both symbolism and film noir, was able to renew the intellectual vision by weaving together poetic and popular traditions.

13. See Douglas Gomery, ed., *High Sierra* (Madison: University of Wisconsin Press, Wisconsin/Warner Brothers Screenplay Series, 1979), shots 14–20, pp. 44–45. Further reference will be made to the shot and page numbers of this edition and quoted in parentheses in the text.

14. More extensive study is taken up in my "Driving on High Sierra," *Eutopías*, 2 (1986), 99–120, and "L'auteur énucléé," in *Hors Cadre*, 8 (1990), 77–95.

15. A reminder of Renoir's suspicions about writing and nature is evinced, since the gap between the title and landscape is as unassailable as that, for example, in the opening of *Partie de campagne*. A difference is established between the sight of a dictionary opened to the definition of *love* that precedes a painterly shot of the countryside. Renoir's opening shot, which contrasts the dictionary and the riverscape, seems to be a reworking of Baudelaire's famous metaphor, in the chapter on "paysage" in the *Salon* of 1859, that berated painters for undertaking nature painting with a "dictionary" in their hands, putting word-shapes from manuals illustrating how to draw "leaves" and "trees" on their uninspired compositions. The credits of *High Sierra* manifest the same gap between image and convention.

16. Walsh had already parodied "authority" comparably in his silent films. In *What Price Glory?* and *Objective, Burma!*, the "law" or the "CG" is always a figure seated behind a desk, his face invisible, arched over a stack of papers. In *The Cockeyed World* (1929), a consummate desecration — hence affirmation — of the icon is performed. In the episode set in the Caribbean, Sergeant Flagg (Victor McLaglen) is called into the commander's office to receive orders about a "dangerous mission" he must soon undertake. A rehearsal for the opening of *Objective, Burma!*, the camera is placed behind the commander's bureau. The officer is seen from the back, his doughboy hat on his head, as Flagg moves frontally into view behind him but facing the viewer. As the sergeant had been at play, he enters with his cotton jacket fully unbuttoned. His upper torso is visible, and his midsection cut off by the commander's hat and body. But the open coat suggests that the "dangerous mission" in question is simultaneously performed by the two men in an act of fellatio. The commander mouths his words (not located *on*) around McLaglen's pubis. The sergeant registers approval with an inimitable grin. The verbal performance of order and command doubles the erotic act that both inverts and respects the play of pleasure and work in the relations of the superior and inferior. Here mockery of the blueprint of the erotic force of authority dictates variations on the same theme in other films.

17. Historically, George Raft was first selected for the role, but as he did not want to die at the end of the film, Bogart got the nod for what became his first commanding feature-length role. Raft and Bogart had similar New York accents and affirmed the aural identity of the signifier. It should be added that in Huston's script care was taken to remove the remark that no doubt made too obvious the connection between *Earle* and *oil*. In shot 220 Huston has Roy utter in joy about being freed of his dumb henchmen, "And I was beginning to think that Art and Larry were giving me the *old oil*" (155). The figure is replaced by "run around" in the final version.

18. On the history of writing as mediation in communication, a theme pertinent in the film, Paul Zumthor writes in *La lettre et la voix* (Paris: Seuil, 1985), 107–29, especially 123: "Writing constitutes a special order of reality; it requires the intervention of authorized interpreters (in the double sense of the term). Before their mediation, it is only virtuality, an appeal to the investment of other values. Without this mediation, it resists, obfuscates, encumbers like an object." Michel de Certeau takes up the same problem in terms of voice "on" and "off" in early modern literature in *L'écriture de l'histoire* (Paris: Gallimard, 1975), chapter 5.

19. The amplification is so shrill that the noise resembles a plaintive cry of Nature emanating from the hillside, like a melancholy Echo or Natura of the tradition of *de planctu naturae*, screaming and lamenting over the impending death of the hero, whose name is contained in the blare of the sirens, in R-O-Y-E-A-R-L-E-R-O-Y-E-A-R-L-E-R-O-Y E A-R-L-E . . .

20. Thus: the mountainside and lake in *Out of the Past,* the flashback and restaurant sequences in bright light in *Mildred Pierce,* the sunbathed shot of the hills over Los Angeles in *Double Indemnity.* Other bright scenes abound.

21. Pardo in fact offers Jarrett a local "cure" for one of his migraine headaches, in the innuendo of the framing, by giving him his penis to suck. When Cody reverts to delirium—he has almost been killed in a plot imported into the prison by a rival member of his gang on the outside—Pardo covers for Cody by taking him under a work table and massaging his head placed on his lap. Calm comes to Cody after a requisite number of caresses (in Patrick McGilligan, ed., *White Heat* [Madison: University of Wisconsin Press, 1984], shot 201, p. 124. All subsequent references to the film will be made to this script and cited by shot and page in parentheses in the text.) The trait of style recalls *The Cockeyed World,* note 16, this chapter.

22. It appears that Ivan Goff and Ben Roberts's script is a literal hieroglyph, a graphic poem that disseminates its meaning all over the surface of its writing. At one point, among others, the typescript supersedes the narrative. When, during the holdup, Cody tells Zuckie to throw the railroad switch, we read: "Cody exits shot toward tunnel mouth. While Het prepares his blasting equipment and Cotton checks his gun, Zuckie tries to throw the switch" (shot 11, 58). Cody is described as pulling away from what he shoots at as an oracle, a "tunnel mouth," and "While Het" becomes an uncanny variant on "White Heat." The jumble of speech and writing is sustained throughout, and constitutes the inner writing of the film.

23. It has been observed in the preceding note that the film has hieroglyphic virtue. In the same fashion, Jarrett can be seen playing the role of the Law that arrests by the inflection of his name when it is subjected to the law of Saussurean *langue:* Jarrett becomes a glimpse of "J'arrête" (I stop), while Cody is not just *Code: D* of Death, but the "coda," "code," or "caudal" sign of the ultimate autograph of fate.

24. Already the sequence parodied its technology in shot 88, when the operator of Car C, his lips pressed to the telephone, says triumphantly, "Got her ["Ma" (Margaret Wycherly)]. Going due east. About thirty . . . *Hold the phone!* She's turning left on Baxter" (81, stress added). The driver is seen holding the phone as he utters the remark, holding the phone that he asks to be held. The gesture collapses the narrative into a rebus identical to the play of letters A, B, and C in hot pursuit of D.

25. Massin, in *Lettre et image* (Paris: Gallimard, 1971), reviews many of the same amphibolic letters in American advertising of the 1950s, such as "FRIGID," with mounds of snow on the top of each cipher, or "LIQUID," whose seven digits are dripping. In the film the heat of the letters contrasts Cody's hot temper and cold blood.

26. Innuendo of the line recurs in the intimate exchange between Pardo and Cody in the night, in the mountains, before the raid on the gasoline refinery. Cody "seems to be straying past Vic to some distant point of his own," toward a vanishing point, when he utters, "Times when I thought I was losin' my grip there was Ma right behind me, pushin' me back to the top again" (301, 168–69).

27. The shadow of the chain over Cody's eye is printed on the cover of the Wisconsin/Warner edition of *White Heat.* In the shots that place Cody (189, 119) and Vic (209, 128–29) before the grill separating them from their visitors in prison (Ma and Vic's fake "wife"), Cody's eyes are sliced by the longitudinal line of the wires; Vic sees through the grid clearly. Other "enucleators" abound, such as the strange print on Ma's dress in the same sequence that multiplies the icon of the characteristic "civil defense" triangle enclosing a "CD." She thus bears the emblem of the civil defender, CoDy, who is a premonition of an atomic bomb. And the family name, Jarrett, is, as noted for polyglot viewers, a sign of a figure who arrests anyone who comes into its path: once again, *j'arrête.*

Epilogue

1. Understood in an archaic sense the role includes that of the mystic traveler who writes by unwriting her world. Usually a female, "She is this dejection, endless and infinite," and remains an

"idiot" who is "entirely in things that can't be symbolized and that resist all meaning." See Michel de Certeau, "Un lieu pour se perdre," in *La fable mystique* (Paris: Gallimard, 1982), 48–50.

2. See Sandy Flitterman-Lewis, "The Impossible Portrait of Femininity: *Vagabond*," in *To Desire Differently* (Champaign-Urbana: University of Illinois Press, 1990), 285–315; Florianne Wild, "Ecriture and Cinematic Practice in Agnès Varda's *Sans toit ni loi*," *L'Esprit créateur*, 30 (Summer 1990), 92–104.

3. The cabbalistic virtue of such an alphabetic sense of the letter is not lost on Claude-Gilbert Dubois, in the important chapter on the graphic plastic force of *logos* in early modern epistemology and literature; see *L'imaginaire de la Renaissance* (Paris: PUF, 1985), 62–65, to which Varda's film responds, as if it were the return of its repressed, over a passage of more than four centuries.

Index

Tom Conley is Lowell Professor of Romance languages and visual and environmental studies at Harvard University. He is the author of *Cartographic Cinema* and *The Self-Made Map,* and the translator of Gilles Deleuze's *The Fold: Leibniz and the Baroque,* Michel de Certeau's *The Capture of Speech and Other Political Writings* and *Culture in the Plural,* and Marc Augé's *In the Metro,* all published by the University of Minnesota Press.